THE ACCIDENTAL PALACE

THE ACCIDENTAL PALACE

The Making of Yıldız
in Nineteenth-Century Istanbul

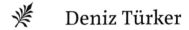 Deniz Türker

THE PENNSYLVANIA STATE UNIVERSITY PRESS
UNIVERSITY PARK, PENNSYLVANIA

Library of Congress Cataloging-in-Publication Data

Names: Türker, Deniz, 1983– author.
Title: The accidental palace : the making of Yıldız in
    nineteenth-century Istanbul / Deniz Türker.
Other titles: Buildings, landscapes, and societies.
Description: University Park, Pennsylvania :
    The Pennsylvania State University Press, [2023] |
    Series: Buildings, landscapes, and societies series |
    Includes bibliographical references and index.
Summary: "Traces the history of the Yıldız Palace in
    Istanbul, the last and largest imperial residential
    complex of the Ottoman Empire"—Provided by
    publisher.
Identifiers: LCCN 2022036144 | ISBN 9780271093918
    (cloth)
Subjects: LCSH: Abdülhamid II, Sultan of the Turks,
    1842–1918—Palaces. | Yıldız Sarayı (Istanbul,
    Turkey)—History. | Architecture, Ottoman—
    Turkey—Istanbul—History—19th century. |
    Palaces—Landscape architecture—Turkey—
    Istanbul—History—19th century. | Royal gardens—
    Turkey—Istanbul—History—19th century.
Classification: LCC DR736 .T87 2023 |
    DDC 949.61/8—dc23/eng/20220816
LC record available at https://lccn.loc.gov
    /2022036144

FRONTISPIECE
Çırağan Palace, artist and date unknown. Gouache on
engraving, 52 × 70 cm. MSİB Painting Collection, Istanbul, 12/2838.

for my mother, İffet Selma Akkor Türker,
forever incandescent

CONTENTS

FIGURES

THE ACCIDENTAL PALACE owes the most to my wonderful mentors, Gülru Necipoğlu, David J. Roxburgh, Cemal Kafadar, and Ahmet A. Ersoy. A novice art historian could not have asked for a more inspiring group of scholars. Gülru Necipoğlu has always guided me back (and still does) to the historical roots of ideas, events, and spaces; that modernity is already there in the early modern is her most invaluable scholarly gift to me. David Roxburgh was and continues to be a steadfast source of academic support and encouragement, a dedicated editor, and an astounding well of information on nineteenth-century cultural and literary history. In research, Cemal Kafadar impressed the pursuit of historical individuals who transcended their time, who either pushed the limits of convention or subverted it in unexpected ways. Tinted by biographical writing, also his doing, the nineteenth-century Ottoman queen mothers and German landscapists of this book have all borne a touch of his finger of wonder. In the process of writing, I found an archival and intellectual companion in Ahmet Ersoy, always a step ahead and always generous in smoothing out my misguided sparks of thought. And without a doubt, in the early stages of this book, my most important bibliographical and linguistic buttress was András Riedlmayer.

Undertaking historical research that requires a lot of traveling is an art. With support from my advisors as well as Sue Kahn and William Granara at Harvard's Center for Middle Eastern Studies (CMES), I was able to complete preliminary research with a Frederick Sheldon Traveling Fellowship, Damon Dilley Funds, and CMES summer grants. From 2014 to 2016 I found an academic home at Dumbarton Oaks as a William R. Tyler Fellow. Here not only chapters took shape and new avenues of research opened up, but, above all, brilliant colleagues became lifelong friends. I would especially like to thank my fellow Tylers, Nawa Sugiyama, Saskia Dirkse, and Julian Yolles, as well as wonderful mentors Yota Batsaki, Anatole Tchikine, John Beardsley, Sarah Burke Cahalan, and Linda Lott for making all of this possible at such a special place. The verdant Yıldız of this book carries a lot of the gardens of Dumbarton Oaks in it.

The bureaucratic hurdles of research and access would make for a fine comic novel. The current and former members of the Yıldız Palace Foundation, Can Binan of Yıldız Technical University, İlona Baytar and Akile Çelik of Dolmabahçe Palace Museum, the archivists of the Presidential State Archives, the librarians of the Istanbul University Library's Rare Works Collection (most important among them Yasemen Akçay), and the research-support team of the Topkapı Palace Museum (especially Esra Müyesseroğlu), all incredibly generous souls, have made the process easier—and even pleasurable. In Cambridge (MA) Julie-Ann Ehrenzweig, Cecily Pollard, and Deanne Dalrymple were always there to provide the necessary watermarked, signed, and sealed letters to unlock both physical and archival doors. Shalimar Fojas White and Joanne Bloom at Harvard's Fine Arts Library responded in milliseconds to copyright queries.

The book took its final shape during my postgraduate life in Cambridge (UK) and later at Rutgers–New Brunswick. I am especially grateful for the continued mentoring friendships of Polly Blakesley, Caroline van Eck, Elizabeth Key Fowden, Vicky Avery, Alyce Mahon, Donal Cooper, Helen Pfeiffer, Khaled Fahmy, Tamara Sears, Laura Weigert, Carla Yanni, Susan Sidlauskas, and Andrés Zervigón. The book's final stages were supported by a Leverhulme Early Career Fellowship, Laura Bassi Grant, and departmental support from Rutgers. In pursuit of this assistance, Neil Cunningham and Geralyn Colvill have been unparalleled in their administrative wisdom.

Marisa Mandabach, Leili Vatani, Elena Papadopoulou, Farshid Emami, and Himmet Taşkömür lent their language expertise to translations of critical passages. Louise Woods, Mertkan Karaca, Murat Göktuna, and Murat Tülek have provided invaluable support on enhancing the book's visual offerings and reference legibility. In times of need, I had the enormous privilege of receiving critical last-minute support from Selim Sırrı

Kuru, Nilay Özlü, Mehmet Kentel, Gizem Tongo, Melike Sümertaş, Erin Hyde Nolan, Buket Çoşkuner, and Bahattin Öztuncay.

Thanks are also due to Hilal Uğurlu, who always undertakes her own research with an eye to help mine and gave me the opportunity to present an early version of my research in my native language in an unbelievably productive forum in Istanbul in 2014. Similarly, much gratitude to Adam Mestyan, Toufoul Abou-Hodeib, Mercedes Volait, Edhem Eldem, Nasser Rabbat, Günsel Renda, and Filiz Yenişehirlioğlu for organizing and chairing panels where they allowed me to introduce some of my preliminary findings. Peter Christensen gave me the chance to share a glimmer of this book with the printed world so that I was able to claim a bit of the contested and coveted Yıldız for myself. I owe enormous thanks to Meredith Quinn, who understood and mollified all my frustrations as a new mother and a scholar-to-be and shared her motherhood wisdom with enviable grace.

At Penn State Press, Ellie Goodman championed what the manuscript had to say and delivered it to a wonderful team of bookmakers. I could not have wished for a better copyeditor than Keith Monley, whose level of professionalism and care even extended to correcting my mistakes in Turkish. Everything fell into place thanks to Brian Beer, Maddie Caso, Jennifer Norton, and Laura Reed-Morrisson, who streamlined the process.

I am eternally indebted to my friend and colleague Yavuz Sezer, in memoriam. If it were not for our mutual joy in trespassing Ottoman imperial haunts, I would never have discovered Yıldız. I hope that he would be quietly pleased to know that, in grief, I have relied on the support of a wonderful circle of his friends, who I am now lucky to call mine: Semra Horuz, Aslıhan Gürbüzel, Ümit Açıkgöz, and Murat Şiviloğlu have made the last stages of writing easier.

I am deeply grateful to my dear friends in Istanbul, Doruk Samuray, Yağmur Nuhrat, Ali Yazgan, Zeynep Tolun, Gizem Ünal, and Emrah Kavlak, who have always enlivened my often extended and difficult stays there. And to the Aras, Bayazıt, and İlter families I owe a lot for their stalwart presence in my family's life through tremendous joy and devastating sadness.

Thanks are due to friends who are family: Nadia L. Marx, the sister I never had, and Hakan Sandal-Wilson, Jesse C. Howell, and Akif E. Yerlioğlu, the brothers I never had.

Above all, boundless gratitude goes to my incredibly supportive family: Tevfik Türker, my heroic, ever-inspiring father; Pınar Türker, my resilient, "greatest" grandmother; Rodrigo Cerdá, my subunit; and Blanca and Jorge Cerdá, my generous, wise, and thankfully always rambunctious in-laws.

All the worthwhile queries and delights that the reader derives from this book are dedicated to my mother, Selma Akkor, who unfortunately did not live to see the end result but during its making entrusted me with her immense willpower, so that I could see it through. I now have the privilege of sharing her unrelenting love and appreciation of creative worlds, ideas, and things with my children, Rui and Siro, hopefully for a lot longer than the time she and I were able to have together.

BOA   T.C. Cumhurbaşkanlığı Devlet Arşivleri (The Republic of Turkey Presidential State Archives)

DBİA   *Dünden Bugüne İstanbul Ansiklopedisi* (Encyclopedia of Istanbul from past to present)

DİA   *Türkiye Diyanet Vakfı İslam Ansiklopedisi* (Turkish Foundation of Religious Affairs encyclopedia of Islam)

İAK   İstanbul Büyükşehir Belediyesi Atatürk Kitaplığı (Istanbul Metropolitan Municipality Atatürk Library)

IFEA   Institut français d'études anatolienne

İÜMK   İstanbul Üniversitesi Merkez Kütüphanesi, Nadir Eserler Koleksiyonu (Istanbul University Central Library, Rare Works Collection)

MSİB   Milli Saraylar İdaresi Başkanlığı Koleksiyonu (Directorate of National Palaces Collection)

PVSE   Pertevniyal Valide Sultan Evrakı (Pertevniyal Valide Sultan Archives)

TCTA   *Tanzimat'tan Cumhuriyet'e Türkiye Ansiklopedisi* (Encyclopedia of Turkey from the Tanzimat to the republic)

TSMAE   Topkapı Saray Müzesi Arşiv ve Dokümantasyon Koleksiyonu (Topkapı Palace Museum Archives)

TRANSLITERATIONS FROM OTTOMAN TURKISH

Transliterations of untransliterated sources are my own and contain complete diacritical markings. Other, previously published transliterations remain faithful to the systems used by the editors of those sources.

I have made sure to provide complete diacritical markings of frequently repeated words like *māheyn* and *selāmlık* the first time they appear, retaining the modern Turkish spelling in their subsequent appearances.

TRANSLATIONS

Translations of Ottoman, Turkish, German, French, and Persian sources are my own, unless a published source or the generous help of a colleague is cited.

Introduction

In late summer 1858 Christian Sester, the Bavarian head gardener of the imperial estates in Ottoman Istanbul, entertained an unusual guest in his hilltop garden, right next to his latest and most ambitious landscape design, the sloping gardens of Çırağan Palace. His guest was Karl Kreil, the Viennese director of the world's first institute of meteorology and geodynamics—founded only a few years earlier, in 1851. Kreil had brought with him to the Ortaköy site a mobile observatory, comprising a sextant, a theodolite, a universal instrument, an inclinatorium, and multiple chronometers and barometers.[1] With the gardener's help, a temporary observatory was assembled on the hilltop, overlooking Çırağan on the shore, to measure Istanbul's magnetic fields.[2] Kreil had already updated the maps of the Habsburg territories with his panoply of precision instruments but had the grand vision of tracking changes in the world's geophysical makeup over long periods by establishing a network of observatories across the globe.[3]

The Istanbul coordinates for Kreil's visionary global project—tracking the Earth's behavior, no less—were taken at a spot that was developing into the new imperial center of the Ottoman Empire, exactly 34 toises[4] (approximately 68 meters) above sea level and 240 toises (480 meters) north-northeast of the

Mecidiye Mosque in Çırağan (today known as the Ortaköy Mosque). An anonymous colored lithograph marks the spot of this transitory but important act of mensuration and also captures the imperial garden in the act of creation that occupies the pivotal space of this book (frontispiece). Through his Habsburg affiliations, Sester put this nineteenth-century royal site on a scientific map, reflecting empirical ambitions beyond mere geopolitics.[5] He had been hired by Sultan Mahmud II (r. 1808–39) in 1836 to invent the reforming empire's representative landscape that would complement the new shoreline palace under construction. By the 1850s this vast green swath, which extended from the shoreline to the ridges of the neighborhoods of Beşiktaş and Ortaköy, had been fashioned by its patrons and makers into a natural amphitheater, opening onto the capital's two older coastal zones: Istanbul *intra muros* and Üsküdar, in the city's Asian quarters.[6] How better for the ambitious Sester to contribute to the making of the palace and garden complex, the capital's new epicenter and the most overt symbol of imperial politics, than by lending its geolocation (*Ortsbestimmung*) to Kreil's international study?

Within the context of the Ottoman state's dramatic political, cultural, and societal shifts, *The Accidental Palace* traces the multiple transformations of this royal landscape, in a newly emergent imperial urban zone in the capital, across the nineteenth century. As Mahmud II's shoreline palace and garden complex of Çırağan, the site was the public face of the sultan's reforms, which laid the foundations for the comprehensive modernization of the empire following the Tanzimat Edict of 1839.[7] The root-and-branch administrative overhauls of the century's first half required representations, matching in scale, in the built environment. The palace and its expanding hilltop gardens continued to be the imperial residence of the Tanzimat regime under Mahmud's son Abdülmecid (r. 1839–61). Although sidelined by the neighboring Dolmabahçe Palace between 1856 and 1878, the site was reinstituted as Yıldız Palace under Abdülmecid's son Abdülhamid II (r. 1876–1909), enlarged to more than fifty hectares (roughly seventy soccer fields), and remained in this incarnation until the empire's dissolution in the 1920s. When Abdülhamid II reimagined it as an imperial center at the end of the nineteenth century, its orientation with respect to the coastline shifted. Now the palace's main structures were nested at the top of the hill, where, since 1795, the mothers of sultans had made their country retreats. This shift asserted the primacy of Yıldız over Çırağan, which would undergo multiple facelifts from the neoclassical to the Gothic-Alhambresque after Mahmud II and whose once iconic garden would be incorporated into Yıldız's now heavily fortified hilltop profile. Yıldız in its earliest instantiation was not conceived as a palace—it became so, accidentally.

During the thirty years it served Abdülhamid, Yıldız never stopped expanding. As late as 1902 various separate imperial lots were appended to its holdings for the construction of a brand-new ceremonial zone. As the Hamidian palace evolved into the empire's administrative center, where all of the state's governing decisions were finalized, it had to make room for a growing cadre of employees of in-house governmental offices and retainers of the many courtly households in Yıldız. Towering walls separated Istanbul from its imperial counterpart in miniature, replete with and ravenous for the period's bourgeois tastes, a utopian microcosm in which a theater, a photography studio, an arsenal, a carpentry atelier, repair shops, kitchen gardens, greenhouses, lakes, grottoes, pavilions, follies, libraries, aviaries, manèges, shooting galleries, and museums had been assembled to satisfy the needs and desires of its occupants.[8]

Although this book does not seek to inventory Yıldız's now-lost spaces, it does recognize the palace's city-like formation at the height of Hamidian rule as one of its staple and most accurate characterizations.[9] The palace's walls were porous for some but not others. The privileged access of some incurred the righteous hostility of those antagonized by the regime, who often inferred the sultan's iniquity from Yıldız's presumed sites of debauchery. Many of their semiapocryphal accounts of the palace during and after Abdülhamid's deposition serve as satirical critiques of his despotism. However, this book is interested neither in qualifying the accuracy of these accounts nor in casting Yıldız as the center of a spy network and international intrigue, no matter how much the sultan enjoyed being read Sherlock Holmes novels before bedtime.[10] Abdülhamid's reign has been the subject of one too many easy metaphors. Instead, *The Accidental Palace* offers granular reconstructions of the site's prepalatine and palatine archaeologies, remaining as close to its archival sources as possible, to read its Hamidian incarnation not as a single moment in the site's lifetime as Yıldız but as part of a longer trajectory of Ottoman formulations and reformulations of imperial identities. The landscape that housed both Çırağan and Yıldız was constantly reshaped to reflect the political motivations of its owners—first as the physical manifestation of a period of reforms and later, under Abdülhamid II, as the very heart of empire and authoritarian rule.

At the time of this writing, the site is apportioned among various Turkish state institutions. Istanbul's residents experience it as various disconnected spaces, all separated by makeshift walls, doors, and guard posts. It is at once a sprawling university campus, a slick hotel from the 1990s, an adequately preserved municipal park, various underwhelming period museums, and a sequence of dilapidated nineteenth-century structures lining two major and often heavily congested thoroughfares: Barbaros Boulevard, which connects the hilly districts with the Bosphorus shoreline and has since 1973 directed traffic to the Bosphorus Bridge, connecting Istanbul's two sides, and Çırağan Avenue, along the shoreline. Until very recently there were more clandestine, inaccessible sections of the former palace, inhabited by branches of the Turkish National Intelligence Organization and the Turkish Armed Forces.[11] Some peripheral and more dilapidated garden segments are cordoned off from public view.

This complex fragmentation is due in large part to the prominence of Abdülhamid's Yıldız as the last stronghold of the Ottoman dynasty; this formidable site, at least in its most immediate afterlife, had to be conquered and its memory expunged by the young Republic of Turkey. Ironically, however, Yıldız's layout also offered functional spaces for some of the republic's new institutions. The palace's appendages, which were designed as discreet Tanzimat offices with subtle classical features, were grouped together to form a campus for the military academy. More palatial structures became sites of secular entertainment. In the mid-1920s, while the new Turkish military trained its young recruits on the site's hilltop, the grand and ornate Şale Kiosk—only a few meters away—was operated as a casino by an Italian-Turkish syndicate.[12] To this day the site is characterized by a peculiar combination of complete public accessibility and absolute inaccessibility; on certain days even the segments reserved as museums are, without notice, closed, to serve formal governmental functions. Despite its partial invisibility in Istanbul's urban memory, Yıldız is still a contested site, exposed to the whims of the current government, fungible and fragile.

Structured chronologically from 1795 to 1909, the book's five chapters are each conceived as a window onto a decisive moment in Yıldız's architectural and landscape history, as the site evolved across a century from an imperial backwater into the center of government. While focusing on physical changes in a royal landscape, the narrative also seeks to identify the site's various designers, from dynastic members to commoners, and the motivations for their architectural choices. Each historical snapshot is selected from a politically charged period in the Ottoman court to highlight the expansion of this landscape into the imperial stage on which sovereignty, visibility, taste, and various forms of self-fashioning were articulated. Nominally, the palace may have belonged to the rarefied realm of the Ottoman elite, but the development of the site was profoundly connected to Istanbul's urban history and to changing conceptions of empire, sovereignty, diplomacy, reform, and the public. The book explores these connections, framing the palace and its grounds not only as a hermetic expression of imperial identity but also as a product of an increasingly internationalized consumer culture, defined by access to a vast number of goods and services across geographical boundaries.

The first chapter begins with a concise historiography of Yıldız as Abdülhamid II's imperial residence. Through critical examination of the sparse, contradictory, and often vitriolic texts written on the last Ottoman palace, the chapter paints a clearer picture of the site's physicality, general layout, and use. To describe this complex and little-understood imperial space, the narrative harnesses the published recollections of three distinct types of palace inhabitants: a scribe in the palace administration, a privileged guest of the sultan, and Abdülhamid himself. Collectively, the composite of three perspectives reveals the palace's tripartite role as the royal residence of the sultan, his center of governance, and a site of royal entertainment. Although seemingly irregular in its plan, Yıldız was deliberately split into these three hierarchical domains, aided by the site's natural geography, on the orders of a hands-on sultan. The first, on the hilltop, was reserved for Abdülhamid and his family. The second physically surrounded the first, rather like a moat, and was reserved for the palace and imperial administration. The third was a vast park on the skirts of the hill, providing leisure activities designed to appeal to the sultan's exclusive visitors.

This chapter's visual sources are the understudied maps drawn by military artists of the state for both completed and projected infrastructural changes on the site. While an unremarkable procedural map of the palace's coal-gas pipes (to provide interior and street illumination) provides the clearest breakdown of the palace's structures, plans for an unrealized railway line inside the palace gardens reveal the sultan's conception of a large segment of his imperial complex as the objects of a sightseeing tour. When taking into account the surprisingly limited number of palace structures that he inhabited on a day-to-day basis (between his small residence and office), the sultan's life within this monumental site was not very different in geographical breadth from that of a young palace scribe.

The second chapter traces the late eighteenth- and early nineteenth-century evolution of the site, looking at the radical transformation of its architecture and landscape from the waterfront to the hillside and extending all the way to the mountaintop. The narrative's principal sources are court chronicles and the records of local diarists attuned to the neighborhood's growth and sustenance. These annals, complementary in their representation of the imperial ceremonies and public events of the time, reveal that the first real owners of this specific geographical space within Istanbul were the powerful mothers of sultans (*valide*s). The chapter suggests that before Yıldız became the last imperial palace, it was a singularly gendered—women-only—space. Although none of the royal residences commissioned by the *valide*s has survived, a number of poetic inscriptions composed to mark their completion remain among the poetry collections of the scribes handpicked by the *valide*s to compose the lines. The chronological timeline of the chapter helps the reader to imagine the physical changes to the site under each of these female patrons, and the narrative reflects in great detail on the varying degrees of competition that arose between consecutive queen mothers, as well as the *valide*s' replication and emulation of their predecessors' modes of patronage and attribution.

Although these women were prolific patrons of charitable institutions, from schools to hospitals and mosque complexes, scholarship has failed to adequately represent them as prominent aristocrats responsible for remarkably visible and grand acts of public philanthropy on par with their early modern predecessors. Through examination of the landscape of Yıldız and the semisecluded yet quite independent lives of the *valide*s on this site in the heyday of reform, the chapter offers a way of understanding these women's social position in the long nineteenth century vis-à-vis the patrimonial palatial structure helmed by the sultan.

The timeline of the third chapter coincides with the period of the queen mothers' gardening efforts on Yıldız's hilltop (1830s), but the chapter looks much more closely at an adjacent segment of the site and the transformative work undertaken by the landscape gardener Christian Sester and his successors throughout the nineteenth century and into the early twentieth.[13] Sester managed to forge a long-lasting imperial career during the early and turbulent years of Mahmud II's reforms—a career outlasting those of Mahmud's two successors. Whereas the first two chapters take a royal cast of characters as the principal patrons of the site, the third chapter introduces this European upstart who had no royal lineage but was well versed in German landscaping techniques and *Sturm und Drang*–infused Romantic literature and leveraged his expertise to gain long-term employment as an Ottoman court official. Even more unusually, he managed to win the trust of a series of sultans and their mothers. In tracing how Sester transformed the barren landscape sandwiched between the waterfront palace and the *valide*s' estates on the site's peaks into a sprawling, deeply forested Romantic garden, the chapter argues that Sester's multistep conversion of a hill puts nature as imperial artifice on equal footing with any palatial architecture. Through his labors, a man-made landscape, too, became "vibrant matter, an agent of historical change."[14]

Sester's political astuteness—his awareness of the central role of a head gardener in the Ottoman administrative structure— allowed him to reshape the post according to his needs by recruiting and training a large and diverse body of gardeners.[15] Some were from Albania and the Black Sea, and others were renegade revolutionaries of the Hungarian War of Independence of 1848–49. Sester's Herculean landscape designs in the imperial gardens of the capital were portrayed in the period's foreign press as the face of a "reforming" empire. His gardener recruits were responsible for maintaining his legacy through the nineteenth century and into the next. Sester and his gardeners reignited a fad for botanical and horticultural competition among the city's higher-level officials, who sought to outdo one another by constructing small-scale versions of Yıldız in the latter half of the nineteenth century.

The main sources for this chapter are the official gardening expenses and gardeners' registers now stored in the Presidential State Archives (T.C. Cumhurbaşkanlığı Devlet Arşivleri) in Istanbul. These documents, although bureaucratic in structure, cast light on the ways in which Yıldız as a garden complex was conceived, compartmentalized, and managed across half a century. On Sester's orders, each segment was assigned to a chief gardener who in turn oversaw a group of novices, and the overall structure of the new corps of gardeners was modeled on Ottoman military rank and file, borrowing relevant army terminology to designate the divisions and individual posts.

The fourth chapter turns to Yıldız's architecture, especially its Alpine aesthetic, which was favored due to the site's unique landscape of hills and ravines. From its earliest appearance in archival documents, Yıldız was described as a mountain, a characterization that appears to have shaped the decisions of all of its subsequent inhabitants.[16] This chapter also traces the history and material sources of Yıldız's disparate yet eccentrically flamboyant timber structures, which were adopted to convey a sense of the Alps, the period's most fashionable tourist destination. Abdülhamid II, the site's ultimate patron and a skilled carpenter in his own right, was familiar not only with the chalet type made popular by the colonial-inflected World's Fairs but also with the Continental appeal of the cottage style, which had already affected his domestic environment; as crown prince, he had been appointed a country residence to which extensive cultivated land and gardens were attached.

This chapter looks simultaneously at the development of the country-house, or cottage-style, aesthetic on the European continent and its traces in Yıldız's building

archives and extant buildings, situating a newly emerging domestic aesthetic and distinct architectural vocabulary in the palace and in Istanbul at large.[17] It explores the nature, use, and adaptation of visual sources that found their way into the libraries of Ottoman tastemakers and consumers, while taking note of imported flat-pack homes inside the palace gardens. It also formulates a relationship between Yıldız and the public space outside the palace walls: certain features of this new palatine domesticity were quickly appropriated by the capital's local builders to cater to the demands of a burgeoning consumer class, whose members competed with one another in a vibrant, if flashy, public sphere through the distinctiveness of their homes. The sources for the chapter's exploration of the architectural features of the Ottoman fiction of country life (in an otherwise rapidly urbanizing environment) are pattern books and mail-order prefabricated-building catalogues. Meanwhile, the preferences of Ottoman homebuyers are most clearly revealed in the period's illustrated novels as well as in local home-management encyclopedias. As a microscale parallel to Suzanne Marchand's study of porcelain's cultural history,[18] this chapter mobilizes the history of the nineteenth-century prefab house, a particularly unusual international consumer good, its transference from the global to the local market, and its Ottomanization.

The fifth chapter brings chronological closure to the study of Yıldız. It centers on a previously unknown photograph album from 1905, whose images constitute the last photographic representations of the palace before its wholesale dismantling in 1909 in the aftermath of Abdülhamid II's deposition. The majority of the album's photographs depict the final expansion of the palace's architecture and landscape under Abdülhamid's initiative to improve the area dedicated to his select guests. The remaining photographs are a deliberate selection of architectural shots of other imperial residences in the capital that were of particular importance to the sultan.

This final chapter's focus on the third function of the palace, imperial sightseeing, complements the first chapter's discussion of the sultan's sightseeing tour, especially in demonstrating his desire to show off his palace as a space of gentlemanly erudition replete with a well-stocked library, a museum, a manège, greenhouses, aviaries, zoos, and artisanal and industrial ateliers. The possible identity of the album's owner opens up room for discussion of late nineteenth-century decorum, imperial access and restriction—in other words, of the ways in which the visibility of the palatial site was controlled.[19] Most importantly, however, the album's photographs, when read together, construct a biography of Abdülhamid II through the imperial spaces he inhabited. The album's storyline is all the more pertinent given that Abdülhamid was the only sultan not to employ a court chronicler with the sole task of glorifying his reign. The album's materiality and its collection of photographs also provide another opportunity to emphasize how much imperial actors were cognizant of new media's layered metamorphic qualities.

Through examination of two buildings, Yıldız's minuscule theater and royal mosque, the book's coda highlights the conception of diplomacy that bolstered Abdülhamid II's thirty-three-year reign. Although archival materials on these buildings are strangely sparse, we do know that their constructions were supervised, at least, by the one-time court architect Yanko Ioannidis, son of one of the most important building contractors in the empire, Vasilaki Kalfa (ḳalfa, "master builder").[20] These two spaces not only showed remarkable physical commonalities but also were the two principal settings for Abdülhamid II's construction of visibility. While the theater was reserved for intimate diplomatic relations, the prayer ceremonies held each Friday in the mosque were intended to display sultanic grandeur. Yet both spaces were designed to entertain carefully selected groups and were thus intimately bound up with the sultan's diplomatic choreography.

The Accidental Palace offers a reflection on late Ottoman visual and textual archives. Each chapter hinges on a set of previously unknown or underused documents, seeking not only to read them against the physical spaces for which they were often blueprints but also to reveal the modes in which they were drafted and used. The Ottoman reforms of the nineteenth century ignited a near obsession with documenting and archiving.[21] Yıldız's imperial library sheds light on the various functions of these newfound practices, administering a dynamic archive in which items such as photographs, lithographs, sketches, and newspapers, along with various other novel media, were continually repurposed to promote the sultan and state as patriarchal protectors.[22] Whether or not they came to fruition, the architectural projects for Yıldız illustrate the ways in which the newest technologies of home building, landscaping, horticulture, and even railway design were incorporated into the complex. Therefore, the book also highlights the ways in which industrial technology was aestheticized and drawn into the domestic sphere.

Although the book's visual sources are undeniably appealing, Yıldız's textual archives seem at first glance disappointingly bureaucratic. On closer inspection, however, they support the nonimperial strand of landscape history that is traced throughout the book. For instance, the minutely kept registers of Yıldız's gardeners not only function as pre-photographic descriptions of individuals for the purpose of state identification but also reveal the history of hundreds of laborers of various ethnic and geographical origins who worked on the palatial land for more than a century. These underused archives also reveal the lasting influence of these individuals on the extrapalatial horticultural networks of Istanbul as well as Cairo, even after Yıldız was fully dismantled following Abdülhamid II's dethronement in 1909. In presenting both the architectural history and, of equal significance, the garden history of Istanbul's imperial fulcrum, the book also underscores the many subimperial actors that contributed to its making.

No academic monograph dedicated to Yıldız's architectural history has previously been published. Like most late-period Ottoman imperial residences, Yıldız has long been overlooked by scholars, who have assumed that its forms are completely alien to vernacular traditions and do not resemble early Ottoman monuments. Yıldız and its nineteenth-century predecessors, such as the palaces of Beylerbeyi, Dolmabahçe, and Çırağan, are featured at the end of architectural surveys as representatives of a contaminated and thus declining imperial taste. Just as unfruitfully, Yıldız is prolifically represented in historical biographies of Abdülhamid II, who had the longest proprietorship over it, as a mysterious Stygian set piece reflective of the sultan's contested rule; it is cast as the shadowy fortress of a hermitic despot, its uneven layout linked with Abdülhamid's various paranoias.

Nevertheless, certain formative texts on Islamic visual cultures and Ottoman cultural history help to establish the book's temporal and methodological framework. As the last palace of a six-hundred-year-old empire, Yıldız serves as a bookend to the Ottoman building of imperial residences. Therefore, the book's natural conceptual model and methodological predecessor is Gülru Necipoğlu's groundbreaking 1991 study of Topkapı Palace, the Ottomans' first royal residence in the imperial capital, Istanbul.[23] My study is indelibly influenced by Necipoğlu's rendering of the interdependence of Ottoman rule and architectural patronage as its prized symbol—the nature of rule made legible in the structure, layout, and ceremonial use of its representative buildings. Of course, Necipoğlu is neither the first nor the last to formulate this relationship. Sussan Babaie conceives of a paradigm that frames early modern Islamic palatine complexes as ideal cities in microcosm.[24] Although a distinctly modern, even protoindustrial site, Yıldız was deliberately constructed to carry echoes of its preceding models: multiple courts that differentiated public from private; gardens and their ephemeral structures designated for the cultivation of various imperial pastimes; ceremonial spaces that substantiated the otherwise elusive body of the ruler; and myriad artisanal facilities to promote the court's artistic patronage.

In differentiating early modern Ottoman imperial patronage from its incarnations in later centuries and situating Yıldız in its urban, cultural, and historical context, *The Accidental Palace* is indebted to the scholarship of Tülay Artan, Shirine Hamadeh, Zeynep Çelik, and Ahmet Ersoy. I position Yıldız—as a space both physical and discursive representing late Ottoman sovereignty—within the urban, architectural, and intellectual histories of Istanbul highlighted in the work of these scholars. Their conscientious and reflective approach to portraying Ottoman patrons' encounters with the new and the nonlocal has helped me to evaluate the syncretic patronage choices of Yıldız's owners. These scholars recover the intellectual rigor behind the deliberations that reformulated the modern visual repertoire of the empire under successive sultans.

Artan's graduate work on the eighteenth-century transformations along the Bosphorus shoreline, although unpublished, remains a staple source for architectural historians of the late-Ottoman empire.[25] Complementing Artan's research, Hamadeh brings a close typological focus to the narrative of urban expansion.[26] The fountains, heavily landscaped public promenades, and manifold commemorative stone inscriptions that strategically populated Yıldız's early incarnations became prominent markers of increased courtly visibility. Both Artan and Hamadeh also laid the eighteenth-century groundwork for discussion of the gendered patronage patterns that orient my study of queen mothers as tastemakers in the early nineteenth century, specifically through their construction and design in Yıldız.[27]

The desire of the court's male and female members to make Istanbul's European shoreline their new residential zone ignited successive infrastructural transformations in this area as well as its immediate hinterland. Yıldız emerged from this very zone, and its shape and use were continually affected by the court's urban restructuring projects. The radical changes in Istanbul's nineteenth-century fabric, especially in this new imperial neighborhood, are the focus of Çelik's guiding study.[28] Examining the dramatic and at times fanciful industrial projects undertaken to "regularize" Istanbul, Çelik writes an infrastructural history of Istanbul during the reform period, into which I insert Yıldız as the capital's last imperial complex.

If Çelik's volume evaluates the nature of the mostly civic (and Western-influenced) structures constituting Istanbul's piecemeal yet grand-scale reformulations, Ersoy's recent study of the visual culture of the late Tanzimat period centers on the rigorously intellectual agency and output of Ottoman bureaucrats, historicizing and defining an imperial architectural idiom "from within."[29] Ersoy's restoration of agency to local actors balances out Çelik's Eurocentric focus on foreign actors and the ideas for projects that they brought with them to Istanbul.

To elucidate Yıldız's expanding role as the empire's administrative center, which culminated in Abdülhamid II's autocratic rule, *The Accidental Palace* crosses disciplinary boundaries to read the period's architectural output through Ottoman political and institutional histories. For my work, the two most enlightening volumes on late-Ottoman imperial symbols, from court ceremony to the language of the chancery and law, which were either revived selectively from old dynastic traditions or originated by sultans themselves to legitimize their regime, are *The Well-Protected Domains*, by Selim Deringil, and *Padişahım Çok Yaşa!*, by Hakan Karateke.

Two earlier but equally groundbreaking studies, Şerif Mardin's *Genesis of Young Ottoman Thought* and Carter Vaughn Findley's *Bureaucratic Reform in the Ottoman Empire*—by examining the structural transformations of the state's administrative bodies through a multitude of sources, both archival (mostly bureaucratic) and biographical (therefore surprisingly intimate)—collectively lay the historical groundwork for exploration of the Ottoman reform era.

As these scholars note, palace structures were not immune to the demands of the period's reforms. Evinced by Yıldız's various physical transformations, such structures and the various functionaries appointed for their upkeep underwent radical makeovers. The Tanzimat also produced a novel bureaucratic system, which created a new type of civil servant. In turn, this new bureaucratic class emulated and replicated the emerging tastes of the court, especially in the design of their homes and gardens. The scholarship of Mardin and Findley, in particular, helps me to trace the relationship between the domestic lives of palace employees and those of members of the court, previously underexplored, through Pierre Bourdieu's sociological constructs of taste, emulation, and adaptation, a method already anticipated by Olivier Bouquet in *Les pachas du sultan*.[30] These studies prompt further examination of what constituted the private material world of this new class of office-goers, whose consumption behavior is often aligned in scholarship with the European bourgeoisie.[31]

Mardin and Findley show that prominent members of this new class were prolific writers of sociopolitical tracts and memoirs. These texts encourage a more nuanced engagement with the notable, if already well-understood, topic of the Ottomans' presumed Western leanings in the nineteenth century. In short, the writings of members of this class of state administrators provide contexts for the mindsets of Yıldız's various imperial patrons. To assume that Christian Sester's recruitment into court employment in the 1830s reflects the same kind of Eurocentrism as the circulation of international pattern books in Istanbul at the century's end is to assume that Westernization is atemporal, unidirectional, and immune to local contingency. *The Accidental Palace* also considers the very intimate, personal spaces in which these bureaucrats, with overt consumer habits, reflected on and wrote about their experiences.

In a happy coincidence, Darin Stephanov has recently published a study that forms the contextual backbone for my own book, covering roughly the same time period (from Mahmud II to Abdülhamid II).[32] Fortifying my argument that the royal dwelling was an important armature for the new identity of the nineteenth-century sovereign, Stephanov reads the reformulated role of the sultans as authoritarian reformists, and the regnal aura they wanted to project to their Muslim and non-Muslim subjects, primarily through the freshly invented celebrations commemorating the ruler's birth (*velādet*) and accession (*cülūs*). Expanded and altered, these empire-wide celebrations continued to be orchestrated by Abdülhamid II, the most spectral of sultans, as his ultimate proxies. Stephanov also highlights the radical changes in the sultan's dress (pared-down military garb), the emergence of imperial portraiture (*taṣvīr-ı hümāyūn*) and a state newspaper, the officialization of the Friday prayer ceremonies (*selāmlık*), and, most important, the royal country trips (*memleket gezileri*) with which the now conspicuously visible ruler aimed to reach a much larger audience. Mahmud II's conception of his palatial garden complex, Abdülmecid's unabated investment in the site, and Abdülhamid II's panoptic retreat into its vastness were all part and parcel of a conscious imperial rebranding that emphasized the sultan's body politic, whether structured on direct visibility or conjured through carefully crafted signifiers of sovereignty.

Yıldız's lifespan also coincides with the historical period addressed by Şükrü Hanioğlu in his *Brief History of the Late Ottoman Empire*. A visual corollary to the period of imperial reforms, the Yıldız of *The Accidental Palace* complements his thematically arranged historical survey of the modern Ottoman era. In writing the history of the palace's syncretic forms, I take as a central tenet Hanioğlu's rendering of Ottoman Westernization as a "complex process of acculturation."[33] Essentially, each of the chapters here unpacks the multiple instances of acculturation through exploration of the architectural, photographic, and landscape design features of Yıldız.

More often than not, novel markers of empire are sought first in a sovereign's image and his immediate surroundings. Predictably, *The Accidental Palace*'s precursory layers trace these most obvious and conspicuous representations. However, the book is emphatic on the notion that the site was equally molded by the accrued expertise, conscious desires, and arduous (physical) labor of others (adopting here the full extent of this designation); the site's image was also later retooled in diverse iterations by nonimperial classes. The potent artistic agency of these men and women can be conceived in Laura Doyle's fertile theoretical construct of the

"inter-imperial," a performative domain or attribute—separate from the ruler's body—through which "the laboring man [or woman] develops a cloaked awareness of the master's dependence on him [her] but also of his [her] own making and laboring powers."[34] Every chapter retains these "inter-imperial" identities in order to expand the list of those who qualify as meaning makers of the nineteenth-century empire's heart and to support the claims of those previously ignored to a place within it.

Lastly, this book does not claim to be the final word on this site or the multiple palaces and imperial residences housed there, and it is especially indebted to the many unpublished Turkish-language theses and dissertations written on Yıldız (see the bibliography). In the way that these scholarly efforts instigated mine, *The Accidental Palace*, through its case-based chapters, hopes to spark further research on the wider and definitively diverse Tanzimat networks of art and architectural patronage, which have until now been eclipsed by the sultanic one.[35] The visual historiography of the empire's last two centuries needs to be populated. Women of the court, who have suffered most from this historiographic oversight, served as prominent civic philanthropists. While they may have been relatively quiet about their personal lives, enough of them recorded their daily lives with descriptive precision, offering insights into their environments unrivaled in the narratives of their male counterparts. Most of this book's visual sources are especially enlivened by the recollections of individuals like Leyla Saz, Ayşe Osmanoğlu, Georgina Müller, Princess Djavidan Hanım (née Marianna Török de Szendrõ), Enid Layard (née Guest), Anna Bowman Dodd, and, to an extent, Bezm-i Alem Valide Sultan. Furthermore, the history of the Tanzimat is often narrated as a sequence of administrative changes helmed by a lineup of Ottoman statesmen; more attention should be paid to the interior worlds of these individuals, the physical environments on which they cast their official identities as state employees, especially because they showed such brio and personality in their home-building choices.[36]

Ultimately, then, *The Accidental Palace* offers inroads into the material culture of the nineteenth-century Ottoman bureaucratic class, exemplifying the recent scholarly attention to non-Western bourgeois cultures, whether or not such sociological designations can be so neatly administered in this context.[37] In this comparative vein, each chapter—whether focusing on patterns of urban patronage, garden and landscape models, the form and function of urban dwellings, bureaucratization of courtly professions, or the imperial court's scaling down into a Victorian family—speaks to such nineteenth-century histories of places outside the Ottoman domain. Besides these thematic global connections, *The Accidental Palace* is designed to encourage scholarly approaches to Ottoman material culture that think through the nature of visual sources not simply to prove the onetime existence of people (names as tallies of foreign versus local) or things (a building, wall, door, garden, or pool) but to reanimate them as documents whose very compositions are worthy objects of scrutiny. The era's bureaucratization, coupled with feverish new forms of record keeping, catalyzed archival production; increasingly, written descriptions were accompanied not only by drawings but also by photographs and other forms of representational media. This awareness that a visual source might have accompanied a written record underlies the book's handling of its primary sources. One is sometimes fortunate enough to find a complete set of records, exemplary of this particular archiving practice, a file in its original multimedia format, but most of the time sources are broken up and dispersed among various repositories, often irreparably so—not unlike Yıldız itself. However, each and every one of these documentary remains signals the possibility of capacious visual histories, providing a clearer sense of how they were created, seen, and used: as versatile, imminently repurposable representational canvases of the constantly shape-shifting modern age, again analogous to Yıldız's centurial making.[38]

Sultan Abdülhamid II's Yıldız Palace

In 1909, when the turbulence accompanying the restoration of the constitution and the deposition of Sultan Abdülhamid II had briefly subsided, Francis McCullagh, a British war correspondent who had lived through these events in Istanbul, reported with excitement that the doors of Yıldız, the mysterious prison-like palace of the mad sultan, afflicted with "the monomania of fear,"[1] would finally be opened, following the government's Young Turk takeover:

> For many years past Yildiz has been regarded by all Turkey as an ogre's den into which the best of the Osmanli were dragged and devoured; as an impregnable stronghold wherein priceless booty was accumulated; as a mysterious residence littered with evidences of a thousand crimes, undermined by secret passages, and provided with all the mysterious chambers, labyrinths, trap-doors, &c., which one would naturally expect to find in the house of a man who has all his life employed a staff of translators to render into Turkish the dregs of the low-class, sensational novels of intrigue and crime that are written in Europe.
>
> The fall of the hoary monster who inhabited this lair constituted therefore, so far as the Ottomans were concerned, one of the most sensational events of their whole amazing history, inasmuch as it laid bare to them all the secrets of Yildiz Kiosk.[2]

As soon as Yıldız's royal inhabitants had left the palace, the Action Army of the Young Turks, deemed liberators, staged photographic scenes to be converted into popular postcards on the vacated grounds (fig. 1). The next task for the new bureaucrats of the constitutional monarchy—the Committee of Union and Progress (the political body of the Young Turk Movement) and Mehmed V (r. 1909–18), the new titular sultan—was to itemize the palace's contents. Aided by one of the palace's eunuchs, whose life had been spared for his knowledge of the locations of safes full of banknotes, company shares, gold, silver, decorations, medals, and jewelry, a commission spent months compiling lists; numbering and reallocating furniture, books, and other objects; dispersing the thousands of animals that made up the imperial menagerie; and classifying the palace's archives, which included countless unopened reports (*jurnal*s) from sycophants seeking Abdülhamid's protection.[3] McCullagh likened this grueling task to "sending a tax-collector to make out a list of the goods in Ali Baba's cave."[4] However, those involved, including McCullagh, were very disappointed with what

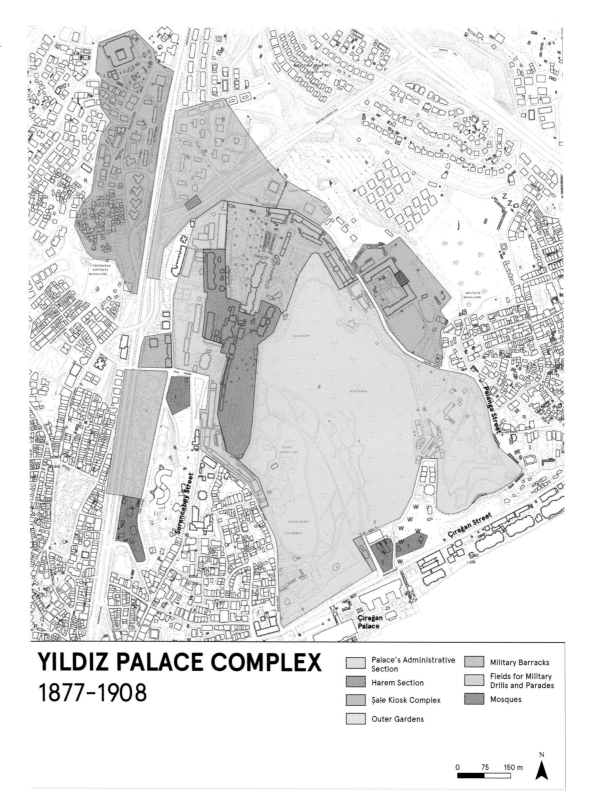

YILDIZ PALACE COMPLEX
1877-1908

Palace's Administrative Section

Harem Section

Şale Kiosk Complex

Outer Gardens

Military Barracks

Fields for Military Drills and Parades

Mosques

0   75   150 m

N

they found. Expecting a treasure trove of secrets and invaluable imperial objects, they were instead confronted with an abundance of Oriental knickknacks, Victorian technological devices, and items easily obtainable from specialized Pera merchants or department stores: "Enough rosaries, sticks, and chibouks . . . were discovered to start a hundred Oriental antique merchants in business, but the only objects in the accumulation of which Abd-ul-Hamid displayed the true zeal of a collector were pianos, gramophones, clocks, shirts, collars, keys, and modern firearms, especially revolvers."[5]

The sultan's interests were not unlike those of a well-to-do European bourgeois. He wanted starched shirts aplenty, ashtrays handy, and American gilt clocks—always synchronized—in all of the rooms he most frequently occupied. The cataloguers discovered many trade journals from which he had bought furniture, locks, revolvers, and even mail-order prefabricated houses. Abdülhamid regarded the quarters he inhabited in Yıldız as his refuge.[6] The structures he built for himself and his family were modest in both scale and cost—he required "little more space than a cat and was evidently not a monarch who delighted in striding up and down lofty halls."[7] Yet their interior furnishings, which in their abundance resembled "an auctioneer's showroom,"[8] displayed an array of styles, from Japanese and art nouveau to Empire and Louis XVI.

Yıldız's architectural historiography is dominated by narratives that align the palace with Abdülhamid, the ruler with the longest residence in and patronage of it. Numerous accounts of the site penned by supporters of the Young Turk Movement read the palace's architectural idiosyncrasies as reflective of Abdülhamid's purportedly twisted mind and the paralyzing fears that made him a prisoner in his own home: "his house is a standing monument to the greatness of his cowardice and the littleness of his mind."[9] The most famous Ottoman version of these accounts is the two-volume ʿAbdülḥamīd-i Ṣānī ve Devr-i Salṭanatı, Ḥayāt-ı Ḫuṣūṣīye ve Siyāsīyesi (Abdülhamid II and the era of his rule: His personal and political life), by Osman Nuri (d. 1909), an obscure military member of the Young Turks, who died before seeing his volumes published. This work, which is indiscriminately cited today in discussions of Yıldız's architectural layout, has often been mistakenly attributed. Contrary to popular supposition, it is not the product of an official court chronicler, nor is it based on archival sources of any kind, let alone the memoirs of individuals who lived or worked at the site. Rather, it is a collage of often grossly exaggerated stories translated from foreign newspaper articles and travel narratives.[10] In another case, Abdurrahman Şeref (d. 1925), the last court-appointed historian of the Ottoman state under Abdülhamid's successor, Mehmed V (r. 1909–18), likens the deposed sultan's Yıldız to the Garden of Şeddād (or Shaddād), a Koranic allusion to the leader of the legendary tribe of ʿĀd in Yemen, whose garden in the likeness of paradise, with lofty pillars, God destroyed as a warning thenceforth against mortal hybrids.[11] A barrage of these kinds of texts, whose impartiality and evidential value are deeply questionable, has continued to cripple our understanding of the palace and its architectural history. This, in part, is why a monograph on this site has never been produced: simply parsing what is real and what is not is a task unto itself.[12]

Some scholars, seduced by these undeniably attractive yet factually dubious narratives, still try to discover secret underground tunnels (of which there are none) and continue to fixate on the notion that Abdülhamid slept in different rooms every night to bewilder his assassins.[13] It is difficult to reinscribe a site designated an "ogre's den" and "the lair of a hoary monster" as one that merits examination within the broader historiography of Ottoman architecture, especially as the cultural output of the nineteenth century is neglected in Islamic-art studies as a period irrecoverably subservient to Western forms, ideas, and modes of representation.[14]

It is true that to many early twentieth-century Ottomans, who sought a parliamentary monarchy, the eradication of censorship, and a level of transparency in the remaining decades of the Ottoman sovereignty, Abdülhamid and his palace were infamously enigmatic and deserving of public enmity. In their eyes, Yıldız had become a "fortress of despotism" and "a synonym for dark misgovernment."[15] Its former occupants and employees frequently laced their accounts with sensationalist stories to appeal to this very audience—an audience that was ready to despise the dethroned sultan and the spaces and symbols of his rule. These narratives quickly cornered a profitable market through the popular dailies. Conveying a spectrum of impressions, from favorable to hostile, and with some written in response to others, they not only collectively dominated the world of newspaper serials but also continued to appear well into the second half of the twentieth century.[16]

Perhaps the single most stirring anecdote reflecting the level of public antipathy to Yıldız comes from a close member of Abdülhamid's family. The atmosphere of greater freedom felt in Istanbul immediately after the sultan's removal allowed his great-niece Mevhibe Celaleddin to visit the palace, which was opened to the public by the Young Turk government for a short period of time before Mehmed V moved in. She provides a description of the public's reaction to Abdülhamid's deposition and Yıldız's place in Istanbul's urban consciousness. When she first entered the site, Mevhibe was struck by the masses touring the palace grounds; Yıldız seemed to have become a tourism attraction (*mesīre*).[17] A handful of photographs by Ali Sami (later Aközer), one of Abdülhamid's former court photographers, illustrates the public's curiosity about and mad rush to the site (fig. 2). Gradually, however, the true nature of this popular interest revealed itself. The visitors were there to display their anger in visceral ways. Mevhibe was horrified to witness a woman encouraging her son to urinate publicly on the Gobelins upholstery in one of the chalets in the palace's private garden.

In the early days of the Turkish Republic, it was precisely the continued enigmatic nature of Yıldız that made it a perfect hideaway for the military school of the new nation, which prided itself on the might of its new army. Presumably in an effort to parallel the Hamidian spy network that was thought to have been at the palace's core (a network not, in fact, as well organized as has been speculated), the republic's intelligence agency also claimed one of the palace's buildings.[18] The absence of extant locally drawn and complete maps of the complex from the reign of Abdülhamid is connected to the site's furtive republican transformation into a military zone and the subsequent redaction of the blueprints of its headquarters. It is also telling that the famous insurance maps of Jacques

Pervititch, which date from the first decade of the republic, gloss over the palace, with an abrupt transition from the busy commercial center of Beşiktaş to the more residential district of Ortaköy.[19] Yıldız's martial inhabitants commissioned a meager first attempt at a monograph on the palace, with indiscriminate borrowings from Osman Nuri's work.[20]

The palace was soon parceled out even further.[21] The Şale compound, which had hosted Abdülhamid II's imperial guests, came to be operated as a casino by an American in the 1920s, while the site's park became a public promenade.[22] The numerous apartments and individual chalets of the sultan's family—the palace's most private, residential section—were turned into a university. A mammoth curvilinear hotel took over a portion of its gardens, towering over the elegant timber Ertuğrul convent, mosque, tomb, and library complex of the North African shaykh Muhammed Zafir Efendi (d. 1903) of the Shadhiliyya Sufi order. Today a modest research institution shares the same space as a building recently converted into a ceremonial hall for the use of the prime minister. What is more, there are plans to restore this fragmented site to its full glory as a garden palace—not to open it up to the public as a museum, like Topkapı Palace, but to convert it into the Istanbul residence of the Turkish president.[23] The official word selected to describe this project is *külliye*, which has historically described Ottoman mosque complexes with many charitable adjacencies; it has never before been applied to secular structures like palaces or civic institutions.

Although Yıldız still occupies a sizable portion of the urban core of Istanbul's European quarter, the complex history of its fragmentation and the incredible volume of its archives have caused scholars to approach the site with astonishing trepidation.[24] Although parts of the site have been reconfigured as museums, including the restored Şale compound (administered by the National Museums) as well as the Istanbul City Museum (converted from the palace's aides-de-camp building by the municipality), on any given day they receive only a handful of visitors. It is both surprising and incredibly sad that such a large and unorthodox site, which bears evidence of nineteenth-century Ottoman material culture, is so willfully forgotten. One scurries along beside its boundary walls, always fearing that one is trespassing in an area belonging to a governmental body; more often than not, guards appear to confirm this suspicion.

ABDÜLHAMID AS AN ARCHITECTURAL PATRON

Abdülhamid was a meditative and frugal architectural patron. Even the most defamatory biographies devote countless pages to his prudent patronage, his "natural taste and talent for architecture," and his "marked preference for the modern and even for the new."[25] One of them highlights his ability to read plans, his insistence on scale models, and his habit of designing his own buildings:

> More than one plan, executed with his own hand, has surprised his architects. He understands their explanations very well, and recognises the correctness of the observations they make....
>
> ... For the smallest building he insists on the construction of a model elaborately studied out, in which all the details are shown with the most conscientious minutiae, so that the building he is putting up is only a mathematical enlargement. He counts himself, in advance, the number of bricks which should be used in building, and keeps this model, after having had it signed by the architect on each of the sides representing the façades of the edifice, in order to be able to see later if his orders have been strictly carried out.[26]

Besides the natural protection provided by Yıldız's location, the site appealed to Abdülhamid for two main reasons: its supposed air quality (shielded as it was against the *lodos*, the warm southwesterly wind that the sultan deemed bad for his health)[27] and its spaciousness, which satisfied the sultan's desire to maintain the active lifestyle in the great outdoors to which he had grown accustomed on the estates of his princely years, such as Maslak and Kağıthane (sites central to chapter 5). Abdülhamid's deeply confessional recounting of his princely years to a physician while in exile often revisits his beloved airy mansions, gardens, and estates. In one case he recalls disagreeing with the suggestion made by his uncle Abdülaziz, the then-reigning sultan, to rebuild Prince Abdülhamid's Tarabya *yalı* in stone: "I do not fancy buildings made of stone and bricks [*kārgīr*]. In my opinion, they are better wooden" (Ben ise kargirden hoşlanmam, böyle ahşap olması daha iyidir).[28]

The understudied railway project upon which I expand later in this chapter reflected Abdülhamid's vision of turning Yıldız into an Alpine estate, with its requisite types. "Above the green slopes, in among the tree-trunks, we passed innumerable châlets," a visitor to his palace observed in 1903.[29] According to another, "the Sultan's own residence [was] a graceful and simple wooden building of the Swiss style of architecture."[30] A somewhat fractious foreign diplomat recalls having shivered in one of these structures during an audience with the sultan: "These houses, built in haste from light materials and barely heated, are glacial. I have rarely been as cold as I was during that audience."[31]

Yıldız's buildings were willfully eclectic and borrowed idiosyncratically from examples found in the period's famed world expositions.[32] They might not have exhibited stylistic unity in the overall effect of the palatial complex, but Abdülhamid used them deliberately to counter the prevailing palatial taste for Tanzimat neoclassicism that he associated with his predecessors. While the sultan's choices were a calculated affront to the architectural culture of the preceding period, he also mobilized these structures as means to display crafts. Instead of reminiscing about the vastness of his palace while in exile, he specifically returned again and again to his mentorship of capable artisans (*erbāb-ı ṣanʿat*) in the ateliers of Yıldız and their skills in carpentry, wood carving, and turnery, as well as to his own creations. Had he not been a sultan, he said, he would have run an arts-and-crafts school.[33]

What follows from here is an architectural overview of Yıldız while it served as Abdülhamid's palace. I show how the sultan conceived it and how some of his closest family members, court officials, and most-intimate guests saw it. Instead of framing Yıldız as a palace built around courtyards, as a handful of short descriptions that identify tenuous linkages to Topkapı Palace seek to do, I discuss prominent segments of the Hamidian compound, whose intended functions were similar to those of its antecedents: functional and ceremonial, public and private.[34] Abdülhamid wanted to appear attentive to his privileged viewers—at times perhaps overbearingly so.[35] Therefore, Yıldız's spaces and their carefully monitored representations, which commemorated these relations and encounters, were always charged and celebratory. Describing a walk through the uninhabited palace, the British journalist McCullagh tellingly observes that "one felt inclined to conclude that the house had been furnished with presents, books and samples of furniture, &c., sent by foreign firms and foreign potentates."[36]

The ensuing section clarifies the physicality of a space that has been the subject of a great number of speculative interpretations. My approach to the description of Abdülhamid's Yıldız is centripetal. Beginning with the broadest possible designations of the site (as a fortress, a city, and a neighborhood) and its relationship with its larger urban environment, I then narrow my focus toward a

definition of its internal parts by means of
the controlled choreographies devised by the
sultan, which delineated the palace's administrative, ceremonial, and domestic/private
sections. As the palace was expanded over
preexisting structures, these three zones did
not have clear physical boundaries. Rather,
they were distinguished by changing use,
etiquette, and circulation. In this regard, the
palace comes closest to the palatine model
of Safavid Isfahan, whose functions, even
within the most private structures of the palace, were circumscribed by the ruler's changing demands.[37]

YILDIZ: A FORTRESS, A CITY, AND A NEIGHBORHOOD

To Yıldız's contemporaries and later historians, Abdülhamid's palace appeared to
carry architectural ambitions beyond those
of a typical imperial residence. For fear of
being dethroned or assassinated,[38] the sultan

retreated from urban life and public visibility and, over the course of thirty years, built
himself a city (map 1). The first visitor to write
about Yıldız as a miniature city was the Qajar
ruler Muzaffar al-Din Shah (r. 1896–1907).
The shah saw the palace in its most complete state, close to the end of Abdülhamid's
thirty-three-year reign. On the return leg of
his third and last trip to Europe, the shah was
hosted by Abdülhamid in the lavish garden
compound of Yıldız's Şale Kiosk, which had
been built and expanded many times over to
accommodate, entertain, and impress foreign
heads of state (fig. 3). The original Şale would
receive a new wing with octagonal towers,
a wing the court documentation referred to
as the "ceremonial office" (merāsim dāʾiresi)
(fig. 4).

A less succinct and expressive diarist than
his father, Nasir al-Din Shah (r. 1848–96), who
had pioneered European diplomatic travel
for the Qajar state, Muzaffar al-Din Shah,
through frequent repetition, highlighted
what he found interesting in his sojourn.
In his travelogue, Yıldız's city-like appearance
receives this kind of emphatic treatment. The
shah observes, "Yıldız is actually a small town
surrounded by walls and is exclusive to the
sultan and the royal family. It is not only a
garden and building but a royal citadel that
is quite vast and extended." A few pages later,
he repeats this point: "Yıldız palace . . . is actually the fortress [*arg*] of government and is a
town unto itself."[39]

As the guest of Sultan Abdülaziz (r. 1861–
76), Nasir al-Din Shah's experience of this
site in 1867 was remarkably different from
that of his son. Then constituting Çırağan's
backyard (discussed in detail in chapter 3),
the many "detached structures" that would be
absorbed into Abdülhamid's palace had just

begun to be built when Nasir al-Din surveyed them during a carriage ride. The buildings whose construction the shah witnessed must have been two masonry pleasure pavilions, the Malta and Çadır kiosks, that occupied the northern and southernmost tips of the imperial park (map 4).[40] According to Nasir al-Din, this site was conceived as Abdülaziz's private zoological garden, boasting specimens that the shah had not previously seen during his European sojourn.[41] Here Nasir al-Din encountered peacocks, a roaring tiger, a leopard, an aviary that housed rare Australian golden pheasants, and dovecotes filled with pigeons. The Azizian version of the site carried architectural echoes of Napoleon III and Empress Eugenie's Jardin zoologique d'acclimatation in Paris's Bois de Boulogne— miniature structures where guests could rest, in the form of dainty gazebos and neoclassical island hermitages, and rustic wooden animal sheds, with wire fencing and thatched roofs. Within two short decades, between one shah and the next, branching avenues, novel buildings, and intricate street patterns had been laid over the landscape, becoming Sultan Abdülhamid's city, as Muzaffar al-Din Shah describes:

> Yıldız garden, which is in the middle of the Ottoman lands, is known as *sarāy*. As we mentioned, it is a town [*shahr*] with several edifices [*ʿimārāt*], a forest [*jangal*], a hunting field [*shikārgāh*], a lake [*daryācha*], and various facilities for excursion [*asbāb-i tafarruj*]. It also includes excellent barracks [*sarbāzkhāna*]; up to thirty thousand regular troops reside in this garden. In fact, it is an enormous citadel [*arg*] surrounded by very solid walls and fortifications. No one without the

FIGURE 4
Abdullah Frères, view of Raimondo D'Aronco's Merasim apartments. MSİB Dolmabahçe Palace Museum, Abdülmecid Efendi Library Collection, Istanbul, 11-1267.

permission of the government is allowed in or out.... A museum, a library, a zoo, a number of workshops [*fabrik*], several private residences for the sultan's family [*haramkhāna*], and all equipment of a great Ottoman royal apparatus [*dastgāh-i salṭanat-i buzurg-i ʿuṣmānī*] is provided in the Yıldız palace complex [*sarāy*].[42]

Indeed, the site's high and mighty walls, which for nineteenth-century observers resonated ominously with the sultan's seclusion, turned the palace into a fortress. Today the congested urban sprawl and modern hotel encroaching upon the palace walls obscure what must have been an intimidating physical presence in the lives of the nineteenth-century residents of Beşiktaş and Ortaköy. Like the shoreline walls of Topkapı Palace, which protected it from possible threats from land and sea, the walls around Abdülhamid's complex shielded his court from a potential siege by Russian battleships on the Bosphorus during the Russo-Turkish War that ended in 1878, and also from insurgents against his sovereignty who might try to storm the palace.[43] The infamous case of the Young Ottoman journalist-theologian Ali Suavi, who in 1878 attempted a coup by charging into Çırağan from its shore in an effort to free and reinstall the deposed sultan Murad V, strengthened Abdülhamid's resolve never to leave Yıldız.[44] It is not surprising, then, that to Muzaffar al-Din, Yıldız resembled a fortress (*arg*). Another factor that probably contributed to his characterization of the site is the fact that Gulistan, the shah's palace complex in Tehran, which like Yıldız was made up of a variety of pavilions, was built inside the Safavid shah Tahmasp I's sixteenth-century fortifications.[45]

Yıldız's interior partitions reinforced the fortresslike appearance created by its monumental outer walls. The American journalist Anna Bowman Dodd (d. 1929), who accompanied the American ambassadorial delegation to Abdülhamid's court a few years before Muzaffar al-Din Shah's visit, was similarly struck by the palace's countless inner walls. To her, Yıldız appeared to be "mediaeval," a "living fortress" made up of "walls within walls."[46] She observed that "the chief residence of His Majesty, the harem, and the pavilions where his younger sons and their households live" were "enclosed within an inner wall," like the keep of a fortress, and set on a terrace atop the highest hill.[47]

The apocryphal descriptions of Yıldız found in *The Private Life of the Sultan of Turkey*, a lurid biography written under the pseudonym Georges Dorys and probably commissioned by the Young Turks as one of many anti-Hamidian narratives at the turn of the century, imagine this segment of the palace as a hexagonal fortress. According to "Dorys," it constituted "what is popularly called the *Small Enclosure of the Palace*, the iron doors of which, opening only on the outside, could not be forced in case of a popular rising or military mutiny."[48] Impenetrable doors, gateways, fences, barriers, and walls were central, both physically and metaphorically, to Abdülhamid's reign. Even the soldiers and guards that lined the palace walls or accompanied the sultan to his highly ceremonial public Friday prayers (*Cumʿa selāmlıġı*) were often described as a "wall of steel" or "fence of glistening muskets."[49] Moreover, Dodd likens the crowded protocol of a diplomatic reception for the American delegation, which the sultan attended with his "aides-de-camp, household guards, officers, courtiers, even priests [imams]," to a silent progression through a "living wall of eyes": "The shapes of uniformed men met one at every turning. A line of tall soldierly figures would be passed, framed in one of the long, damask-hung passages. Groups of others, close to the doorways of salons, stood as if posing for caryatids . . . young officers in showy uniforms caught the eye and held it, though the groups were rooms and rooms beyond, in the distant perspective."[50] Located outside the palace's northern and northwestern walls, the Ertuğrul and Orhaniye military barracks, named after the founder of the dynasty and its second sultan, respectively, provided further protection for the palace's inhabitants. Along with the smaller barracks for the Turbaned Regiment (*ṣārıḳlı zuʿāf ālāyı*), composed of military recruits from Baghdad, Yemen, Hejaz, and Tripoli, these structures were erected mainly to house the regiments that guarded the sultan during the *selamlık* ceremonies. During these events the regiments took up a complex formation along the narrow strip along the hill between the palace gates and the Hamidiye Mosque (fig. 5). In this condensed space, the various ethnic compositions of the regiments were meant to perform the roles of loyal Turkic, Arab, and Albanian subjects of Abdülhamid's empire.

Yıldız's most circumspect historiographers are those who have built their observations on Muzaffar al-Din's repetitive rendering of the palace as an urban settlement. In the only useful, albeit still limited, encyclopedia entry on the palace, Afife Batur's analysis stresses its growth over time and organic acquisition of an urban layout: "a milieu unlike that of a palace, was it intended as a town?"[51] Batur reads the palace as made up of interwoven streets and buildings, devoid of axiality or any other form of geometry. Neglecting its prepalatine history as a much smaller imperial site, which formed the kernel of its subsequent growth and reconfiguration, she concentrates on its unsystematic planning. She is quick to argue that additions to and connections between buildings were constructed spontaneously and without premeditation, whereby a fabric of streets and small irregular piazzas emerged to give the palace the appearance of a "medieval city."[52] François Georgeon, the historian who offers the most balanced biography of Abdülhamid II, also calls the palace "a town within a town,"[53] which like any growing city appeared to be a permanent construction site. Yıldız was always in need of another building to accommodate a new government office, or an additional residence to house a family member or an imperial guest. The lands around it—most

FIGURE 5
Abdullah Frères, photograph of the Hamidiye Mosque during the *selamlık* ceremony, with a Bosphorus view in the distance, from the album "Palais Imperiaux," 1891. Ömer M. Koç Collection.

of which were privately owned gardens and orchards—were often seized to allow for this continual development. Countless official documents show how the palace gradually engulfed its surroundings and grew piecemeal into a fifty-hectare complex by the turn of the century.

Another of Muzaffar al-Din Shah's perceptive descriptions of Yıldız notes its centrality with respect to surrounding neighborhoods. In a diary entry, the shah describes the neighborhoods of Ortaköy, Dolmabahçe, and Beşiktaş as irrevocably and symbiotically linked with the palace in a constant circulation of goods, services, and people. These people and places, he says, constitute "Yıldız's neighborhood" (mujāvir-i qaṣr-ı Yıldız).[54] To the shah, not only the houses and shops of ordinary locals but also Dolmabahçe (recently demoted to the status of mansion ['imārat], as opposed to palace), its mosque, and the imperial foundry of Tophane seemed to have been subsumed under the authority of Abdül-hamid's Yıldız.

Yıldız's innumerable employees, from the members of its regiments to its eunuchs, its chief bath keepers, and its quilt makers, populated Beşiktaş's bustling marketplace, its ramshackle coffee shop that "hung like a cage above a lumber warehouse,"[55] and its bakeries, butchers, and other food sellers. The palace's affluent bureaucrats, however, were given sumptuously endowed mansions on the plateaus of Nişantaşı, which Georgeon calls the "town of pashas."[56] Since Yıldız under Abdül-hamid had upstaged the Sublime Porte as the empire's administrative center, the ministers were strongly encouraged to live close to the palace, because they could be called upon at any hour.[57] The imperial treasury covered the cost of constructing and furnishing the mansions for the grand vizier, the chief religious official, and the minister of war, and even subsidized rents for the homes of many low-ranking officials.[58]

The sultan commissioned photographs that meticulously documented the process of building the houses of his viziers. The expenses of the imperial treasury include room-by-room furniture lists for their interiors.[59] Unsurprisingly, one of these lists begins with the furnishings for the grand vizier's study (*yazı odası*)—its bureau, library, and requisite cigarette stand—one room in a well-appointed residence befitting the dedicated and industrious governmental work that the vizier was expected to undertake. A contemporary insider reports that these mansions were often preferred over Yıldız to host the ministerial gatherings at which important decisions regarding the state were discussed, because they often offered a degree of privacy

that the palace's Mabeyn Kiosk did not.[60] To encourage these bureaucrats to remain as close as possible to the newly designated governmental palace (where members of the administration were always on call and viziers, scribes, and aides worked in twenty-four-hour shifts in times of emergency), the sultan's calculated benevolence extended beyond the appointment of opulent mansions and luxurious furnishings to landscaping and the provision of greenhouses and delicate wooden pavilions to keep his officials content in their domestic worlds.

Even more than the many military barracks situated on the high plateaus of the palace, the police station in Beşiktaş's square and its chief, Yedi-sekiz Hasan Paşa (who killed Ali Suavi during the latter's Çırağan raid to reinstall Murad V), were responsible for the surveillance around Yıldız. The station controlled all of the properties surrounding the palace and handpicked their tenants, from the Hasan Paşa creek to Ihlamur and Yenimahalle, from Ortaköy to the entrance of the Şale Kiosk, and from the hillside street of Serencebey to Yıldız's Mabeyn. A palace scribe recalls that this station was where Yıldız really started: "it was the beginning, door, and lock of the palace" (Burası Yıldızın mebde-i kapısı, kilididir).[61] The station's personnel were often covertly integrated into the neighborhood, posing as shopkeepers, tailors, cobblers, or beggars.

Amid the urban chaos of the capital's new center, Yıldız imposed an implicit hierarchy on its neighborhoods. A baker with an oven in Beşiktaş had to abide by this hierarchy when distributing bread via his itinerant vendors (*ṭablakār*): starting with the devout attendees of the sixteenth-century mosque–dervish convent of Yahya Efendi, then moving to the mansions of the sultan's closest aides bordering the palace—Tahir Paşa, the imperial head guard; Rıza Paşa, the minister of war; and Ali Bey, the sultan's secretary—and finally proceeding to the stately homes of viziers, ministers, and scribes in Nişantaşı. Yıldız's kitchens, their stone buildings located beside the Mecidiye Mosque, not only fed the palace's own inhabitants and employees but also delivered large round trays full of food covered in dark cloth three times a day to the *yalı*s (shore mansions) of the court's extended members, which dotted the shoreline from Kuruçeşme and Ortaköy to Fındıklı.[62] When about forty *tablakar*s (tray-carrying waiters), dressed in their pitch-black, high-collared stambouline frocks, walked in single file along the avenue behind Çırağan, "they cast long shadows on the sidewalks."[63] The court's savvy food vendors also sold large quantities of leftovers to Beşiktaş's locals, while broughams carrying the court's female members crisscrossed the roads connecting Yıldız with the waterfront mansions of their relatives.[64] This deeply enmeshed quotidian economy that spanned the palace and its surroundings was also constantly invigorated by the spectacle of Abdülhamid's Friday prayer ceremonies. The shopkeepers of Beşiktaş served halvah and zythum (*boza*) to the immense crowds that gathered each week to witness the sultan's grand unchanging devotional display.[65]

THE *SELAMLIK* AND MABEYN

To understand the eventual palatial evolution of Yıldız's architectural layout, it is important to recognize that for a long time the hilltop Yıldız estate and its buildings served as an imperial retreat in the form of an urban mansion (*ḳonāḳ*). This mansion, with all of its appendages, was the fulcrum around which the Hamidian palace would evolve. Shared between the sultan and his mother, this small royal estate consisted of administrative quarters allocated to the sultan and his male retinue (*selāmlıḳ*) and more-private residential ones for the female members of the court (*ḥarem*, or *ḥaremlik*) (map 2). When Abdülhamid selected it as his palace, its two zones were already bisected by a still-extant high and undulating, exaggeratedly rusticated wall bearing heavy reliefs of flowers arranged inside bulbous vases (fig. 6).

The Mabeyn Kiosk, the primary *selamlık* structure at the core of this urban estate (map 2, no. 35), was built over an earlier imperial structure (the *valide* compound discussed in detail in chapter 2; see fig. 34) during Abdülaziz's reign, at a time when a type closely resembling eighteenth-century French urban mansions with subtle neoclassical trimmings was being adopted especially for such royal retreats.[66] This estate was allocated for the use of Abdülaziz's mother, Pertevniyal Valide Sultan (d. 1883), and an almost identical version was simultaneously built for her in the woods of Acıbadem, known today as the Validebağı ("orchard of the sultan's mother") Kiosk. The shared trademark features of these simple cross-axial structures, with their central halls (*sofa*), were the pronounced cornice that separated the two floors, Serlian fenestrations, composite double pilasters as quoins, blind crenellated balconies with consoles, and banded friezes between every aperture. There might have been plans for a Mansard roof with oeil-de-boeuf windows for the Mabeyn, a differentiating feature of the Validebağı Kiosk. Pertevniyal Valide Sultan was an earnest architectural patron and directly involved in

MAP 2
Administrative (*selamlık*), residential (*harem*), and *şale* zones of the Yıldız Palace complex and its adjacencies under Abdülhamid II. Courtesy of M. Tülek.

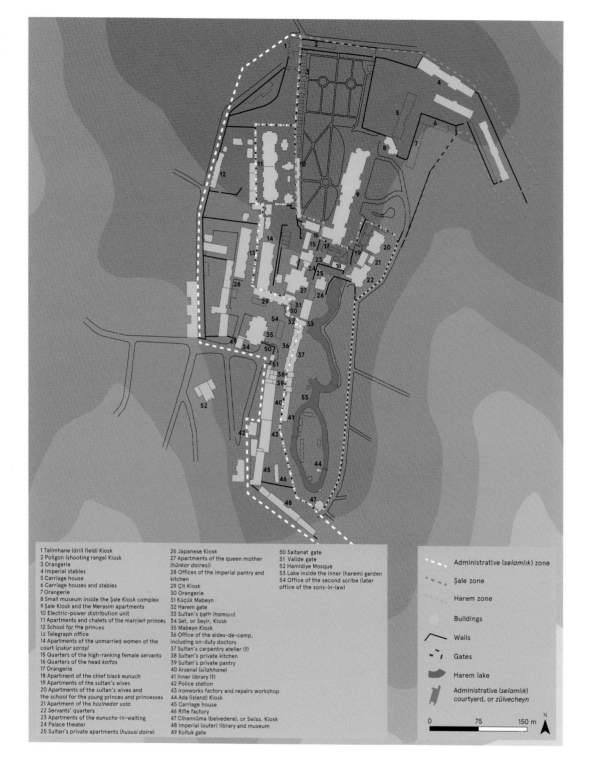

1 Talimhane (drill field) Kiosk
2 Poligon (shooting range) Kiosk
3 Orangerie
4 Imperial stables
5 Carriage house
6 Carriage houses and stables
7 Orangerie
8 Small museum inside the Şale Kiosk complex
9 Şale Kiosk and the Merasim apartments
10 Electric-power distribution unit
11 Apartments and chalets of the married princes
12 School for the princes
13 Telegraph office
14 Apartments of the unmarried women of the court (*çukur saray*)
15 Quarters of the high-ranking female servants
16 Quarters of the head *kalfas*
17 Orangerie
18 Apartment of the chief black eunuch
19 Apartments of the sultan's wives
20 Apartments of the sultan's wives and the school for the young princes and princesses
21 Apartment of the *hazinedar usta*
22 Servants' quarters
23 Apartments of the eunuchs-in-waiting
24 Palace theater
25 Sultan's private apartments (*hususi daire*)

26 Japanese Kiosk
27 Apartments of the queen mother (*hünkar dairesi*)
28 Offices of the imperial pantry and kitchen
29 Çit Kiosk
30 Orangerie
31 Küçük Mabeyn
32 Harem gate
33 Sultan's bath (*hamam*)
34 Set, or Seyir, Kiosk
35 Mabeyn Kiosk
36 Office of the aides-de-camp, including on-duty doctors
37 Sultan's carpentry atelier (?)
38 Sultan's private kitchen
39 Sultan's private pantry
40 Arsenal (*silahhane*)
41 Inner library (?)
42 Police station
43 Ironworks factory and repairs workshop
44 Ada (island) Kiosk
45 Carriage house
46 Rifle factory
47 Cihannüma (belvedere), or Swiss, Kiosk
48 Imperial (outer) library and museum
49 Koltuk gate

50 Saltanat gate
51 Valide gate
52 Hamidiye Mosque
53 Lake inside the inner (harem) garden
54 Office of the second scribe (later office of the sons-in-law)

···· Administrative (*selamlık*) zone

- - - Şale zone

Harem zone

Buildings

── Walls

Gates

Harem lake

Administrative (*selamlık*) courtyard, or *zülvecheyn*

N

0   75   150 m

the upkeep of her properties. It is likely that the type of the French *hôtel particulier* often observed in sites associated with her is reflective of her stylistic preference for retreats. A much simpler building with a pedimented roof belonging to an earlier period—either Mahmud II's time or his son Abdülmecid's—formed the main structure of the estate's harem section (fig. 7). Abdülhamid II's palace expanded around these two preexisting sections of a single estate, with other structures gradually built within and around them to accommodate the growing needs of the court at the end of the nineteenth century.

Especially in the memoirs of foreigners, the palace complex is often treated as equivalent to the Mabeyn Kiosk. This structure, along with the mosque, was the most visible to the palace's visitors. It is not surprising that a postcard commemorating the twenty-fifth anniversary of Abdülhamid's enthronement selects these two, the secular and religious hallmarks of the palace, as stand-ins for the sultan (fig. 8). As an architectural term, *mābeyn* denoted the central *sofa* that separated the women's quarters from the men's in a large and affluent home. The *mabeyn*, as a structure serving as a transitional space between the private residential quarters and the relatively public administrative offices of the sultan, seems to have emerged during the reign of Abdülhamid I, when he erected a Mabeyn Kiosk next to the Privy Chamber in Topkapı Palace, a pattern also repeated in Edirne Palace.[67] In the eighteenth-century Ottoman court, the *mabeyn* replaced the *enderūn* (denoting the sultan's private quarters and attendees in the palace) in its physical space, its function, and the palace functionaries assigned to it. The principal result was the constitution of a separate, private

FIGURE 6
Ahmed Münir, photograph of the gate leading to Yıldız's harem from the Mabeyn courtyard, repairs attributed to Raimondo D'Aronco. İAK, Bel_Mtf_001271.

scribal unit that serviced the sultan's communications with the vizierate and other ministerial offices.[68] It was also a site of homosocial entertainment, where the sultan could rest, watch musical performances, pray, eat, be groomed, and receive delegations. The members of the sultan's *mabeyn* included his sword bearer, footman, equerry, private secretary (*sırkatibi*), *müezzin*, turban winder, key bearer, wardrobe attendee, coffee maker, barber, and table setter.

As a hallmark of early structural reforms in the palace, as well as in state institutions, Mahmud II institutionalized the *mabeyn* strictly as a scribal/administrative office, whereby the sultan's personal scribe became first secretary (*başkātib*). His supervisory role was expanded to cover the sultan's privy purse (*ceyb-i hümāyūn*). Mahmud's pre-Tanzimat palatial restructuring reduced the number of attendees responsible for the sultan's private entertainment, instead appointing protocorporate civil servants. Thus began the politicization of the *mabeyn* as a chief

palace institution; it became the Hamidian era's most powerful state agency, as well as its most crowded, boasting more than four hundred employees of various ranks carefully selected from the Imperial School of Public Service (*mekteb-i mülkīye-i şāhāne*).

Yıldız's structures realized the bifurcation of the *mabeyn* office into the sultan's personal attendees (*ḫuṣūṣī dāʾire*) and scribes with official duties (*resmī dāʾire*). While the latter were allotted various closely clustered buildings in the palace's public segments, those who cared for the sultan's person had rooms inside his private study (Küçük Mabeyn), located in the harem quarter. The lord chamberlain (*başmābeynci*) headed a team dedicated to the sultan's personal needs, while the first secretary oversaw the scribal office.[69] Both of these top appointees held ministerial ranks—a novelty for the period.

It is important to stress here that the Mabeyn Kiosk was not a singular administrative structure but one of a series of interdependent structures servicing the functionaries of the state, collectively constituting the nexus of the empire's informational networks. Abdülhamid used the Mabeyn Kiosk and its one-story, administrative appendage, the Çit Kiosk, both overseen by the members of the *mabeyn*, to host formal receptions. The office

FIGURE 8
Postcard commemorating the twenty-fifth anniversary of Sultan Abdülhamid II's accession. İAK, Krt_012294.

of the marshal of the palace, a ceremonial post created for Gazi Osman Paşa (d. 1900), a seasoned military mastermind and hero of the Russo-Ottoman War of 1878 who was the highest-ranking member of Abdülhamid's palace administration, was allocated an entire floor of offices in the Mabeyn Kiosk.[70]

A good number of the administrative structures were located around a courtyard next to the Mabeyn (map 3, nos. 1–20). The Cipher Secretariat (Şifre Kitabeti), which boasted a telegraph line for direct communication with governors and embassies outside the palace, the administrator of the sultan's privy purse, and offices for the palace's kitchen staff, occupied a row of conjoined apartments abutting the office of the falconers. The office of the first secretary (başkitābet), no longer extant, was housed in the same courtyard, in the largest of these neoclassical apartment complexes (map 3, no. 21). As the

paper output of the palace secretariat grew, the courtyard obtained a library that acted as a bureaucratic archive (ḫazīne-i evrāḳ dāʾiresi) (map 3, no. 16).[71] What is remarkable about this oft-forgotten courtyard, today part of a university campus, is that it accommodated the same educational function as the private segment of Topkapı's enderun (which contained a school for the education of the princes and promising janissary recruits) by housing two schools for the children of the court and palace elite (map 3, no. 27). Sharing the same zone of the palace with these schools, Tahsin Paşa, Abdülhamid's first secretary after 1894, who served until the sultan's deposition in 1909, observed that their instructors lacked merit and competence and that most of the princes received their teaching unenthusiastically.[72]

The başkitabet, which has often been misidentified as located in the Mabeyn Kiosk, had its own building adjoining this courtyard. Young scribal recruits working under the first secretary were not allowed to venture beyond this segment of the palace except to attend the Friday ceremonies (fig. 9). The workday atmosphere of the *başkitabet* was dismally bureaucratic due to its cramped rectangular rooms with heavy, gilded furniture recycled from old palaces and previous decades, over-flowing paperwork and unpalatable food, for which administration members retained sodium bicarbonate on their desks.[73] This courtyard remained active through the night; official petitions received late in the day were copied and sorted for the sultan overnight by two scribes on evening shifts, who slept on makeshift beds in the same rooms. The memoirs of these young people often com-pare their experience of the office to that of a boarding school, with their stifling obliga-tions alleviated by games, jokes, and wres-tling competitions.

Other members of the *mabeyn* institution were given rooms on the top two floors of the Merasim annex to the Şale Kiosk, which also contained an office for the grand vizier (map 2, no. 9; map 3, nos. 37 and 38). It is dif-ficult, therefore, to draw precise physical boundaries for the palace's *selamlık*, Abdül-hamid's public domain inside Yıldız, under which all of these administrative bodies fell. At times, state functions operated out of offices in the private segments of the palace (like the viziers' offices in the Şale's ceremo-nial extension, Merasim). As the number of personnel constantly grew, new recruits had to be accommodated ad hoc. Yet most remarkably, this male-only administrative zone, despite its lack of spatial distinction, lent its name to the most public event in the capital, Abdülhamid's Friday prayer, which

every week offered the outside world a much more organized and controlled glimpse of the chaotic and crowded daily life of the *selamlık*.

YILDIZ'S UBIQUITOUS *DAIRES*

The word *daire*, which denoted a government office in the spatially and functionally hyper-compartmentalized Tanzimat bureaucracy, was also adopted in the palace to describe individual floors, rooms, and apartments of buildings, as well as pavilions designated for particular people, offices, or functions. The dictionary definitions of *daire* from the period highlight its application both to a professional office and to a segment of the domestic residence. *Ḳāmūs-ı Türkī*, a diction-ary compiled by the Ottoman Albanian writer Şemseddin Sami (d. 1904), at one point scribe to the Military Inspection Commission in Yıldız's Çit Kiosk, defines *daire* first as "a col-lection of rooms inside a large mansion" (bir ḳonāḳ vesā'ir binānıñ münḳasım olduġu aḳsāmıñ beheri ki bir ḳaç oda vesā'ireden mürekkebdir) and second as "each of the gov-ernmental departments responsible for the affairs of state and the buildings that house their offices or assemblies" (umūr-ı devleti idāre eden şu'bātıñ beheri ve beheriniñ aḳlām ve mecālis vesā'iresini ḥāvī ebnīyesi).[74]

The preference for this word over other spatial demarcations in Yıldız's bureau-cratic archives reflects not only the unusual integration of imperial residences and gov-ernmental offices on this site—a blurring, of sorts, of the boundary between domestic and administrative spaces—but also Abdülha-mid's way of showing his partiality toward his close retinue. Although *daire* was used to refer to well-known Ottoman governmental insti-tutions, such as the office of the grand vizier, scribes, and members of the *mabeyn*, it was

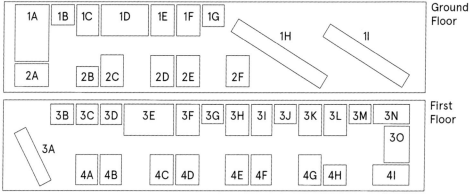

Ground Floor

First Floor

1A Clerical office of the *mabeyn*
1B Servants' quarters
1C Room of the first secretary
1D Guestroom
1E Kadri Bey's bedroom
1F Room for the imperial retinue of the war council
1G Dining room
1H Office of the sultan's gentleman-in-waiting
1I Office of the chief black eunuch
2A Office of the *başkitabet*
2B Dining room
2C Kamphofner Paşa's room
2D Head librarian's room
2E Room for the head of the war council
2F First dragoman Kara Todori's room

3A Office of official ceremonies
3B Room of the sultan's private aide Mehmed Paşa
3C Depot (archive) for clerical documents
3D Ahmed Ali Paşa's room
3E Parlor
3F Bedroom for the on-duty aide
3G Dining room
3H Room for the on-duty lieutenant general (*ferik paşa*)
3I Room for the sultan's private aide Mehmed Ali Bey
3J Dining room
3K Ahmed Celaleddin Paşa's room
3L Bedroom for the deputy of the treasury
3M Chief black eunuch's rooms
3N Chief black eunuch's room
3O Pantry
4A Room for the sultan's private aides
4B Kadri Bey's room
4C Room for the sultan's librarian
4D Room for the tobacconist
4E Room for the on-duty aide
4F Room for the queen mother's chief eunuch
4G Chief black eunuch's room
4H Room for the member of the deputy of the treasury

also used to describe incredibly idiosyncratic ones created by Abdülhamid himself—institutions that transformed his *paşa*s and close acquaintances into his private political advisors and informants. Outlining the civil offices of Yıldız, Tahsin Paşa equates some of these institutions with the officials who were appointed to run them, rather than the specific functions of the offices. For example, he mentions the *daire*s of İzzet Holo Paşa (the second scribe of the *mabeyn*, head of the revenues office, and high commissioner of the Hejaz Railways), Derviş Paşa (an Albanian politics expert), Kamphofner Paşa (a German military expert), Aleksandr Kara Todori Paşa (an experienced diplomat), Şakir Paşa (head of the military commission), and Dragoman Nişan Efendi (an Armenian translator of French newspaper articles on issues regarding the Ottoman state).[75] İsmail Müştak (later Mayakon), a clerk working under Tahsin Paşa, notes in his memoirs, serialized in the early years of the Turkish Republic, that if given a bird's-eye view of Yıldız under Abdülhamid, one would see "a gloomy neighborhood composed of tiny offices [*daire*s]."[76]

In Yıldız's archives and the memoirs of its bureaucrats and members of the court, the names of individual buildings are rarely mentioned; instead, the word *daire* is frequently used to indicate an administrative office serving a palace function or the quarters designated to its inhabitants. Şadiye Sultan, another of Abdülhamid's memoir-writing daughters, describes Yıldız as "a palace broken up into apartments" (dairelere taksim edilmiş saray).[77] All of the palace's inhabitants thought of their assigned lodgings in terms of collections of rooms or apartments within a larger complex, rather than as independent structures. Even Abdülhamid's

own residence, a stately Victorian home, was referred to as his personal quarters (*ḫuṣūṣī dāʾire*, as discussed in detail in chapter 4).

Some of these *daire*s were more idiosyncratic than others, resulting from Abdülhamid's brand of generosity, or his personal whims and preferences. For years he hosted a Dr. Blane—a French physician who had formerly practiced his trade on transatlantic ships—in "an office made up of two rooms" (iki odalı bir daire)[78] in the Küçük Mabeyn, as he found the doctor's medical wisdom and quirky habits (carrying around two bags full of antique artifacts and leaving his room only for short strolls in the palace park) to his liking. Blane became "a personal doctor and mentor" (hem doktorum hem akıl hocam idi) to Abdülhamid, according to the sultan's recollections, and was one of the few advisors who dined with him every night.[79]

High-ranking state employees were not the only recipients of Abdülhamid's tactical munificence, distributed as part of a strategy he called *isticlāb*, or the act of drawing near.[80] He also hosted influential Arab and Kurdish notables in the Double Palaces (Çifte Saraylar) in the Teşvikiye quarter of Nişantaşı for considerable lengths of time, keeping them occupied with gratuitous state protocol, honors, and gifts to weaken their control over populations and regions that he wanted to consolidate under his caliphal authority.[81] The Double Palaces, which had been constructed by Abdülmecid to house the lord chamberlain and first secretary and were the first residential buildings in what would become the town of pashas, were transformed under Abdülhamid II into guest apartments (*misāfirīn dāʾiresi*). Their inhabitants, despite their sumptuous accommodation, were exiles in the empire's capital, subject to the sultan's constant surveillance. The memoirs of government officials label them quite caustically as provincial tyrants (*ṭaşra müteğallibesi*) or bandit chiefs (*sergerdeler*), whose family members seem to have led palpably sober, interiorized lives (*nā-maḥremlik*) amid the vibrant sociability that had emerged in Yıldız's residential extensions in Nişantaşı. According to an itinerant local food vendor, it was difficult to communicate with the non-Turkish-speaking residents of these conservative households; female members would speak in whispery tones and were glimpsed only when they extended their hennaed hands through doors to receive meals.[82]

The most conspicuous architectural example of Abdülhamid's strategic detainment of influential Arab notables in Istanbul and close to his palace was his commission of a stately devotional and residential complex for Muhammed Zafir, the aforementioned North African shaykh. The Ertuğrul convent mosque—"an adorned and modest prayer space" adjacent to the palace's western walls[83]—was appointed to Zafir's Sufi order, and members of his extended family were moved into two monumental timber mansions in the same garden. His family continued to occupy these residences in the city's republican years, and the memoirs of one of his last descendants indicate that Abdülhamid's surreptitious overprotection eventually severed the family's ties with its North African origins. (I return to the importance of this shaykh to the sultan in the following chapter.) Gazi Osman Paşa was also given an urban estate, on the same imperial street as the shaykh's complex.[84] This still-extant street, named Serencebey Yokuşu, held considerable prestige in the hierarchy of Yıldız's surrounding neighborhoods, and

the most influential members of Abdülhamid's cabinet, responsible for decisions on matters of the state, religion, and warcraft, were made to reside there. The sultan's commemoration of figures important to his life and rule continued even after their deaths; after Zafir's passing, for example, Abdülhamid commissioned the Italian architect Raimondo D'Aronco to build a small domed tomb and adjacent library in front of the timber dervish convent. The small scale of these pavilion-like twin structures was in line with Abdülhamid's patronage of person-specific, customized buildings in which he conducted his own brand of intimate diplomatic gatherings (discussed further in chapter 4).

THE PALACE GATES

The impenetrable "high walls of Abdülhamid's fortress" (*ḳalʿa sūru*), which to many were a source of tremendous consternation, were punctured by heavily guarded gates to the different segments of the palace complex (map 2, nos. 49–51).[85] The gates were patrolled by Albanian *tüfekçi*s (guards) of the Second Squadron, who in their frequent unruliness seemed little different from the pre-Tanzimat janissary corps in the eyes of the palace officials.[86] Three main doors, clustered around the Mabeyn Kiosk, were used most frequently. One of these, which remained open every day from morning to midnight, was located immediately below the Set (or Seyir) Kiosk and its terrace, an elevated pavilion and dais reserved for foreign delegates invited to watch Abdülhamid's *selamlık*. Off to the side and at the foot of the hill that climbed up to the other two ceremonial gates, this portal was referred to as the "servant's entrance" (*koltuk kapı*) by the palace's royal residents. However, for the numerous clerks

FIGURE 10
Yıldız's office of the aides-de-camp on duty, attributed to Raimondo D'Aronco, after 1894.

European garb, and the requisite small-time informants.[87] One of these scribes provides a particularly colorful breakdown of these visitors according to the degree of recognition they received from the palace's doormen, who to him represented "the plainest of measurements of what the palace was" (sarayı anlamak için sadeliği ile beraber en doğru mikyaslardan biri kapıcılardır).[88]

According to Osman Nuri, Abdülhamid's contentious and obscure biographer, this door opened onto the now broken-up first segment of the palace.[89] This expansive area fronting the Mabeyn Kiosk included the *daires* charged with the upkeep of the palace and the most important offices responsible for communication between the sultan and the ministries. Once inside, visitors saw the stately Mabeyn Kiosk and its enclosed viewing platform, the Set Kiosk, on an elevated terrace to the right. The palace's mammoth imperial kitchen and pantry, which fed the multitude of palace employees several times a day, were on the left, on lower ground reached via a slope.

The majority of the heavily traversed palace buildings were constructed as understated gallery-like apartments with discreet, often tediously undifferentiated neoclassical façades. They were elongated for practical reasons, to accommodate the internal separations of the various *daires* that served as the quarters of individuals or subgroups within an administrative office. These structures were often placed in barrack-like parallel blocks, one after the other, resting on the sloping terrain's ridgelines. For instance, parallel to the imperial kitchen and separated from it by a large courtyard stood a building allocated to the countless aides-de-camp who were not on active duty inside the palace.

employed in the Mabeyn office, who had to pass through it every day, it was the palace's main door (*cümle kapı*).

When the highest-ranking students of the Imperial School of Public Service were recruited to coveted scribal positions within the palace, they entered Yıldız through this portal and were immediately taken into the office of the first secretary to be told the requirements of their post. The memoirs of these recruits provide the best descriptions of the human traffic through the portal. The crowded pageantry that paraded through day and night included grand viziers (Saturdays and Tuesdays), ministers (Mondays and Thursdays), officeholders of all levels, dragomans accompanying first-time visitors, rich provincials, concession-seeking foreigners, formidable contractors, robed members of the *ulema* (merchant class), nondescript middlemen, jewelers, Ottoman dandies in

Those working, meanwhile, were given lodgings in a chalet-like building on the other side of the Mabeyn (fig. 10) (map 2, no. 36), conveniently adjacent to the harem gate (map 2, no. 32).

Although, as previously mentioned, the palace's *selamlık* section may have lacked ceremonial linearity in its organization, it was physically bisected by the Mabeyn Kiosk, separating the more public zone into which the *koltuk kapı* led its visitors from a more private one allotted to the sultan's closest retinue. This section, elevated and relatively private, was often inaccessible even to employees of the scribal offices and housed only the officials on duty, whose responsibilities were divided between the sultan's study (Küçük Mabeyn) and Mabeyn (map 2, nos. 31 and 35). The cluster of buildings around this segment was much smaller; most were made of timber, had residential appeal, and boasted far more inventive wooden ornamental decoration as a marker of the rank of the officeholders who occupied them.

The central structures of the *selamlık*'s more selective zone were the office (no longer extant) of Abdülhamid's beloved second scribe, İzzet Holo Paşa (d. 1924); the lodgings of the aides-de-camp on duty; and the Çit Kiosk (fig. 11), which served multiple intimate functions, from emergency wartime convocations to theological discussions in the presence of the sultan during Ramadan (*ḥużūr dersleri*) and post-Friday-prayer gatherings with foreign ambassadors (map 2, nos. 54, 36, and 29). If a visitor who had entered the palace through the *koltuk kapı* was allowed into this second section of the *selamlık*, he was required to pass through the office of the head guard (*sertüfekçi*), situated between these two zones and aligned with

FIGURE 11
Yıldız's Çit Kiosk, 1867–76, attributed to the Balyans.

the Mabeyn's elevated basement floor, right below the Çit Kiosk.

In many ways, the division of the public zones according to a gradation of closeness to the sultan can be thought of in terms of the traditional splitting of Islamic audience halls into public and private chambers (*dīvān-ı ʿāmm* and *dīvān-ı ḫāṣṣ*). Perhaps even more important, Abdülhamid's use of the Mabeyn (from which he was largely absent) and his private study, Küçük Mabeyn (where he was available only to a small circle of officials), is reminiscent of the sixteenth-century sultans' absent presence in the crowded Council Hall in the second courtyard of Topkapı Palace and of their secluded dwelling in the Privy Chamber in its third courtyard.[90]

The palace's second and third portals opened into the more private section of the *selamlık* zone. The one known as the imperial gate (*saltanat kapısı*) was roughly in line with the *koltuk kapı*. Both portals faced the

Hamidiye Mosque (map 2, no. 52). Directly in front of the slope that led up to the Mabeyn was the third and last portal, the gate of the sultan's mother (*valide kapısı*). With the exception of the "gate of sovereignty," the names of these portals were not fixed; different inhabitants of the palace knew them by different names. While a scribe may have known the main entrance as the *koltuk kapı*, indicating a kind of servitude, to Abdülhamid's daughter it was the *aş kapısı* ("stew gate") because of its proximity to the kitchens and the constant circulation of its *tabla-kars* in and out of the gates, carrying food to Yıldız's employees, guests, and affiliates on the peripheries of the palace. The sultan's daughter recalls the gate of the sultan's mother as the gate of departure, or "official journey" (*gidiş kapısı*), a door that was used only by the members of the court.[91] However, this portal was (as this book's second chapter shows) most likely named after Yıldız's pre-palatine owners, the queen mothers of the previous sultans; the tradition of preserving the names of sites in memory of their owners meant that it retained this designation.

Bearing composite pilasters identical to those found on the façade of the Mabeyn, the imperial gate was probably also erected during the reign of Abdülaziz (fig. 12). After Yıldız became a palace, this gate was reserved specifically for Abdülhamid's use on days when he ventured beyond the palace walls: for the Friday prayer ceremonies in the Hamidiye Mosque, the official greetings (*mu'āyede*) for the two religious festivals (*bayrām*) in the domed ceremonial room of the Dolma-bahçe Palace, and the imperial visitation to the mantle of the Prophet Muhammad in Topkapı Palace (*Ḥırḳa-i Şerīf*, or, interchange-ably, *Ḥırḳa-i Saʿādet*) on the fifteenth day

of Ramadan.[92] The *valide* gate was used by the members of the household who lived in the palace, and like the imperial gate, it received its name from its use by the sultan's adopted mother and her retinue on Fridays, when they left the palace in her carriage to witness the pomp and circumstance of the sultan's public appearance.

The foreign guests of the sultan, who were invited to see the palace and were granted the privilege of meeting him informally, were also brought into Yıldız through this gate, because it provided easy access to Abdülhamid's sightseeing route (discussed below). It was the very spot from which the imperial railway, an unrealized addition to the imperial tour, would have begun. A right turn from this gate and down the slope toward the shore led the visitors to the imperial library, fronted by a dovecote (used later as a rifle factory and until recently the headquarters of the Turkish State Intelligence Agency), and the Çadır Kiosk, with its lake and island in the palace's park (map 3, nos. 4, 83–84, 78).

ABDÜLHAMID'S SELF-DESIGNED SIGHTSEEING TOUR

Inside Yıldız, Muzaffar al-Din Shah showed great interest in a particular group of palatial structures: the museum, library, zoo, and factories. In 1894, similarly, Georgina Müller, wife of the German Orientalist Max Müller, remarked, "The Sultan had said that we were to see his museum, library, and garden."[93] Another female visitor vibrantly recalled her experience on the palace grounds as follows:

> A manufactory of porcelain . . . ; an arsenal; a museum containing the Imperial library and a magnificent collection of minia-tures, enamels, and jewels. . . .

Palais Imperial de Yildiz (Résidence de S. M. I. le Sultan)

FIGURE 12
Mabeyn Kiosk and "the imperial gate" (*saltanat kapısı*), photographer and date unknown. İÜMK, 90815–0001.

Meanwhile, as on and on we had been driven, past lawns, lakes, gardens, and kiosks, we came, in due time, to an archway, beyond which a number of low buildings within an inner courtyard proved to be the Imperial stables.[94]

Conducted by a courtier, Abdülhamid's privileged visitors were first shown the museum inside his private garden, in which the sultan preserved and displayed the treasured gifts of his foreign counterparts:

Here are collected and beautifully arranged all the presents that he has received, as well as innumerable valuable objects that belonged to some of his predecessors. Countless clocks and watches, inlaid armour, objects in jade, caskets, wonderfully bound books, china of all sorts, pictures, miniatures, jeweled ornaments of every kind, all so arranged in their cases that one could examine and enjoy them, a delightful contrast to the confusion in which treasures of the old Seraglio are heaped together. One upright case contained four dozen of the most perfect deep blue Sèvres plates, a present from the Emperor Napoleon, sunk into velvet, twenty-four on each side of the

The ou Ferkhan - Kiosque situé dans le Parc Impérial de Yildiz

stand. Each plate was a picked and perfect specimen.... We could have spent hours in examining everything, but time was limited, and we were taken on to the private stables, still within the Harem walls, holding twelve of the most perfect Arabs, used by the Sultan for riding and driving in the park of Yildiz.[95]

In the imperial stables, close to the Malta Kiosk, the sultan's many prized Russian, Austrian, and Arab steeds were "put through [their paces]" for guests (fig. 13) (map 3, no. 56).[96] If scholars and bibliophiles were

part of the retinue, they would also be led to the library at the edge of the Mabeyn courtyard, staffed by a "devoted" librarian, along with "six or eight intelligent assistants," and containing "a carefully prepared and very full catalogue"; "exquisite Persian mss."; "modern [Indian] works on [Indian] music"; "fine mss. of the Korân with glosses and commentaries"; "bookcases ... of the best construction, with movable shelves"; "a very good collection of English, French, and German classics"; "glass cases, filled with gorgeously bound, illustrated works, chiefly gifts to the Sultan"; and "photographs of places in the Sultan's

كتبخانه همايون داخله گريته

٩٠٥٥٢

dominions and of public buildings in Stam-bûl" (fig. 14).[97]

Guests also walked across the suspended footbridges—including "the sultan's favorite rickety bridge"[98] (fig. 15)—hovering above the park's lakes, or took a carriage across its valley to the porcelain factory (fig. 16). Muzaffar al-Din Shah reports that three Qajar students were apprenticed in the factory. Depending on which side of the park the visitors began their tour, either the Çadır Kiosk or the Malta Kiosk was often outfitted for their respite. For some time, Çadır also served as an annex to the imperial Hereke factory; looms were

installed in the kiosk to supply necessary furnishings and repairs for the palace, augmenting both the palace's self-subsistence and its image as a facilitator of local craftsmanship.[99] Indeed, the structures inside the park were seen as stations for artisanal work. When the Italian artist Fausto Zonaro (d. 1929) received his court appointment, the Çadır Kiosk was assigned to him as a private atelier (see fig. 39).[100]

Although most of the palace's buildings were not geometrically ordered and its courtyards lacked a linear sequence (thus, to Batur, resembling a medieval town), the

FIGURE 15
Vasilaki Kargopoulo, *Pont à
Yeldez*, 1878. İÜMK, 90751–0048.

Pont a Yeldez (303)

experience of its grounds followed a systematic courtly order. The palace's sightseeing
tour was expressly choreographed by the
sultan and implemented by his master of
ceremonies (*teşrīfāt nāẓırı*), who was also the
head dragoman of the court (*divān-ı hümāyūn
tercümānı*).[101] The sultan would later attribute
his lavish posttour gift-giving—especially to
the wives of foreign ambassadors—and the
controlled intensity of his hosting on the palace grounds to the timeworn decorum upheld
by the "wisdom of the government, and the
government of wisdom" (böyle hareket etmek
'hikmet-i hükûmet, hükûmet-i hikmet' icabı
idi).[102]

To the palace's most important guests, for
whom the Şale Kiosk was reserved as royal
lodgings, Abdülhamid opened the doors of
his private residential space and his theater
(fig. 17). Inconspicuous from the outside, the
theater (on which I expand in the book's coda)
was located in the transitional zone between
the sultan's personal residential quarters
(*hususi daire*) and study (*küçük mabeyn*) and
the gate that opened into the compound of
the Şale (map 2, nos. 24–25).

At that time the exceptionally discreet
and narrow interstitial zone between two
royal residential compounds, the harem and
Şale, acted as a private ceremonial domain

FIGURE 16 (*top*)
Exterior view of the imperial porcelain factory. Photographer unknown. İÜMK, 90552–0083.

FIGURE 17 (*bottom*)
Nondescript façade of the palace theater, with the gate leading into the compound of the Şale Kiosk. SALT Research, IFEA Archive, Istanbul.

in which the sultan could bestow on visitors privileged access to his most intimate domain and introduce them to a particular Ottoman brand of courtly entertainment. This transitional area, according to Muzaffar al-Din Shah, contained an enclosed gallery that connected the sultan's Victorian residence with the Şale (fig. 18). A surviving cross-sectional representation of the gallery's paintings in situ suggests that the gallery was arranged into ten discrete units, each full of imposing glass cabinets, in the style of an imperial curiosity cabinet (fig. 19). The first unit contained medals and coins, and the second, minerals and semiprecious stones; visitors went on to view, in order, Sèvres and Capodimonte porcelain; imperial gifts and weapons; bronze- and silverware; rare bookbindings, carpets, prayer mats, and illuminated folios; European porcelain; shells; and, finally, Chinese and Japanese porcelain tableware and enameled porcelain. Abdülhamid reserved the center of this gallery for dynastic portraits and battle scenes. The sultan's visual glorification of his dynastic past in the space reserved for his most exclusive guests certainly seems to have impressed Muzaffar al-Din Shah. "Most of this gallery's walls," he recalls, "are decorated with paintings of the Ottoman sultans' wars, which are really spectacular and reveal the high dignity of this family."[103]

This grand display of gifts and glories, as well as the sultan's museological impulse, must have had a lasting impression on Muzaffar al-Din's father, Nasir al-Din Shah, who designed a small museum called *gāh-ı abyaż* (white palace) inside Gulistan Palace to store the gifts he had received from Abdülhamid. With its classical pilasters and subtle floral stucco window frames, this Qajar repository of gifts may have shared architectural features with Abdülhamid's museum or imperial library; it may even have been a small replica of the Mabeyn Kiosk. The sultan spent hours personally showing Nasir al-Din's son and successor, Muzaffar al-Din, the most valuable manuscripts from his collection of "twenty thousand books" and presented him with a Koran handwritten by the eighteenth-century court calligrapher Yedikuleli Seyyid Abdullah Efendi. Muzaffar al-Din also read his own fortune in the pages of an album (*muraḳḳaʿ*) of calligraphy by the sixteenth-century Persian master of the *nastaliq* script, Mir Emad Hasani.[104]

As noted above, the buildings that Abdülhamid most wanted his guests to see were distributed across the palace's park. The guests were taken on this sightseeing tour in a carriage. To transport visitors rapidly between these structures, an elaborate railway line—sixteen hundred meters long—carrying an imperial coach (*rükūb-ı şāhāneye maḥṣūṣ vaġon*) was conceived (fig. 20). This novel mode of travel must have been expected to offer visitors an easy way to traverse the steep slopes of the park, which were, moreover, bisected by a natural gorge containing cascades and lakes. Although the railway project was ultimately unrealized, the royal presentation copy of its plans reveals it to have been dramatic.[105] A topographic cross section detailed how the tracks were to be laid out, the locations of the bridges and tunnels along the route, and the design of the imperial coach, including its interior fittings of sumptuous local Hereke carpets and Orientalist furniture.

Tracing almost exactly the route taken by Yıldız's many foreign visitors, the coach was set to pick up the sultan's guests from a spot between the Mabeyn and Çit kiosks. Not by coincidence, this was also where foreign dignitaries awaiting an audience with the sultan gathered after the *selamlık*.[106] The railcar's journey would commence by crossing the Mabeyn courtyard, following the downward slope of the ridge along the imperial arsenal (*silāḥḥāne*), clad in a densely columned façade (fig. 21), before stopping in front of the palace's main library. From here the coach was to travel along a short bridge resting on arcaded piers, crossing the artificial lake in front of the Çadır Kiosk (marked as *köşk* on the plan, possibly in reference to its earliest incarnation as an open structure not intended for overnight habitation; the Malta Kiosk, in contrast, is marked here as *ḳaṣır*). After the first bridge depicted on the map, the rails curve toward the north as they enter a tunnel running along the high walls that separate the sultan's private garden from the park. This tunnel leads the railcar onto a second, longer bridge (with high castellated towers bearing the Ottoman banner) to reach the final site of the tour, the imperial stables, before depositing passengers at their lodgings in the Şale Kiosk.

FIGURE 19 (*above*)
Yıldız Palace Museum, around
1880. Watercolor on paper,
39.5 × 232 cm. MSİB Painting
Collection, Istanbul, 121/543.

FIGURE 20 (*right*)
"The general plan of the railways that are conceptualized
for the garden of the imperial palace of Yıldız" (Yıldız
sarāy-ı hümāyūnu baġçesinde
inşāsı mutaṣavvir olan demir-
yollarınıñ ḫarīṭa-ı ʿumūmīye-
sidir). İÜMK, 93283.

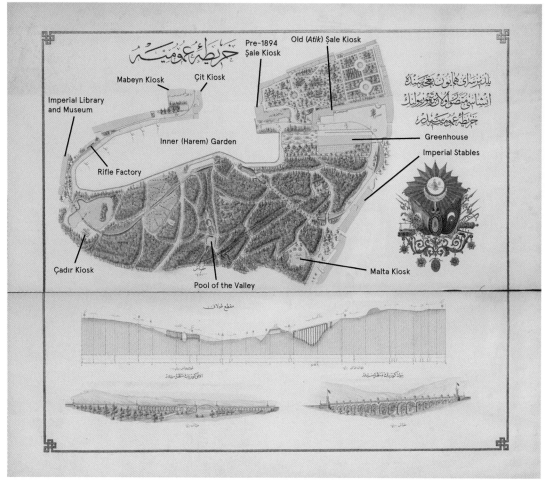

Batur mentions this railway project only briefly, as part of her argument that the palace was conceptualized as an industrializing city unto itself.[107] Since then, surprisingly, no close analysis of this unconventional palatial addition has been undertaken, although the plans contain a detailed map of the sightseeing segment of Yıldız under Abdülhamid, one of only a handful that survive. Although undated, the project must have been conceived before 1894, because the layout of the Şale on the map appears to date from a period before D'Aronco's double-towered ceremonial extension to the structure. The partial map of the grounds—covering almost the entirety of the external park, the Mabeyn courtyard, and the environs of the Şale—features minute topographical measurements and painstaking representations of the park's diverse flora (flatter grounds were reserved for kitchen gardens and formal flower parterres, while the slopes were densely wooded), which must have necessitated an intimate knowledge of the site. The terraced platform of the sultan's private harem garden is conspicuously left

out, but its walls are carefully demarcated. Therefore, this project for the park may have been developed at around the same time that Abdülhamid was designing his personal gardens, which would have commanded spectacular views of the train and tracks traversing the grounds below.[108]

During Abdülaziz's reign, each time a railway line was completed in the imperial domains, often by a European company that had received concessions for its construction, the sultan received an imperial railcar and its scale model as gifts.[109] The abovementioned unrealized prestige project for Yıldız was the recreational byproduct of a similar international deal struck with the newly unified German Empire during Abdülhamid's time to finance and lay out the Anatolian railway line that would connect Istanbul to Central Anatolian towns.[110] To signal the start of the negotiations, the sultan had sent Chancellor Otto von Bismarck (d. 1898) a three-volume set of photograph albums that depicted the towns, monuments, landscapes, and peoples populating the would-be trajectory of the

railway.[111] The photographers, selected from instructors in the imperial military and engineering schools in the capital, undertook the Yıldız railway project for the sultan to commemorate the completion of the regional railway line.

These artists of the imperial military, who often also served as the court's unofficial artists, knew the sultan's tastes well. The imagined interiors of the coach were upholstered in his beloved Hereke fabrics, and the furniture featured the kind of Damascene inlays that he himself was skilled in crafting. The artists were evidently also attuned to Abdülhamid's overall conception of his palace. The project's map not only demarcates the key stops along the sultan's sightseeing tour but also conveys the appeal that the site's Alpine topography held for the sultan, overemphasizing it in drawings. The backdrop

to the watercolor perspective renderings of bridges, as well as the views depicted through the imperial coach's window, dramatizes Yıldız's hills, reimagining them as mountains with deeper valleys and denser forests (fig. 22).

THE ATELIERS

A gas-piping map from after 1902 provides a clear view of the outer courtyard's ateliers (map 3, nos. 84 to 86), reminiscent of the sixteenth-century layout of Topkapı Palace, where the craftsmen's workshops were located in the former palace's outer courtyard.[112] Inside Yıldız the workshops were clustered beside the main (outer) library. The ironworks atelier (*temürḫāne*) and repairs workshop (*taʿmīrḫāne*) shared a wall: wrought iron was brought from the former to the latter to produce furniture, an example of which is itemized, in the report of the commission overseeing the liquidation of the palace, as a table with engraved iron shelves and grilles supporting an onyx top.[113] The extant photographs of the *tamirhane* in the Yıldız photograph collections display a large, well-oiled workspace outfitted with steam engines (fig. 23). A rifle factory (*tüfenk fabrikası*), too, was located across from the *tamirhane*, potentially sharing materials with the ironworks atelier. It is not by chance that the library was among this industrial assemblage of buildings; the contents of the library, open to consultation by the palace's craftsmen, boasted catalogues and manuals on metal fixtures, furniture, buildings, revolvers, and so forth that had often made their debuts in the world's fairs.

Later, while in exile in Thessaloniki, the deposed sultan recalled this site more often and with greater fondness than any of the other craft facilities he had installed in Yıldız. He praised its steam-operated machinery and metal-casting technologies for objects such as locks, bolts, keys, and coins, and explained how he had tirelessly recruited talented apprentices from the Tophane imperial foundry to run the atelier's diverse operations, ranging from the building of royal carriages to the manufacturing of furniture and a small boat made of imported aluminum planks for the palace's artificial lakes.[114]

The armory (*silahhane*), also located in the Mabeyn courtyard and connected to the *tamirhane-temürhane* complex, followed the interlinked gallery typology of the palace's many buildings. The 1909 palace-liquidation lists, mentioned at the start of this chapter, paint an elusive picture of this building's functions. It was designated primarily as a grand two-story arsenal for the palace's

ركوب شاهانه يه مخصوص واغونك داخلى منظره سى

guards. The gas-piping map marks the many areas to which these guards were dispersed—to gates as well as along the heavily protected inner and outer walls of the palace. However, the liquidation lists of the *silahhane* record divers objects pertinent to construction: wood samples, carving knives, plumb lines, saws, toothing planes, various miter squares and compasses, paint samples, a Mariotte's bottle, lockmaker's clamps, voltage regulators, surveying gadgets (such as sextants), paint

FIGURE 22
"Interior view of the imperial coach" (rükūb-ı şāhāneye maḫṣūṣ vaġonuň dāḫilī manẓarası). İÜMK, 93283.

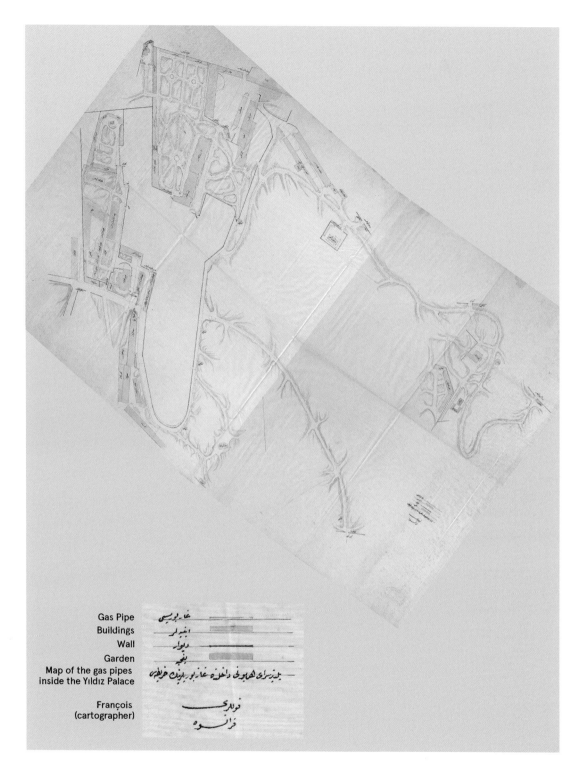

Gas Pipe

Buildings

Wall

Garden

Map of the gas pipes
inside the Yıldız Palace

François
(cartographer)

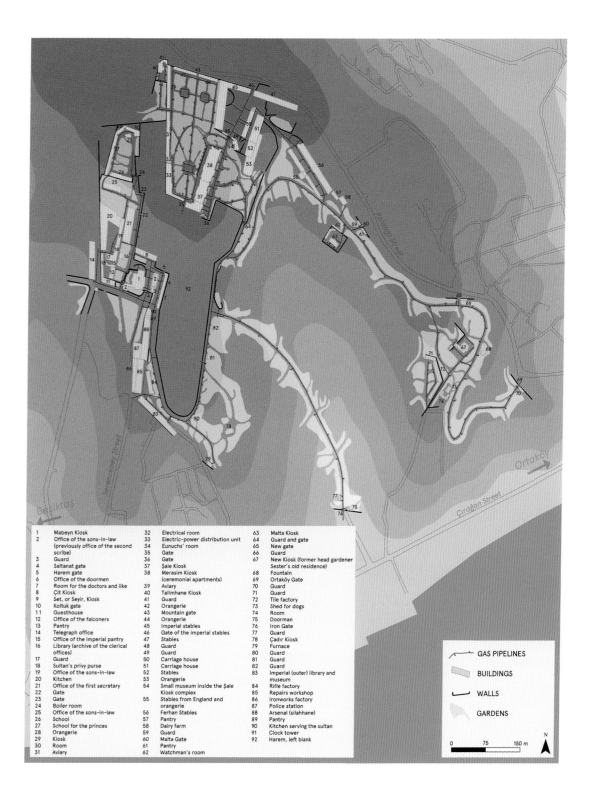

1	Mabeyn Kiosk	32	Electrical room	63	Malta Kiosk
2	Office of the sons-in-law (previously office of the second scribe)	33	Electric-power distribution unit	64	Guard and gate
		34	Eunuchs' room	65	New gate
		35	Gate	66	Guard
3	Guard	36	Gate	67	New Kiosk (former head gardener Sester's old residence)
4	Saltanat gate	37	Şale Kiosk		
5	Harem gate	38	Merasim Kiosk (ceremoniai apartments)	68	Fountain
6	Office of the doormen			69	Ortaköy Gate
7	Room for the doctors and like	39	Aviary	70	Guard
8	Çit Kiosk	40	Talimhane Klosk	71	Guard
9	Set, or Şeyir, Kiosk	41	Guard	72	Tile factory
10	Koltuk gate	42	Orangerie	73	Shed for dogs
11	Guesthouse	43	Mountain gate	74	Room
12	Office of the falconers	44	Orangerie	75	Doorman
13	Pantry	45	Imperial stables	76	Iron Gate
14	Telegraph office	46	Gate of the imperial stables	77	Guard
15	Office of the imperial pantry	47	Stables	78	Çadır Kiosk
16	Library (archive of the clerical offices)	48	Guard	79	Furnace
		49	Guard	80	Guard
17	Guard	50	Carriage house	81	Guard
18	Sultan's privy purse	51	Carriage house	82	Guard
19	Office of the sons-in-law	52	Stables	83	Imperial (outer) library and museum
20	Kitchen	53	Orangerie		
21	Office of the first secretary	54	Small museum inside the Şale Kiosk complex	84	Rifle factory
22	Gate			85	Repairs workshop
23	Gate	55	Stables from England and orangerie	86	Ironworks factory
24	Boiler room			87	Police station
25	Office of the sons-in-law	56	Ferhan Stables	88	Arsenal (silahhane)
26	School	57	Pantry	89	Pantry
27	School for the princes	58	Dairy farm	90	Kitchen serving the sultan
28	Orangerie	59	Guard	91	Clock tower
29	Kiosk	60	Malta Gate	92	Harem, left blank
30	Room	61	Pantry		
31	Aviary	62	Watchman's room		

GAS PIPELINES

BUILDINGS

WALLS

GARDENS

0   75   150 m

N

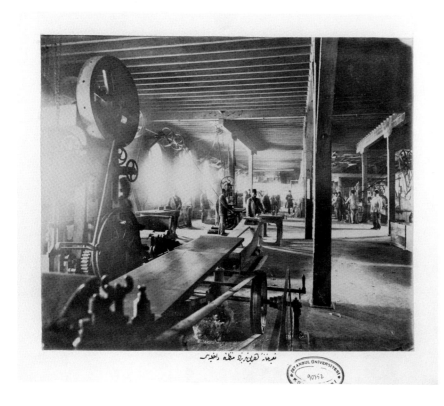

FIGURE 23
"Interior view of the imperial ironworks" (taʿmīr-ḫāne-i hümāyūnlarınıñ manẓara-ı dāḫilīyesi). İÜMK, 90552–0038.

brushes, a photography reflector, a hand drill, and a magic lantern to project slides with dissolving images.[115] Parts of the *silahhane* may have been reserved for overflow tasks involving carpentry, building, photography, and the like; alternatively, by 1909 some of the factories in the inner and outer courts may have been reassigned.

To a great extent Yıldız's sites of production were located close to its sites of display. The museum, of which there is no photographic record, was adjacent to the offices of the palace aides but accessible from the harem garden. The museum's inventory grew over time. The transcriptions of its contents published by the commission responsible for the liquidation of the museum reflect its crowded diversity. The lists prepared by the commission itemize the requisite features

of a nineteenth-century royal cabinet (coins, jewelry and precious stones, clocks, globes, snuffboxes, taxidermy, revolvers, swords, rare porcelain, gifted medals and orders, sultanic eulogies in gilded containers or on banners), symbols specific to a Muslim sovereign (Korans, scrolls, talismanic objects, Kaʿba covers, portraits of sultans and other courtly members in various media and their seals), and symbols specific to Abdülhamid's rule (a multitude of gifts from both his imperial domains and around the world sent to commemorate the twenty-fifth anniversary of his enthronement). However, other objects, similar to the magic lantern stored in the arsenal, spoke of a deep interest in the experience and consumption of visual representation through novel means. For example, the museum contained elaborate gilded stereoscopes resting on columns and accompanying scenographic plaques provided by the Lumière brothers, the French pioneers of the moving image.[116]

The side of the museum closest to Abdülhamid's personal quarters housed his carpentry atelier. At the other end of the museum was a library referred to as the "personal" (*hususi*) library. Although the contents of the museum were undoubtedly heterogeneous, the commission reports make them seem even more so by treating the carpentry studio as part of the museum, probably because of the interlinked layout of the two spaces.[117] Positioned between the atelier and library and spatially more prominent than either, the museum seems to have lent its designation to these two adjacent spaces, at least in bureaucratic documentation. Again, although the large volumes of bookbinding materials and equipment (from cardboard to a lithographic stone, pared leather, and a milling press) listed by the commission appear to have been found in the museum, it is more likely that either the carpentry workshop or the inner library sheltered a bookbinder's operation. Some of the equipment might have even been shared between the carpenters and binders.

The most paradoxical feature of the palace's inner zone of display and production was its location within the harem gardens, seemingly reserved for the sultan's family members. Starting at the nymphaeum under the sultan's private residence (map 2, no. 25), an inhabitant of the court could board an electric launch on the garden's meandering lake, rest in one of the many one-room lakeside pavilions, and ultimately visit the aviary (full of exotic birds, but mainly reserved for pigeon breeding—a curious site of collection and display of a different kind).[118] Yet the itemized lists made by Yıldız's dissolution commission indicate that this inner garden was also, at times, home to a flurry of artisans. For example, a considerable number of bookbinding tools are itemized in a room next to the Cihannüma Pavilion (map 2, no. 47). A Carl Cruze cardboard cutter, a chisel, a press for gilding, a trunk full of various letterpresses, a stove for glue, a bookbinder's table and chair, and various printing presses of different dimensions from the same Leipzig brand all suggest that a well-equipped second bookbinding atelier was in operation in the palace in 1909.[119] Immediately adjacent to the pigeon house and not too far from the bookbinding atelier was a small two-story photography studio with small rooms allocated for the development of images and storage of equipment, including glass negatives (fig. 24).[120]

Books and objects were in constant circulation within the palace, and smaller libraries (in the form of large bookcases) were installed inside some of its buildings, most prominently the Mabeyn and Merasim. In the late spring of 1909, when the palace was vacated, dispersed among its various buildings were volumes such as an Egyptian antiquities catalogue in French, a treatise on the Karakeçili tribe, an album of paintings by Fausto Zonaro depicting the Greek War, a biography of Metternich, a Hicaz yearbook (*salname*), a manuscript containing an Ibn Khaldun translation, a list of burned books and pamphlets, photographs of individuals exiled to the provinces under Abdülhamid, a printed hagiography of Battal Gazi, a printed edition of *A Thousand and One Nights*, a scientific report on an earthquake in Aydın, and a memorandum on the need for a history of Circassia.[121] A copy of the full catalogue of the outer library was also circulated—always, it appears, readily available for consultation by various members of the court without having to visit the main library.

THE HAREM

If the palace's administrative quarter (*selamlık*) was bifurcated by the Mabeyn Kiosk into two segments, one for workaday employees and one more exclusive, its harem was similarly divided (see map 2). The zone reserved for the sultan's immediate family, consisting of his wives, young and unmarried children, and the servants allocated to their individual *daire*s, was closest to his own residence. This was a startlingly small, closely bounded area that could be considered the palace's real harem. As an extension to the harem, individual apartments within the palace grounds were also allocated to married members of his family; these residences were located

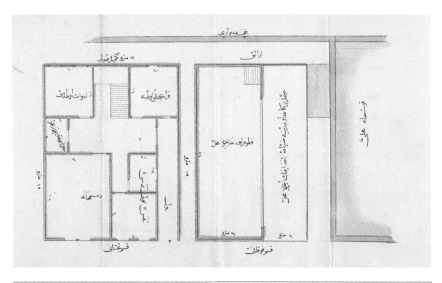

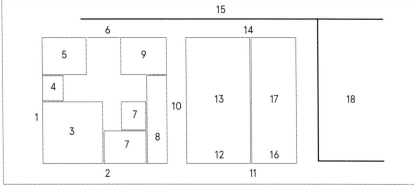

1 Ten meters	**10** Ten meters
2 First floor	**11** Ground floor
3 Drawing office	**12** Six meters
4 Storage room for the glass negatives	**13** Photography studio
5 Equipment room	**14** Gap
6 Completed height twelve meters	**15** Garden wall
7 Recreation room	**16** Four meters
8 Path	**17** Picture-developing room
9 Darkroom	**18** Aviary

FIGURE 24
Undated plan of a photography studio inside the palace's harem garden. BOA, PLK. P. 4609.

(*muhit*) of its own. He ponders, "What kind of life they led in this neighborhood was unknown to me, but it was certainly not one where they [the princes] strove to perfect their personhood."[122]

A curiously narrow gate through the wall separating the harem from the Mabeyn courtyard led the sultan's family members and his closest aides, scribes, and handpicked visitors into a relatively cramped courtyard, an exterior antechamber to the harem. This outdoor waiting room was often called the *zülvecheyn*. This word, used interchangeably with *mabeyn* and meaning "two-sided" or "bidirectional," was generally applied to transitional zones between the men's and women's quarters in affluent Ottoman households. In the case of Yıldız, this designation implied not only that the zone offered access to these two segments of a wealthy residence but also that it provided the only passage between the sultan's quarters and the Şale—that is, between the sultan's family quarters, his most intimate space, and the court's royal guest lodgings. It was also this quirkily cramped and physically unmarked *zülvecheyn* that provided access, via an archlike opening between the sultan's private residence and his workspace (*hususi daire* and Küçük Mabeyn), to the harem's oblong, heavily landscaped English garden.

For the female members of the court, who saw the area bordered by the harem wall with high sculptural reliefs as the threshold of their private residences, the small courtyard of the *zülvecheyn* constituted the actual *selamlık* of their home.[123] This was the quarter in which the head of their family always conducted his business; the sultan hardly ever ventured into the two zones of the Mabeyn. To the women, the Mabeyn courtyard, with

farther up the complex's hilltop and constituted their own neighborhood, together with parks, ponds, chalets, and servant quarters (map 2, no. 11). In his memoirs, the sultan's first secretary describes this harem extension as a remarkably interiorized neighborhood all of its administrative and service facilities, was a separate entity, a distinct neighborhood of government employees and offices removed both physically and hierarchically from the privacy and sanctity of their home. Thus, as a spatial and functional designation, the *selamlık* indicated different zones for the members of the harem and the government officials on the other side of the wall.

Abdülhamid's private residence, his workspace inside the Küçük Mabeyn, and the residence of the *valide* (previously the Azizian Mabeyn's main harem structure) were—perhaps unusually—located in this transitional zone (map 2, nos. 25, 31, and 27). Yıldız's real harem, where the sultan's immediate family and their numerous attendees resided, was clustered inside a small terraced area on the northeastern border of the sultan's private garden. Its largest structure was a conglomeration of three interlinked two-story apartment blocks, which were built for the female servants (*cariyeler dairesi*), the female supervisor of the harem and her retinue of *kalfa*s (*hazinedar usta dairesi*), and the wives (*kadınefendiler dairesi*) of the sultan, respectively (map 2, nos. 20–22). These three connected units were compressed into a small area, limited from the north by the Şale Kiosk. Indeed, the earliest version of the Şale, probably commissioned by Abdülaziz and extant during the site's palatial conversion under Abdülhamid, dictated the eventual irregularity of the harem's layout and its spatial confinement. A steep declivity to the east limited its expansion but allowed a citadel-like border in the form of a natural belvedere from which the private harem garden enjoyed a commanding outlook over the palace's park below.

The quarters allocated to the servants of the harem were designed as transitional spaces, often squeezed between the two zones or apartment units that they serviced. An archway underneath the residence of the sultan's eunuchs-in-waiting (*musahib ağalar dairesi*) marked the harem's threshold on the Şale side (map 2, no. 23). This transitional structure was connected to the sultan's private residence to allow eunuchs, the foremost harem chamberlains, to scurry between the sultan and the *selamlık* on the Mabeyn side to report Abdülhamid's needs to the office of the head scribe. The eunuchs also took turns keeping vigil in the sultan's private residence (*hususi daire*) to communicate Abdülhamid's orders to the members of the harem. As mentioned at the beginning of this chapter, Nadir Ağa (d. 1935), the third *musahib*, who became Abdülhamid's favorite due to both his devotion to the sultan and his athletic daring (he tested the first automobile to be brought into the palace and operated the barges on the harem's lake), was able to evade persecution in the aftermath of the sultan's deposition by showing the commission formed by the Young Turk government the numerous hidden safes in the harem apartments.[124]

Similarly, the apartment of the *hazinedar usta*—who, as the female counterpart to the sultan's head chamberlain in the Mabeyn, was responsible for the management of the harem—was situated between and connected by enclosed bridges to, on one side, the apartments of the sultan's wives and, on the other, the apartments of the female servants in her purview (map 2, nos. 21, 19–20, and 22). Within the harem, the *hazinedar usta* wielded "considerable discretionary powers" (selahiyet-i vâsi'a sahibi),[125] was held in higher esteem even than the sultan's wives, and had direct access to the sultan. She was the harem's financial accountant, its master of

FIGURE 25
Present state of the residence
of the chief black eunuch,
surrounded by greenhouses
and the terraces of the inner
garden.

instructors, favorite among them the celebrated artist and sultan's aide Şeker Ahmed Paşa (d. 1907).

Perched like a jewel box on the first tier of these staggered sets, and between the apartments of the eunuchs-in-waiting and the rest of the harem structures, was the residence of the chief black eunuch (*kızlarağası* or *darüssaade ağası*) (map 2, no. 18) (fig. 25). With its Roman windows, high-relief sculptures of flower vases in place of keystones, pronounced quoins, and strikingly small scale, this delicate two-floor building carries echoes of Ottoman pleasure pavilions from earlier decades, such as those at Göksu, Küçüksu, and Ihlamur, and may be one of the last remaining fragments of the site's prepalatine history as a much smaller royal estate.[127] It is no surprise that this standout structure from the recent past was repurposed to fit the office of the chief eunuch, who held the same rank as the grand vizier and chief religious officer in the court hierarchy (although this rank seems to have been merely titular in the Hamidian era).[128]

To ease the busy circulation between the various *daire*s inside the harem, almost all individual buildings were physically linked with their service quarters. Indeed, from the multipurpose Çit Kiosk of the *selamlık*, which offered access to the harem's antechamber (*zülvecheyn*), a visitor could walk all the way to the lofty turreted ceremonial hall in the Şale Kiosk without once having to step outside. Similarly, Abdülhamid could move easily between his study in the Küçük Mabeyn and the Şale, where he visited his royal guests or met with the grand vizier, who was assigned a set of rooms there for his twice-weekly audience with the sultan. Not only was Abdülhamid's private residence (*hususi daire*)

ceremonies, and often the preferred bearer of the sultan's decrees over his eunuchs, who were, in turn, relegated to acting as the *hazinedar*'s personal messengers between the harem and the offices within the Mabeyn—especially the one in constant communication with the accountants of the imperial treasury in Dolmabahçe Palace.[126]

The outdoor space between the residence of the eunuchs-in-waiting and these three apartments was incredibly tight, labyrinthine, and tiered, defined overall by a cluster of terraces that ended with a wall separating the harem from the grounds of the Şale. Three iron-framed greenhouses with grottoes once ran along the harem side of this wall (map 2, no. 17). In the family photographs shot inside the palace's interiors, these greenhouses and their elevated rostra-like grottoes frame the poses of the sultan's young children and their connected to the quarters assigned to the eunuchs in his service, but it also had private access through a gallery to the already interconnected apartments of the female servants, the *hazinedar usta*, and, finally, the sultan's wives.

Until they were old enough to continue their learning in the separate school for the princes, the younger sons and daughters of the sultan received coeducational instruction in the otherwise nondescript apartments appointed to the sultan's wives. The main entrance to these apartments supported a dome painted with a map of the Ottoman territories. A reflective pool of water immediately below it (which was later removed) reversed the mural and made it available for close-up study.

Life inside the Hamidian harem was often quiet and understated. Abdülhamid followed a strict and unchanging schedule of work, repose, and repast, along with the oft-cited bedtime ritual of having detective novels by the French writer Émile Gaboriau (d. 1873) read to him by the keeper of his wardrobe (*esvapçıbaşı*). The monotony of the sovereign's day-to-day existence was so ingrained in Yıldız's administrative functioning that in their publications each of his aides-turned-biographers dedicated a chapter to the sultan's daily life.[129] The inhabitants of each of the apartments within the harem lived their own nuclear lives. To a great extent their social activity mimicked that of Ottoman elites outside the palace walls. Despite their uncomfortable physical proximity, communication between the *daire*s allotted to the sultan's wives, daughters, and married sons was still highly formal, regulated by myriad servants and written invitations.

The various members of the sultan's extended family had to see a lot more of one another during religious holidays or on the anniversary of Abdülhamid's accession to the throne, when they were required to participate in associated ritual practices. Often, the large reception rooms (*sofa*s) dividing the individual apartments became stages for musical or theatrical performances, including re-creations of the operas that the members of the harem watched in Yıldız's theater.[130] The children enacted pantomimes based on popular Victorian fairy tales.[131] On warmer days, the performances were held outside, on a small stage built on the garden side of the sultan's private residence.

One of the memoirs from the time describes the remarkable, if little known, occasion on which the members of the harem devised an elaborate "public exposition" (*umumi sergi*), a globally popular, if demanding, nineteenth-century phenomenon of consumption, to celebrate the twenty-fifth anniversary of the sultan's accession.[132] Reportedly, the women, dressed as merchants, turned the *zülvecheyn* overnight into a bustling marketplace, selling everything from grain and cheese to soaps, drapery, haberdashery, and sweets. A separate exhibition of imperial jewelry (not available for sale) was also curated, with dramatic electric lighting installed to enhance the pleasure of viewing. All of the palace's royal production facilities and those beyond, in İzmit—its dairy farm, kitchen gardens and greenhouses, the private safes of its members, its on-site porcelain factory, and the Hereke textile factory—were mobilized to contribute goods for the night market.

The small palace theater, located in the *zülvecheyn* and squeezed between the residence of the sultan's mother and that of the eunuchs-in-waiting, served as another recreational site for the members of the harem. Whenever a *daire* hosted an important visitor, such as a high-ranking female living outside the palace—like Abdülhamid's sister Cemile Sultan, the Egyptian khedive's mother (*valide paşa*), or the wife of a foreign ruler or ambassador—the *hazinedar usta* and her servants would organize and execute the visit following an admixture of European and traditional protocol.[133] The sultan would order a performance to be staged in the theater following the harem visit, and the sultan's wives, daughters, and other close female relations would be expected to attend, looking on from the harem's grilled second-floor balconies. Inconspicuous as the theater was, its location meant that it served as an important ceremonial threshold for the palace. A stripped-down triumphal arch next to its entrance conducted the privileged guests of the Şale into the palace's harem, and passing through it, the harem's women were allowed to spend a day in the royal guest lodgings after the *bayram* ceremonies.

On the first day of each of the major religious holidays, the Şale was reserved for the sultan's immediate family to host their relatives. These prolonged visits always commenced with a tour of its multiple rooms and apartments. In many ways, in fact, the female members of the harem replicated the tour that the sultan had devised for his royal guests. The Şale, referred to more often as the "ceremonial apartments" than by its typological designation, was the tour's shining glory. The first and only palace building to be supplied with electricity in 1889 (its massive generators still stand inside its

garden compound), it was also furnished with lavish Hereke textiles and enormous carpets and housed Yıldız's painting and clock collections. The Şale appeared to members of the court and palace officials alike as a permanent world exhibition, with each of its apartments designed in the style of a different nation. It was intended to appear as a kind of *Gesamtkunstwerk*: "the Arab style, the work of the English, or the French and German styles, with furniture equipped with the adornments of that people [*kavim*]."[134] While men enjoyed the sultan's shooting range (known as the Poligon Kiosk) on the far corner of this complex or watched military parades from its adjacent miniature Gothic castle, the Talimhane Kiosk (map 2, nos. 1–2), women took walks around the Şale's grottoes, ponds, round palmhouses, and monumental greenhouses, which were fronted by bronze animal sculptures, gifts from the compound's first guest, the German emperor Wilhelm II.[135]

The urban make-believe played out in Yıldız's harem was also observed inside its private garden. The members of the court referred to this site as the inner garden (*iç bahçe*) or the garden of the *selamlık* (given that members of the harem thought of the transitional zone of the *zülvecheyn* as the sultan's administrative quarters). This garden, which was designed in the shape of "an attenuated ellipse" (*ṭūlānī bir beyz*),[136] was laid out on a shallow gradient between the platforms carrying the *hususi daire* on its north and the Cihannüma (Belvedere) Kiosk to its south (map 2). A thick retaining wall on the garden's eastern side separated it from the palace's park below and bore a discrete portal that provided private access between these two heavily landscaped spaces. The centerpiece of this private garden was a serpentine lake, built in the late 1880s, which formed a moat around an island and supported docking stations for barges and launches, along with pavilions for relaxation along its shores. Each of the docking stations was named after a Bosphorus neighborhood, and in keeping with the desire to bring as much of life outside the palace into the harem as possible, the single-room art nouveau pavilion on the island (Ada Köşkü) was conceived as a neighborhood coffeehouse.[137]

Abdülhamid's critics used the artificial lakes, grottoes, cascades, rustic bridges, railings, and gazebos (all poured concrete over iron)[138] of this picturesque garden as a metaphor for the sultan's ever-suspect mental state. In their eyes, the garden's landscape, like its owner, was "strangely crooked in form" (ġarīb bir ṣūretde iʿvicāclı).[139] Georgina Müller, the first and possibly the only foreigner to record her time inside the (then newly landscaped) harem garden with relative impartiality, describes it as it was intended, as a space that was "as well kept as … the best English gardens":

> Yildiz stands on the summit of the highest hill of the capital, and here before us lay a large lake or artificial river, covered with kaïks and boats of all shapes, an electric launch among others. The gardens sloped to the lake on all sides, the lawns as green, the turf as well kept as in the best English gardens. Exquisite shrubs and palms were planted in every direction, whilst the flower borders were a blaze of colour. The air was almost heavy with the scent of orange blossom, and gardeners were busy at every turn sprinkling the turf, even the crisp gravel walks, with water. The Harem wall, now on our right, rose no longer bare, but covered to the top with yellow and white Banksia roses, heliotrope, sweet verbena, passion flowers, &c. Thousands of white or silvery-grey pigeons—the Prophet's bird—flew in and out of a huge pigeon-house, built against the walls, half hidden by the creepers.[140]

For individuals with intimate access to this inner garden, it was a place of miniature pavilions, architectural landscaping feats, and aviaries, all housing the period's most "precious novelties" (bedāyi).[141] The rarest of bird breeds, trees, plants, and flowers, as well as the most popular architectural styles of the day, were reserved for this space. It contained the best that the recreational world of the nineteenth century had to offer.

THE PARK

The narrow southern strip of the Mabeyn courtyard (where the main library and Çadır Kiosk were situated), along with the Şale compound on the complex's northeast, formed an imperfect crescent around the grand park of Yıldız. Two pathways at the tips of this crescent led members of the harem and Abdülhamid's guests into the park's woods and pavilions. However, the real experience of the palace's park—or "outer garden" (dış bahçe), as it is termed in narrative accounts of the site—commenced after one had passed through Yıldız's oldest gate, the Portal of Mecidiye, situated behind Çırağan Palace. This gate had once provided access to the gardens when they had served this waterfront palace. The female members of Abdülmecid's and later

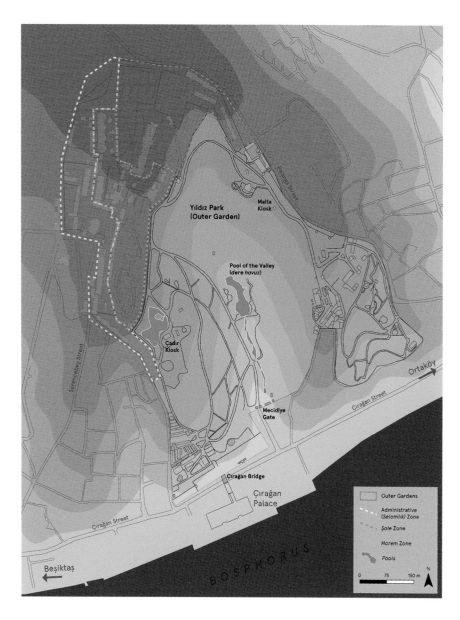

and fifty meters long, with a cascading stream varying in width from ten to thirty meters; the waters feeding the park's lake were pumped from the lake at a higher elevation in the harem gardens. Due to its placement between the two hills of Yıldız, this artificial body of water was called the "Pool of the Valley" (*dere ḥavuż*).[142] Water for the palace was brought from the city's heavily wooded northern valley, called the Forest of Belgrad. An 1895 map of Istanbul's water system and dams, drawn by a member of the Military Inspection Commission, illustrates, using a thick red line, the Taksim waterways, which were fed by three early nineteenth-century dams and reached elevated grounds of the palace (fig. 26). Once Abdülhamid had established Yıldız as his palace, its water usage increased to about one third of the overall supply to this region of the capital—evidence of the site's quick transformation into its own town.[143] When usage at his palace threatened Istanbul with major water shortages, the sultan sought alternative sources in the north of the city (Karakemer Aquaduct, near today's Kemerburgaz) and established the Hamidiye waterways in 1902.[144] In the last years of his rule, Yıldız and its surrounding neighborhoods were maintained by approximately thirty fountains.

The Çadır and Malta kiosks, the two neoclassical pleasure pavilions built during Abdülaziz's conversion of the site into a miniature Bois de Boulogne, were surrounded by the heavy foliage of trees, and occupied the peaks of this ravine's two hills. These pavilions afforded protected views that allowed their royal occupants to repose in a contemplative daydream (*meşġūl-ı ḥayālāt*).[145] From their earliest incarnation as part of the grand

MAP 4
Yıldız Park, with the central "Pool of the Valley" (*dere havuz*), the artificial lake in the outer garden, and the pond in front of the Çadır Kiosk. Courtesy of M. Tülek.

Abdülaziz's harems, however, used a bridge rather than this gate, which was level with the street. Abdülmecid's understated Mecidiye Mosque flanked it on the right, and the stone barracks of the imperial guards, on its left.

The park's natural ravine (*dere*), or gorge (*boğaz*), contained a large lake, one hundred

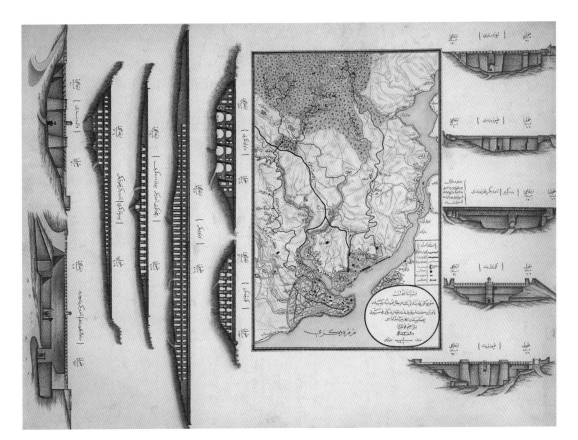

FIGURE 26
Major General Ibrahim, map of
Istanbul's main waterways and
renderings of its aqueducts
and dams, 1894–95. 50 × 67 cm.
İÜMK, 92577.

project to convert the hills of Çırağan into an
English garden (discussed at greater length
in chapter 3), these structures were conceived
as hermitages complementing the Romantic landscape. Their secluded siting worked
in Abdülhamid's favor again in 1881, when
he used them to imprison the high-ranking
political representatives of Abdülaziz's
reign—most famously the influential Tanzimat statesman Mithat Paşa (d. 1883), who
was one of the creators of the first Ottoman
constitution of 1876—under prosecution by
the new government for conspiring to assas-
sinate the late sultan.[146] Whenever Murad V's
mental illness visibly disrupted his ability to
govern during his short and ill-fated reign,

in the spring and summer months of 1876,
he was rushed to the Malta Kiosk, which also
functioned then as a kind of asylum or sanatorium. Here he was treated and hidden away
from the prying eyes of a curious public and
the bewildered members of his household at
Dolmabahçe, especially his ambitious mother,
Şevkefza.[147]

Like that of his scribes, Abdülhamid's life
within the palace during his thirty-year reign
was largely contained within a few structures
inside the harem. Memoirs of his daughter
Ayşe and his first secretary Tahsin identically
refer to the sultan's day-to-day experience
of this grand site as monotonous (*yeknasak*).

After an early rise in his cozy Victorian residence, he would bathe in his private *hamam*, perform his morning prayer, and be dressed by the keeper of his wardrobe. He would then enter the *selamlık* (*selamlığa çıkmak*) and in his office inside the Küçük Mabeyn meet his first secretary. He took lunch with his family in the harem and returned to work with his scribes and ministers in his office. As expanded on in the following chapters, only on ceremonial occasions (often after the Friday ceremonies) could he venture out into the park, ride a horse, and visit the theater. Otherwise, in the evenings, he found solace in carpentry inside his tiny atelier or reading in the outer library.

Yıldız Kiosk and the Queen Mothers

If we were to seek a uniquely gendered space in the Ottoman capital between the late eighteenth and early nineteenth centuries, the area demarcated by Çırağan Palace on the waterfront and extending up to the valley between Beşiktaş and Ortaköy would fit the bill. This particular imperial segment of the nineteenth-century capital, which eventually developed into Abdülhamid II's Yıldız Palace complex, was reserved for the powerful mothers (*valides*) of the sultans for almost a century. Selim III's mother, Mihrişah Sultan (d. 1805);[1] Abdülmecid's mother; Bezm-i Alem Sultan (d. 1853); and Abdülaziz's mother, Pertevniyal Sultan (d. 1883), all focused their philanthropic activities on this hilly site, in line with the sultans' growing preference for the waterfront palace of Beşiktaş (later known as Dolmabahçe) over the grand but secluded Topkapı.

Here, the *valide*s first erected fountains, infrastructural requisites for any newly urbanizing neighborhood and readily placed markers of ownership. Most important, however, they pioneered a taste for imperial structures in the form of countryside retreats and farming estates. This development, which has been surprisingly overlooked, demonstrates the existence of a "pastoral ethos" that scholars have long hoped to see more vividly exemplified in the eighteenth-century revival of the Ottoman court's *villeggiatura* practices.[2] From the beginning of the nineteenth century to the moment at which Abdülhamid II made it his palace in 1878, Yıldız was inhabited by a succession of these charitable, architecturally discerning mothers of sultans, who frequented the site not only to enjoy its privileged views but also to inspect their adjoining farming estates while remaining close to the sacred sites of Beşiktaş, which resonated with their spiritual and religious sensibilities— sensibilities that, due to the women's inherently circumscribed and private lives within the patriarchal system of the Ottoman court, were necessarily constrained.

WOMEN OF THE OTTOMAN COURT AND THE LURE OF BEŞIKTAŞ

The site's first proprietors were the daughters of sultans. The consummate mid-seventeenth-century traveler Evliya Çelebi witnessed the allocation of its waterfront, later known as the *yalı* of Çırağan, to one of the court's high-ranking women. In his voluminous description of Istanbul, Evliya records that the mansion and a garden previously known as Kazancıoğlı, located next to the imperial garden of Beşiktaş, were granted to Kaya Sultan, daughter of Murad IV. Evliya, a devoted member of the intimate courtly circle of Kaya Sultan's husband, Melek Ahmed

Paşa, knew this residence reasonably well, describing it as "a mansion that needs to be seen" (*vācibü's-seyr bir yalıdır*). Its singularity, according to this diligent observer, lay in its unusual two-story fountain (*fevḳānī şāẕrevān*).[3]

It is very likely that a pattern of property succession was put in place soon thereafter, or had already been partially established, to reserve this waterfront lot (with its ever-changing buildings) for the daughters and sisters of sultans. A parallel can be drawn with the designation in perpetuity of a cluster of *yalı*s along the landing dock of Eyüp to the same group of high-ranking women.[4] Although the celebrated nighttime festivals held around illuminated flowerbeds in the mansion's gardens by Ahmed III's grand vizier Nevşehirli Damad İbrahim Paşa forever sealed the mansion's name as Çırağan (after the word *çirāğ*, meaning "lamp," "light," or "candle") and suggested ownership by the vizier, the residence's real proprietor was Fatma Sultan, the sultan's daughter and the grand vizier's wife.[5] Ahmed III's letters to his vizier inquiring after the health of the princess Fatma Sultan, who was suffering from smallpox, offer an unusually close-up portrayal of a father deeply anguished by his daughter's sickness and desperate to discover antidotes.[6] This intimate glimpse of a father's concern for his daughter is evidence of the belief—widely held by members of the court and promoted by the paterfamilias himself—that a princess held a crucial position in the imperial hierarchy as a figure with political and institutional agency. Once married, she was, along with her own household, a symbolic extension or satellite of the sultan's court and had to conduct her married life as such.[7]

Skarlatos Byzantios, the nineteenth-century Phanariot chronicler of Istanbul, ascribes a kiosk curiously called Gülhane (modeled, he writes, on a Byzantine predecessor in Topkapı Palace) to Ahmed III, which was situated on the mountain plain (οροπέδιον) of Beşiktaş and above his daughter's wooden palace below. This delicate architectural folly, which was covered in marble with gilded Koranic inscriptions, stood for the paternal-sultanic gaze and might have been the erstwhile structure on the Çırağan hills that would later become the Çadır Kiosk, first depicted in a marquetry landscape on a pen box (discussed in the following chapter).[8]

Sedad Hakkı Eldem, who left behind the most comprehensive study of the Ottoman waterfront residences to date, shows how the Çırağan mansion might have looked in the time of Kaya Sultan and how it may have changed over the course of the eighteenth century. As evidence, he compares the descriptions and architectural sketches created by Franz Philipp von Gudenus, a member of the Austrian delegation that visited Mahmud I's court in 1740, with an engraving from the expanded second edition, published in 1842, of the French ambassador Marie-Gabriel-Florent-Auguste de Choiseul-Gouffier's *Voyage pittoresque de la Grèce* (fig. 27).[9] Like Evliya Çelebi's verbal description, Gudenus's sketch of the property's layout and his accompanying narrative focus on the site's most distinctive feature: Kaya Sultan's double-tiered fountain, featuring flower-shaped brass waterspouts whose waters collected in a large marble pool embellished with prominent fish reliefs.[10] The former structures at this site appear less like components of a hardy mansion than like light, porous buildings to be used for temporary stays.

Superimposing Gudenus's plan onto Choiseul-Gouffier's engraving of the mansion's waterfront façade, Eldem finds remarkable similarities between the two, especially in the layout of the central assembly hall projecting over the water. At the time of the ambassadorial visit, the site contained two small kiosks, one with the reception hall on the water and the other set back against an arbor of vines and separated from the former by a central marble pool. Overall, the site seems to have been used first for semi-informal court ceremonies on its lawns, at which high-ranking officials like the vizier and grand admiral hosted and entertained foreign delegations with theatrical and circus performances. Although heavily gilded, according to Gudenus, the kiosks were meant to provide only temporary shelter; they were not generally intended for overnight stays. They were light, open, and ephemeral timber buildings. Outdoor structures such as the fountain, pool, terraces, and flower parterres were more central to the use and overall experience of the space than the buildings themselves.

Selim III's sister Beyhan Sultan (d. 1824) was the owner of the wooden mansion when Choiseul-Gouffier saw it a few decades later.[11] Her residence was a considerably enlarged version of the waterfront kiosk outlined by Gudenus, with two wings added to its sides in place of the two large flower parterres that had once served as makeshift stages for performances before foreign delegations. The expansion of the kiosk into a mansion reflected the privatization of the property in the time of Selim III, marking the point at which the princesses began to take real

Vue d'un Kiosque entre Defterdar-Bournou et Kourou-Tchechmè.

ownership of their designated Bosphorus properties—forming their own subcourts and inhabiting their *yalıs* for long periods of time rather than allowing them to remain in regular use for court ceremonies. This was especially the case for widowed princesses like Abdülhamid I's daughter Esma Sultan (d. 1848) and Selim III's sister Beyhan Sultan, neither of whom remarried and both of whom enjoyed unprecedented levels of independence in presiding over their own households in their designated waterfront mansions.[12] They entertained individuals such as the celebrated poet and shaykh of the Galata Mevlevî dervish lodge, Şeyh Galib (d. 1793), and brought in decorator-architects and landscape designers to reinvent the *yalıs'* interiors and outdoor spaces.[13] The period's most prominent female tastemaker was, of course, Selim III's charismatic sister Hatice Sultan, who notably employed the German draftsman Antoine Ignace Melling as her stylemaker for the construction of a

FIGURE 27
Louis-François-Sébastien Fauvel, *Vue d'un Kiosque entre Defterdar-Bournou et Kourou-Tchechmè*. From Marie-Gabriel-Florent-Auguste de Choiseul-Gouffier, *Voyage pittoresque de la Grèce* (1782–[1824]). Getty Research Institute, Los Angeles (84-B22325).

tripartite Empire addition to her Defterdar Burnu waterfront mansion in Ortaköy.[14] Hatice Sultan's numerous letters to Melling repeatedly and forcefully list her decorative needs, reflecting a dogged, if temperamental, discernment.[15] Among a plethora of visual symbols, pediments, garlands, crests, monograms, eye-catching colors, heavy gilding, and copious silks and porcelain objects were the decorative markers of choice for these princesses, and in acquiring and displaying them, they appear to have created a lively culture of collecting and self-fashioning.[16]

The busy social lives of the princesses and the spaces they inhabited were intimately bound up with their locations in specific neighborhoods of the imperial capital: the women continually crisscrossed between their mansions in Eyüp and others along the coastline from Tophane to Kuruçeşme. Both the residential properties tenurially ceded to the female members of the imperial household and the revenue sources assigned to them, such as agricultural land and tax farms, retained a remarkable degree of continuity in their inheritance. The *yalı*s in Eyüp, originally allocated exclusively to the daughters of Ahmed III and Mustafa III, offer a useful example.[17] After the death of Ahmed III's daughter Esma Sultan the Elder (d. 1788), a progressive host able to speak her mind to Baron de Tott's wife about her dissatisfaction with arranged marriages between young princesses and elderly statesmen, her agricultural properties were passed on to her namesake, the abovementioned daughter of Abdülhamid I: Esma Sultan the Younger. The latter was an even more independent woman, who sustained a lively, autonomous court with her bevy of female courtiers, and was prominent enough to be considered a

regent, albeit sardonically, when Mahmud II remained the sole male heir.[18] A similar transfer of inherited wealth occurred between Selim III's sisters Hatice Sultan (d. 1821) and Beyhan Sultan (d. 1824) and between Abdülhamid I's wife Şebsefa Kadın and daughter Hibetullah Sultan—an understudied pattern of property handoffs that I believe continued into the nineteenth century.[19]

In a calculated move to curb the rising power of the military-administrative elite, Ahmed III revived this revenue-redistribution model and encouraged the princesses "to engage in public manifestations of dynastic sovereignty" in the capital, enabled by the enormous economic independence the model conferred.[20] A remarkable study of the sources of revenue for the eighteenth-century princesses links this targeted redistribution of imperial wealth with the burgeoning of the imperial female patronage of lavish residential architecture along the Bosphorus.[21] It asserts that the increased visibility of these women, as pioneers of taste and consumers of novelty, was connected with the state's assignment to them of the invaluable yet increasingly precarious Rumelian properties as tax farms. This was done to safeguard the state's most important revenue-generating sources by keeping them within the family and out of the reach of increasingly powerful local landlords. The princesses were also married off to influential dignitaries to secure the latter's allegiance to the sultan, as in the case of Fatma Sultan and Nevşehirli İbrahim Paşa. By the turn of the century, however, the imperial princesses had attained unprecedented agency in the ways in which they conducted their lives, which had tangible repercussions for the layout of their mansions. The central spaces were designated as the apartments of the sultan, who often frequented the courts of his sisters or nieces. Even the stewards (*kethüda*s) hired to manage the incomes of these women received statelier lodgings than the princesses' husbands, whose apartments were comparatively humble and inconspicuous.[22]

The wealth of the daughters and sisters of the eighteenth-century sultans was seemingly so vast that they were able to retain substantial disposable incomes to spend on their own sizable households, residential architecture, and luxury objects, which they had no need to protect through monumental pious endowments. In contrast, the *valide*s of the eighteenth century are curiously less visible as patrons and consumers. Only with Selim III's mother, Mihrişah, does the status of the *valide* as a prominent personage of the court and a savvy builder of residential and civic structures begin to reemerge. The most monumental work attributed to Mihrişah is the Valide Dam (Valide Bendi) in Belgrad Forest; the most intriguing, in terms of its overall baroque schema, is her tomb and interconnected *imaret* in Eyüp.

The activities of the two powerful *valide*s of the nineteenth century, Bezm-i Alem and Pertevniyal, reveal—albeit unobtrusively, as little is known about their lives, let alone their patronage patterns—a definitive turn toward the patronage of monumental civic and religious architecture. While they did indeed build personal residences (and the developments in and around Yıldız estate are prime examples), these buildings did not exhibit the degree of ostentation seen in the previous century, perhaps due to a shift in courtly decorum that favored the channeling of personal wealth into public service. A change in the *valide*s' resources may have

resulted from the loss of the lucrative Balkan territories, rather than from the kind of profligate spending often attributed to female members of the court or from the fraudulence of financial advisors in league with scheming non-Muslim moneylenders. For example, the fact that the majority of the properties assigned to Bezm-i Alem's largest endowment, her hospital complex in Fatih, were olive orchards in Edremit, on the west coast of Anatolia (probably among the most profitable lands then remaining in the empire's domains), suggests that geopolitical changes were behind the geographical shifts in the income sources assigned to the powerful women of the court.[23] These women may have had to rethink their self-presentation with respect to both their fiscal capabilities and their roles as the mothers of reformist sultans; however, their architectural presence alongside that of their sons and daughters on the Bosphorus waterfront persisted well into the reign of Abdülhamid II.

THE FIRST YILDIZ KIOSK AND ITS ECHOES ACROSS THE SHORE

If Ahmed III revitalized the courtly practice of frequenting the royal suburban mansions and gardens through his daughters, sons-in-law, and various high-ranking officials, the patronage of Mahmud I (r. 1730–54) consolidated this practice by meeting the infrastructural needs of the European shoreline of the Bosphorus, which stretched from the imperial foundry of Tophane to the Çırağan Palace.[24] Mahmud built his monumental waterworks project of 1732 on his predecessor's foundation by constructing a dam in Sarıyer's Bahçeköy neighborhood. From the wooded hill close to the Black Sea the water was brought by aqueduct to Taksim, named after its distribution facility, and from there down to Fındıklı. An observer of the period notes that, before Mahmud I, the boroughs (*kasaba*s) of Tophane and Fındıklı had been blessed with good weather, proximity to the walled city of Istanbul, and a propitious orientation toward the *qibla* (indicating the cardinal direction of Mecca, to the south); their only shortcoming was a lack of drinking water.[25] Furthermore, by rallying many of the city's elites, including his mother, to endow fountains and *sebil*s (structures for water distribution) in Tophane and Fındıklı, Mahmud I distributed water to a larger swath of the shoreline and the suburban villages on its hills. The same observer estimates that as many as eighty fountains benefited from this collective effort.[26] What had started out as an effort to improve a very specific segment of the shoreline resulted in the increased habitability of many neighborhoods of the imperial capital, from Galata to Kasımpaşa, Dolmabahçe, and Beşiktaş.

In the late eighteenth-century chronicle by Cabi Ömer Efendi, Yıldız Kiosk first appears as a structure built by Selim III at the tail end of two colossal building projects completed in 1795: the restoration of the arsenal and the construction of the Imperial School of Engineering, both along the Golden Horn. Lauding its views, the chronicler describes Yıldız as a belvedere, "the world-showing kiosk" (köşk-i cihānnümā).[27] A few subimperial pleasure pavilions in Arnavutköy and Akıntıburnu were constructed alongside this building. Built in succession, these residences were all sited on privileged higher ground as belvederes (*nezâreti şâmil*) overlooking the increasingly populated and lively waterfront of the Bosphorus. Aware, perhaps, of the trendsetting patronage of Selim III's

sister Hatice Sultan and cousin Esma Sultan, Cabi Ömer lists their upland pavilions before the sultan's own. For these competitive patrons, the principal motivation to build these belvedere-like structures was to enjoy their glorious vistas. Selim III's Yıldız Kiosk was given its name after the powerful north wind, *Yıldız*, that blew at this very spot and was coveted for its strength by Selim and his retinue of expert archers and riflemen.[28]

A concern for safety may have been another reason for the court's pursuit of shelter in the imperial hills. Notoriously, Selim III's reign was plagued by janissary insurgencies in the capital. A historian of a slightly later period speaks of the precarious position of the *yalı*s, noting that they were often easy targets. A particular battalion of five thousand janissaries (Beş Ortalar), greatly feared among Istanbul's inhabitants, fled the capital by merchant ships, but not before riddling with bullets the windows of the waterfront mansions of notables living in Ortaköy and Beşiktaş—starting with the *yalı* of the famous diplomat and minister Halet Efendi (d. 1823)—turning the residences into "sieves" (misâl-ı gırbâl).[29] Although this may seem merely a colorful anecdote, events like this may have precipitated the building of Mahmud I's first belvedere behind Beşiktaş Palace, aptly named *sāyebān* (lit. *gölgelik*, meaning both "baldachin tent" and "shelter") for the shade and refuge it provided.[30]

Beginning with Selim III, a pronounced display of reverence toward the family matriarch became evident; the *valide* reclaimed her position above the sultan's sisters. Her patronage became complementary to the sultan's empire-wide reforms, and her position next to the sultan clearly suggested an attempt at dual rule that would become much more pronounced in the nineteenth century. In contrast with Mahmud I's personal upland refuge, Selim III's Yıldız Kiosk was remarkable for the fact that it was built for his mother, Mihrişah Sultan, as part of a comprehensive royal project to redesign all of her residences.[31] When the kiosk was erected, Selim III had already restored his mother's apartments in Topkapı Palace and renovated its harem gardens to her liking.[32] Yıldız Kiosk was to be her retreat, positioned at the top of the hill both literally and metaphorically; it took prime position in a hierarchy of buildings that belonged to the princesses, which were located on the shores below and bracketed the sultan's residence at Beşiktaş. To no one was this architectural hierarchy—aided by the site's topography—more central to the experience of this imperial quarter than to Selim III, who spent an astoundingly large proportion of his days shuttling between his official summer residence and the waterfront residences of his sisters.

From 1803 Mihrişah's Yıldız Kiosk rapidly grew and transformed into an estate. A day-to-day account of Selim III's life records that it was his mother (and not the sultan acting on his mother's behalf) who initiated the building of a "garden pavilion" (bağ kasrı).[33] This building was not at the very summit of the hill, a position held by the Yıldız Kiosk, but downhill and on the meadows to its southwest. It occupied the neighborhood of Yahya Efendi, named after the sixteenth-century theologian and Sufi shaykh who had built his convent there. A fountain inscription from 1797, which was later inserted into the façade of a modern apartment building, attests to Mihrişah's patronage of this segment of the site: "Our Mistress, the illustrious Mihrişah Sultan,

the mother of the sovereignty's highest [Selim III], may glory be upon her, granted and ordained to be included in her noble endowment half a *māṣūra*[34] of fresh water to this fountain from the large aqueduct that she had built as a duty to God's munificence" (Mehd-i ʿulyā-yı salṭanat, devletlü Mihrişah Vālide Sulṭān ʿaliyyetüʾş-şān efendimiz haż-retlerinin li-vechillāhüʾl-kerīm müceddeden binā buyurdukları bend-i kebīrden işbu çeş-meye daḫī yarım māṣūra māʾ-i lezīz iḥsān ve vaḳf-ı şerīflerine ilḥāḳ buyurdular).[35] Her monumental aqueduct fed the fountain of her estate.

Soon after this kiosk and orchard estate had been built, Selim III added them to his busy recreational itinerary in Beşiktaş, visiting his mother at least as often as he did his sisters.[36] Çırağan also came to be Selim's preferred summer residence. It presumably offered a more intimate *mabeyn* for his male retinue than the sprawling and unwieldy Beşiktaş Palace next door, which by then, with its collection of pavilions from different periods, had become a version of Topkapı. He used Beşiktaş only for official meetings with his ministers. Often the sultan and his prized halberdiers (*serhengān*) would take a quick trek up from Çırağan to the sultan's mother's new estate to practice archery and musketry, play the game of jereed, and watch wrestling, javelin throwing, and log cutting (*kütük darbı*).[37] If his mother joined the sultan in observing these courtly pastimes, fireworks would follow until the early morning hours, when the estate would be prepared for their overnight stay, with neither returning to their waterfront palaces.

On any given day in Selim's court, leisure activities intended to display physical prowess and strength were paired with religious rituals for the contemplation of the other-worldly. The neat and balanced cohabitation of these two courtly spheres was facilitated by the positioning of the three royal properties—Çırağan, Mihrişah Sultan's estate, and Yıldız—which were physically layered on top of each other from waterfront to hilltop. The Mevlevi lodge, of which Selim III was a devoted member, was also located adjacent to Çırağan.[38] In a way, the new imperial strip in Beşiktaş replicated the conjoining of worldly pleasure and material effusiveness exhibited by the female members of the court in and through their Golden Horn *yalı*s, which were similarly clustered deliberately close to the mosque complex of Eyüp Sultan, a holy site central to the ceremonial legitimation of the Ottoman house.[39]

The appearance of Mihrişah's pavilion and the overall layout of her farm estate are currently unknown. However, the pavilion's typological designation as a *bağ kasrı* (garden or orchard pavilion) appears to be a novelty in court chronicles otherwise preoccupied with waterfront palaces and mansions. To translate the site's designation as "garden pavilion" is to deny its singularity as a newly formulated property type probably more analogous to the rural Palladian farming estates of sixteenth-century northern Italy, where austere but luxurious small-scale neoclassical villas perched commandingly above cultivated lands full of fruit trees and vineyards. While the existing records fail to explain why Mihrişah Sultan chose this kind of estate instead of a waterfront palace or an inland urban *konak* (was it conceived as an infirmary or a private sanatorium, for example, or simply as an income-generating farm?), it served as a model for many other buildings constructed by the mothers of successive sultans. The most prominent among its successors is the still-extant Validebağ Kasrı in Acıbadem, a vast wooded retreat on a hilltop on Istanbul's Asian side, attributed to Sultan Abdülaziz's mother, Pertevniyal; but a few decades earlier, in 1813, Mahmud II's mother, Nakş-ı Dil Sultan, had built a lesser-known pavilion in Çamlıca's hills that was also celebrated during its time.[40]

Although very little is known about the person and patronage of Nakş-ı Dil Sultan, she also seems to have preferred elevated sites on which to build her extrapalatial residences.[41] It has been suggested that Mahmud II's court began to commission highland retreats in the capital for medical purposes.[42] Since the sultan and his mother both suffered from tuberculosis, and later from a mystery disease with varied symptoms (which was therefore impossible to diagnose without an autopsy), they sought curative airs in Istanbul's hills, especially in the forested segment of Çamlıca perched above the Beylerbeyi Palace.[43] It is unclear whether they believed that tuberculosis was contagious. The physicians of the era were split in their approaches to the etiology of the disease; the majority still believed that it was hereditary. If, however, the Ottoman court was aware of the disease's transmission from person to person, the construction of and subsequent retreat to these imperial hideouts represented a smart move on the part of the court's most prominent members, allowing them to quarantine themselves and protect the other inhabitants of their crowded palaces.[44]

Yıldız Kiosk and its association with the mothers of sultans factored greatly into Nakş-ı Dil's residential commission in Çamlıca, where she appears to have built a

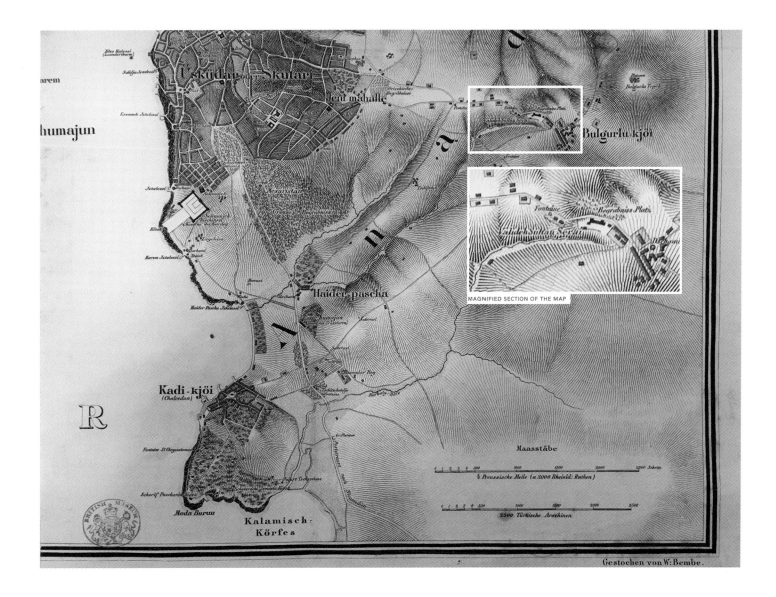

MAGNIFIED SECTION OF THE MAP

near-identical structure. By constructing a similar garden pavilion on the hill exactly opposite the hill and residence linked with her predecessor, Nakş-ı Dil may have sought to instate herself as the new *valide*. Yet with two of these royal sites in her name, she may also have been laying claim to the imperial capital's two prominent hilltops; while the palaces of Beylerbeyi and Çırağan were her son's properties, the elevated sites above them were her own. Although the first topographic map of Istanbul, drawn up by the Prussian officer Helmuth von Moltke (d. 1891), neither demarcates the estate's boundaries nor provides its layout, it still generously labels Nakş-ı Dil's Çamlıca estate as the "Palace of the Queen Mother" (Valideh Sultan Serai) (fig. 28). On the German map, this imperial site is the only residence reserved specifically for the *valide*.

FIGURE 28
Nineteenth-century map of Istanbul and its surroundings, detail showing the Valideh Sultan Serai. From Helmuth von Moltke, *Karte von Constantinopel, den Vorstaedten, der Umgegend und dem Bosphorus, im Auftrage Sr. Hoheit Sultan Mahmud's II.: Mit dem Messtisch in 1:25,000 aufgenommen in den Jahren 1836–37*. British Library Board, Maps 43999.(2). © The British Library Board.

An ode (*kaside*) composed by the renowned court poet Vasıf to commemorate Nakş-ı Dil's Çamlıca pavilion—allegedly built in her son's name—stresses the fact that in its hilltop siting, the pavilion was modeled on Mihrişah's Yıldız Kiosk and presided over the Asian slopes like a beacon of light. "If the Kiosk of Yıldız brought radiance to the neighborhood of Beşiktaş," wrote the poet, "this [building] bestowed grace to the quarter of Üsküdar" (Eğer verdiyse Yıldız Köşkü fer semt-i Beşiktaş'a, Bu sūy-ı Üsküdār'a zīb-baḫş-ı iftiḫār oldu).[45] Playing with astrological imagery, the poet finds that with respect to its high altitude, this royal pavilion is no different from Yıldız in its closeness to the Pleiades, the star cluster most visible to the naked eye. He therefore likens it to its predecessor in their mutual resemblance to a light-scattering moon ("Bunuñ beyne'ş-Şüreyyâ ve'ş-serâ yoḳ farḳı Yıldız'la, Bu ḳaṣr-ı Yıldız'a nisbet meh-i pertev-niṣār oldu").[46] Although this unusually long ode provides no detailed architectural information beyond the usual Persianate allusions to the four-quarter gardens of Isfahan and the forty-columned pavilion, it is still replete with imagery befitting a fecund rural villa. Vasıf revels in the color and taste of the estate's cherries, its freshly sown dewy saplings and moist earth, its pleasant balmy winds, and the overall capaciousness of its structures. It is with this kind of imagery that the ode signals the typological novelty of the imperial estate, and indeed defines it quite precisely as such with the word *me'vā*, meaning "shelter" or "retreat."[47] These pastoral allusions were as much about the court's desire to be close to nature, a Romantic appeal, as they were reflective of the tubercular imperial family's pursuit of recovery through nature's restorative potential.

FAVORABLE WINDS, MAHMUD II, AND ARCHERY AT YILDIZ KIOSK

The Yıldız Kiosk and especially its adjacent farming estate are almost completely absent from records of the early years of Mahmud II's reign. Only in 1811 does evidence of the ruler's use of Yıldız appear, as the fifteen-year-old watches through binoculars the destruction of more than a hundred bachelors' rooms across the shore in Üsküdar, part of an effort to crack down on prostitution and what appears to have been a surge in venereal disease. In the same year, a historic deluge seems to have caused significant disruption to the court's visits to Yıldız. The deluge that "gushed forward a whirlpool of water" not only destroyed many buildings and bridges on the famous promenade of Kağıthane but also flooded streams in Beşiktaş, turning the latter into a sea ("Beşiktaş gûyâ bir deryâ olmağla").[48] Many properties located in these two suburban villages were severely affected, and many ordinary lives were lost. Ottoman chroniclers record the destruction of the old stone bridge of Beşiktaş, along with the local mill, public baths, shops, and the barracks of the gardeners' corps. The deluge was strong enough to flood all of the upland gardens and orchards close to the Yıldız estates. Had Nakş-ı Dil lived longer—she died in 1817—she surely would have restored and repurposed this area for her own use, just as she had undertaken the construction of the Çamlıca estate and her modest yet exquisite baroque tomb and adjacent *sebil* in Fatih.[49]

Mahmud II's preoccupation with perfecting his archery and his relentless desire to compete with the most skilled men in his retinue led to the reinstatement of Yıldız as a prominent imperial retreat after 1818, when the sultan first picked up the sport.[50]

A curious little diary, kept only to document the record-breaking ranges—measured in *gez*[51]—achieved by the sultan and his bowmen, reveals that Yıldız was second only to Okmeydanı (meaning "archery field"), the traditional imperial site for the sport established by Mehmed II (d. 1481).[52] To document the sultan's fledgling hobby, professional archers began to publish detailed how-to guides,[53] and court panegyrists quickly shifted their focus to Mahmud II's mastery of bowmanship. Poets popularized the phrase *Yıldız havası*, referring to the strong north wind that blew across the hilltop site and provided ideal currents for the longest shots. In one of many such couplets, the statesman and poet Sadık Ziver Paşa (d. 1862), the court's most prolific chronogram composer, lauds the sultan's talent, aided by the wind of Yıldız: "By delivering his opening arrow with the Yıldız wind, the shah made it apparent to us that he was the moon to the sign of majesty" (Tīrine Yıldız havāsı ile virüp ol şeh güşād, Māh-ı burc-ı şevket oldığın bize kıldı 'ayān).[54]

The physical boundaries of the imperial retreat of Yıldız were expanded by Mahmud II's frequent archery gatherings. Numerous stone inscriptions marking and celebrating his records can be found in the meadow of Ihlamur, northwest of the Yıldız Kiosk and the future site of another royal retreat, built by Abdülmecid, named Nüzhetiyye.[55] As the group moved around in search of the best wind conditions, portable arbors (*gölgelik*) traveled with them and were put up to provide shade at the selected spots. The archery diary also refers to places around Yıldız with specific, often highly localized names. It provides the first mention of a still-extant door belonging to this property, the "mountain gate" (dağ kapısı),

which apparently faced the main road leading to Kağıthane (the property meanwhile had another, south-facing door). The diary also refers to a smaller structure, a kiosk next to the fountain of Selim III, which was visited for brief excursions (*biniş köşkü*) on the estate and had a porch (*sundurma*) from which the sultan shot arrows in the direction of the non-Muslim cemetery by the Ortaköy stream.[56] From the *biniş* kiosk, the archers enjoyed shooting toward a granary (*harmanlık*), a storage facility that was probably connected with the *valide*'s farming estate. Mahmud II often shot from the corner of the orchard of Gazzazbaşı, next to the Yıldız Kiosk, where he had placed an archer's column (*ayak taşı*) called the "orchard's worth" (bağ bedeli), toward a cemetery locally known as Güvercinlik (meaning "the pigeonry"). On days when the sultan wanted to practice (*meşk*) and not compete, he gathered his archers in front of a coffeehouse close to Yıldız and took aim at a group of mastic trees. The coffeehouse occasionally also served as an informal shooting range, with arrows fired in the direction of the extant Muslim cemetery in Ortaköy. Reflecting the importance of this kiosk to Mahmud II, von Moltke's map depicts it as a structure with a pronounced cross-axial layout set inside a walled garden. The map also marks spots that were important shooting locations for the archers, as identified in the sultan's archery diary, such as the smaller pavilion with the porch, the coffeehouse, and the surrounding cemeteries (fig. 29).

The Yıldız estate fell from favor with Mahmud II in the tumultuous period of the Greek Uprising of 1821. During the uprising, while the state searched for the Greek clergymen who had been sent to Istanbul from

MAGNIFIED SECTION OF THE MAP

various European cities to incite support for their independence movement, the court chose not to relocate to its summer estate on the hills of Beşiktaş and Ortaköy, two neighborhoods traditionally inhabited by the capital's Greek Orthodox subjects.[57] Şanizade Mehmed Ataullah Efendi, a historian born and raised in Ortaköy, witnessed the rounding up and execution of six priests in the area.[58] These executions drew tremendous crowds (made up especially of women), which prevented the executioner from finding sufficient public space for his acts and delayed the court's move to Mahmud II's summer palaces, Beşiktaş and Çırağan.[59]

YILDIZ AS THE QUINTESSENTIAL *VALIDE* ESTATE

The hilltop property was revived once again under the patronage of Abdülmecid's mother, Bezm-i Alem Valide Sultan. Sensationalist histories of the Ottoman harem as a site of continual competitive scheming belie the fact that, like their male counterparts, the affluent women of the house of Osman were eager to model their dispositions, legacy, and architectural influence on those of their female antecedents. This remarkable but understudied genealogical intent is most visible in one of Bezm-i Alem Sultan's first architectural undertakings: erecting an open-air mosque (*namāz-gāh*) in Yıldız for Nakş-ı Dil Sultan, the mother of her husband, Mahmud II. A short chronogram, again composed by the court favorite Ziver Paşa, refers to Bezm-i Alem's successor as Nakşī Kadın, a name used only in the intimate setting of the harem.[60] It is also important to note here that when Bezm-i Alem took the title, more than twenty years had passed since the death of Nakş-ı Dil. This was a very long time

for the harem to remain without a head, making it all the more important for Bezm-i Alem simultaneously to commemorate her predecessor, the mother of her husband, and to present herself as the new queen regent.

History presents a clearer picture of Bezm-i Alem's public-oriented endeavors than that of her predecessors.[61] The trope of love that Darin Stephanov identifies in the post-Tanzimat imperial image tailored for Abdülmecid's relationship with subjects seems also to have been catalyzed by his mother in reformulating hers with the empire's populace.[62] Her seal, longer and more intimate than most imperial seals, shows her understanding of public charity as a devotional act stemming from her boundless, uncontested love toward Prophet Muhammad. Embedded in the seal's verse, her name, which means "the feast of the world," alludes more to selfless and abundant giving to her subjects than earthly conviviality: "From love [*muḥabbet*] emerged [Prophet] Muhammad / Just as there is no love without Muhammad / From his appearance emerged a feast for the world [*bezm-i ʿālem*]."[63] She was a prolific builder of fountains and a patron dedicated to the improvement of public health and education in the capital. Her most significant contribution to Istanbul in the mid-nineteenth century was a richly endowed hospital in Fatih. This large complex was the first health-care institution to be called a hospital (the modern term *ḥastaḥāne* as opposed to the outdated *şifāḥāne*), and its focus was treatment for smallpox and cholera, which were responsible for the worst global epidemics of the period. As smallpox, especially, was believed to be a disease carried by the poor, Bezm-i Alem's demographic target for the hospital was Muslim men in need.[64] She also founded the first civil high school, which prepared its students for university in the capital (under construction at the time), and a preparatory school for girls, to which she donated her own manuscript library and for which she established a lithographic press to print textbooks.[65] The construction of a second bridge between Galata and Eminönü was also undertaken at her initiative, to relieve congestion on Mahmud II's first wooden one.[66]

Bezm-i Alem's numerous and grand public works made her very popular with Istanbulites. In a moving account of her funerary procession, Adolphus Slade (d. 1877), the British admiral of Abdülmecid's navy, highlights the queen mother's links with women and the poor, the capital's most underprivileged demographic groups: "As the procession passed along the streets, lined at intervals with troops, numerous female spectators in open spaces sobbed audibly; and although Eastern women have ever tears as well as smiles at command those shed on this occasion were sincere, for the sex had lost that day an advocate, the poor a friend."[67] The curative powers of water undergirded Bezm-i Alem's charitable institutions in the capital. She endowed the hospital complex with the revenue of Lake Terkos, which fulfilled a large proportion of Istanbul's water needs.[68] Poems dating her fountains and *sebil*s refer to her as a person of purity (*zāt-ı pāk*), alluding to both her virtuousness and her attention to health and cleanliness.[69] Her surviving letters to her son, Abdülmecid, indicate that she frequented the natural springs of Yalova, whose fresh air helped her to breathe (*ferah ülemek*), and enjoyed the facilities there, bathing and receiving mud treatments (*suya girdi, çamura süründü*).[70] Like the contemporary German

Romantics, she found storms and gales exciting subjects for her letters to her son, which were peppered with references to sublime meteorological events. It was unusual for members of the harem to take this kind of balneological trip at such a considerable distance from the capital. Bezm-i Alem's stays in Yalova reflect a further opening-up of the court's previously guarded private entertainment and medical practices, as well as the growing public presence of the queen mothers.[71]

From 1842 onward, Bezm-i Alem was definitely engaged in restoring Yıldız as the *valide* estate. She not only erected the abovementioned open-air mosque in honor of her predecessor but also built a considerable number of fountains on the boundaries of the walled estate and around the shrine complex of Yahya Efendi, which aided in the neighborhood's urban transformation.[72] The fountains' inscription poems praised her as a benefactor who had improved living standards in Beşiktaş. The grandest of her five fountains around Yıldız, a *meydan* fountain with pronounced quoins and four embellished and inscribed façades, provides an inauguration date of 1839, accompanied by the following line by Ziver Paşa: "With water the Queen Mother brought contentment to this quarter" (Bu semti kıldı Vālide Sulṭān āb ile dil-şād) (fig. 30).[73]

Most significantly for the architectural expansion of Yıldız, Bezm-i Alem built a second kiosk next to the one constructed during the time of Selim III. Two commemorative poems, by different poets, from 1842—both referring to the site again, after Mihrişah's time, as a *bāğ* (an orchard or cultivated land)—competed for the status of the new kiosk's epitaph. The competition pitted the court-endorsed Ziver Paşa against a lesser-known poet, İbrahim Raşid Efendi (d. 1892). The latter poet, who kept his day job as a lowly bureaucratic scribe, fashioned his artistic persona as that of a commoner, interspersed his poems with urban patois, and was beloved by an extracourtly readership.[74]

Bezm-i Alem did not choose Ziver's poem, laden with sharp-witted and complex celestial metaphors, because it failed to remark on the prominence of her urban project to rejuvenate the hilltop. Her landscaping in Yıldız was in tandem with the rest of her efforts to build and restore fountains in Beşiktaş to improve the neighborhood's water facilities. She surely also knew that Yıldız's name came from the north wind and not the star; therefore, to her, Ziver's astrological imagery was a misreading that overlooked the most important fact about the site: its function as a royal archer's favorite retreat. The poet had changed the meaning of the site's imperial designation, and that was unacceptable to Bezm-i Alem, who was clearly driven by a commemorative impulse to preserve the legacy of Yıldız's former inhabitants, male and female. The *valide*'s rejection of this poem must have been especially hard for a poet who prided himself on his knowledge of astronomy and had even authored a treatise on comets.[75]

In Ziver's discarded poem, the new pleasure pavilion ("meserret-gāh") on the summit of a hill ("rütbe-mürtefiʿ") and the adjacent Yıldız Kiosk replicate the twin stars of the Ursa Minor constellation, Pherkad and Kochab. "That elevated building of this lofty pavilion, / Is worthy of being a noble constellation for the stars in the heavens" (O rütbe-mürtefiʿ bünyānı bu ḳaṣr-ı berīnüñ kim, / Felekde yıldıza burc-ı şeref olsa sezā her ān).[76] Sublime

FIGURE 30
The Bezm-i Alem Valide Sultan Fountain, Maçka, Istanbul, 1839. Photograph courtesy of M. Göktuna.

astral imagery derived from the adjoining placement of these two highland pavilions, with a play on the meaning of Yıldız as the polestar, forms the poem's lyrical apex: "Together with this pavilion, the pavilion of Yıldız is like Pherkad,[77] / It is as if this place were made indistinguishable from the apogee of the sphere of the heavens" (Bu ḳaṣr ile berā-ber ḳaṣr-ı Yıldız Ferḳādān-āsā, nola eylerse evc-i çarḫ ile bu mevḳiʿyi siyyān). The poem ends with only the briefest allusion to the site's strong winds: "The new kiosk's windows chime each time the Yıldız winds stir with a rhythm that instills joy in Venus in the sky" (Ṣadā virdikçe her bir revzeni yıldız hevāsıyla, o aheng ile lā-büdd eder gökde zühreyi şādān).

Bezm-i Alem's desire to connect with her public is also apparent from her choice of the commoner's poet over the upper-class court favorite. Linguistically, Raşid's invocation of the site is much more accessible than Ziver's and centers on the concrete changes that the queen mother had made to this particular segment of the imperial Beşiktaş neighborhood. Raşid's poem—whose wooden plaque still exists—aims to describe the new building, and rather than make clever astrological connections with the site's name, it emphasizes the patron's piety and generous philanthropy.[78] It reads as follows.

> Abdülmecid Khan of celestial rank, king of
>   the kings of the world,
> the mother of this Shah is Bezm-i Alem,
>   of the noblest name.
> When she, who is as virtuous as Hācer,[79] as
>   chaste as Ṣıddīḳa,[80] and of the disposi-
>   tion of Rābiʿa,[81]
> extended her munificent hand, it became
>   a fount of benefaction to the garden of
>   the world.

> When she bestowed her favor on Yıldız,
>   it is wondrous how a mountaintop
>   turned into an orchard.
> There she also built an ornate mansion, of
>   lofty structure,
> whose gentle breeze is so soul-reviving,
>   its water so delicious, and its views so
>   grand
> that next to it the Arch of Chosroes[82]
>   remains but an aged edifice.
> What a sublime pavilion, its appearance
>   so exalted, and its garden so exquisite
>   that
> if Sinimmār[83] were to see its layout,
>   he would place his finger on his mouth
>   [in wonderment].
> As long as that munificent [lady] dwells
>   there, grant o Lord, in good health,
> that each moment spent inside it may
>   bring nothing but pleasure.
> The one who utters this prayer is her slave
>   Rāşid,
> as do the singing nightingales that always
>   keep watch over its rose garden.
> Seven planets came and told the following
>   chronogram:[84]
> The mansion of the sultan's mother is as a
>   moon to Yıldız.[85]

Raşid portrays Bezm-i Alem as a builder who has transformed an otherwise arid mountaintop. The poet alludes to the sudden verdancy of the site by calling it an orchard with an exquisite layout ("baġ-ı raʿnā"), a world of gardens ("riyāż-ı dehre"), and, using a recurrent and familiar trope, a rose garden (*gülistān*). It appears that Bezm-i Alem initiated the first radical transformations of the site, and it is with her that Yıldız's history as an important imperial garden complex really began. She was also the origin of the quest

FIGURE 31
Mıgırdıç Melkon, *Marmara
Strait*, ca. 1844. Oil on canvas,
wood, and silk, 60 × 90 cm.
The Naval Museum, Istanbul,
507.

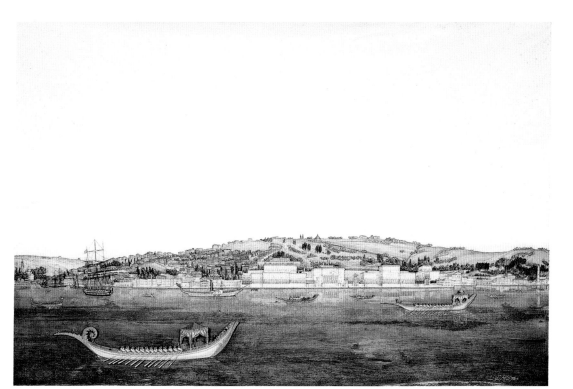

to outfit this *sui generis* hilltop estate with
the requisite farm typology—a quest that
continued to shape Yıldız's palatial development, which featured unceasing architectural
experiments with chalets, suburban cottages,
and French *hôtels particuliers*.

The model for the hilltop orchard estates
of both Nakş-ı Dil and her devoted successor, Bezm-i Alem, was perhaps the garden
palace of Nurbanu Valide Sultan (d. 1583), the
formidable wife of Sultan Selim II (d. 1574).
Indeed, Nakş-ı Dil may have inherited the
actual property of this sixteenth-century
valide. Nurbanu's extrapalatial summer residence accompanied her hilltop mosque in
Üsküdar, which came to be known as Atik
Valide Sultan ("Old Queen Mother").[86] Having
outlived her husband, Nurbanu became the
first queen regent to take the title of *valide*,

and her mosque complex was the first *valide*
project designed by the court architect Sinan.
A sixteenth-century Ottoman geographer
reported that Nurbanu's building project in
Üsküdar attracted interest in the suburb,
a phenomenon (and literary trope) also evident in response to the charitable acts of her
nineteenth-century successors.[87]

A waterfront view of Çırağan executed in
marquetry on a pen box provides a glimpse
of Bezm-i Alem's estate and her new pavilion, erected next to the Yıldız Kiosk, both of
which were circumscribed by a wall (fig. 31).[88]
Her endowment measures this complex of
two pavilions at around eighteen hectares.[89]
The pen box also depicts a fragmented view
of the farm building adjacent to (not included
in) the walled complex of the two pavilions.
A later Ottoman reworking of von Moltke's

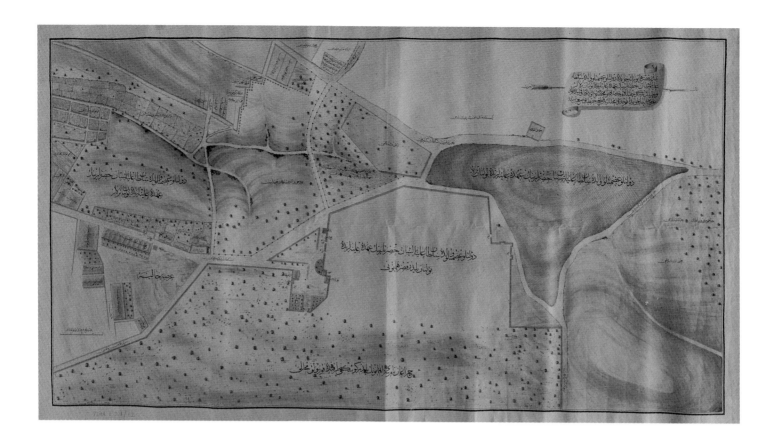

map calls Bezm-i Alem's farming estate *valide çiftliği* and marks the site with an elongated building fronted by a fountain. This farming estate was probably an expanded version of the one to which Selim III's mother, Mihrişah, retreated to convalesce when in poor health. Unlike her predecessors, Bezm-i Alem was a keen and respected horticulturalist, personally involved in producing as many varieties of each fruit and vegetable as possible, and hence always in need of more land. The products of her farm at Yıldız were substantial enough to be sold, to great demand, in the city's markets.

Another map, which was drawn to formally demarcate the fields designated for Bezm-i Alem's use and accommodate her farm's expansion, shows that the fields were large enough to surround the walled-in Yıldız Kiosk to its north (to the right on the map), west, and south; the east was divided between the endowment of the Yahya Efendi convent and the grove cascading down to Çırağan (fig. 32). This map also highlights the coffeehouse indicated both on von Moltke's map and in Mahmud II's archery diary, which fell outside the south-facing walls of the Yıldız Kiosk, aligned with the open-air mosque that Bezm-i Alem erected for her predecessor, Nakş-ı Dil.

The court's head physician, Hekimbaşı Salih Efendi (d. 1895), sparked Bezm-i Alem's horticultural interest. Salih Efendi was one of the first graduates of the imperial medical school founded by Abdülmecid, and an expert botanist, whose mansion and botanical gardens in Üsküdar were renowned for their production of herbal remedies.[90] He was also a celebrated instructor of natural sciences in the capital's imperial high schools, who bewildered even students of civil service, such as Ahmed İhsan—future journalist and founder of newspapers—with his extensive knowledge of botany.[91] The physician and the *valide* collaborated not only on the latter's hospital project but also on establishing the capital's largest collection of fruit specimens. All of the gardens in Istanbul and beyond were mobilized to contribute to Bezm-i Alem's orchard, which in its completed state boasted 581 kinds of fruit: among them "206 types of pears, 98 types of apples, 25 quinces, 43 peaches, 13 sour cherries, 31 cherries, 21 apricots, 9 pomegranates, 11 figs, 11 mulberries, 15 medlars, 59 grapes, 31 oranges."[92] Each variety had a particular name conjured up by the *valide* and her botanical advisor, Salih, in accordance with its color, weight, country of origin, taste, or scent. Thirty-one types of cherries came from a certain İbrahim Bey's garden in İstinye; a medlar the size of an egg from the plot of the gardener İzzet Ağa (but grafted from Europe); Lebanese peaches from Beirut; large, smooth-skinned, tart pope's peaches from the Tarabya Pavilion; apple-scented pears weighing three hundred drachmas from Varna; and grapes from as close as Erenköy and as far as Erzurum. Seeds and flowers circulated continuously between the imperial gardens of Istanbul for Bezm-i Alem and Salih Efendi's joint ventures. And although there is currently no indication that Abdülmecid came to inspect the produce of his mother's farms, his father, Mahmud II, did so regularly on the imperial estates with cultivated lands.[93]

To date, no information has come to light on the appearance of Bezm-i Alem's new wooden pavilion next to the Yıldız Kiosk (besides the pedimented roofs shown on the pen box), but a grand marble fountain (later moved to the district of Topkapı outside the city walls) in the form of a triumphal arch that Bezm-i Alem had erected beside these two structures reflects a taste for a classical idiom with simple but striking iconographic sculptural reliefs (fig. 33).[94] Two Corinthian columns carry the inscription stone, and five oval medallions framed by floral wreaths crown the fountain. A niche created by a high-relief arch on the ornamental slab above the spout bears a classroom globe resting on a sturdy pedestal and surrounded by a halo of rays.[95] Although at present smoothed by erosion, the globe can easily be imagined to have once born an outline of the imperial domains. Bezm-i Alem's iconographic intent with this fountain was to convey her philanthropic drive as complementary to her son's institutional reforms, and in accordance with this vision of dual rule through shared patronage, the inscription poem by Ziver Paşa lauds their collective charitable acts and not just those attributed specifically to Bezm-i Alem.[96]

To the artists under the sultan's and the *valide*'s joint patronage, this dual rule was evident. When Guiseppe Donizetti (d. 1856), the Italian composer and director of the imperial band, composed a hymn in "the new style" (*şarḳı-i cedīd*) for Abdülmecid I, he also created one for Bezm-i Alem.[97] The presentation copy of the song for the *valide* is embellished with depictions of garlands and bouquets bursting with flowers, a knowing nod to her green thumb and her own brand of imperial imagery, while the Turkish lyrics of the song allude not only to her mirage-like

FIGURE 33
Bezm-i Alem Valide Sultan's
fountain, originally near
Yıldız, 1843, but relocated to
the Topkapı district of Istanbul
in the late 1950s. Photograph
courtesy of M. Göktuna.

gardens (*serāb*) but also to her beneficence as
a patron (*elṭāf, feyż, cūd*, and *ʿināyet*).

YILDIZ, OTTOMAN WOMEN, AND PROFLIGACY

Ahmed Cevdet Paşa (d. 1895), perhaps the
shrewdest historian of the nineteenth-
century empire, attributes its economic
downturn in part to the increase in competitive consumption by the women of the
Ottoman court and the female members of
the Egyptian viceroyalty. The latter group,
having grown suddenly richer from cotton
production during the worldwide shortage
caused by the American Civil War, displayed
their family's newfound fortune in building
lavish residences along Istanbul's shores and
so fueled their rivalry with their Ottoman
counterparts, inciting conspicuous profligacy,
especially in the acquisition of European
goods.[98] The death of Bezm-i Alem, the principal authority in the economic and social life
of the harem, was an important factor in the
emergence of this unchecked extravagance,
which led Abdülmecid, a sultan portrayed by
Ahmed Cevdet as subservient to the whims of
his women, to seek the empire's first foreign
debt.[99]

According to Ahmed Cevdet, the main
offender among these women was a wife of
Abdülmecid's named Serfiraz.[100] This shock-
ingly libertine woman apparently lodged
herself unannounced in the newly unoc-
cupied Yıldız, took up lovers from Beşiktaş's
marketplace like a Victorian demimondaine,
appeared unchaperoned in the capital's public
promenades and gardens, and led Abdülmecid by the nose, often refusing to allow him
to enter her hilltop mansion. We will never
know whether all of these allegations are
true or whether they were part of a recurrent

trope in patriarchal history writing that takes aim at women, especially those with considerable power, as easier targets than their male counterparts and derides them as figures of debauchery, moral decay, and, in the same vein, unbridled spending.[101] Selim III's sisters were criticized by their contemporaries in exactly the same manner, as was Abdülhamid I's daughter Esma Sultan.[102] However, this incomplete story of a woman who in one way or another declared her independence from the court still underscores an important fact about Yıldız. This imperial property held a coveted position among the female members of the harem because it was an autonomous space with spacious gardens and farms designed for and used specifically by women, not part of a small segment of a palace with a much more congested shared harem quarter.

The public prominence of the *valide* reemerged—and Yıldız's rightful ownership was once again restored—during Pertevniyal's tenure (1861–76). Information on Pertevniyal's life, like that of most of her antecedents, is fragmented; and like those of Bezm-i Alem, Pertevniyal's sizable charitable donations and monumental endowments are overshadowed by the opulent expenditures of her son.[103] Even her mosque in Aksaray—a structure unique for its time due to its church typology, with two minarets and unusual Gothic ornaments covering all of its surfaces—is discussed most often as the best example of a new state-sanctioned architectural idiom, not as an instance of a *valide*'s participation in formal and stylistic decision making.[104] One of many popular history narratives, a genre to which the lives of high-ranking Ottoman women are all too often relegated, states that Pertevniyal wanted her mosque's courtyard to surpass that of Bezm-i Alem's

mosque in Dolmabahçe, and employed her *kethüda* Hüseyin Hasib Bey to see the project through.[105] However, unlike Bezm-i Alem, who was not present at the opening of her hospital, Pertevniyal attended the inauguration of her mosque.[106] Another publication mentions that this *kethüda* was also appointed mayor (*şehremini*) of Istanbul and consulted the dowager queen on matters related to the capital's infrastructure.[107] In navigating such disparate pieces of insight, one should not lose sight of the fact that Pertevniyal lived during the heyday of Queen Victoria's long reign and was aware of her European counterpart's popularity. Inhabiting the monumental apartments built specifically for her use in the Dolmabahçe Palace, Pertevniyal surely saw parallels between her own matriarchal role and that of the British monarch, especially after her son, Abdülaziz, personally met the English queen during his European trip— a historical first for the Ottoman court.[108]

The *valide*'s frequent employment of the Bavarian gardener Christian Sester and her practice of tipping him for performing services that lay outside the duties of his official post as head gardener of Çırağan imply that Pertevniyal sustained the farming activity next to her Yıldız estate. Some understanding of her taste in residential structures may be gleaned from the Yıldız estate and its almost identical counterpart on the hills of Üsküdar (fig. 34; for comparison, see fig. 12). She selected the same type, that of the eighteenth-century French urban mansion, for her two wooded estates—much as her predecessor Nakş-ı Dil had once seen the two as a pair, Yıldız serving as a model for her pavilion in Çamlıca.

Selim III's much-publicized attachment to his mother was in all likelihood part of

FIGURE 34
Photograph of Validebağı Kasrı (the mansion of the queen mother's orchard), 1861–76, construction attributed to the Balyans, Koşuyolu, Istanbul. 48 × 40 cm. BOA, PLK.p_01022.

his new imperial self-fashioning: a dual rulership based on filial piety. This pairing continued to be highlighted in the reigns of all of the succeeding sultans. Abdülaziz and his mother, Pertevniyal, made the strongest impression on the Ottoman public, not only in their copatronage of mosques, palaces,

and mansions but also and most importantly during the sultan's tumultuous and very public dethronement. News quickly circulated that Pertevniyal's harem quarters had been ransacked, the jewelry she was wearing forcibly removed, and the deposed *valide* dragged without her veil to the police station.

Istanbulites became even more preoccupied with the grieving Pertevniyal after her deposed son committed suicide, so much so that a brief but dramatic fictionalized memoir of her recollections of her son's tragic death, entitled *Sergüzeştnāme* (An account of events), was published soon thereafter.[109] The parallels are uncanny between the former dowager, who dedicated her life to children, prayer, and flowers after the death of her son, and Queen Victoria, the widow who lived in mourning for the rest of her life following the death of her husband, Prince Albert, in 1861.[110]

During their short but memorable corule, Abdülaziz and Pertevniyal cohosted banquets celebrating high-ranking governmental appointments. The sultan's favorite retreat, the farming estate in İzmit, was the preferred setting for these royal celebrations, and Pertevniyal coordinated the preparations there ("İzmid tarafında kâin çiftlik-i hümâyûnda Vâlide Sultan hazretlerine mahsûsen ziyâfet tertîbi").[111] In the Ottoman official histories, Pertevniyal also appears as a central figure in the court's frequent diplomatic encounters with the khedivial family of Egypt.[112] When Abdülaziz officially sanctioned the title that the Egyptian governors had selected for themselves, he bestowed on the newly appointed khedive Ismail Paşa (d. 1895) the right to succession from father to son, rather than from brother to brother. With the Ottoman acknowledgment of their title, the Egyptian family attained an elevated status in the Ottoman courtly order and a tangible presence in Istanbul's social life. When the Egyptian viceroys initiated their prolonged summer sojourns in Istanbul, Pertevniyal would welcome them to the capital and undertake the first of many gift exchanges in familial recognition. Personal family ties

also bolstered Pertevniyal's role in this otherwise novel diplomatic task, as she was the sister of Khedive Ismail Paşa's mother, Hoşyar Kadınefendi (d. 1886), who was the first to carry the title *valide paşa*.[113]

Ottoman men of letters were very much aware of Pertevniyal's centrality to Ottoman politics and administrative decisions. In an ironic twist of fate, Ahmed Cevdet, the otherwise ruthless critic of women's improvidence (especially in the Ottoman and Egyptian courts), sought a patronage relationship with Pertevniyal. In the same advice manuals that he would eventually present to a newly enthroned Abdülhamid II, he mentions sending her lavish textiles from Aleppo and a pony for her grandson, the future heir to the throne Yusuf İzzeddin; but perhaps more unusually, he made sure that she received the first copy of each of his voluminous works.[114] By ingratiating himself with the sultan's mother and appearing often at political gatherings in her Dolmabahçe quarters, Ahmed Cevdet eventually obtained his desired post of governor of Syria, although Abdülaziz's deposition forced him to relinquish it soon afterward.

THE YAHYA EFENDI CONVENT AS YILDIZ'S SPIRITUAL CORE

As noted above, an important factor that made Yıldız and its waterfront dwellings so compelling for the female patrons of the Ottoman harem was the connection that these women felt with this neighborhood's principal spiritual nexus: the tomb, mosque, and dervish convent of the sixteenth-century Sufi scholar and polymath Yahya Efendi (fig. 35). A foster brother to Sultan Süleyman, Yahya Efendi acted as an adopted father to the sultan's daughter, Raziye, who was the

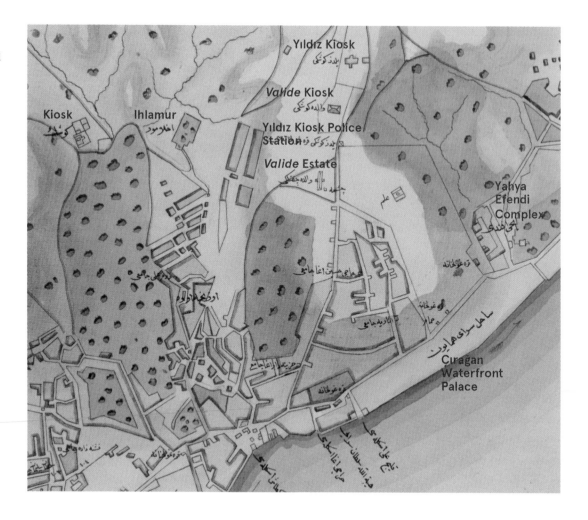

first female member of the court to be buried there.[115] This devotional bond between the revered Sufi scholar and a courtly female disciple must have strengthened the spiritual significance of the site for the succeeding women of status, because the cemetery of the shrine complex eventually developed into one exclusively reserved for the women and children of the court during the nineteenth century.[116] There is a compelling parallel between the attachment that the nineteenth-century dowager sultans felt to this holy site and the tendency of eighteenth-century mothers, sisters, and daughters of sultans to build

their royal waterfront retreats in Eyüp, near the tomb and mosque of the seventh-century saintly figure Ayyub al-Ansari.[117]

Legends portray Yahya Efendi as an ascetic who, after falling out of favor with Sultan Süleyman, chose to live out his days as a recluse, building his home outside the imperial capital. An auspicious dream would guide him to Beşiktaş, where he cheaply purchased a sizable property from a poor man and built himself a dervish lodge that also served as a makeshift medical facility.[118] The land owned by Yahya Efendi was much larger than the tiny walled-in park that his complex inhabits today. According to seventeenth- and eighteenth-century literary surveyors of Istanbul's coastlines, the only structure on the hill between Beşiktaş and Ortaköy was the little domed tomb of Yahya Efendi.[119]

Well into the last decades of the eighteenth century, Yahya Efendi's property still covered a large swath of land that extended from the waterfront Fer'iye Palaces into the valley that stretched behind them.[120] Gradually, segments of the property were absorbed into the imperial projects that within a century became the parkland of Abdülhamid II's palace. Aşık Çelebi, the sixteenth-century biographer of poets, describes the formidable building efforts that Yahya Efendi personally undertook on the uninhabited hilltop of Beşiktaş. "For years, he built buildings and took them down, made landfills, dug the earth, and carried stones" (Niçe niçe yıllardur ki ol diyārda gāh yapup gāh yıkup deñizler ṭoldırup ṭopraḳlar ḳazdırup ṭaşlar ṭaşıdur).[121] Describing his choice of a life in seclusion, Yahya Efendi wrote about himself in the third person as someone "playing with soil in his Beşiktaş."[122] Evliya Çelebi describes the property of Yahya Efendi, apparently a miracle-working gardener, as a vast mountainous meadow into which sunlight never penetrated and which was adorned with grand plane trees, willow trees with their heads turned down, mastic trees, cypresses, and walnuts of Rum ("Greek" walnuts).[123] It is quite tempting to think that the site and its landscapist owner served as models for the queen mothers as they conceived of their own verdant retreats.

Yahya Efendi believed that his newly adopted home was where Moses, guided by God to find the one man wiser than he, had encountered the "Servant of God" widely understood by exegetes as Hızır (Khidr). Much like Moses, Yahya Efendi saw himself as a disciple of Hızır in his theological pursuits. He must have reveled in imagining the topography of Beşiktaş as the exact embodiment of the rocky junction at which Hızır finally revealed himself to Moses. The latter was a meeting site that, like Beşiktaş, saw the convergence of the two seas (mecmū'a-tü'l-baḥreyn) described in the Koran. Yahya Efendi stipulated in his will that he should be buried at the exact spot at which he imagined the two prophetic figures to have met. For the courtly figures of later centuries who frequented his tomb inside the complex, the Koranic story must have resonated and imbued the site with talismanic power—not just for the *valide*s and their sons but also for outsiders like the Bavarian landscape designer Christian Sester, who, when hired by Mahmud II to transform this hill into a Romantic garden, was asked expressly to find water sources, as Moses and Hızır had been, to accommodate more fountains, lakes, and ponds.

Furthermore, the poetic chronograms of the era—especially those installed by the sultans and their mothers in the neighborhood of Beşiktaş—allude to Hızır, given his association with springs, as the discoverer of the "water of life" (āb-ı ḥayāt) or "spring of life" ('ayn'ül-ḥayāt) on a "mountaintop" (Ḥıżırlıḳ ṭaġı), that gave this elusive prophetic figure immortality. These chronograms often also refer to the origin story of Hızır as a vizier to Alexander (Ḥıżır-ı İskender), who at the end of Alexander's life went on a quest to find the source of immortality, only to upstage his king and vanish, and was expected to reappear, according to mystical-religious narratives, to steer the spiritually misguided.

The *valide*s continually contributed to the restoration of Yahya Efendi's shrine, whose lands gradually shrank into a hamlet nestled inside a garden full of trees, those beyond absorbed by the *valide*s' surrounding pavilions and farmlands. A chronogram composed by the court poet Vasıf, the earliest reference to the patronage links between the mothers of sultans and the shrine complex, speaks to this give and take. It states that Selim III "beautifully restored" (ra'nā-ı tecdīd) the mosque in 1806, using funds from his mother's endowment.[124] The court's piety did not always mean that it left properties belonging to a different endowment untouched. The large parcel of land that once belonged to the sixteenth-century dervish seems to have been gradually taken over by the imperial properties. The first Yıldız Kiosk, farming estate, and fountain of Mihrişah Valide Sultan were all parceled out of the high plateau that belonged to Yahya Efendi.

Bezm-i Alem also took great interest in the upkeep of this complex. As stipulated in an addendum to her endowment deed from 1842, a shaykh in the dervish convent of Yahya Efendi in Beşiktaş had to recite the Koran in accordance with the practice of the Naqshbandi sect and mention Bezm-i Alem's name during the prayers. The mosque's imam, cantor, and caretaker were also required to participate in the recitation, each reading a surah.[125] Pertevniyal followed suit in taking an active role in repairing the mosque-cum-shrine. On ascent to the mosque, a visitor would pass through a portal bearing an inscription that not only announced Pertevniyal's repairs to the mosque but also listed her four most visible public works as *valide*: a *sebil*, a school, a mosque, and, apparently most exciting for the poet Hayri,[126]

a state-of-the-art pool in the arsenal to receive the imperial battleships.

While serving as Abdülhamid II's palace, Yıldız continued to be surrounded by small religious convents of symbolic importance, a circumstance that should not necessarily be ascribed solely to Abdülhamid's reinstitution of his caliphal role and his desire to unite all Sunni Muslims under his leadership. Pertevniyal was a politically adept queen mother, and having foreseen that Abdülhamid was a likelier candidate for the throne than the clinically anxious Murad, she cultivated an intimate relationship with Abdülhamid during his time as crown prince and retained considerable sway over decisions regarding his family life as well as his personal religious affiliations. Although free access to the harem quarters was forbidden to princes who had passed adolescence, Pertevniyal encouraged Abdülhamid to pay her frequent visits to converse and play the piano.[127] It was during these visits that she introduced the future ruler to Müşfika, an orphan girl she had fostered from a young age, who would eventually become Abdülhamid's favorite and most devoted wife.

Prince Abdülhamid found spiritual guidance in the teachings of Shaykh Muhammed Zafir Efendi of the Shadhiliyya Sufi order from Tripoli, also through Pertevniyal's mediation.[128] Pertevniyal was the patron of the order's first convent in Unkapanı, but soon after Abdülhamid became sultan, he moved the order's headquarters close to Yıldız and assigned the shaykh two large mansions in the same garden as the dervish convent's mosque—one for the shaykh's immediate family and the other for his incessant stream of North African guests. In maintaining such a close relationship with Abdülhamid, bound both through marriage and through faith,

Pertevniyal could remain in the imperial center by living in one of the Fer'iye Palaces in Ortaköy instead of suffering confinement to the cramped harem quarters of the Topkapı Palace, and maintain her attachment to the two convents on the outer limits of Yıldız.

It is also important to note here that women of rank, especially the *valide*s, were political agents—not necessarily in the international arenas of war, debt, or trade, but certainly in maintaining marriage alliances indispensable to the court's order and the continuation of tradition. Even in the nineteenth century, the sultan's wives (*kadınefendiler*) and most of the other women employed to serve the members of the harem were selected exclusively from certain Circassian families from the North Caucasus. This continued to be a region of strategic importance, which the nineteenth-century Ottomans maintained as a buffer against Russia as the latter intensified its encroachment upon the Orthodox Christian subjects of the Ottoman state.

Tribal affiliations contributed greatly to the composition of the retinues of the sultans' mothers, sisters, and principal wives. Loyalty to their family members often prompted the wives to secure administrative posts for their male relatives, and many of those who retained their familial ties channeled their charity work solely to their villages of origin.[129] Recent scholarship on a modest scale, based on the recollections of the wives of the last sultans, highlights the fact that most of these wives were the daughters of Circassian tribal nobility. The women maintained their inherited aristocratic ranks even after joining the Ottoman court, most visibly in the preservation of their family crests and in their exclusive patterns of socializing.[130] In line with this exclusivity, the *valide*s

groomed members of their own retinues, daughters of their own tribes, for their reigning sons as well as future heirs. Once adopted by the harem, these girls were given elaborate new names by the most erudite bibliophilic women of the court.[131] Mahmud II's sister Esma Sultan's presentation of Bezm-i Alem to her brother Mahmud II, and later her presentation of Perestu—who would become Abdülhamid II's beloved foster mother and the empire's last *valide*—to her nephew Abdülmecid, as well as Pertevniyal's abovementioned introduction of Müşfika to Abdülhamid II, are among the more conspicuous examples of such in-house marital politics.

After encountering a few assassination attempts in rapid succession soon after his accession, Abdülhamid II decided to make Yıldız his palace. He moved his immediate family and personal servants to the modest pedimented two-story mansion that functioned as the harem structure to Pertevniyal's *hôtel particulier*, which in turn became Abdülhamid II's administrative quarters, the Mabeyn. The site did not yet have enough accommodation to support a large household, so before the move the harem was downsized: the retinues of the wives, unmarried sisters, and married sons shrank, as did the number of the sultan's household attendees. Abdülhamid had appointed his foster mother, Perestu, to the post of *valide* immediately after his accession ceremony (*cülus*). At that moment, this extremely reserved woman became the head of his harem, obliged, apparently much to her dismay, to preside over all court ceremonies. Her carriage was always first in line in a harem cortège, and every diplomatic visit to the harem had to begin with a reception at her apartments. As more structures were fitted into Yıldız's harem, the building into which Abdülhamid had initially moved was appointed for her use. But Perestu, capitalizing on the freedom that her predecessors had secured for the post of *valide*, frequently retreated to her mansion in Maçka. The latter was a building that her husband, Abdülmecid, had appointed for her years ago, when another of his wives, the presumed libertine Serfiraz, had chosen Yıldız for her own residence.[132]

The Ottoman gardening culture in the first half of the nineteenth century revolved around these women as much as their male counterparts, if not more so. Yıldız, in particular, which they created and used for almost a century, was manifestly a product of the women's personal efforts. It was also a visible architectural signifier of their status as queen mothers, often paired with their estates in Çamlıca. While Bezm-i Alem and her botanist advisor, Salih Efendi, expanded the Yıldız estate, her son, Abdülmecid, continued in his father's footsteps in converting the hills between his mother's residence and Çırağan into a grand Romantic park. The next chapter follows the landscape history of Çırağan's gardens under Mahmud II and Abdülmecid and, through a description of the site's physical transformations, discusses the evolution of the court's gardeners' corps at that time. Like the *valide*s, Mahmud II and Abdülmecid saw this vast and central site as ripe for rebuilding. With a complete redesign, it would be the poster palace for a new imperial image, of which the court was in dire need after the elimination of the janissaries and the subsequent initiation of empire-wide reforms. A court poet and early witness to the project of making Çırağan and its gardens the royal residence nonpareil, built to reflect the state's radical restructuring, praises Mahmud II alternately as a renovator (*müceddid*) and as a capable architect (*miʿmār-ı ḳudret*), referring to both his building of the palace and his governance of the empire at large.[133]

Yıldız and Its Gardeners

Christian Sester (d. 1866) was the ambitious European head gardener (*bostāncıbaşı*) who installed a large portion of the landscaping on the grounds that would become the Yıldız Palace. His horticultural legacy in the Ottoman capital goes hand in glove with the evolution of the site. Sester's involvement in developing the property in parallel with the *valide* estate described in the previous chapter and the backyard of Çırağan Palace speaks directly to the quest for a new imperial image, embarked upon by the century's first two rulers, Mahmud II and his son Abdülmecid. As reform-oriented sultans, they eagerly sought out advisors to help them transform their environments to befit the enlightened, politically engaged, and overtly public role they had cast for themselves. The site they chose as their new residence would become emblematic of this imperial refashioning.

Yıldız and its makers, most of whom were recruited and taught by Sester, instituted a predominantly German dynasty of gardeners—a new kind of corps crafted from the long-established Ottoman state institution of the *bostancıs*—which was disrupted only at the end of the nineteenth century, when the court began to value different modes of horticultural expertise and directed its attention toward France. If, in very broad strokes, nineteenth-century Ottoman garden history

was characterized by grand landscaping projects modeled on Yıldız, the twentieth century saw an obsessive attention to the cultivation and acclimation of plants in the intimate spaces of the most technically advanced greenhouses and palmhouses. Ultimately, these shifts of interest were not only related to matters of taste but invariably also tinged with the competitive spirit of changing diplomatic alliances within national and international political networks.

Until Mahmud II's overhaul of the janissary corps in 1826, Ottoman imperial gardening history, from its variegated designs to numerous aspects of its production and associated expenses, was tied to one of the corps' most prominent branches, the *bostāncı ocağı* (imperial corps of gardeners), whose members were conscripts largely of Christian origin (ʿacemī oġlan).[1] From their inception, the *bostancıs* were an indispensable part of the military state organization; when needed, they graduated into the janissary corps. It is no coincidence, then, that on August 5, 1826, a few months after the janissaries were violently disbanded, the gardeners' corps was completely (albeit much more innocuously) restructured under a military charter (*niẓāmnāme*). The eldest members were made to retire with lifetime pensions (*ḳayd-ı ḥayāt*), and the able-bodied ones were redeployed to train with Mahmud's new army ("'asākir-i manṣūre-i Muḥammediye") and serve as officers (żābiṭ) on gates and in barracks and police offices on the Dolmabahçe-Ortaköy shoreline, where the court now resided full-time.[2] A decade later, members of Sultan Mahmud's retinue took ambassadorial trips to European capitals and returned with an idea for ensuring the upkeep of the many imperial gardens: a European garden director, a professional who understood the latest practices and trends in landscape design, botany, and horticulture, would fill the vacant post of the court's *bostancıbaşı* (head or chief gardener), restoring the post to its erstwhile métier and bringing the imperial gardens back into the spotlight. This garden-centered practice continued until World War I, and Yıldız, the longest-serving imperial palace of the nineteenth century, became its operational headquarters within just half a century.

In the relative political calm of his last decade, Mahmud II began the construction of his palace on the Beşiktaş shore, on a landmass different from Topkapı's, which was nevertheless always in his sight. Nicola Carelli, an Italian architect hired by the Balyan family to sketch and model the new structure, noted in his letters that the sultan wished it to be in the European manner (*sul costume d'Europa*) but "much less imposing" (*alquanto meno grandioso*)—"not only to avoid reproaches from Muslims who, since the massacre of the Janissaries, had been looking unfavorably on him," but also because "in the last period he had not a clear picture of his finances."[3]

Mahmud's desire to curtail the grandeur of his new palace finds a precedent in his leveling of official rank among the state elite in 1829, when he decreed that the fez must be worn by all without distinction. Arguing that this sartorial law instantiated the new undifferentiated subjecthood of the Tanzimat era, Donald Quataert powerfully articulates its repercussions as follows: "In using clothing laws to erode distinctions based on religion and create a new base for this regime, Mahmud II offered non-Muslims and Muslims a common subjecthood/citizenry."[4] The sultan actively promoted this radical shift in the fashion of the bureaucratic state apparatus by increasing his own public appearances, wearing a nondescript Western military suit and the inevitable tasseled fez. To affix his new imperial image in the minds of his subjects more permanently, he also commissioned full-length portraits in oil to be displayed inside civic buildings, along with ivory medallions (*tasvir-i hümayun*) to be worn by his court officials.[5] One of the earliest known of these portraits, painted by a French artist of German origin named Henri-Guillaume Schlesinger, places the sultan next to one of the columns of his new palace in Beşiktaş. His new army, parading right below him, signals the dawn of a new age, while Topkapı in the far distance stands in for the old guard, now abandoned.

Carelli was not able to complete the project, but it is likely that his suggested design in the Empire style influenced the end result in 1834. Mahmud's new imperial residence, known interchangeably as the toponymic Beşiktaş Palace and as Çırağan, commemorating the previous palace on the site where it had stood, rose as a tripartite unit: the *selamlık*, a temple-fronted audience hall, and a harem (fig. 36). The palace, like the empire's administrative body, conformed to Mahmud's political transformations. He subsumed the *mabeyn* under his command, reduced the number of its members, and gave its functions a distinct type in the cruciform *selamlık*. Only a few paintings, engravings, and fragmentary plans of this palace remain. Jean-Michel Dalgabio, a France-based Italian architect, drew what appears to be a segment of the harem's plan in 1843 (during Abdülmecid I's reign).[6]

The "peripteral" audience hall, planned as the centerpiece of the shoreline palace, was elevated on monumental stairs and contained a pediment bearing Mahmud's *tughra*.[7] What is less well known is that the hall also boasted a small theater with views of both the sea and the hills behind it. The grander landscaping project that would start soon in this hilly backyard after the palace's completion was aimed at mitigating the structure's perceived "customhouse-like coldness"—an apt description of the audience hall.[8] A type of landscape that was new to the onlookers and not symbolic of an *ancien régime* had to be created to complement Mahmud's monumental, if pared-down, royal aesthetic.

CHRISTIAN SESTER AND THE ENGLISH GARDEN IN THE OTTOMAN CAPITAL

While serving as ambassador to Austria, Fethi Ahmed Paşa (d. 1858), Mahmud's Anglophile son-in-law, an enterprising industrialist in glass and longtime marshal (*müşīr*) of the Tophane armory, signed a contract with a Bavarian named Christian Sester.[9] According to the loosely worded agreement, once the thirty-one-year-old landscape gardener arrived in Istanbul, he would begin "ordering the grounds" (arżıñ niżām ve intiżāmına mübāşeret eylemek) allotted for the sultan's imperial gardens, "draw out the plans appropriate for growing multifarious trees" (gūnā-gūn eşcār yetişdirmeğe iḳtiżā iden zemīn ve resimleri çıḳarmaḳ), and "closely supervise all

aspects related to gardens and their walkways himself" (bāġçe ve yollarıñ her bir ḫuṣūṣuna kendüsi bi'n-nefs neżāret itmek).[10] Promised a generous annual stipend of 2,000 florins, comfortable lodgings, candle wax, coal and firewood, "protection from any hindrances to his work" (bāġçe tanżīmine dāʾir ḫuṣūṣla-rıñ icrāsıyçün kendüsine bir ruḫṣat-ı kāmile olaraḳ hīç bir ṭarafdan kimesne mānic ve müzāḥim olmamaḳlığı), and the option to quit with six months' notice, Sester duly arrived in Istanbul in 1835 with an assistant (*mucāvin*). He was given—rightfully borrowing from his European precedents—the lofty title of "imperial garden director" (*großherrlicher Gartendirektor*).[11] Until his death in 1868, Sester would remain in the service of three of the four sultans of the nineteenth century, Mahmud, Abdülmecid, and Abdülaziz, and transform most of Istanbul's imperial gardens of the period.

FIGURE 36
Thomas Allom, *The Sultan's New Palace on the Bosphorus*. From Robert Walsh, *Constantinople and the Scenery of the Seven Churches of Asia Minor* (1838). Courtesy of the Rare Book Collection, Dumbarton Oaks, Washington, DC.

The Bavarian parvenu's résumé played a significant role in his selection for the Ottoman post. Born and raised in Aschaffenburg, he descended from a family of gardeners employed for the upkeep of the picturesque park of Schönbusch Palace, then belonging to Karl Theodor von Dalberg (d. 1817), the prince-primate of a confederation of Rhenish states that, in alliance with Napoleon I, had declared their independence from the Holy Roman Empire. At a very young age, Sester abandoned his training in Latin to devote himself completely to "the noble art of gardening."[12] He grew up in a world of affluent provincial patrons and their German garden experts, who traveled around Europe to master the various branches of the practice.[13] His obituary, published in a local Aschaffenburg newspaper, mentions his hereditary attraction to the garden arts at a very young age: "The seed that slept in him suddenly awoke to unfold itself into a blossom, which shone forth as alone in its kind."[14] With this familial predisposition, Sester first apprenticed in his hometown under Schönbusch's head gardener, Christian Ludwig Bode. Under Bode's supervision, Sester honed his skills "as a gardener in general, and as a landscape gardener [Landschaftsgärtner] in particular."[15] Soon afterward, the young Sester began his scholastic grand tour (often referred to as his "journeyman years")[16] with the botanical gardens of Munich-Nymphenburg, which had been conceptualized by Schönbusch's first landscape gardener, Carl Ludwig von Sckell (d. 1828), as extensions to the baroque summer palace of the Bavarian rulers.[17] Bode was a disciple of Sckell's, and had been entrusted to create English gardens with a German bent—a complete turn to nature and an economical use of garden structures—that he must have imparted to his apprentice at Schönbusch. Following his training in Munich, Sester was appointed head gardener of Dalberg's smaller country estate in Bohemia—his first venture into the Habsburg domains—and then returned to Bavaria in 1832, tasked with "the supervision of the gardens of Frauendorf's horticultural society" (dem Sitze der praktischen Gartenbaugesellschaft). He had only just been hired as a head gardener (Obergärtner) by Prince von Dietrichstein to lay out the gardens of the prince's new Viennese summer residence—a neoclassical structure with an uncanny resemblance to the Dolmabahçe Palace, if the latter had been stripped of its sculptural reliefs—when his Eastern adventure beckoned. Dietrichstein, moving within diplomatic circles, had recommended him to Sultan Mahmud II.

Although I have yet to identify a drawing or plan in Sester's own hand of the Ottoman gardens he created, he left behind a short ekphrasis from 1832, which appeared in Frauendorfer Blätter on July 3, 1845, on how he envisioned the gardens while serving as head gardener. Following the hackneyed European trend of describing the Tanzimat courts of Mahmud and Abdülmecid as stalwartly progressive, Sester's erstwhile hosts in Frauendorf heralded him in this news item as the artistic counterpart to the two reform-oriented sultans. As published in 1845, the piece came with a lengthy prologue praising Sester's international success.

A letter from Constantinople that was printed in the daily newspaper on the 12th of last month emphasized that the young Sultan [Abdülmecid], like his father [Mahmud II], found a great deal of pleasure in everything new and better. For example, when setting up his palaces, the Sultan on numerous occasions expressly ordered that he no longer wanted the Old, but rather the New, according to better European taste. Thus, the garden at Tscheragan Palace, which was installed some six years ago by one of our countrymen, Herr Sester of Aschaffenburg, pleased the Sultan so extraordinarily that while he was recently moving from his palace to Beylerbeyi, he ordered that Tscheragan be outfitted for the next winter so that he could spend fall and also the winter there.... We are pleased by this news all the more because we have not heard from our old friend Herr Sester for quite some time. What a wonderful direction human fate can take! In 1832 Herr Sester was still helping to install the gardens in Frauendorf. While this garden was later destroyed by high winds and hail, we can take solace in the fact that the spirit of progress managed to transplant [*verpflanzt*] a refined taste for gardens in Turkey in the form of Herr Sester, placing him at the summit of that country's artistic reform.[18]

In Sester's ekphrasis, entitled "On the Cliff Bench in Frauendorf, May 8, 1832," appended to this flattering précis, the gardener describes a walk through a garden of his own creation in a manner resembling a musical composition. The sentimental tone of the narrative, which the gardener intends to evoke with his garden, is modeled on earlier works by C. C. L. Hirschfeld and Hermann Ludwig von Pückler-Muskau, who were his literary companions, both in their sentimental tone and in the way they were written as walkthroughs. From a vast stagelike clearing, Sester enters a steep and narrow path lined by a thick mass of conifers, with only a "handrail made of bark-stripped branches" to hold on to, having been seduced by violets under the shade of a spruce tree below. As he descends, he gently discloses his horticultural knowledge by pairing plants that share symbiotic relationships: cherry trees against a pine, hardy berries with delicate dayflowers, primrose entwined around a pear tree. However, the environment is presented as so immersive and natural that it belies the human hand that put it together. At one point Sester comes across a bench, on which he sits to listen to the sounds of starlings, blackbirds, and a rushing creek and contemplates a moss-covered precipice and what lies beyond. As night descends and nature's sublime takes over, Sester reveals his philosophical inspiration: Herder's short prose work entitled *Kalligenia, die Mutter der Schönheit* (1803), which inquired into the aesthetic qualities of nature and its laws, and the happy convergences between an artist and a scientist when studying them.[19] The gardener, who crafted himself from both of these professions, writes, "The philosopher should hurry to this spot, disdaining the trinkets of the masses, and devote serious contemplation to the purpose of man; and [a] celebrated goddess will come to him (as Kalligenia did to Kallia) in the dreams of Herder." The article ends with the author's appeal to the Persian king to hire a professional of Sester's caliber to "refine their taste for decorative garden arts among the masses there," because, he suggests, "progress in the garden arts and garden culture is in all countries a measure of the level of cultivation of their people!"[20]

The *Frauendorfer Blätter*'s push to connect the English landscape garden with liberal rule echoes the sentiment of the era. The German writers of garden treatises, who were Sester's contemporaries as well as the authors of his literary and technical primers, believed in the close correlation between an enlightened, benevolent ruler and the manner in which he laid out his estate. One of the most widely read of these figures, a member of the landed nobility from the North and himself an obsessive landscape designer, Prince Hermann Ludwig von Pückler-Muskau (d. 1871), propounded that the best garden model for an estate owner was the English one because with all of its philosophical connotations it offered the best contrast with the gardens of Le Nôtre's Versailles and Vaux-le-Vicomte, which had become preeminent symbols of French autocratic rule alongside the structures they circumscribed.[21] In deliberately including the working lands of the ruler— a hint of a peasant here, a farm there—*yet* emphasizing untouched nature, the English landscape garden was for Pückler-Muskau a "microcosm of the civilized world."[22] So if Mahmud II and later Abdülmecid strove to make distinctive visual claims about their reinvention as reform-oriented sovereigns eager to instate a completely new administrative, judiciary, and cultural system for the public, they may well have selected for their surroundings an aesthetic scheme similar to that of the benevolent German gentry to best fit their newfangled, reinvented image.

It is not surprising that Sester was acquainted with the writings of German philosophers. Excerpts from their most popular texts were printed and circulated even in Frankfurt's monthly gardener's almanacs. Herder's *Kalligenia*, written close to his death, was one of these short but evocative narratives that also made its way into the homes of the working classes.[23] Starting with Kant, figures like Herder, Goethe, and Schiller upheld garden art's position among the highest plastic arts of their time. For them, and for their role model in all things related to landscape art, C. C. L. Hirschfeld, author of the popular *Theorie der Gartenkunst* (1779 to 1785), a gardener was equal to, if not more privileged than, a landscape painter in his command over space, light, and sound. Hirschfeld would write as follows:

> On the strength of these comparisons of the two arts, it is easy to see that at base the art of gardening is as superior to landscape painting as nature is to a copy. None of the mimetic arts is more entwined with nature herself, which is to say more natural, than the art of gardens. Here the portrayal is merged with the actual. Movement is not merely perceived as suggestion but truly felt. Water, which in a landscape painting is animated only through reflections, offers the pleasure of its presence through sight and sound. The eye is offered colors glowing or shimmering with a luster, gaiety, and warmth unrivaled by the magical power of any Titian. The gradual experience of garden scenes offers more protracted and entertaining pleasure than the most lovely and detailed landscape painting, which the eye can only quickly encompass.[24]

These thinkers of aesthetics not only gave the gardening profession incredible agency in shaping nature but also fueled the garden artist's creative powers with the German protonational ideas of the freedom of the mind and creative expression. Rustic, seemingly untouched landscapes were the perfect backdrop for, and the best visual representatives of, their fiery ideas. Sester was also geographically close to these members of the *Sturm und Drang* movement of arts and letters, themselves preoccupied with the shackles of Enlightenment rationalism, and was certainly spurred on by the Romantic fervor of their aesthetic inclinations.

Sester's obituary also recounts his first interactions with Mahmud II, who, unlike Selim III, did not want orange trees in his gardens—an eighteenth-century fad, now too commonplace—and instead desired something that "others did not have." During their four-year interaction, Sester installed a spacious portico on the side of Mahmud's wooden Dolmabahçe Palace. Under this section, and protected from the "icy winds that the Pontus not so seldom sends, a fantastical artwork [*fantasiereiches Kunstwerk*] arose, whose depiction we encounter only in a *Thousand and One Nights*." He installed waterfalls with alcoves molded out of grottoes, and planted flowering evergreens—azaleas, rhododendrons, and only recently acclimatized dryandra, a native of Oceania—alongside his beloved exotic conifers, the araucaria. The gardener's undertakings did not end with gardening; he won a building commission for a garden house, favored over the more costly proposition of the unidentified imperial architect. When it was discovered that the new garden lacked the necessary running water—whether a stream, a lake, or a channel of water for the newly built pavilion—Mahmud asked Sester to find closer wells or springs (*Quellen*). Sester's response, which the translator was reluctant to convey to the sultan, was, "Lord, I am not Moses."[25] The obituary claims that Mahmud took this statement as a sign of honesty, but he must also have appreciated Sester's biblical reference to Moses, who struck a desert rock from which water flowed. This story from the life of a prophet also found in the Koran was certainly familiar to, and must have resonated with, the Ottoman ruler. This nineteenth-century anecdote unknowingly but compellingly adds to the tradition of the Ottoman saintly narratives (*menāḳıbnāme*s), especially that of the sixteenth-century architect Sinan. In his "autobiographies," Sinan is compared to the miracle-working, immortal Hızır for his discovery of "life-giving springs" and the hydraulic feats he achieved when building the Kırkçeşme aqueducts.[26]

From the start of Sester's tenure, Mahmud's commissions to him went beyond garden projects and seem to have allowed the gardener to take initiative. During a cholera outbreak, Sester helped establish lazarettos along the straits of Bosphorus and Dardanelles. As a recruit from Austria, he acted as a conduit between the two empires by facilitating the arrival of quarantine experts from Zemun (now a municipality of Belgrade, Serbia).[27] Sester's second extraprofessional undertaking was to alleviate a citywide water shortage by fixing some of Istanbul's late eighteenth-century reservoirs (*bend*s) located in the Belgrad Forest, in Istanbul's Northeast. Signaling the end of the repairs, the *Allgemeine Zeitung München*'s report from 1852 suggests that Sultan Abdülmecid chose Sester over the minister of public works for the considerable difference in cost between the two. The article also mentions more than five hundred workers from Croatia, Montenegro, and Serbia, who were employed under him, and among them he had a reputation of being "just, selfless, and generous" (Rechtlichkeit, Uneigennützigkeit, Freigebigkeit).[28]

Sester also laid out the designs for the Ihlamur Pavilion, in the valley behind

Dolmabahçe, which would later serve as a favorite inland retreat for Abdülmecid, and restored his predecessor Jacob Ensle's additions to the Topkapı Palace during Selim III's reign.[29] His horticultural contributions to Saʿdabad (in present-day Kağıthane) are recorded in the construction expenses from the summer of 1863, which state that the chief gardener (*bāġçıvānbāşı*) supplied the site with rose and linden trees and a set of rustic railings.[30] Sester was also assigned semi-imperial commissions from wealthy bureaucrats such as Abdülmecid's minister of war (*serasker*), Rıza Paşa, who wanted an identical version of the sultan's English-style garden for his own residence.[31]

On various occasions the *valide*s, too, sought Sester's expertise. Ceremonial preparations for Sultan Abdülmecid's return from his Rumelia trip in July 1846 saw his mother, Bezm-i Alem, organizing a festive celebration spanning three days and multiple stations, starting with the Topkapı and the shoreline palaces of the sultan's sisters, ending at Çırağan, his imperial residence. The queen mother employed Sester to orchestrate the illuminations in not only Çırağan but "all public buildings, the country houses of important personages, and the houses of emissaries in Bujukdere [Büyükdere] and Tarapia [Tarabya]."[32]

The monthly domestic expenses of Abdülaziz's mother, Pertevniyal Valide Sultan, consistently place "the gardener from Austria" (Nemçeli baġçıvān) at the top of the ledger from 1857 to 1858. His work on Pertevniyal's residence in the walled-off hilltop estate that contained sizable market gardens, especially for strawberries, was yet more expensive than hiring boatmen, kavasses (armed attendants of an ambassador or consul), and maintainers

of water conduits (*şu yolcu*).[33] The earliest relevant map drawn up by the Ottoman-employed Prussian officer Baron Helmuth von Moltke, from 1839, which also exists in the Imperial Engineering School's redeveloped version from 1845, identifies two small structures perched on the elevated grounds behind Çırağan. One is labeled the kiosk of the *valide*, and the other, smaller, cross-axial one is Yıldız (see fig. 35). These two structures were the earliest incarnations of what would develop into a country estate (labeled as *çiftlik* on the 1845 map), surrounded by a multitude of arable fields (*tarlā*) and protected by guard posts (*karaġolḫāne*). This estate, among those allotted to the mothers of sultans from Selim III to Abdülaziz, is shown on the ca. 1861 map reproduced in figure 32. The latter map, although drawn without topographic conventions, not only shows the generous sprawl of the nineteenth-century *valide*s' income-generating properties in the new imperial zone of the capital but also clarifies the site's relationship with Çırağan on the shore: they are connected by a grove ("Çerāġān nām sarāy-ı hümāyūnuñ Yıldız Köşkü ṭarafında koruluk maḥalli"). By the time the map was made, the wall that separated the two kiosks on the hill, belonging to the *valide* estate, from the waterfront palace had been taken down. The map's drafting must have coincided with the second stage of Sester's landscaping of the grove during Abdülmecid's reign, when the gardener connected the two sites to form a majestic garden-boasting complex.

Indeed, Sester's biggest contribution to the capital's outdoors was his gradual two-step transformation of the ravine-bisected hills behind Mahmud II's marble-colonnaded Çırağan Palace—hills that cupped the shoreline between Beşiktaş and Ortaköy—into a sprawling Romantic landscape. Under Sultan Mahmud, Sester had to work within the bounds of the traditional terraced aesthetic, but he also naturalized these spaces as much as he could by turning the large flower parterres into uneven lawns and adding multiple bodies of water with undulating frames. Ziver Paşa composed an ode to mark the completion in 1839 of the first round of landscaping under Sultan Mahmud for the garden behind Çırağan. The ode was once inscribed on the gate opening into the garden and is unusual not only in its placement on a garden gate—perhaps suggesting that the court wanted to emphasize the importance and physical centrality of the garden's construction—but also because it highlights, briefly but eloquently, the site's terraced architecture.

> The exalted Mahmud Khan, the spring
>   season of the garden of imperial
>   grandeur,
> Made a new rose garden full of embellish-
>   ment and glory.
> When he commanded this meadow to be
>   adorned in layers [ḵat ḵat],
> Without a doubt, it became the envied and
>   agreeable [ṭıbāḵ][34] garden of paradise.[35]

An undated color-tinted lithograph offers a view from this hillside garden onto the back of the crenellated Çırağan, the delicate footbridge connecting the palace to the garden, and the walled elevation of the terraced parterres (frontispiece). It captures the early phase of Sester's work, comprising the swelling ha-has that held up the two ponds, a white classical monopteros-like *fabrique*, which must have been one of Sester's architectural commissions, and mounds

of soil occupying the foreground, removed to open up the pools. Sester's round temple is poignant, because it invokes the location's Byzantine past, when, according to the sixteenth-century French topographer Pierre Gilles (d. 1555), a temple to Apollo standing on this part of the hill popularized this suburb (Diplokionion) of Byzantium, but also because such neoclassical rotundas (one specifically for Apollo) dotted the English garden of Sckell's Munich-Nymphenburg. Sester must have read Gilles's *De Bosphoro Thracio* in Latin, an indispensable handbook for foreign visitors to Istanbul's shoreline, to discover the palimpsestic nature of his work site and new home.[36] It also cannot be a coincidence that he named his second child, and first to be born in Istanbul, Apollonia.

On the flatter ground, immediately behind Çırağan's central hall, the lithograph reveals a fragment of a garden developed for private use with similar pools. Julia Pardoe, who likened the gardens of Beylerbeyi to a Tower of Babel built in layers by gardeners of different nationalities, also witnessed the frenzied activity behind Çırağan. Sester and his assistant must have started on the projects within months of their arrival, as Pardoe's travel account was published in 1836, only a year after Sester signed his contract. Her description of Sester's horticultural activity behind Çırağan animates the content of the undated painting as well as the engraving corresponding to the traveler's account (fig. 37): "The gardens of the palace are extensive, but will require time to make them worthy of description; at present, a great portion of the hillside behind the building is left in its original state, boasting for all ornament sweeps of fine cypresses, and here and there a tuft of almond trees, a group of acacias, or a majestic

SCENE FROM ABOVE THE NEW PALACE OF BESHIK-TASH.

FIGURE 37
W. H. Bartlett, *Scene from Above the New Palace of Beshik-Tash*. From Julia Pardoe, *The Beauties of the Bosphorus* (1839). Harold B. Lee Library, Brigham Young University, Utah.

already extant walled-in parterres that Sester had to work with and the earliest phase of the gardener's attempt at building up the foliage with trees and shrubs.

The pleasure garden Wiegenstein (Beschiktasch) ... boasts an excellent location between two ravines. A stream flows through each of these ravines. Adjoining this garden is Tschiragan [Çırağan] Palace, which was built by Sultan Mahmud II. It is here that the current sultan [Abdülmecid] lives during a portion of the hot summer months with his royal retinue. A German gardener was commissioned with the job of landscaping in European style the inner areas that are enclosed by walls. And as far as one could see from the outside, the gardener seemed to have a particular liking for green lawns, while trees and shrubs were relegated to the background. Viewed from our distant vantage point, the garden did not appear to be particularly handsome, due to the stark contrast between its spartan appearance and the surrounding naturally thick vegetation. Yet it was said that the garden was particularly beautiful up close. Mahmud II spared no expense in order to improve the gardens that he had created. The servant of the church, Abdul-Medschid [Abdülmecid], had bountiful shipments containing seed stores and decorative bushes sent each year to Constantinople from Vienna.[39]

maple; while the white tents of the Bulgarian workmen employed upon the walls, give to the scene the picturesque and cheerful appearance of a summer encampment."[37] Sester's obituary expands on his accomplishments in this "great compound [*große Anlage*] of Ortaköy," the region in which the palaces of the royals were located—hence the connection with the queen mothers in nearby Yıldız. Under his supervision, "mounds had to be removed, rocks blown up, and basins filled in" to properly realize "the conceits of painterly garden scenes, and to faithfully imitate the images of nature."[38]

The famous Weimar botanist Karl Koch (d. 1879) included a visit to Turkey in one of his three pioneering scientific quests to collect plant specimens in the Caucasus. In 1843, he was perhaps the first to leave an account of Sester's gardening work in Çırağan. With a horticulturalist's eye for landscaping, tempered with a bit of hearsay, he spotted the

Foreign visitors privileged enough to visit the site with the imperial gardener in tow stress the pre-Sester aridness of its terrain and provide insight into the stages of its development under his command. Before Sester began the second phase of forestation for Abdülmecid, and only seven years into his directorship, Countess Ida von Hahn-Hahn (d. 1880), a novelist commissioned by German aristocrats and a pen pal to Prince Hermann von Pückler-Muskau, met Sester by chance at the lodgings of the Pera proprietress Madame Balbiani in the fall of 1845. The gardener, a frequent guest of the Balbiani boarding-house, offered to take his compatriot on a tour of Mahmud's Çırağan. In a letter to her mother, the countess first provides a lengthy description of the interior of the palace, from its porcelain collection to its sundry mirrors and clocks, then gives the letter's recipient a glimpse of the garden, whose development was still at an early stage.

> The garden of this palace is quite new, situated on the steep and totally bare side of a hill, where as yet, nothing is to be seen that would give us the idea of a garden—no flowers, no shade, no verdure, no water, nothing but the heavenly view of the Bosphorus; perhaps in ten or twelve years it may be transformed into a garden. In the centre, between the pavilions, is a parterre of flowers, where, however, you see nothing rare or handsome but what you find in ours—climbing roses, dahlias, and the like. Orange and lemon trees stand in pots, as with us, and are kept in winter in hot-houses.[40]

Prince Leopold, Duke of Brabant (and the future king of Belgium), who was hosted by Abdülmecid in 1860, took a guided tour of the palace garden with Sester and recorded its transformation in his travel diary on April 13: "After lunch, we went down the Bosphorus by boat to the gardens and kiosks of Çırağan. This garden, drawn by a German,

is large and handsomely created. One sees Constantinople, the Bosphorus, and even a bit of the Sea of Marmara. The soil, rocky here, is not overly favorable for vegetation; also, the garden provides no shade. Near here, in the lower part of the garden, is another kiosk of the Sultan, all in white marble and richly adorned, but in bad taste."[41] Both the countess's and the duke's observations on the garden's barrenness and lack of shade find their representation on the lid of an Ottoman writing box. Executed in oil by the Armenian artist and marquetry specialist Mıgırdıç Melkon, the painting is not only a rare local depiction of Mahmud's version of Çırağan but also the only midcentury visual proof of Sester's completed output (fig. 38).[42] An earlier version by Melkon (see fig. 31) depicts the site before the central circular pavilion has been added. However, the pavilion represented on Melkon's pen box has distinct *chinoiserie* features, recently confirmed as a later folly that Abdülmecid commissioned from Nigoğos Balyan, architect and spirited proponent of Ottoman Armenian rights, in 1846, which stands out from the overall Doric stoicism of Mahmud's palace-garden complex.[43] Melkon's painted lid shows the full span of the garden, extending all the way up to a second, larger kiosk painted in green, whose billowy roof resting on thin columns is exactly the same as the roof of the tent (*çadır*) kiosk once perched right next to Sa'dabad's canal. The green kiosk was likely the earliest incarnation of the brick and stone pavilion also called the tent kiosk (Çadır Köşkü, map 4) that would later replace it during Abdülaziz's additions to the garden, although maintaining its original shape-derived designation (fig. 39). In the artist's evocation, Sester's winding paths and burgeoning saplings present a sharp contrast

FIGURE 38
Mıgırdıç Melkon, pen box
depicting the Beşiktaş Palace,
undated. Oil and papier-mâché,
60 × 90 cm. MSİB Calligraphy
Collection, C.Y.454.

with the more arid hilltops to the garden's
right and the urban sprawl to its left. A curious dun-colored wall behind the southern
wing of the palace—the same structure
shown in the undated oil painting in the Dolmabahçe collection (frontispiece)—appears
to support a greenhouse, whose glass panels
are visible next to the temple-like garden
folly. Small greenhouses indeed began to be
imported from England on Fethi Paşa's initiative in Abdülmecid's time.[44]

A recently discovered painting by the
Italian painter Carlo Bossoli (d. 1884), which
takes more or less the same bird's-eye-view

side glance at the reworked backyard as the
aforementioned undated painting, depicts
Mahmud II's first terraced segment and
the English garden behind it under brilliant, saturated sunlight (fig. 40).[45] To access
this terraced section, palace inhabitants
had to use either a covered footbridge that
crossed the public road or, if on horseback
or in a carriage, a ramp level with the road.
Bossoli's painting also shows that the heavily
landscaped terrace was separated from the
Romantic garden above it (where figures are
depicted strolling the grounds) by a stately
one-story stone greenhouse with a façade

consisting of pediments and pilasters and punctuated with potted plants. The terrace itself is shown to contain a carefully arranged set of round flower parterres with a central pool bearing a cascading fountain. It is very likely that in his unusual ode to Mahmud's new garden, "adorned in layers," Ziver refers to the site that Bossoli foregrounds in his painting.

The internal layout of the Çırağan, especially its central grand hall, purposefully boasted two vistas: the Bosphorus on one side and the terraced landscape on the other. Contrary to popular belief, the palace's patrons deliberately sought the double view, of water and greenery, instead of singling out the Bosphorus. An actual theater within this hall—constructed by a German carpenter, Seefelder, and featuring specially designed latticed screens through which the *valide* and her retinue could watch performances and later socialize with the female performers—mimicked and augmented the imperial staging of natural scenery.[46]

What these paintings do not show, however, is how Sester filled the barren valley sandwiched between the *valide*s' walled-in hilltop residence and the thicket of cypresses surrounding the saintly precinct of Yahya Efendi's tomb, nestled to the northeast of Çırağan. This was the second phase of Sester's expansion, commissioned under Abdülmecid. No surviving paintings like the two previously mentioned depict what would become first the forested extension of the Çırağan gardens, with lakes and waterfalls, and later the centerpiece of Abdülhamid II's Yıldız Palace. However, seventy-five single-page expense accounts covering weekly work that started on February 5, 1849, indicate intense gardening activity in the area. Each of these

expense accounts only sparsely fills a single page and lists the day laborers' rates (*rençber yevmiyesi*) without, unfortunately, providing a detailed plan of Sester's overall undertaking. However, they all bear his Ottoman seal, "Çerāġañ sāḥilsarāy serbaġçıvānı Sester," which identifies his position in Abdülmecid's court as the chief gardener of the Çırağan waterfront palace, embellished with a single stemmed flower.[47] They also provide a general overview of the landscaping project by describing it as the "leveling" (tesviye) of the new garden between Çırağan, its mountains ("Çerāġān ṭāġları"), and Yıldız Pavilion, as well as the construction of the gardener's home ("baġçıvānbāşı mösyö Sestār'iñ ḫānesi") adjacent to the Ortaköy side of the new garden. "Leveling" most likely meant the razing of walls that divided the garden of the shoreline

FIGURE 39
Çadır Pavilion in the Imperial Park of Yıldız, 1880–93. Photographer unknown. İÜMK, 90815–0011.

FIGURE 40
Carlo Bossoli, *Çırağan Palace, Topkapı Beyond*, undated. Tempera on linen canvas, 116 × 180 cm. Private collection.

Çırağan Palace from the barren site behind it, as well as from the Yıldız estate, once intact and outlined on Melkon's writing box. Finally, some of these accounts document the aggregate cost of multiple weeks' worth of work: for example, under the oversight of Selim Efendi, the sultan's head chamberlain (*mābeyn ferīḳi*), the treasury disbursed to Sester more than 2 million *ġurūş* from its 50th to its 130th week.[48] Photographs of Yıldız's forested park from the late 1880s more than compensate for the lack of visual and written proof of Sester's overall vision (fig. 41).

The Austrian Jewish writer and ethnomusicologist Ludwig August von Frankl (d. 1894), who followed the recommendation of the Ottoman ambassador to visit Naples and met with Sester in Istanbul on his journey to Jerusalem in 1856, had the opportunity to spend time in the chief gardener's one-story stone house, perched close to the imperial gardens, which contained "a large hall, the windows of which framed the low-lying Bosphorus, offering a huge picture."[49] Frankl emphasizes that a house made of stone reflected a certain kind of privilege

"in Constantinople, where conflagrations are a regular feature," and adds that the beautiful house "had been constructed by the Sultan for Sester, whom he loves and holds in high esteem." (The house's foundations still exist on the northeastern edges of Yıldız's park, adjacent to the porcelain factory. The space of his house and garden is now occupied by haphazardly built dormitories for the employees of the neighborhood's fire department.) It was in this intimate space that the Austrian traveler was able to observe the gardener, in full Oriental garb, convalescing from a poisoning attempt by an unidentified

"jealous" underling. Sester, seated, entertained his guests with his Armenian Catholic wife, Rosa (née Askerian). Frankl describes him as "a man with a serious demeanor, a demeanor that exudes an Oriental calm that is pleasant, as it is not caused by thoughtlessness." Almost two decades into his service as a gardener at the time of Frankl's visit, Sester seems to have created inside his home a familial environment that combined native practices with touches from his homeland. "We were presented with food and drink in an Oriental fashion; yet we were also given the opportunity to think about our German

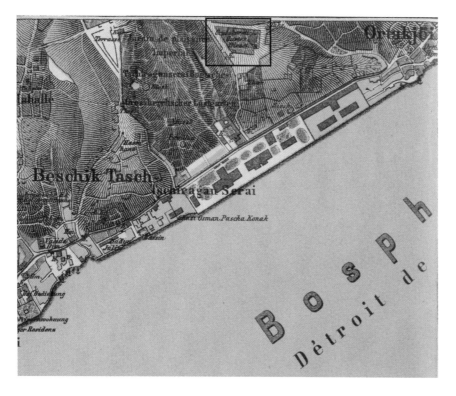

homeland, thanks to an extremely fine wine
from Rhineland."[50]

Overall, Sester had better luck than his
predecessor, Ensle, in integrating into the
Ottoman court: the gardener from Bavaria
cultivated a deeply personal relationship with
Sultan Mahmud and his successors in the
somewhat more forbearing atmosphere created by Selim III's reform efforts. Although
a foreign member of the court, Sester held
considerable authority over a large group of
workers. A short memo exchanged between
the office of the grand vizier and the Ministry of Superintendence in 1852 reports that
an unruly gardener, a Croatian named Zey-
nel, was brought over to the head gardener,
accompanied by the capital's gendarme.[51] Sester's obituary adds that while working on his
ambitious Ortaköy project, he strengthened
his fluency in the Turkish language, so he

must have been able to communicate directly
with his staff.[52]

Sester seems, nevertheless, to have been
subject to a few remaining requirements
of the role of the pre-1826 *bostancıbaşı*. One
was the adjacency of Sester's home to Çırağan, the court's preferred residence in the
first half of the nineteenth century, which
paralleled the traditional practice of assign-
ing the *bostancıbaşı* an official office in Topkapı palace and later one in Kuruçeşme, close
to Beşiktaş Palace.[53] A Stolpe map drawn up
between 1855 and 1863 (and expanded in
1882) provides a cartographic sense of Sester's
gardening feats in the area labeled "Gross-
herrlischer Lustgarten" and of his adjacent
residence as the imperial garden directorate
("Grossherrliche Garten Direction," outlined
in red) (fig. 42). Whereas most other expatriate court officials, such as Sester's contemporary Guiseppe Donizetti, instructor general of
the Ottoman imperial music band, chose to
reside in Pera, the garden director combined
his office and family home in the privileged
zone around the palace.[54] This was probably
also where Sester and his gardeners kept their
plans and drawings.

In keeping with earlier designatory practices, Sester retained militaristic control over
his gardeners by arranging them into squad-
rons (*bölük*) in accordance with their posts in
the various imperial gardens of the capital.
Salary registers still referred to each gardener
as *nefer* (individual, soldier), and salaries
continued to be documented and paid by the
Ottoman imperial treasury.[55] However, the
martial terminology found in registers of
these late nineteenth-century recruits seems
to have become merely formalistic, maintaining such designations for bureaucratic ease
rather than indicating a direct link between

the conscripted members of the pre-1826 gardening corps and the janissaries, with the former expected to join the latter.

Sester's reputation, at least in the imperial neighborhood of Beşiktaş, survived posthumously. Two maps of Ortaköy produced by members of the imperial army under Abdülhamid II identify the site of the garden directorate as belonging to the former head gardener, Sester ("sābıḳ baġçıvānbaşı Sester Efendiniñ ḫāne ve bāġçesi").[56] These maps were drawn between 1899 and 1900 at the sultan's behest as part of a project to expand Yıldız's gardens into Ortaköy by absorbing the gardens of the Ferʿiye Palaces and the small plots of land owned by the neighborhood's tradesmen. The goal was to create a palatial extension replete with a new imperial mansion to host and entertain diplomatic guests around a porcelain factory and a completely new picturesque garden. One of the maps details the lodgings for Abdülhamid's trusted Albanian *zouave* regiment[57] ("fesli zuhāf birinci ṭabūrunuñ iki bölük efrād-ı şāhānelerıñ iḳāmetine maḥṣūṣ bārākalar"), and the other focuses on the immediate surroundings of Sester's house, pinpointing its commanding location in a small town square with a fountain in the middle and the house of the head gardener's assistant (*bāġçıvān ḳalfa*) sandwiched between the head gardener's residence and that of the caretaker (*türbedār*) of the Yahya Efendi convent. The mansion built over Sester's residence under Abdülhamid would continue to be known among the palace officials as the head gardener's pavilion well into the reign of Mehmed V (r. 1909–18), probably indicating its function as an official structure (fig. 43). When Mehmed V chose to make Yıldız his palace after a brief and unpleasant stint in the drafty Dolmabahçe,

his sons would host banquets for the palace officials in this mansion.[58] Twice in his hefty memoirs, Sultan Mehmed's head scribe, Halid Ziya, talks about the new building's banqueting function and how it retained the name of the site's famous former inhabitant. Initially, Halid Ziya wonders why the name "Bahçıvanbaşı Sesvter [*sic*] köşkü" was

FIGURE 43
The new Yıldız pavilion that replaced Sester's residence. Photographer unknown. İAK, Alb. 156.

adopted, but later on, having found out the backstory yet still unsure of the foreigner's name, he describes it as "a pavilion that was built for the head gardener Chester [sic] on the clearing in the forest cascading from Yıldız to Ortaköy, and these days referred to as the world-viewing, or Belvedere [Cihannüma] Pavilion," for its resplendent views of the Bosphorus.[59]

The persistence of his name in the new building's designation might have had something to do with a few unusual remnants from the site's original owner. According to a renowned Hungarian ornithologist, István Nogel, who stayed at Sester's home, the gardener had an insect collection, which the visitor reclassified, and Nogel also mounted several birds for him.[60] Likely as an homage to the site's great transformer, these taxidermy specimens (including canaries, pigeons, cranes, and cockroaches) were later displayed in the banqueting hall built over the gardener's residence, recorded in detail in the palace inventories in the aftermath of Yıldız's liquidation in 1909, and last noted to have found their place in the Ministry of Education.[61] Moreover, these inventories suggest that Sester's natural-science cabinets—the displays of which were also documented and preserved—included geological samples as well as a great variety of conifer leaves, his choice evergreens.

ISTANBUL'S GERMANIC NETWORKS AND ROYAL GARDENERS AFTER SESTER

In the empire's new century, when renegades and émigrés could acquire privileged posts, Sester fashioned himself as an aristocrat— at the very least among the capital's foreign residents—through his professional title as garden director of the Ottoman court. Frankl describes a salon-like gathering in the gardener's home during which the government's reforms were discussed by a diverse group, ranging from the doctor of the German Hospital in Istanbul, Dr. Stolle, and his entourage to the gardener's wife and niece. Although Sester's visitors were in agreement that the "Hat Humajum" (Ḫāṭṭ-ı Hümāyūn, or Islahat Fermanı, of 1856) was bound to fail due to great opposition from conservative members of the Turkish government, the gardener, to Frankl's dismay, remained quiet. He would light up only when his wife and daughter walked into the room, and declare, "Do you see, my good men! This is my Reich, where permanent peace reigns, which one cannot say of every Oriental peace treaty."[62]

Sester's political reticence was a different matter, however, when dealing with the embassy through whose agency he had first been brought to the empire and under which he was therefore registered. Taking advantage of the gardener's access to Mahmud II and Abdülmecid, the Austrian ambassador to Constantinople, Anton Graf Prokesch von Osten (d. 1876), during his time in the diplomatic service, from 1855 to Sester's death in 1866, seems to have employed Sester as a palace informant. Jotting the gardener down as *Hofgärtner* in his diaries, Prokesch von Osten encouraged Sester to visit him regularly to share his views on the newly appointed Sultan Abdülaziz. The gardener must not have been in the new ruler's good graces or may have been disappointed by the fact that Abdülaziz did not permit him the same courtly intimacy that he had shared with the two preceding sultans. In 1863 Sester would describe Abdülaziz to Prokesch as "ignorant, fickle, heartless, and spiteful."[63] (Counterclaims by confidants of the new sultan would characterize the gardener to Prokesch in much the same terms.) Prokesch feared that Abdülaziz would thwart the reform efforts aimed at allowing more rights for the empire's Christian population, a topic continually on the competitive agendas of the Austrians and the Russians. According to Prokesch's diary, Abdülmecid seems to have forewarned his gardener—immediately before the sultan's death, in dramatic fashion—that his chosen successor was against granting privileges to the Christians. The status of the empire's religious minorities also affected the gardener's life personally. As a Catholic Armenian, his wife and her family must have experienced the often-violent outcomes of the schism between and among the empire's Apostolic, Catholic, and Protestant Armenian populations in the early half of the century with respect to rightful representation and the involvement of external bodies (Rome and the European protector powers) over local ones (sultan, patriarch, the Mekhitarists, and wealthy and influential Catholic *amira* families like the Balyans and Bezciyans, who were members of the Armenian National Council).[64]

Sester might have relied on Austrian protection for his foreigner's rights, but in his private hours he worked for the German community in Istanbul. For example, in May 1855 he petitioned the German Federal Assembly (Bundesversammlung) for the purchase of a hospital building in the Ottoman capital that would be financed by German mutual-aid societies of the governments of the various member states of the German Confederation (*hohe deutsche Bundesregierungen*).[65] The petition was for the German Hospital, founded in 1846, which had been repeatedly relocated until a permanent building was established for it through the aid of the German federal charity funds to which Sester appealed. In the aftermath of the Hungarian uprising of 1848–49 and the influx of émigrés into the Ottoman lands, Sester also provided gardening employment in Çirağan's expanded grounds for six deserters from the Hungarian army, who were all German volunteers from Baden and Württemberg fighting for the Magyar cause.[66]

Istanbul's expatriate clubs enabled the formation of these kinds of networks. Hundreds of Hungarian soldiers found their way into the colony-like club run by Balázs Orbán, a young Hungarian-expatriate baron, who would find jobs for them in the capital.[67] As a facilitator, Orbán commended Sester's dedication to these individuals in their acquisition of a completely new professional skill: "It is true that only one [of the refugees] knew anything of gardening, but he taught the others so that they worked to full satisfaction."[68] Among them, a renegade named Dániel Sipos would show great promise and be selected as head gardener for the Kanlıca residence of Mehmed Fuad Paşa (d. 1869), one of Tanzimat's founding fathers, and later Khedive Ismail Paşa's world-renowned gardens in the Gezirah Palace, Cairo.[69] Similarly, for German-affiliated émigrés, the Teutonia Club, which was established in 1847, fostered a lively community of Germans, Austrians, and Swiss. The proactive and resourceful head gardener probably presided over this convivial pan-German community, of which he was a perfect representative.[70] After all, he had been born in Bavaria, trained in Austria and Switzerland, and employed on both Prussian and Habsburg estates.

In European courts, the office of the head gardener was much respected, as Sester was well aware from his apprenticeship with Bode and intimacy with Sckell, as well as with the latter's mentee and Sester's contemporary Peter Joseph Lenné (d. 1866). The latter was the illustrious garden director of Prussia's imperial palaces (with Sanssouci as its ultimate pride and glory) and the landscape engineer of its cities (Potsdam and Berlin). During the nineteenth century this occupation became indispensable for every European ruling house that maintained grand parks and gardens as much as palaces.

There can be no doubt that Sester bolstered his garden directorship with his knowledge of the now-defunct role of the *bostancıbaşı*, once powerful within the Ottoman system of governance, which he had partly inherited. In 1845, when he took the waters in the German Baden-Baden and then the Austrian Bad Gastein and convened with the rest of the European Sesters in Aschaffenburg, he was also granted an audience with the Bavarian king, Ludwig I, as well as his daughters, Grand Duchess Mathilde and Princess Alexandra. Sester would later lunch with the Bavarian keeper of the royal silver collection (*Oberstsilberkammerer*), a palace employee whose courtly status most likely paralleled that of a royal head gardener.[71] Sester's visit to Ludwig I earned him a "valuable golden watch." A year later, when Ludwig's son Luitpold was Abdülmecid's guest in Istanbul, Sester would conduct him on a private tour of his grand garden designs behind Çırağan.[72]

A small news item that appeared on October 23, 1845, traces Sester's five-month vacation from Istanbul. Permission to leave was granted to him after eight years of service in the Ottoman palace. He started his journey in the early summer months and arrived first in Baden-Baden, "the queen of the Spas of Germany,"[73] right on time for the lively bathing season. Sester had already been decorated with an Ottoman order,[74] and the news report eagerly highlights the fact that he "had received splendiferous gifts from the deceased Sultan Mahmud, from the current Sultan Balide [*Valide* mispelled], and from Abdul Medschid, and ... had also been awarded the Turkish medal of honor."[75] It was important to display one's status markers in the lively social scene of Baden's promenade, a site visited daily by kings, queens, and their retinue, but even more so to distinguish one's courtly bearing from the pretensions of the moneyed bourgeois upstarts who occupied the seasonal tabloids.[76] Sester stayed in Baden-Baden for seven weeks before leaving for Bad Gastein, where "he was honored with great attention and homage."[77] The gardener's ill health following his poisoning by an underling, an incident to which Frankl alludes in his observations in 1856, may have been the main reason for his long leave of absence from courtly service in 1845. Baden-Baden's *Ursprung* and its "vegeto-animal deposits,"[78] however, seem not to have been restorative enough (and indeed Baden was a town less for convalescence than for luxury vacations), so Sester was probably advised by the town's physicians to try his luck on the remote, hard-to-reach heights of Bad Gastein. The social scene of this Austrian town had very little to offer compared with Baden's weekly balls, but its caloric waters were known to "excite, disturb, [and] agitate the nerves"[79] and would perhaps rouse the gardener's legs into action, as they had famously done those of a lame Bavarian cavalry officer.[80] The waters must have revived the royal gardener enough to allow him to press on to

Switzerland and thence to Frankfurt, where he picked up his siblings to journey to his parents' final resting place, in Aschaffenburg. The local report praises the family's filial affection as a stalwart small-town trait. "They [the Sesters] also went to the cemetery, where they honored their dear parents with tributes of childhood love."[81]

Penned by an anonymous author, Sester's obituary confirms the gardener's degenerative health problems and remarks on the futility of his frequent trips to the various European centers of balneology.

A Turkish tobacco pipe that was bestowed upon him as an honor by a visiting Armenian was designed first and foremost to destroy him. Various signs alerted Sester to the danger, and he had the pipe extinguished. Yet he was nevertheless unable to avert his fate: a cup of coffee and later the ingestion of a type of candy called Glico by the Greeks were sufficient to fulfill their purpose—arsenic had been intermixed in these items in such quantity that despite medical attention and visits to various European spa towns, Sester's lower extremities were afflicted by permanent paralysis. As a result, he was forced to ride a small horse in order to conduct his rounds in the royal gardens. The Sultan did not overlook this dastardly deed, which was motivated by envy. We know from Sester's own mouth that the Sultan summoned a high-ranking official who had been generally suspected of committing the poisoning, who was then stripped of his honors, offices, and medals.[82]

Sester's predecessor, Ensle, also experienced poisoning attempts. In the first case, he was rushed out of the palace by Antoine Ignace Melling and treated in the artist's summer residence in Büyükdere by an old Armenian woman. The second attempt occurred when the sultan asked Ensle to attend to the garden of one his wives in Topkapı Palace. Her eunuch "handed [Ensle] a cup of coffee, along with a cloth that had a coat of arms stitched onto it." Ensle testifies, "What he intended by handing me these things … I am not sure, and I poured the coffee out onto the ground, instead of drinking it, for fear that it was tainted."[83] The palace eunuch's wrath may very well have been a fabulist's trope employed in foreign accounts, coupled with racist sentiment. Ensle places this animosity toward him in the context of the widespread xenophobia directed against expatriates that erupted in the Ottoman domains after Napoleon's conquest of Egypt. It is unclear why and by whom Sester was targeted, but in both cases a foreigner employed in the court's most intimate surroundings (palatial gardens that were used only by the sultan and his family) attracted strong resentment.

Both Frankl's travelogue and Sester's obituary mention the gardener's inability to attend to his work on foot, reporting that he used an equine or a small wagon to survey the grounds. Frankl describes a "train" (*Zug*), possibly a horsecar, imported by Mahmud II from Europe on Sester's recommendation.[84] This vehicle must have been one of the commodious horse-drawn carriages called *Britschkas* (or *Britzsckas*) that were used to shuttle visitors between spa towns—and even for overnight journeys across the Alps, as the versatile interiors could be turned into bedrooms—before the midcentury arrival of the railways.[85] The gardener must have experienced its comforts during his palliative quests and may have thought it best to install one in the hilly garden he constructed for Mahmud and later expanded for Abdülmecid. The very short distance between his home and his workplace also made his physical handicap slightly more bearable.

La Turquie announced Sester's passing a day after he died from an ambiguous "attaque d'apoplexie" on December 17, 1866.[86] This was an undifferentiated diagnosis given to all sudden deaths at that time. He was interred in a marble tomb in the catacombs of the Catholic Cathedral of St. Esprit in Pangaltı in 1867, sharing a central aisle with the empire's eminent dragoman families and consuls and with Giuseppe Donizetti.[87] This small neoclassical church, built by the Swiss architect Giuseppe Fossati in 1846, was the main ecclesiastical site for the city's Catholics (often referred to as "Latins"). The sultan's gardener had donated stately sums to the upkeep of this church since its inception.[88] There he also maintained a family chapel, whose chaplain, Nicholas Perpignani from the Aegean island of Tinos, had been summoned to Istanbul by the British admiralty to provide "spiritual services" at the British hospital in Tarabya (along the Bosphorus) during the Crimean War.[89] The family chapel must have had special significance for Sester's wife, because for a long time Catholic Armenians had not had their own churches, instead using sites designated by the state for the Catholic Levantine communities.

Rosa was buried next to her spouse in 1896. Sester must have obtained the interment permissions required for a family tomb with the help of the grand vizier of the time and the preeminent Tanzimat bureaucrat Mehmed Emin Âli Pasha (d. 1871). Cholera outbreaks and the Vatican's often-refractory protocols made burial in prestigious catacombs,

especially in foreign lands, difficult.[90] Another indication that a lot of planning went into the tomb's making lies in its sculptural marble reliefs, which stand apart from their relatively austere neighbors. A knight's helmet, a stand-in for invulnerability and protection, and four swans, representing grace, wisdom, or harmony, furnish the prominent baroque crest of the tomb (fig. 44). The eminent garden director created the reliefs for his family: the knight's helmet for himself, and the four swans for his wife and three children. The larger swan is perched on top of the helmet as a devotional gesture toward Rosa's role in the family. Behind the crest once stood a stained-glass depiction of Christ's resurrection, noted for its beauty in the church's chronicles.[91] Below the crest, the tomb's two roundels preserve Victorian reliefs of the husband, with his stately mustache, and the wife, in her creased blouse, both with expressions speaking of hard-earned lives. They face each other in the fashion of a marriage portrait, under the flowering branches of a holly, the heraldic symbol of truth. They are festooned with the literal fruits of their service to the court: apricots, apples, figs, and poppies hang from garlands around the couple. The centralized placement of the poppies among the fruit is intriguing. In this extremely autobiographical iconographic scheme, Sester may very well be alluding to the fact that he cultivated these opiates to relieve himself of the debilitating pain caused by arsenic.

Soon after Sester's death, his post was taken up by his assistant Steffel, who had accompanied him to Istanbul in 1835. Archival evidence, though scarce, indicates that Steffel's wife had pleaded, following his passing in 1870, to recover the amount promised to him from the imperial treasury for the construction of his Ortaköy residence, which he had designed and built in the vicinity, again, of the imperial gardens of Çırağan. The residence had been deemed "too intrusive in its proximity to the palace" (Çerāğañ bāġçesine neẓāreti var), and its second floor had thus been completely demolished.[92] A Hakkı Paşa had bestowed the site on Steffel ("ḥadāʾiḳ-i şāhāne direktörü mösyö Steffel") for his satisfactory work in "leveling and laying out" (tesvīye ve tanẓīm) the Kağıthane garden and park—the latter word referring to the segments of the riverside strip at the head of the Golden Horn that were reserved for public promenades.

From Sester's time to Steffel's, the relationship between the head gardener and his royal patron appears to have shifted from personal to ceremonious; as a result, the gardener's proximity to his site and the sultan was widened. It is unclear whether the site granted to Steffel was Sester's former home or the existing one allocated to the head gardener's assistant, but it was definitely in the vicinity of the square made famous by Steffel's predecessor. Also certain, however, is that Steffel grew in skill from the palace's young tiller (sarāy ekincisi) to its garden director under Sester's careful tutelage.[93] In 1865 the *Allgemeine Zeitung München* published a telegraphic dispatch that celebrated the work of the "artistically gifted" (*kunstsinnig*) *Obergärtner* Steffel on the gardens and park—which had become an inseparable landscaping pair on every Ottoman imperial outdoor site and in corresponding documents—of Abdülaziz's newly built Beylerbeyi Palace. The dispatch notes that Steffel achieved paradisiacal results under the supervision of the head inspector, "Chevalier von Sester," whose many achievements had finally won him his noble

accreditation as both a "chevalier" and a "von."[94] Anticipating Abdülaziz's move from Dolmabahçe to Beylerbeyi, the dispatch also reports that many *yalı*s were rented in the vicinity of the new palace for court officials.

Under Abdülaziz, the Ortaköy *Lustgarten* that Sester and Steffel had built for Mahmud and Abdülmecid as a refuge for

FIGURE 44
The Sester family tomb, St. Esprit Cathedral, Istanbul. Photograph courtesy of T. Türker.

quiet, philosophical contemplation increasingly became a site for the sultan's harem. This is perhaps why Steffel's residence was deemed obtrusive. The closest observer of life in the imperial harem of that period, the preeminent female composer Leyla Saz (d. 1936), records detailed recollections of the German duo's Çırağan garden. Her memoirs carry an awareness of the garden's different building stages: Mahmud II's terraced backyard succeeded by Abdülmecid's expansion into the hills beyond, the connection with the *valides*' rural country retreat later converted by Abdülaziz into the neoclassical Mabeyn Kiosk, and the site's ultimate conversion into Abdülhamid's sprawling garden-city, Yıldız.[95] She highlights the role of the garden's amenities in providing precious outdoor entertainment for the women of the harem. If for the preceding two sultans the site's appeal had lain in its varied vistas from different sectors of the gardens (which German garden treatises, as well as Frankl's account, call *Räume*), its chief attractions for the women were its greenhouses, gazebos, exotic plants, artificial lakes connected by moving footbridges, and the shade cast by monumental plane and fruit trees.[96] It also seems from Saz's account that before the still-extant monumental bridge connecting Abdülaziz's Çırağan to the park was built to accommodate a street below for the public tram, the terraced garden was accessed first by stairs—the ruins of which remain to this day—and later via the bridge's first incarnation, visible in the abovementioned colored lithograph and the oil painting by Bossoli (frontispiece and fig. 40).

The land sloped behind the Palace, the garden was on a small terrace to which one had access by stairs placed in front of the gate. A vast courtyard full of big trees came before the actual garden and was always open, while the entrance to the garden was closed by a grill in order to keep the little girls from entering without surveillance. This grill was opened two times each week and then everybody could walk around freely under the vigilant eye of the *kalfa*s.

A big lake surrounded by layers of flowers and fruit trees had a little island in the middle and was shaded by ancient plain-trees. This was the main ornament of the garden. The island was connected to the garden by four turning bridges covered with lawns and which could be opened or swung to the side in such a way as to completely free the lake for rowboats.... [97]

The Yıldız Park, or rather the gardens of the Mabeyin, were connected to the garden of the old Çırağan Palace by a bridge enclosed with grills. This bridge crossed the street just like the present passage only with the difference that the street was far more narrow in those days than it is now.[98]

Foreign accounts tinged with Oriental fantasies of garden orgies talk of Sester's annoyance at the women's disregard for his handiwork, manifested in their indiscriminate plucking of newly planted flowers: "the most precious and rare flowers were ripped asunder by these women and used as missiles; they writhed around in wild lust on the flower beds, and in one night the product of months of the most careful horticultural labor was thoroughly devastated."[99]

After Sester and Steffel, the posts of the head gardener and his assistant became a well-oiled system in the palace's roster of employees. Having taken in German renegades after the Hungarian Revolution of 1848–49, Sester continued to bring in a steady stream of his compatriots to expand his royal horticultural team with experts best equipped to service the expanded gardens of Çırağan under Abdülmecid. For a brief period, Fritz Wentzel was Sester's secretary, following a meeting between the two while Wentzel was convalescing from rheumatism at the German Hospital, the very institution that Sester had helped to fund.[100] Wentzel would later take up the position of head gardener at the recently inaugurated German Consulate of Istanbul, after Abdülhamid granted the shoreline site that he had once occupied as a prince in Tarabya to the unified German Reich.[101]

At this consular site, Wentzel implemented a program of forestation similar to that undertaken by Sester in converting the barren hills of Çırağan into the grove-like park of Yıldız.[102] His collaborator on this landscaping project in Tarabya was Eduard Petzold (d. 1891), who had been trained in Park von Muskau in Germany, the erstwhile English landscape garden of the influential aristocrat landscapist Prince Hermann von Pückler-Muskau.[103] Of all of Sester's students, Wentzel seems to have most faithfully preserved his master's tenor, both in the way that he fashioned himself and in his gardening practice. The young Wentzel was a childhood friend of the renowned pathologist Rudolf Virchow (d. 1902), later fought in the Crimean War, and learned the combined arts of gardening and landscape design through experience and under Sester's close supervision. In his postwar Istanbul days, while convalescing from war wounds, Wentzel took care of Sester's children and was initiated in the practice of the man who had taken him under his wing. Wentzel, too, like Sester, chose to go native in his sartorial choices, appearing at the Düsseldorf botany exhibition sporting a fez, which he was required to wear while working in the Ottoman gardens. And Wentzel, too, was eager to orient his expatriate compatriots looking to find gainful employment, "who would otherwise be lost in the colorful tumult of people and languages in Constantinople."[104] In the recollections of Árpád Mühle from Temesvár (now Timişoara, Romania), one of Sester's renegade trainees from Hungary, who would become an important landscapist and rose expert, Wentzel appears as a monkish recluse, attending to his nursery of rare plants—a secluded verdant Ciceronian Tusculum to his intimates.[105]

An anonymous reporter for the weekly journal *Gartenwelt* happened upon a few of Sester's pupils, including Wentzel, in Istanbul in 1907 and inquired about the legacy of their tutor, their professional lives in Istanbul, and the state of gardening in the Ottoman capital. In the neighborhood in which Sester's residence was located, Wentzel and the old German gardener J. D. H. Koch from Darmstadt, who also spoke with the reporter, had opened nurseries to serve the city's ever-increasing gardening enthusiasts. Koch ran a family business with his two sons, had a branch in Kağıthane, and took private commissions to design the parks of the capital's grandees. The Levantine-Croat Jacques Pervititch's impressive insurance maps from the first half of the twentieth century indicate that Koch's large Ortaköy orchards ("grand jardin d'horticulture de Mr. Koch") at the bottom of the valley below the Jewish cemetery, where he lived and, according to *Gartenwelt*, "enjoyed a well-earned rest," survived well into the 1920s.[106]

One of the many foreign *kalfa*s who had joined Sester's team along the way, Adam Schlerff of Frankfurt, who had entered into service as a foreman in 1857, took the helm as the garden director after Steffel and Wentzel. Like Sester before him, Schlerff was given a home in Ortaköy's green valley, in the vicinity of the Armenian Catholic church and the Greek cemetery, as well as Koch's residence and nursery.[107] Having long served as a residential and devotional refuge for the city's many minorities, this neighborhood now also had to make room for the court's foreign gardening experts.[108] In 1882, in the early years of Abdülhamid's reign, Schlerff would receive the Mecidiye Order of the fourth degree as the head gardener of the imperial gardens (*ḥadāiḳ-i ḫāṣṣa serbāġçıvānı*).[109] The German horticultural journal *Gartenflora* dutifully reported this news, calling Schlerff the *Hofgartendirektor* and his assistant August Wienhold the *Hofgärtner*.[110] Along with the Lombard Romeo Scanziani, Wienhold was also the principal caretaker of the greenhouses in Abdülhamid's *Lustgarten*, enclosed within the harem quarters.[111] Schlerff's son was also employed in the imperial gardens, first working in the greenhouses (*şobacı*), which were located in front of the ceremonial apartments, the extension appended to the Şale Kiosk, and later appointed to the gardens of the Maslak estate.[112] Schlerff and Wienhold's collaboration appears still to have been going strong in 1901, when the German-Baltic reporter Bernard Stern interviewed various employees of the palace complex and left a thorough account of its various aspects.[113] Each gardening assistant would eventually

supervise a different segment of Yıldız's garden, each segment compartmentalized according to the main kiosk or pavilion within it, so the gap in status between each of the head gardeners and their *kalfa*s became less pronounced than that between Sester and Steffel. For example, a *kalfa* appointed to the harem gardens of Yıldız, depending on his seniority and years of service, would be paid substantially more than the head gardener of the Mabeyn gardens.[114]

Along with the growth of the gardening corps, a new kind of professionalization began in its conduct and associated documentation. These foreigners and the men who worked under them would fall under the supervision of an Ottoman bureaucrat who was assigned to keep systematic ledgers for all the gardening expenses and salaries and to present them directly to the imperial treasury. During Stern's inquiries, a Rauf Bey was appointed to the task. Rauf Bey was joined by a site inspector named Reşid Paşa. Four years later, these two separate bureaucratic posts were combined to form a single post, the superintendent of the imperial gardens (*ḥadā'iḳ-i ḫāṣṣa-ı şāhāneleri nāẓırı*), which was assigned to a high-ranking member of the scribal office, its vice-director İzzet Holo Paşa (d. 1924).[115]

Schlerff's Ottoman seal marks a register of gardeners employed in the imperial sites in 1883. This particular register seems to list only the 252 Muslim members of the troop, but perhaps most intriguingly, it itemizes every individual's physical attributes—height, age, eye color, and even facial hair, distinguishing between a mustache and a beard—as well as the village, settlement, city, and province from which he hailed.[116]

From the village of Kızara[117]
in the Safranbolu district of the province
of Kastamonu
tall, with hazel eyes, brown hair and a
mustache
Hüseyin Ağa son of Hasan
Age 40
Joined on June 13, 1880, salaried on
April 13, 1884

From the village of Nikšić[118]
in the province of Shkodër
of middling stature, with hazel eyes and a
sparse mustache
Haşim Ağa son of Abdullah
Age 28
Joined on December 9, 1884, salaried on
December 9, 1884

From the village of Bar
in the province of Shkodër
of middling stature, with hazel eyes,
brown hair and a mustache
Rüstem Ağa son of Edhem
Age 55
Joined on February 24, 1881, salaried on
February 24, 1881[119]

The dates of their entry into service and of
their first wage payments were also jotted
on the sides of their tags. The physiognomic
detail in the registry reflects a prephoto-
graphic practice that can be traced back to
early Ottoman times. The registry is also proof
of the nineteenth-century imperial practice of
recruiting gardeners from either Kastamonu,
a central Black Sea province, or Shkodër,
in northwestern Albania. Given Abdülhamid's
deep trust in his Albanian bodyguards, this
choice of Albanian caretakers for his most

immediate surroundings should not come as
a surprise.[120] However, the fact that more than
half of the gardeners were selected from two
specific districts of the empire is indicative
of the continuation of an earlier recruitment
pattern, probably undertaken for the *bostancı*
corps that were folded into the gardening
corps of the nineteenth century.[121] Reinforcing
the idea that a martial language was maintained for these employees, other ledgers list
a "corporal" (*onbaşı*) appointed as a buffer
between the *kalfa*, or head gardener, and the
rest of the gardeners in a particular imperial
garden or section of a garden.[122] Each squadron enlisted five to twenty men. They received
rations of food, summer and winter uniforms,
shoes, and haircuts, and their dormitory units
were arranged according to their lands of
origin and, relatedly, the types of food they
cooked. "The Turks from Asia and Rumelia, Albanians, Montenegrins, Bosnians, and
Greeks," who were defined by the last imperial
head gardener as "shirkers" (*embusqués*), had
jobs on the side or owned shops in the city.[123]
Members of Abdülhamid's Albanian battalion
(*Prizren taburu*), too, spent their free time
working the land in the fields of Ortaköy, close
to their assigned barracks. They were happy
members of this diverse gardening neighborhood, which, according to the recollections
of one of these soldier-cum-gardeners, was
Yıldız's principal produce hinterland.[124]

That a majority of these individuals were
brought in to work in the imperial gardens
in 1877 or soon afterward—immediately
following Abdülhamid's ascension to the
throne—speaks to an effort to expand gardening activity in the imperial gardens in
general, and in Yıldız, the shining example,
in particular. Another important indication

that Abdülhamid was eager to attend to the Crown's green spaces instead of commissioning costly palatial structures appears in the announcements of Adam Schlerff's death in German and English horticultural journals of 1907, in which lists of the late director's achievements boast of his superintendence of sixteen imperial gardens.[125] Bernard Stern describes Abdülhamid's deep and abiding love of the natural world and of greenery and his penchant for decorating diplomatic banquets and court ceremonies with flowers and fruits, especially out-of-season ones, cultivated in his own lavish surroundings: "Fresh plants have to be available at all times, not least because of the colossal effort that is put into providing decorative flowers and plants for dinners and receptions that are hosted by the Sultan. The Sultan loves transforming the salons in which he receives guests or hosts a dinner into gardens full of the rarest plants and flowers, and he takes great pleasure when his guests admire the living decorations more than the dead luxury of the marble or the colorful sheen of the carpets."[126]

A CHANGE OF HANDS IN THE FINAL YEARS OF THE CORPS

Through the insights provided by his two seasoned interviewees, *Gartenwelt*'s patriotic reporter laments the demise, after more than half a century, of the influence of "German industry" (deutscher Fleiß) on the gardens and parks of Istanbul's ruling elite. Charles Henry soon took the position of head gardener from the septuagenarians Schlerff and Wienhold.

Henry was a French greenhouse expert who had first been brought to the imperial gardens to operate a greenhouse built with a hot-water system in favor of the preexisting inefficient ones heated by hot air. *Gartenwelt*'s

reporter, albeit disheartened by the German fall from grace in the garden arts, concedes Henry's "superior ability in rearing exemplary plant cultures in forcing houses" (ein ausgezeichneter Leiter der Treibereien und Kulturen) (fig. 45).[127] Although the old Germans stayed on without a salary reduction, they became *kalfa*s under Henry, the new head gardener ("Serbāġçıvān Mösyö Hanri"). His French seal read, "Jardinier en chef de S. M. I. le Sultan."[128] To help him command more than three hundred gardeners in the final years of Abdülhamid's reign, Henry was appointed two Ottoman scribes to keep the books: a *kātib* named Osman Şadi Efendi and Mehmed Tahir Efendi bin Mustafa.[129]

If garden laborers belonging to the same nationality really did show solidarity, it is tempting to think that Henry preferred to work with Gustave Deroin, who was "responsible for carrying out the plans and drawings for changes that [were] to be made to royal gardens, as well as for arranging ornaments and decorations,"[130] on the turn-of-the-century Ortaköy expansion of the palace around Sester's old residence. Deroin was hired by the court in 1882 but had started his professional life as a horticulturalist in Istanbul in 1856, serving the obscure "chez MM. Gabared et Karakiaya" as a "chef des cultures,"[131] and later owned his own nursery on Büyükdere Road. The nursery supplied European-imported mushrooms, seeds, and saplings of trees bearing fruits such as wild pears, cherries, almonds, and plums for the consumption of the inhabitants of Yıldız.[132] Although employed in the court's gardens, which were overseen by Henry, Deroin was later recorded as "a gardener without a specific placement inside Yıldız's building-centered garden compartments" (mevāḳiʿ

ḫāricinde ḫidmeti olan bāġçıvānlar), possibly because his expensive services were requested only on occasion and he often acted as an agent for European horticultural products.[133]

The "blond, fez-donning, and sweetly affable" Monsieur Henry was Yıldız's head gardener for its best and worst decade.[134] In the early years of the new century, the functions of the different sections of the palace's outdoors were settled, along with the attendants allotted to them. (Henry explains why the archival documents identify Yıldız's gardens solely in terms of the structures they enclosed: "contrary to [European gardens], which we regard as sites of rest and pleasure, the Orientals see them as annexes to buildings, hermetically enclosing them.")[135] Under his jurisdiction, the imperial gardens saw their largest number of employees. And although he complained in retrospect of their organizational incoherence, he was satisfied with the results of their work overall.[136] Furthermore, a few years before Abdülhamid's thirty-year reign came to a crashing end and the Salonican army of the Committee of Union and Progress descended upon the site in 1909, Henry was asked to take a botanical expedition to the environs of Bursa to identity specimens for a royal botanical garden (nebātāt bāġçesi) in the capital, whose climate was similar to that of its neighboring region across the Marmara Sea.[137] It is unclear from the account he leaves behind whether this garden was intended solely for the palace; nevertheless, it coincided conceptually with Abdülhamid's many projects undertaken to educate his urban subjects in zoology, botany, and other natural sciences.

The account of Henry's trip, available only in the Ottoman translation but still bearing his seal, is filled with descriptions of the various kinds of indigenous trees, shrubs, and

ش ه نصه قصرها مایه ی لیمن لقان نظر عمویة

90552

flowering plants that grew around Bursa's Mount Olympus (Uludağ, then referred to as Keşiş Mountain, where Henry locates another Yıldız Pavilion); Lake Uluabat (the gardener uses its ancient Greek name, Apollonia), with its striking peninsular town of Gölyazı; the well-fortified İznik; and the gardener's favorite, the thermal springs of the mountainous regions of Çitli and Olyat, close to İnegöl.[138] He is struck by the destruction of forests in these regions and warns his imperial audience of the "unrestrained [Balkan] refugee settlers with their axes" (muhācirler bilā-pervā bālṭa çalmaḳtan çekinmiyorlar) and the shepherds with their flocks that grazed on the saplings of oak trees. In his medical knowledge, Henry appears as thoroughly a man of the nineteenth century. He believes that miasmic airs are a cause of malaria,

FIGURE 45
View of a greenhouse in the garden of Şale Kiosk (Şāle ḳaṣr-ı hümāyūnları civārındaki limonluġun manẓara-ı 'umūmīyesi), undated. Photographer unknown. İÜMK, 90552–0040.

a disease by that point proved to be mosquito borne but perhaps not yet commonly accepted as such, which he detects in the yellowed faces of İznik's lakeshore inhabitants. Like Sester, he seems to have been indebted to his visual memories of Europe's best sites, for his description of two thermal springs reads like that of a pristine Alpine landscape of cliffs, winding roads, deep valleys, pine and beech forests, invigorating waters, and curative airs. He encourages the sultan "to consider transforming [the area] into a spa town, bedecked with thermal baths and hotels, with ample potential to surpass its European counterparts" (sāye-i muvaffaḳıyet-vāye-i ḥażret-i şehriyārīde mükemmel bir ḳāplıca ve oteller binā ve teʾsīs edilürse Avrupāʾnıñ bu yoldaki olān müʾessesātına ezher cihet teveffuḳ edeceği şüphesizdir).[139]

However, Henry's entrepreneurial enthusiasm and managerial jurisdiction over the gardening corps were brought to an abrupt end with a complete overhaul of Abdülhamid's established court order in Yıldız. Thousands of its employees and objects were first itemized by a commission and then disbanded to prepare for Mehmed V's nominal rule under the Committee of Union and Progress. During this transitional phase, when the coffers that financed the smooth running of this mammoth imperial complex were dwindling, the much-loved French novelist Marcelle Tinayre visited the ghostly, decaying grounds and was led on a tour by Henry, her countryman. In the gardens, Mme Tinayre was struck by how quickly "real nature" had taken over its carefully manicured imitations. "The fittings of the greenhouses are rusting, water in the basins is stagnant, grass has started infesting the walkways, dead tree branches block the thicket." The palace functionaries

had all cleared out; the gardeners were on strike, because no one was paying them; and more than two thousand lemon trees in the orangery that needed to be brought out for the spring and summer were rotting indoors.[140] However, Henry soon enough found gainful employment in Cairo, managing the gardens of Egypt's last khedive, Abbas Hilmi Paşa (d. 1944). He would later sign his extensive review of the once grand gardens of Yıldız, which he published in the *Revue horticole* under "Ch. Henry, ex-jardinier en chef du Sultan, jardinier en chef de S. A. le Khédive, Palais du Koubbeh."[141] Henry found himself working for the Ottoman elite's biggest competition in aesthetic matters.

The khedive considered Koubbeh Palace his "real home," a sprawling site enfolding a bizarre Italo-Mediterranean palazzo outside Cairo, agricultural facilities, schools, stud farms, brick kilns, and extremely lucrative cotton plantations. Of the khedive's many lavish palaces in and around Cairo, this place, with its vast territories, best allowed him to fashion himself—like his nineteenth-century peers, including Abdülhamid—as a "gentleman farmer." He had started completely remodeling the gardens surrounding the palace when in 1905 he received the French-American reporter Amédée Baillot de Guerville for an interview. Their interaction stretched over a few days, during which Abbas Hilmi, after first unrolling "a large colored plan of his property, on which he showed [the reporter] the tour [they] were to take together," took the reporter to inspect his grand estate on foot, horseback, and by boat. Guerville begins his report of the tour by noting that "the garden was in a state of confusion," with "huge ditches, heaps of stones, and a hundred or so men busy with picks and shovels."[142] The khedive boasted that he had hired the "greatest master of modern gardening," the French landscape architect Édouard-François André (d. 1911), to refashion his leisure grounds. The head gardener of the city of Paris, André was also an accomplished botanical explorer in the Humboldtian tradition, who had traveled extensively in equatorial America to collect rare specimens, and a practitioner with immense global renown and reach, responsible for laying out private and public parks everywhere from Uruguay to Russia, and now Egypt.[143] Also a scientist, André edited *Revue horticole*, to which Henry contributed articles. They were probably in correspondence, facilitating the gardener's placement in the Koubbeh project André had undertaken.[144] Henry disappears from all records at the onset of the First World War. Later, the British deposed his patron and installed a sultanate in Egypt. Abbas Hilmi, who ended up having to side with the Ottomans during the war, had to spend his later years in exile in Switzerland. Both Yıldız after Abdülhamid and Koubbeh after Abbas Hilmi quickly began to serve their new inhabitants under new regimes, although the former site displayed considerably less pomp than the latter, which became the Egyptian kings' favorite residence throughout the twentieth century.

In brief, the influence of these landscapists during their lifetimes as foreign garden experts was to incite frenzied interest among Istanbul's landowners, along with competition in botany, horticulture, and their many accessory arts. Among the Ottomans, garden arts became an almost academic preoccupation and therefore provided employment to some foreign expatriate experts as well as their trained personnel. If some of the Germans

remained in the city as successful nursery owners, Albanian and Black Sea migrants working in the Ottoman imperial gardens dominated the gardening profession in the city's many market gardens. Throughout the nineteenth and early twentieth centuries, affluent Ottomans presided over the delicate contents of their own greenhouses, collected gardening books for their private libraries, imported rare seeds from around the world, and converted their overgrown groves into picturesque parks, which they dotted with ambitious rockeries and miniature pavilions. Since this hobby had become competitive, each of these sites reflected not only its designer's training and creative prowess but also its patron's discretion and tastes, which played an immensely important role in the variegated architectural profile of the city. No site ended up looking like another. Ultimately, however, Yıldız—first as the grove and gardens of the shoreline palace of Çırağan, then during its transformation under Abdülmecid and Abdülaziz, and in its final incarnation as the last Ottoman imperial palace complex—remained at center stage of the city's overall fascination with the picturesque and represented a transformative rediscovery of the Bosphorus's topography that would result in the city's play on novel, experimental, and ultimately refreshingly hybrid residential types.

A one-of-a-kind publication entitled *Rehber-i Umūr-ı Beytīye: Eve müteʿalliḳ bi'lcümle umūruñ rehberidir* (A guide to household matters: This is a guide to all matters related to the home), by Mehmed İzzet, a member of the palace's translation office, beautifully illustrates the trickle-down effect of consumption patterns from Yıldız's inhabitants to the capital's city dwellers. Inspired by North American and European practical-advice publications on home economics, the palace bureaucrat-cum-author intends to provide Ottoman families with useful information—from recipes, basic pharmacology, and medical triage to gardening and home building—the second of the three volumes tellingly distributed by the publisher of the *Women's Journal* (*Ḫānımlara Maḥṣūṣ Ġazete*). Although the structure of the guide may have followed that of European models, Mehmed İzzet deliberately uses specific examples from Istanbul to illustrate his entries. Among these, the renowned local examples for his entry on the "waterfall" (*çāġlāyān*) directly relate to horticultural competition among Istanbul's elite. Mehmed İzzet implies that his readers will instantly recognize the sites he enumerates alongside their owners, pointing to a landscaping obsession with imitating nature, and the niche jobs that emerged through this popular interest.

In the gardens of our city, beautiful waterfalls imitating natural cascades [*ʿādetā ṭabiʿī bir ḳāṣḳād taḳlīdi*] are constructed next to central pools or against walls in corners.... Moreover, in our city individuals called cascade builders [*ḳāṣḳā-dcı*] have made this their sole occupation and craft.

In Istanbul [Dersaʿādet], mostly in large mansions [*ḳonāḳ*] and some homes [*ev*], there are waterfalls both big and small. Especially the waterfall in the Kuruçeşme waterfront mansion [*yālı*] of the late Abdullah Efendi,[145] the head of calligraphers [*reʾīsüʾl-ḫaṭṭāṭīn*], and the ornamental fountain in the shape of a ruin [*selsebīl ḫarābesi*] from which the water drops down from fifty meters in the Çengelköy home of the late Selim Paşa, a high-ranking member of the artillery,

are considered to be among the most delightful works of this art [*enāfis-i āṣār-ı ṣanāʿiyye*].[146]

The origins and nationalities of these specialized landscapists, such as the cascade builders to whom Mehmed İzzet refers in passing, are unknown. However, the protonationalist rumblings heard at the turn of the century with respect to the empire's cultural agents—characterizing the class of architects, for example, as not "Ottoman," "Turkish," or "Muslim" but made up of religious minorities, Levantines, or foreign expatriates easily swayed by European trends—seem to have permeated the discourse on landscape design. Cevat Rüştü (d. 1939), an agriculture expert who wrote prolifically on the history of native garden culture during the War of Independence, laments that German and French nursery owners had blunted the traditional tastes of their local clients and that the "Turkish" gardening heritage was long lost.[147] According to the incensed author, the Koch brothers and Gustave Deroin promoted their skills as landscape engineers only to sustain a demand for expensive imported—and regionally inappropriate—seeds. It was high time, argues Cevat Rüştü, to set up agricultural and horticultural institutions, closely study past practices such as competition to produce rare flower specimens, and shed all foreign-inspired artifice. Although atavistic impulses and burgeoning xenophobic sentiment were serious and to some extent inevitable in the aftermath of the war and collapse of the empire, the publications that attained widespread popularity were the ones incredibly nostalgic about a past in which the gardens of waterfront mansions and townhouses were as important as the people inhabiting them.[148]

The Architecture of Yıldız Mountain

Neither sources from the nineteenth century nor modern studies reveal much about Yıldız's Alpine appearance, especially after its conversion into a walled palatial complex under Abdülhamid II.[1] Nonetheless, the site's topographic designation—it is recorded as a mountain (*ṭāġ*) in court registers from the first half of the nineteenth century onward—factored greatly into its later conceptualization as a hilltop palace. Typological choices made during the site's architectural transformation from hilltop retreat into garden palace were attuned to its topography. Although very little is known of the structures that constituted the Yıldız estate when it served as the summer retreat of the *valide*s in the early 1800s, Istanbul's upland imperial residences in that period were designed as pastoral hamlets to complement their rural woodland settings. For instance, the French poet Alphonse de Lamartine (d. 1869) was most taken by Abdülmecid's small hermitage in Ihlamur's verdant glen, which he likened to a Swiss valley.[2]

The Ottoman court's official practice of continuing to use the original designations of its buildings even after the structures themselves had been replaced by new ones suggests that at the very least a light wooden kiosk made of twigs (Çit Köşkü) was one of the Yıldız estate's dependencies (fig. 46).

An early member of Abdülhamid's scribal office, who would have experienced Yıldız before it was transformed into a palace complex, refers to this structure as "rustic" (*rustaî*) and likens it to a gossamer birdcage among lofty trees and delightful meadows.[3] For a French diplomat visiting the site at around the same time, the estate's main residential structure resembled a *Maison du champagne*, elegant and restrained in its luxury.[4]

Christian Sester's landscaping project on the "mountains of Çırağan" (Çerāġān ṭaġları) and the attempts made by queen mothers to irrigate their arid, rocky soil to transform the property into gardens ("ṭāġ üstü bāġ oldu") heralded a particular kind of building aesthetic under Abdülhamid's patronage. Soon after his relocation from Dolmabahçe Palace to Yıldız's hills, the sultan found the latter's extant masonry buildings as humid and airless as those of their statelier shoreline neighbor. Taking his cue from Yıldız's precipitous geography, its successful forestation under his immediate predecessors, and the prevalent medical sentiment that advocated for the salubriousness of higher altitudes,[5] Abdülhamid started to construct a multitude of wooden residential structures with pitched roofs, irregular plans, and intricate fretwork. These buildings reflected the Ottoman take on a pervading global taste for the

FIGURE 46
Vasilaki Kargopoulo, *Tchair kiosque à Yeldez* (possible precedent to the Çit Kiosk), 1878. İÜMK, 90407–0034.

"cottage style." From European spa towns and sanatoria to the Himalayan hill stations of the British Raj in India, the country cottage, due to its formal and stylistic versatility, had become the structure of choice, especially for affluent highland sanctuaries.[6] An imperial estate, Yıldız functioned as a summer retreat (ṣayfīye) for members of the Ottoman court, but the architectural vocabulary of its hilltop siting was definitively established during the reign of Abdülhamid.[7]

ABDÜLHAMID II, WOODWORK, AND A TASTE FOR TIMBER CONSTRUCTION

Captions in the Hamidian photograph albums and official palace documents often acknowledge the origins of these structures, which are referred to as chalets (phonetically recorded as şāles) or Swiss kiosks (İsviçre ḳaṣrı) (fig. 47). While some of these commissions overtly

imitated chalets, others were constructed to look like their close typological relatives: the Victorian cottages and suburban villas popularized by the Scottish landscapist John Claudius Loudon (d. 1843) in his numerous publications, such as *A Treatise on Forming, Improving, and Managing Country Residences* (1806) and *An Encyclopaedia of Cottage, Farm, and Villa Architecture and Furniture* (1836). These commercial publications fashioned the persona of the nineteenth-century gentleman farmer, advising him to balance his life in the city with studious work and contemplative rest in nature. The diverse residential specimens presented in these prescriptive volumes were suitable for all pockets.

Among the earliest "lifestyle" publications, these volumes propounded comfortable suburban living, and their sizable readership of estate owners rapidly shifted to one of amateur architects and landscape designers.[8] The villas and the dependencies reproduced within them were inspired by the notion of a scaled-down picturesque: the structures were surrounded by irregular terrains, while their internal configurations, intimately domestic, accommodated the individual needs of household members. They were playfully asymmetrical in their arrangement and easily customizable in the placement of their apertures, roofs, balconies, verandas, towers, and chimneys. Each particular style—noted in these publications as a building's "expression," the manifestation of the owner's taste in its exteriors—was defined by its architectural projections (e.g., French Mansard roofs, Swiss gables, Italianate towers) and its revivalist cladding (e.g., Gothic moldings, Tudor beams, Grecian columns). For Loudon, Gothic features prevailed among a wide array of historicist styles of domestic architecture; indeed,

FIGURE 47
"A view of the island and Swiss
pavilions, from the island,
inside the imperial garden"
(ḥadīḳa-ı şāhāneleri dāḫilinde
adadan ada ḳaṣr-ı ʿālīsiyle
isviçre ḳaṣr-ı hümāyūnlarınıñ
manẓarası), after 1894. Photographer unknown. İÜMK,
90552–0031.

Gothic during this period was deemed most indigenous to English architecture and saw a revival for most of the civic and ecclesiastical monuments of the Victorian era.[9]

Abdülhamid's Yıldız library collection evinces a preference for the publications of Victor Petit (d. 1874), Loudon's French counterpart. Petit was an archaeologist and restorer of medieval French architecture. The idiosyncratic way in which the Ottoman imperial librarian catalogued Petit's titles in Ottoman Turkish shows how the court and its patrons, builders, and craftsmen prioritized the content of these volumes.[10] The cataloguer did not translate the titles verbatim but instead created his own versions based on descriptions of the volumes' illustrations. This classification system enabled the user rapidly to identify the model for the building he was planning to construct. For instance, what must have been Petit's 1848 *Habitations champêtres; recueil de maisons, villas, châlets, pavillons, kiosques, parcs et jardins* was listed as "designs for kiosks, country homes, chalets, pavilions, gardens, arbors, and orangeries in different architectural styles" (Her ṭarz

FIGURE 48
The office of İzzet Holo Paşa (*center foreground*), in a photograph titled "The view in the direction of Beyoğlu from the conservatory of the new noble pavilion" (yeñi ḳaṣr-ı ʿālīniñ cāmekānından Beyoğlu cihheti görünüşü). Photographer and date unknown. İÜMK, 90552–0021.

frivolous, insubstantial, or downright ugly: "shacks" (baracche), as an Italian journalist would observe.[12] On the contrary, however, the sultan was deliberate in his selection of this pliable domestic typology. His architectural penchant for this type of building stemmed in part from the artisanal hobbies he had cultivated in his princely years. He was a skilled carpenter, producing intricate pieces of neo-Mamluk and Alhambresque furniture, from bookcases to cabinets that resembled small architectural objects, all adorned with tiers of cupolas, crenellations, niches, pilasters, reliefs, and columns.[13] His feel for wood—its properties and the potential it offered to render movement and detail on façades—must have contributed to his preference for these light residential structures that displayed their craftsmanship through their elaborate carpentry work. The buildings were legible to him—structures that he himself could easily construct.

mimarīde köşk, köy ebniyesi, şale, pavyon, bağçe, ḳemeriye, limonluḳ resimleri). The architectural words and phrases most frequently indexed by the Ottoman court in these compilations were "farms" (çiftlik), "models and plans for rural homes" (köy ebnīyesi modeli ve planları), and "chalets in the French, German, and Swiss styles" (Fransa, İngiltere ve İsviçrekārī şale). The most commonly indexed garden accessories were "waterfall," "cascade," or "rockery" (ḳasḳad), "pool" (ḥavuż), "arbor" (ḳamerīye), "aviary" (ḳuşluḳ), and "orangery" (limonluḳ). Throughout the late nineteenth and early twentieth centuries, versions of these architectural structures were assembled in the "most beautiful and airy" (en güzel ve en havadar) spots of the palace grounds.[11]

To some visitors to the palace, Abdülhamid's architectural choices appeared

Abdülhamid did not limit the use of this type to residential buildings. Often the sections of the palace in which these structures were most conspicuous were occupied by the government officials closest to the sultan. Indeed, his commissions often served as an affront to the monumental neoclassicism of the Azizian Mabeyn.[14] For example, he intentionally crowded the courtyard of the Mabeyn with two parallel pavilions in the form of unusually attenuated chalets: one for the office of the second scribe (the defunct kātib-i s̠ānī dāʾiresi, built solely for the sultan's right-hand man and director of his prized Hejaz railways project, İzzet Holo Paşa) (fig. 48),[15] and the other for his aides-de-camp (an extant structure built by D'Aronco).[16] These two gallery-like structures were simply laid out but delicately embellished; like exhibition pavilions, they bore repetitive sequences of dormer windows framed by lacy timber fretwork, each demarcating an apartment unit assigned to an individual or group of palace functionaries. Aware of Abdülhamid's crowding of the Mabeyn courtyard with his preferred buildings, his successor, Mehmed V, would order the removal of these "lousy timber offices from the square" (ahşaptan kötü kötü daireler).[17]

Under Abdülhamid's patronage, Ottoman courtly decorum continued to be reflected not only in the forms of buildings but also in their ornamental features. The building assigned to İzzet Holo Paşa was topped with pronounced gable crowns and displayed square wood panels of art nouveau floral carving between each of the second-story windows, below the roofline.[18] Its rich ornamentation echoed the *paşa*'s authority over the aides-de-camp, whose building was considerably more subdued. D'Aronco quoted these square, florid ornamental panels in the exterior decoration of the Küçük Mabeyn, which functioned as Abdülhamid's private study (described in chapter 1) (fig. 49). In these two structures, the Italian architect retained the domestic scale, predominant use of wood, and expressive ornamentation that Abdülhamid had sought in his palace commissions. But the architect also calibrated the nature and hierarchy of the relations between the sultan and his favored officeholders.

Reinforced by period photographs of Yıldız, the Mabeyn and the Hamidiye Mosque together presented the de facto face of the palace to the outside world. However, the lighter, smaller pavilions in this governmental courtyard best defined Abdülhamid's personal taste. In their longitudinal forms, the office of the second scribe and that of the aides-de-camp sat on a leveled platform on the ridge of the hill and ran along the gradient of the site's topography. Placed between the busy governmental court and the idyllic pleasure gardens of the harem, they formed a permeable wall dividing the public part of the palace from its private zones (map 2, nos. 36 and 54). The siting of the pavilion for the aides-de-camp as a "go-between" was especially well matched to the official role of its inhabitants, whose principal task was to carry imperial decrees between Abdülhamid's personal quarters and the scribal offices in the Mabeyn courtyard. These two pavilions also contained private sleeping quarters for the aides on guard duty. Accordingly, the structures' homelike scale and ornamental schema were deliberately chosen to fulfill the dual roles of workspace and accommodation.

FIGURE 49
Küçük Mabeyn, attributed to Raimondo D'Aronco, from the lake inside Yıldız's inner garden, after 1894. İÜMK, 90552–0005.

If the sultan meant to convey an architectural connection between his private workspace (D'Aronco's Küçük Mabeyn) and the studies of his closest officials through the flexible typology of the chalet, he sought a similar formal and functional unity between his private residential quarters (the *hususi daire*, built by the sultan's favorite *kalfa* Vasilaki and the members of the palace's carpentry atelier) and the Şale Kiosk (map 2, nos. 25 and 9).[19] These two buildings were built at around the same time and were meant to be identified as a unit, especially when the sultan hosted important guests. Abdülhamid's residential quarters, a Victorian villa with pitched roofs and balconies, were completed soon after the birth of his daughter Ayşe in 1887, while the first version of the Şale—listed as the old Şale Kiosk in the registers of the privy purse—appeared almost a decade earlier, around 1879.[20] As soon as these two imperial lodgings were complete, period photographs recorded their intentional formal dialogue, with the Victorian Gothic roofs of Abdülhamid's residence blending into the broad eaves of the Şale. One of these photographs, shot by the Swedish-expatriate photographer Guillaume Gustave Berggren (d. 1920) and reproduced in the widely read French journal *L'Illustration* in 1889, best illustrates the typological transformations that Abdülhamid undertook on his palace grounds (fig. 50). The photographer's chosen viewpoint in Ortaköy shows an awareness of the sultan's turn away from the Tanzimat-ordained bureaucratic classicism that had previously marked the site and toward a homier, more lighthearted, more picturesque idiom.[21] Through this image, the photographer also highlights the new form of diplomacy, increasingly intimate and informal, that Abdülhamid sought to

nurture with his foreign allies (especially the German emperor Wilhelm II, for whom the original Şale was twice expanded). The sultan's "home" was placed immediately next to that built for his European ally, the structures were formally alike, and together they occupied the highest and most privileged point of the palace complex. This pair of royal residential structures also participated in a contrarian architectural dialogue with neighboring structures that had once constituted the site's Tanzimat-era harem quarters.[22]

The Şale compound was accessed from a steep road along Ortaköy that led to its private entrance, labeled the "mountain gate" (*ṭaġ ḳapısı*) (map 3, no. 43). The building and its gardens most likely fell within the former grounds of the *valides*' mountaintop estate, based on the gate's designation, which hinted at its earliest users, once actively preoccupied with its topography. The Şale divided the compound into a section reserved for the imperial guest's *vita activa* and another for his *vita contemplativa*, modeled on the vocational duality expected of a visiting head of state, who would quickly identify with the space's functions. This structure—heavyset due to its many expansions—separated the flat and orderly ceremonial grounds to its north, which were used for military drills and as a shooting range by the privileged occupants of the compound, from the cascading Romantic gardens to its south. Unlike the sultan's *selamlık* ceremonies, the ones held inside the grounds of the Şale, in keeping with the scaled-down intimacy of its structures, were always kept private. The sultan accessed this compound through an enclosed private gallery between his personal quarters and the small palace theater without having to traverse the northwestern section of the

Vue générale du Palais de Réception dans le Parc Impérial de Yildiz

FIGURE 50
Guillaume Gustave Berggren,
photograph of Abdülhamid II's
private residence (*far left*) and
the Şale Kiosk (*center*), 1889.
İÜMK, 90815–0013.

complex to reach the ceremonial roadside gate.[23]

Abdülhamid's princes followed suit in lining up a multitude of small, irregularly shaped timber-framed chalets for their private use, which were built along the narrow but forested garden alongside their official row of apartments (map 2, no. 11).[24] Separated from each other by thickets of trees and landscaped cascades, the cozy kiosks gave the young princes individualized and personal zones "in nature," which their monolithic and interconnected apartments could not provide. Each of these chalets was unique

and reflected the interior arrangements and decorative choices of its owner. The buildings' walls were covered in murals depicting snowy landscapes, waterfalls, lakes, and mountain cottages. Although the 1894 earthquake directly attenuated the preference for these structures, their enabling of an autonomous family life sustained their popularity among members of the court for another decade. After Mehmed V and his court returned to Yıldız, his princes continued to reside in these kiosks with their immediate families.[25]

The family units that supported communal life in the Hamidian harem began to grow smaller, suggesting the court's turn toward a bourgeois lifestyle and habits: each of the married members would play house.[26] For instance, as soon as his private Victorian residence had been constructed, Abdülhamid moved in with only one of his seven wives, Müşfika Kadınefendi—replicating, as noted by their daughter Ayşe, a nuclear family life. Furthermore, the exteriors and interiors of Yıldız's domestic spaces under Abdülhamid were decorated separately to cater to their inhabitants. Şeker Ahmed Paşa, the beloved court aide to Abdülhamid's children and an established painter with a military-school background, decorated the increasingly privatized interiors of this family residence with his trademark still lifes, while the main room in Müşfika's quarters contained painted iconographic representations of the four seasons.[27]

The court's appreciation of seasonal changes in nature went hand in hand with the siting of the sultan's family residence. The murals of its interiors were intended to reflect the building's surroundings. From its large set of windows, Ayşe Sultan and Müşfika Sultan enjoyed commanding views of the sloping gardens and forests of the palatial complex. A series of rare photographs of this private residence and its landscaped gardens, from the private collection of the last caliph, Abdülmecid Efendi (d. 1944), further speak to the court's recognition of (and even obsession with) Yıldız's privileged topography and the theatrical atmosphere produced by the site's complementary buildings. These photographs are intriguingly selective in their depiction of the chalets in the sultan's private garden, under a climate felicitous to such types. It is as if a photographer had been quickly mobilized to capture the fleeting moment, crafting

a visual narrative that validated the typological choices of its patron. They are also among the best available representations of the sultan's defunct private residence when it was built in the late 1880s, providing close-ups of its windows, balconies, eaves brackets, and one-piece mahogany doors; the expensive materials used had a lasting impression on Ayşe Sultan (fig. 51).[28]

The Ottoman court's penchant for chalets, the globally popular architectural vocabulary of suburban villas, and for their accompanying landscape designs did not begin with Abdülhamid's reign. What was to become a trademark Hamidian typology in Yıldız's buildings began with a taste for its representation in planar art. Abdülaziz Efendi, a high-level bureaucrat in the judicial offices of the nineteenth century, who left behind a detailed but underused ethnographic study of the daily practices of Ottoman urban life, identifies Mahmud II's reign as a transformational period in terms of domestic details.[29] Abdülaziz Efendi observes that along with a complete overhaul of interior furnishings, such as the replacement of divans with clustered arrangements of sofas and chairs, there came a change in wall display in favor of framed or painted vignettes of cottages in floral and sylvan settings. The imperial Maslak estate, which is made up of two distinctly Loudonian Gothic villas, displays the best examples of ceiling paintings of waterfalls, snow-capped mountains, and rustic cabins.

Sultan Abdülmecid's decorative instinct was to exhibit all kinds of European products on tables and mantelpieces in his palace's public zones; these objects were paired with "colored lithographs, exhibiting views of Switzerland, hung in gold frames against

FIGURE 51
Abdülhamid II's private residence (*hususi daire*). Photographer and date unknown. MSİB Dolmabahçe Palace Museum, Abdülmecid Efendi Library Collection, Istanbul, K 86-30.

the brightly painted walls of many apartments [in Çırağan]."[30] The German aristocrat and prolific novelist Countess Ida von Hahn-Hahn, who was shepherded around the interconnected waterfront pavilions of Çırağan by the head gardener Sester in the 1840s, was quick to identify the central European source of these images, as she had only recently taken a tour of Switzerland's mountainous regions. Petit's lithographs of Alpine towns such as Bern, foregrounding chalets, shed some light on the kinds of framed images that the countess could have seen on the walls of Abdülmecid's palace. These lithographs (stripped from their original volumes and collected in new bindings) may very well

have been the ones exhibited in Çırağan's galleries (fig. 52).

The representational appeal of the Alps in the Ottoman court did not fade; Mehmed V and Vahdeddin, the two sultans succeeding Abdülhamid, quickly returned to Yıldız's high grounds at the start of their respective reigns. The collection of the School of Fine Arts (ṣanāyiʿ-i nefīse mektebi) contains watercolors by V[iktor] Olbrich, all dated between 1917 and 1918, which depict multistoried rustic chalets basking in sunlight, with exposed broad gables supporting consoles, balconies, and verandas.[31] One of these watercolors reveals that the basement below the first-floor veranda housed the homeowner's carpentry

workshop, containing wooden beams, wheel-
barrows, and window frames; this suggests
that the chalet had been crafted and remained
under construction by its owner.

The Ottoman court constructed its earliest chalets at the end of Abdülaziz's reign
(1861–76). In his political memoirs of 1912,
entitled *Mir'āt-ı Şu'ūnāt* (The mirror of
events), Abdülaziz's head scribe, Mehmed
Memduh Paşa (d. 1925), records the sultan's
patronage of a great many wooden imperial
pavilions along Istanbul's popular meadows
of Kağıthane, Alemdağı, and Karakulak.[32]
Probably built by Abdülaziz's court architect Sarkis Balyan, these structures were
placed in the most public spots in the city's
suburbs, apparently eliciting great censure,
as an attempt to conceal the empire's fiscal
downturn.[33] Abdülaziz's imperial pavilions in
Kağıthane—the grand cross-axial İmrahor,
with its heavy clipped gables, and the smaller
of the pair, Koşu—have survived only in photographs but were the earliest products of the
court's interest in and experimentation with
Alpine types (fig. 53). The mathematician-
illusionist Léon-François-Antoine Aurifeuille
(d. 1882), who went by his *nom de plume*
Alfred de Caston, published an interview
with Sarkis Balyan in which he listed all of
the buildings that the architect had constructed for the court, including a chalet on
Abdülaziz's farm in İzmit ("le chalet dans la
ferme du Sultan à Ismidt").[34] The predecessor
to Abdülhamid's Şale in Yıldız, referred to as
the "old" or "small" chalet in building-repair
documents, was probably also from the early
1870s. An expansion of the corpus of building types for pleasure and courtly pastimes
during Abdülaziz's time—Sarkis Balyan's list
mentions not only *kiosque*, *palais*, and *serail*
but also *maison*, *chalet*, and *ferme*—coincided

FIGURE 52 (*top*)
Victor Petit, *Châlet du canton
de Berne*, undated. Chromo-
lithograph. İÜMK, 93220.

FIGURE 53 (*bottom*)
Abdullah Frères, photograph
of Mirahor Kiosk at Kağıthane,
from the album "Palais Imperiaux," 1891. Ömer M. Koç
Collection.

with the increased circulation of volumes by draftsmen like Loudon and Petit, who introduced these new domestic specimens.

Portable versions of these structures arrived in the capital in iron-reinforced crates from northern European countries and Russia along with building manuals.[35] From simple hospital barracks to much fancier, fully fledged villas, these portable buildings quickly acquired the Ottoman Turkish designation *ḳābil-i naḳl* (and less frequently *seyyār* and *ḳurma*).[36]

Inspired by these imported architectural aids, residences large and small, portable and moored, modest and stately, began to compete with each other through their pronounced features and the ways in which they reflected the tastes of their owners. Yıldız's archives, albeit fragmented, cast light on how this flexible typology became popular among the members of the court and the bureaucratic class and how it opened up a vibrant world of home building—engendering a "boundlessness of design in a country free of European architectural tradition and conventions,"[37] as the architectural historian Doğan Kuban observes. In the nineteenth century Istanbul's property owners showed an incredibly lively interest in the appearance and expressiveness of their homes. If Abdülhamid's version of Yıldız was the trigger, the growing agency and creativity of a consumer class very quickly carried this eclecticism of types and features into the capital's domestic architecture.

NORDIC "FRAME HOUSES" AND THE GLOBAL TYPOLOGY OF DOMESTIC BLISS

The popular British architecture journal *The Builder* ran an inconspicuous series of correspondence between its readers in 1877.

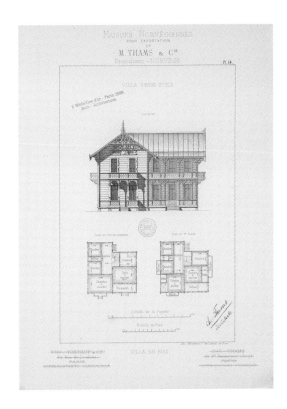

FIGURE 54
"Villa Swiss Style," after 1889. From M. Thams & Cie.'s catalogue of Norwegian houses. İÜMK, 92352.

An initial inquiry on the "effect of time" on a house "bodily imported from Norway" to Britain's West Country quickly instigated from the journal's transatlantic audience a flurry of arguments over its cost, durability, and comfort.[38] Within less than a decade, this seemingly marginal debate between builders and (potential) buyers of prefabricated timber houses had made such structures popular with consumers worldwide.[39] During this period Norway's leading architects and architectural theorists studied the ethnography of the generic Nordic house and—predictably for the time—lauded its medieval building techniques, style, and ornaments as the "Norse Renaissance."[40] However, this quintessential Nordic structure was quickly extracted from its primordial northern home and given a range of façades, from that of the Swiss chalet to that of the Tuscan villa (fig. 54).[41]

Newly recognizable to the railway traveler, tourist, and patient of European spa towns and sanatoria, the adaptable frame house became central to any country estate whose owner sought to bring home the health-giving mountain experience.

Nordic prefabs would become attractive not just to the prospering middle class but also to the European monarchy. In the same long journey of 1843 that brought her to Abdülmecid's Istanbul (and his Swiss lithographs), the Countess Ida von Hahn-Hahn visited a small cross-axial Nordic stave church with dragon-headed ridges in Brückenberg, Prussia. In her travelogue, she remarks on the fact that the Prussian monarch Friedrich Wilhelm IV (r. 1840–61)—a medieval-architecture enthusiast—had brought this twelfth-century building in pieces from Norway and reassembled it in his Silesian domains.[42] The Prussian monarchs' interest in the dragon-style Norwegian timber structures continued under the architectural patronage of Wilhelm IV's nephew Kaiser Wilhelm II.

The Prussian rulers' preservation of Norwegian churches was tied to the period's prevailing fascination with medieval building modes, which was in turn due to the growing conviction that such modes manifested the utmost structural legibility and rationality. Scholarly enthusiasts from kings to architects and preservationists studied medieval buildings and made the case that they should be understood as technological achievements and therefore emulated. Eugène-Emmanuel Viollet-le-Duc (d. 1879) was perhaps the most influential figure to seek in a nation's medieval past the origins of its building techniques, including the underlying materials and structural essence. His theories were incorporated into the scientific quests undertaken by various empires to analyze and restore their medieval architectural heritage and thereby forge a national architectural idiom. Viollet-le-Duc's polygenetic classification of historical dwelling types allotted the Aryans, the progenitors of the European nations, buildings made of wood. This connection, based on natural affinities, incited Prussian rulers to covet "savage" Nordic churches but also to commission secular variants like their monumental, if deliberately rustic, log cabins.[43]

The Ottomans were equally caught up in locating their nation's architectural apogee in its medieval past.[44] Viollet-le-Duc's theories were introduced to the official Ottoman architectural discourse through his disciple Léon Parvillée, a ceramics specialist recruited to restore fourteenth- and fifteenth-century buildings in Bursa, the empire's first capital.[45] Although very little is known about their production, the earliest prefabricated structures to be built in Istanbul, based on the designs of the Levantine-Italian architect Giovanni Battista Barborini with modifications by Parvillée, were a mosque, a bath, and a pavilion for the Ottoman display at the 1867 International Exhibition in Paris.[46] Parvillée's assessment of early Ottoman monuments as having been constructed based on universal geometric principles, and his alignment of their forms with those of the European Gothic tradition, permeated the language of a state-sponsored architectural treatise produced for the 1873 World Exposition in Vienna, *Uṣūl-ı Miʿmārī-i Oṣmānī / L'architecture ottomane*. The formal and historicized interconnections established by *Uṣūl*'s collaborators between early-Ottoman monuments and Spanish "Arab" and Gothic traditions were studiously displayed in the formal and ornamental schemas of the Azizian and later Hamidian mosques.

If structures like the Aksaray Valide Mosque (1871) and the Hamidiye Mosque (1886) offer ecclesiastical examples of this medievalizing discourse, the court's novel palatial structures were distilled versions of the same Romantic desire to express truth, transparency, and virtue in one's dwelling. Loudon's and Petit's villa specimens were rooted in the period's idealization of medieval building traditions. Although the Ottomans may not have intellectualized their residential types as intensely as *Uṣūl* did the imperial monuments, readers of these architectural books were aware of the cult of virtuous mountain peasants and their timeless hearty habitations. Indeed, before the decision was made to produce an exact replica of Ahmed III's fountain for the Vienna Exposition, Pietro Montani, a member of *Uṣūl*'s production team, prepared a preliminary project comprising four buildings, including a farmhouse modeled after "traditional peasant homes in Thrace and the Balkans" and an urban Ottoman house.[47] Although the plans for these two buildings have not survived, it is clear that *Uṣūl*'s intellectuals were deep in thought about not only the form of the empire's civic architectural monuments but also the aesthetic conventions of its domestic dwellings.

Many empires may have been eager to retrofit the Gothic tradition to their architectural heritage for its pristine geometric rationality, but wooden mountain cabins held a universal validity and appeal of another spiritual kind: the features of these structures were found to resemble the human anatomy. An American reader of Viollet-le-Duc, after taking a tour of the most prominent prefabricated chalet producers in Switzerland, composed a guidebook on that building type, which he prefaced with the French theorist's espousal of the Alpine home as the *Ur*-form of domestic typology.[48] To this chalet aficionado, it was not surprising that chalets were found over a wide swath of the world's highlands, because they replicated the human form.

> The internal adjustment of the châlet ... is that of an enlarged and simplified human body. The body itself is a home; with its organs, machines, tubes, it may be said to be a moving home for the human spirit; and in the arrangements which Nature has planned for its adaptation to life....
>
> Externally, too, ... the part of the châlet which comes in contact with the earth being the purely utilitarian part, and the topmost part being the part of thought and retirement; the part between being that of the ordinary mechanics and intercourse of daily life.
>
> Moreover, it is symmetrical and in its alternation of voids and wall spaces, gaily decked with nosegays, its bands and strips of wooden lacework or embroidery, its overhanging bowers, the element of feminine humanity is strongly marked. Standing on the mountainside, upright, its face shaded by the wide brim of its hat-like gable, its eyes peering across the wide valleys, the châlet has a look surprisingly and mysteriously human.[49]

THE FIRST PORTABLE STRUCTURES IN THE OTTOMAN DOMAINS

Among the European imperial patronage networks of the industrializing age, Mahmud II's court was exemplary in recognizing the

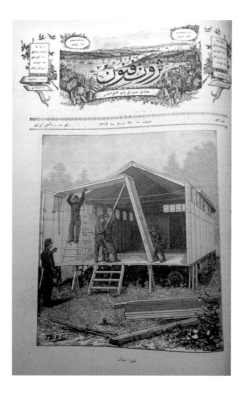

potential of prefabricated buildings to answer the growing needs of the public. In his chronological history, Gilbert Herbert identifies Mahmud's commission of an iron corn mill from the Scottish shipbuilder William Fairbairn (d. 1874) as among the first of such large-scale purchases.[50] At the forefront of the development of modular building technologies, owners of English shipbuilding companies manufactured iron-framed greenhouses in the aftermath of the construction of Paxton's iconic Crystal Palace in 1851. Continuing his interstitial role as cultural agent, Fethi Ahmed Paşa, who had previously recruited Sester, purchased one from London's Westwood, Baillie and Company for Abdülmecid's expanded Çırağan gardens.[51] The official Ottoman documentation of this purchase referred to the building as a "crystal palace" (*billūr sarāy*).

The Ottomans' third encounter with prefabs, which was a consequence of the Crimean War (1853–56) and therefore much more publicly visible, was occasioned by the erection of the British Renkioi (Erenköy) Hospital. The hospital complex, composed of a large group of wooden and canvas wards, was designed by the British civil engineer Isambard Kingdom Brunel (d. 1859) and was produced, delivered, and assembled in only five months.[52] Replete with ventilation and drainage systems to prevent infectious diseases, the structure was built on the initiative of Florence Nightingale when contagion became rampant in the Selimiye Barracks, initially designated for the treatment of wounded soldiers.

The practicality of these portable structures remained of public interest into the second half of the nineteenth century. In 1892 *Ṣervet-i Fünūn* made the assembly of a prefab its cover story.[53] The full-page image under the caption "Cardboard Construction" (Muḳavvā İnşāʾāt) depicts soldiers hoisting up part of the pitched roof of a bare-bones military barracks, temporarily raised on wheels, which was intended as a hospital (fig. 55). The roof and walls appear to have been delivered in panels that were then inserted into frames (hence their earlier designation in *The Builder* as "frame houses"). Parts of the frame remain in the image's foreground. The image also highlights the fact that no additional tools were required for the construction of the barracks: each panel rested on the last with no visible hinge or joinery, and the soldiers worked with nothing but a few simple scaffolds.

In its cover story, the journal promoted this new building material—essentially "paper pressurized into attaining the hardness of wood"—as that which would finally supplant iron, which had hitherto been at the forefront of the production of "exemplary works of [today's] civilization" (demirden numūne-i medenīyet).[54] Lightness and portability, the cover story argues, would soon take over from the monumental heaviness that had marked the century's ironclad building projects, from railways and bridges to the "famous tower in Paris" (Paris'iñ meşhūr ḳūlesi). It is reasonable to assume that this materials-based face-off was put to the test in the 1889 International Exposition of Paris, which is referenced in the report in *Servet-i Fünūn* and at which a Norwegian village constructed of timber-framed houses won its builders many gold medals and, for the first time, patents for their portable inventions.[55] Mindful that the prefab could easily be disparaged as a makeshift folly, the Ottoman report emphasizes the efficacy of such structures in responding to urgent civic needs by, for example, enabling the swift erection of hospitals. The report's anonymous news writer whimsically adds that prefabs allowed buyers to "change the location of their homes whenever they desired a change of scenery" (ḫāne ṣāḥibi ṣıḳıldıġı gibi evini söküb başḳa ṭarafa götürüyor ne āʿlā), likening this process to "turtles' carrying their homes on their backs" (ḳāblunbāġalar gibi meskeni ṣırṭında ṭaşımaḳ).

Within just a few years of the publication of this news item on light and portable construction, the Ottomans had incorporated the wartime technology into their daily lives. To treat the soldiers who fought on the Macedonian front of the 1897 Greco-Ottoman War, Abdülhamid set up an elaborate prefabricated hospital much like its predecessor Renkioi on the uninhabited and elevated flatlands between the Balmumcu Pavilion, an early nineteenth-century upland

imperial estate, and his palace.[56] Named Yıldız Hospital, it was made up of fourteen barracks and employed more than three hundred people, including a head surgeon, six doctors, and twenty-three pharmacists. It is unknown how long this large complex remained intact and in the service of Istanbul's military personnel. However, *Servet-i Fünūn*'s firsthand coverage of the site in 1897 indicates that it provided high-quality care, complete with an X-ray machine.[57] The journal's photographs suggest that the hospital's most important building was its operating pavilion, which boasted large windows, dado-like ornamental panels that resembled small hanging carpets on its entrance façade, and faux rusticated pilasters (fig. 56). It is unclear whether these buildings were constructed locally or imported. However, the stylistic similarities between the operating pavilion and the pavilion later assembled by Ottoman craftsmen to stage the first meeting of Abdülhamid and the Qajar shah Muzaffar al-Din hint at the possibility that it was locally built.

If wars provided the opportunity for prefabrication to demonstrate to the Ottomans its efficacy in producing quick and affordable shelter, the Suez Canal enabled the France-based company at the helm of this colossal engineering project to present to the Egyptian viceroys their own imported chalets at the end of the 1850s.[58] Ferdinand de Lesseps, the French project developer, installed his own in the newly inaugurated town of Ismailia.[59] The French engineers involved in the project, too, lived in little chalets set inside gardens in the three station towns along the canal's north–south: Port Said, Ismailia, and Suez.[60] The unconventional French gift to the Egyptian viceroys,

FIGURE 56
"The operating room belonging to the Yıldız Hospital, among the charitable institutions of the Sultan Yıldız Hospital" (mü'essesāt-ı ḫayriyet-i ġāyāt cenāb-ı ḫilāfetpenāhīden olan Yıldız ḫastaḫānesiniñ ʿamelīyāt dāʾiresi). From *Servet-i Fünūn*, no. 331 (1897).

مؤسسات خيريت غايات جناب خلافتپناهيدن اولان يلديز خسته‌خانه‌سنك عمليات دائره‌سی)

Le pavillon d'Opération de l'Hopital de Yildiz

a chalet surrounded on all sides by a large iron veranda, was erected on high ground next to Timsah Lake in Ismailia to oversee the project and host the frequent visits of Europeans. With its prominent veranda intended as a viewing station—a circumambient belvedere adorned with dainty woodcarving and iron filigree work—this version soon emerged as the preferred style of prefabricated building for colonial settlements (fig. 57).[61]

Christian Marius Thams (d. 1948), the principal Norwegian supplier of portable structures to Yıldız, presented this model as the colonial prototype in his mail-order catalogues (fig. 58). Thams, a wealthy mining heir and ambitious nineteenth-century industrialist with training in architecture, operated the first large hydroelectrically powered mill for prefabricated buildings. Aside from his entrepreneurial ventures, he served as the Belgian consul general in Norway, and when the Belgian king Leopold II turned the Congo into his personal colony,[62] it was Thams's prefabs that supplied the colonial officers with the comfort and warmth of home.[63] His *petites villas en bois* of the Free State of Congo are displayed extensively in his catalogue, along with other variants, which were configured for functions required by a colonial settlement, such as hospitals, schools, military barracks, and churches, all bearing the flag of the Free State on their roofs and set in the tropical vegetation of the Congo Basin.

Yıldız's architectural patrons quickly added another supplier to their lineup of exporters. A Russian polymath engineer/physician by the name of Shcherbakov (Щербаковъ), who appears to have owned a facility producing mostly concrete building parts in Odessa,[64] sold them a chalet for the palace's harem gardens. Although the building has not survived, Shcherbakov's chalet catalogue is listed among the books in the palace library (*Odesa Şehiri'nde Sitterbāḳof'uñ şale ṭarzında ḳābil-i naḳl köşkler "imāline maḫsūs fabriḳası ḳataloġu*),[65] along with a document tabulating the payments to workers employed in the chalet's installation. This enterprising Russian engineer first found patronage in the Ottoman court by making a case for building a prefabricated hospital that

FIGURE 57 (*top*)
Édouard Riou, *Chalet du vice-roi*. From Marius Fontane, *Voyage pittoresque à travers l'isthme de Suez* (1870). Getty Research Institute, Los Angeles (1389-108).

FIGURE 58 (*bottom*)
"Small wooden villas for the Independent State of Congo," after 1889. From M. Thams & Cie.'s catalogue of Norwegian houses. İÜMK, 92352.

would specialize in the recently discovered treatment of diphtheria. Within three years of presenting his case and receiving permission for its construction, he had assembled the pavilion in the harem quarters ("Mösyö Çerbākof maʿrifetiyle ḳurulan köşk"), but Ottoman officials lost track of him shortly thereafter.[66] It took the office of the grand vizier five years to confirm his death and recover the amount paid to him in advance of the hospital's construction—700 Ottoman lira of 1,000 allotted for its completion.

When a functional prefabricated building such as a hospital was exported to the Ottoman territories, its patrons often requested a fancier version for their personal enjoyment. The khedive Ismail Paşa did not limit himself to his chalet in Suez but installed another—with lacelike woodwork and a central sun

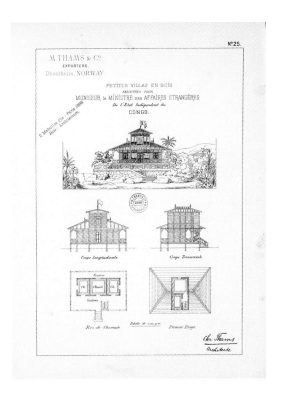

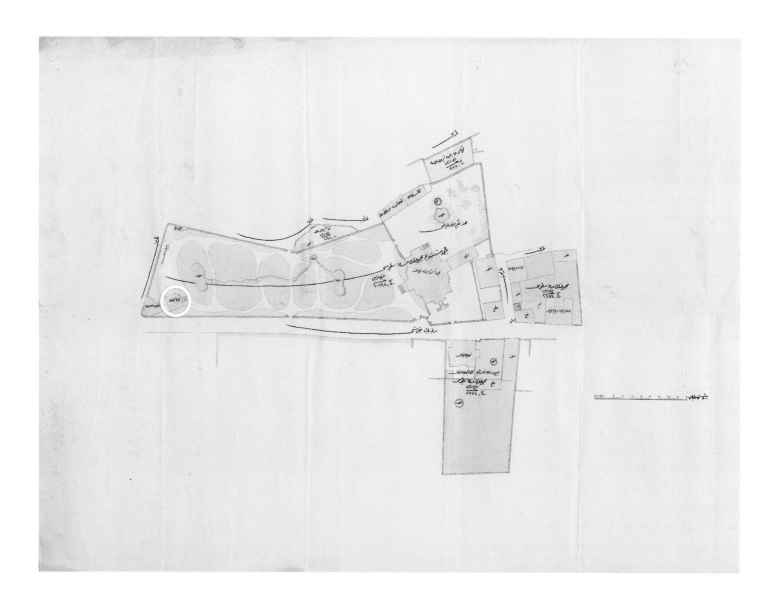

FIGURE 59
Beşiktaş garden estate for a palace official, with a prefabricated kiosk (*kurma köşk*) in a corner of the garden (*lower left*). BOA, Plk_p_02036.

motif on its gable louver—at the highest point of his English gardens in Istanbul's Emirgan. Gingerbread versions of this colonial morphology quickly became the quintessential accessories to Istanbul's hilly estates. A map illustrating the construction of an urban mansion (*konak*) and its garden offers a rare and early example of such a prefab in a landscaped garden setting, intended to replicate Yıldız on a smaller scale (fig. 59). Undertaken on an imperial order, a new *konak* was built alongside the Serencebey ramp on the Ortaköy side of the palace for an unidentified royal appointee.[67] The cross-axial main residence sits at the top of the ridge of an elongated plot overlooking two lakes joined by a miniature river and pool. At the other end of the garden rests a "prefabricated kiosk" (*kurma köşk*) and its later extension alongside a greenhouse for flowers and an orangery.

The chalet that Abdülhamid purchased from Thams was assembled on a platform immediately above a waterfall-fronted, faux-stone nymphaeum, one of the centerpieces of the sultan's heavily landscaped private garden and the point of embarkation for his electric boat. All that remains of this structure is photographs and catalogue renditions in Yıldız's library collection. An incomplete and undated *defter* from the imperial treasury that itemizes the hardware locally procured for the structure's assembly calls it the "Swedish pavilion" (*İsveç kaşrı*).[68] A photograph taken from across Abdülhamid's artificial lake, commissioned to foreground the pavilion over the nymphaeum, helpfully shows that this structure was one of the first to be built by Abdülhamid after the completion of the landscaping project in his harem gardens (fig. 60). It may even have initiated the sultan's architectural program of countering Yıldız's preexisting Tanzimat masonry buildings with his preferred type.

Abdülhamid lived in this prefabricated cottage while his *kalfa* Vasilaki and the palace's carpentry atelier devised plans to build the sultan a more permanent Victorian residence in its place.[69] Attempts to identify the sultan's residence within the palatial complex—which often evince something close to an obsession with where he might have slept—mistake this temporary structure for its more permanent successor. This Norwegian import served as a place marker and partly also as a small-scale replica for the statelier building that followed. Thams's prefabricated design lent its irregular plan, as well as its gable and finial motifs, to the private residence that the sultan would soon inhabit with his nuclear family.

Imports as three-dimensional exempla and their sales catalogues were studied and used as building aids by the architects, carpenters, and contractors of the court.

FIGURE 60
Garden view of the Swedish pavilion. İÜMK, 779-34-0057.

Depending on the financial scope of an imperial architectural project, the builders would be asked to construct chalets in the capital's local building facilities or import them directly from European factories. For instance, when planning to institute a zoological garden in the capital, Abdülhamid commissioned Vasilaki to draw up a

FIGURE 61 (*top*)
"Châlet no. 222." From Kaeffer & Cie.'s catalogue, *Châlets suisses bois découpés* (1884). İÜMK, 92007.

FIGURE 62 (*bottom*)
Swiss (Şale, later Cihannüma) Pavilion, undated. İÜMK, 90469–026.

feasibility report on the chosen site, providing a detailed survey of the layout of the zoo and plans for structures crucial to a pedagogically yet palatably rustic environment for his public, like Paris's acclaimed Jardin d'acclimatation. Vasilaki's site survey of 1885 for this eventually unrealized project demands that the little pavilions be made of "natural wood" (*natürel odun*) and that the overall effect of the place be created in the "English manner" (*İngilizkâri*).[70] The imperial decree mandates that the requisite timber structures be acquired from Switzerland rather than produced and assembled in Istanbul's imperial cannon foundry in Tophane should the former option prove cheaper.

The newer chalets erected in Yıldız's gardens, however, those installed soon after the arrival of the Norwegian and Russian imports, began to diverge from their catalogue versions. This indicates that the later chalets were most likely built in the palace's workshops or the sawmills of the imperial arsenal and foundry. The chalet known today as the Cihannüma Pavilion, which rests on the wall separating Abdülhamid's harem garden from the vast park below, was modeled after one from a Franco-Swiss company called Kaeffer Cie. et Successeurs. The marginalia on Yıldız's copy of Kaeffer's 1884 catalogue reveals the court's selection: the page containing prefab no. 222 is earmarked with a placeholder that contains a handwritten note indicating its selection (fig. 61).[71] In its courtly adaptation, this simple, midrange chalet with two floors and two fireplaces was raised on an elevated ground floor laid out in stone, with narrow imperial stairs in front and winged extensions on its sides (fig. 62). Kaeffer's most expensive prefab (200,000 francs), a twin chalet listed as containing four rooms on each floor, twelve fireplaces, two attics, a boudoir, a salon for the madam's flowers, and billiard and smoking rooms for the monsieur, was built on Yıldız's grounds with visible modifications.[72] The builders retained this structure's stylistic eclecticism. They replicated its Gothicized rooflines, ridge crenellations, and baroque oeil-de-boeuf windows, eliminated an entire floor and two side entrances, and added two small side balconies on the second floor and rounded out the ones on its main façade (figs. 63–64).

In its gender-specific allotment of social spaces to the male inhabitant and private ones to the female inhabitant, this particular chalet in Kaeffer's catalogue resembled the traditional layout of large Ottoman mansions of the period, in which a central room, or *sofa*, divided public from private quarters. The fact that the chalet had a familiar layout but preserved the intimacy indicative of a nuclear family must have appealed to Abdülhamid. The sultan had sought an analogous interior configuration in designing his private residence, in which his wife had her own above-mentioned boudoir-like quarters.

The devastating 1894 earthquake turned these chalets into an immediate and appealing necessity inside the palace.[73] Ayşe Sultan reports that her father commissioned a Japanese-style kiosk to be placed above an artificial grotto in the palace's harem gardens. She recalls that this single-room structure, made from bamboo, was used by her father as a bedroom (fig. 65).[74] The bamboo for and construction of the now-defunct structure have been attributed to a Japanese teacher of tea ceremonies with whom Abdülhamid maintained close ties, who resided in Istanbul during a period of increased diplomatic relations between the two empires, ran a

Japanese goods store for more than twenty years, and supplied the sultan with all sorts of rare objects from the Land of the Rising Sun—a land similarly beset by frequent earthquakes.[75]

The postearthquake findings of an international group of experts provide further evidence of the overall downscaling of Yıldız's Hamidian structures and of the court's increasing preference for the wooden chalet form.[76] A comprehensive initial report written under the leadership of Demetrios Éginitis, director of the Athens Observatory, expresses astonishment at the sturdiness of wooden buildings ("aḫşāb ḫāneler zelzeleye ḫayretbaḫş

FIGURE 63
"Châlet no. 274." From Kaeffer & Cie.'s catalogue, *Châlets suisses bois découpés* (1884). İÜMK, 92007.

Kiosque Impérial à Yildiz

FIGURE 64 (top)
"An imperial pavilion at Yıldız" (Yıldız'da
kāʾin ḳaṣr-ı hümāyūn), undated, attributed
to Abdullah Frères. Abdul-Hamid II Collection, Library of Congress, Washington, DC,
Lot 9534, no. 14.

FIGURE 65 (bottom)
Japanese Kiosk in the inner garden of Yıldız,
undated, attributed to Vasilaki Kargopoulo.
İÜMK, 90407–0034.

derecede ṭayanmışlardır") and proposes that "the majority of the buildings having been of wood has reduced the scale of the calamity" (ekṣer ḫāneleriñ aḫṣāb olması meṣāʾibiñ az olmasına ḫiẕmet etmiştir).[77] In contrast, "the well-built, beautiful and new brick and stone structures with iron reinforcements had collapsed" (āʿlā yapılmış güzel ve yeñi ve ḥatta demirler ile baġlanmış olan kārgīr ḫāneler münhedim olmuşdur).[78] Two little-known chalets with their own gardens and glasshouses, nestled behind the pavilion of the heir apparent in Dolmabahçe, were constructed by Abdülhamid for his brothers Mehmed Reşad and Kemaleddin,[79] and another, with a prominent second-story balcony, was assembled for Abdülaziz's son Yusuf İzzeddin in the gardens of the Ferʿiye Palaces.[80] The Beşiktaş mansion of Gazi Osman Paşa, the sultan's chief chamberlain, was outfitted with a chalet—whose likely plan is recorded without the owner's name in figure 59—that was attached via a windowed gallery (cāmekān) to a previous prefabricated structure with ogee and horseshoe arches (see fig. 71).[81]

SCALED-DOWN ARCHITECTURE, INTIMATE DIPLOMACY

Abdülhamid began to build "bijoux," one-room pavilions, not only for his private use or for earthquake safety but also to house intimate diplomatic encounters.[82] The best-known example of this ceremonial practice is his erection of a kiosk next to the imperial Hereke carpet factory in İzmit to receive the German emperor Wilhelm II and empress Augusta-Victoria on their second visit to the Ottoman lands, in 1898.[83] The extant Hereke Kiosk, a one-floor tripartite structure with wiry bracketed double columns that hold up broad eaves, and two low-drummed, lead-covered Ottoman domes on either end, is believed to have been built in Yıldız's ateliers in preparation for the visit of the German royalty.[84]

However, an article published in *Le Monde illustré* on the emperor and empress's time in the factory complex, with images provided by the Swedish photographer Berggren, foregrounds a building that is morphologically a likelier candidate for the Yıldız-manufactured prefab (fig. 66). The photograph's caption identifies this pavilion as the banqueting hall of the Hereke Kiosk. Perched on a platform resting on piles driven into the shore and shallow water immediately adjacent to the domed kiosk, this new structure was a cross between the hospitals of Yıldız and Renkioi but had the intricately carved gable decorations of the chalet designated for İzzet Holo Paşa or the Japanese Kiosk built after the earthquake. If, indeed, the Hereke Kiosk had been the pavilion prefabricated for the imperial visit, the article would surely have included it among the documentary photographs. The Hereke Kiosk seems to have served rather as an embarkation station (formally analogous to Istanbul's small Neo-oriental ferry stations, such as Haydarpaşa), while the simpler chalet—quickly assembled for the occasion—hosted the imperial entourage for lunch after their visit to the factory.

A small pavilion was also custom built in Yıldız's Şale compound to receive the Qajar ruler Muzaffar al-Din Shah on the last leg of his European tour, in 1900. Before his arrival, the shah had requested that his Istanbul visit be modeled after the highly publicized itinerary of the German emperor's most recent stay.[85] The Şale and its gardens were prepared to welcome him, along with the capital's cannons, the imperial battalions

FIGURE 66
The prefabricated kiosk in Hereke assembled for the visit of the German emperor and empress. From *Le Monde illustré* (1898).

and band, and the sultan's dispatch vessel İzzeddin. However, for Abdülhamid, who had renewed his role as caliph of the Sunni Muslims, hosting the Shia shah proved more difficult. How should his initial encounter with a Muslim ruler of an opposing denomination be arranged? To stress his caliphal role, Abdülhamid sent his princes and viziers to the Ortaköy dock rather than greet the shah himself. The relationship between the two states had soured since the growth of anti-monarchic sentiment in Iran, which Qajar statesmen blamed on the political activism of Sayyid Jamal al-Din al-Afghani (d. 1897), who had sought asylum in Abdülhamid's court, and which they linked to the assassination of Muzaffar al-Din's predecessor, Nasir al-Din Shah, in 1896. In addition, Iran's political allegiance to Russia in the Russo-Ottoman War

FIGURE 67
Persian ('Acem) Kiosk at
Yıldız. Photographer and date
unknown. İÜMK, 90508–0008.

of 1877–78 must have contributed to the ultimate reluctance displayed by the Ottomans in staging the encounter between sultan and shah. The sultan greeted the shah in a boxy single-room structure with art nouveau trimmings called the Persian Pavilion ('Acem Köşkü), which would serve as a neutral, makeshift stage for their complicated alliance (fig. 67). It is no wonder, then, that the shah remarked in his travelogue on the building's placement at the "threshold" (*sar-dar*) of a garden, or that the photograph albums commissioned by the Ottoman court gave the structure the impartial designation of "the meeting spot" (*mülāķāt maḥalli*).[86]

A photograph album depicting Wilhelm II's large hunting lodge in the verdant East Prussian forest of Rominten (today a logging camp between Poland and Russia) may also have intensified Abdülhamid's interest in chalets and their portability.[87] Enclosed within a carved-wood binding featuring

reliefs of deer antlers, rifles, pine cones, and leaves, the album offers a tour of the grounds, with photographs showing the building from every angle (e.g., fig. 68). Once the gift had arrived from Germany, it was prepared for the sultan's private perusal. An Ottoman representative who had visited the site inserted extensive Ottoman Turkish captions below photographs describing the architectural vignettes. One of these captions reveals that the building's "premade parts were bought from Norway" (işbu köşküñ bi'l-cümle aķsāmı Norveç'den ḥāżır olaraķ celb olunmuşdur).[88]

Behind the widespread popularity of these buildings was an idealization of rural life, of stoic peasants and their unadulterated connection with nature. These Romantic sentiments had emerged through novels, plays, and philosophical theories foregrounding Alpine settings.[89] To the developers and consumers of chalets, the organic morphology and materials of rustic residences reflected the savage nobility of their original inhabitants. Affluent estate owners and royalty identified with protagonists like the philosopher-huntsman of Friedrich von Schiller's play *William Tell* of 1804 and fashioned their recreational surroundings in the manner of these figures revived from medieval annals. It is no surprise that the Ottoman captions also inform the album's viewer of Wilhelm II's inspiration: "The Emperor built this lodge in the likeness of peasant homes after his visit to Norway, where he encountered and liked these structures beyond measure" (İmparāṭor hażretleriniñ Norveç'e ettiği seyāhat esnāsında ziyādesiyle beğendiği Norveç köylüleri ḥānelerini taķlīden cesīm bir orman dāḫilinde inşā ettirdikleri Rominten Köşkü).

Holm Hansen Munthe, a prolific Norwegian architect credited with the revival of the dragon style from Viking history during the Nordic Renaissance, was awarded the commission to fashion a prefab as a massive hunting lodge for the Kaiser's hideaway.[90] Indiscriminately replicating versions of Muntheian architecture, the industrial impresario Thams would then include a look-alike of this wide H-plan log cabin in his catalogue, as a reproducible "Norwegian casino—style" house (fig. 69).

Wilhelm II's interest in Norway's medieval history went beyond a mere hobby. He was an avid reader of its legendary sagas and was particularly fascinated by the thirteenth-century mythic figure Frithjof. A mammoth statue of Frithjof was erected in Norway under Wilhelm's patronage, and epic poems, operas, and symphonies were composed based on the legends surrounding his life. Wilhelm's near self-identification with this figure was not lost on Abdülhamid, who received a leather-bound and illustrated German translation of the *Frithiofs saga* (published as an epic poem in the 1820s by the Swedish classicist Esaias Tegnér) from the German ruler.[91]

Aside from the catalogue, the gifted photograph album, and the illustrated saga, Ahmed Midhat Efendi (d. 1912), Abdülhamid's most trusted *literatus*, fueled the sultan's interest in the expressive capacity of portable residences. In 1889 Abdülhamid sent Ahmed Midhat to participate in the International Congress of Orientalists in Stockholm.[92] The product of Ahmed Midhat's observations, his monumental and richly detailed travelogue *Cevelānnāme* (An account of wanderings), which was both presented to the sultan and published, contains a minute description of the oldest Norwegian portables.[93] Urged on by the organizers of the congress, Ahmed Midhat and

روشنده که شکلك امیر الوسع تابر بابر نظره عوسی . نرو دیرهامی

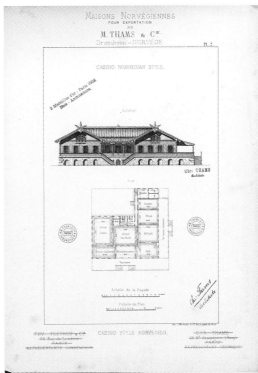

FIGURE 68 (*top*)
View of the prefabricated lodge in Rominten, undated. Photographer unknown. İÜMK, 91380—0008.

FIGURE 69 (*bottom*)
"Casino Norwegian Style," after 1889. From M. Thams & Cie.'s catalogue of Norwegian houses. İÜMK, 92352.

نشان طاشنده ثريا پاشا قوناغی وكوشكی

سر لایی علی سامی خور دیله

matches the chalet lithographs in the sultan's library. For Ahmed Midhat, these examples of Norway's oldest buildings were, in their solidity (*metānet*) and constitution (*hey'et*), ultimately far superior to any of Istanbul's masonry structures. The longevity of their woodwork was even on par with that of the East's Greco-Roman city of Palmyra (which the journalist refers to by its Arabic name, Tadmür) and the Achaemenid capital Persepolis, two sites renowned for their stone reliefs.

HAMIDIAN BUREAUCRATS AND THEIR HOUSE AND GARDEN COMPETITION

The new courtly embrace of portable architecture quickly spilled out of the palace and into the domestic lives of the Ottoman bureaucratic elite.[94] Many of the sultan's ministers followed suit in adorning their newly appointed properties (all in the neighborhood of Nişantaşı, near Yıldız) with miniature pavilions during their service. Yanko Ioannidis, the palace architect, constructed the mansion of the grand vizier Küçük Said Paşa, also located in this bureaucratic town, in the image of the palace, comprising a harem building, a separate *selamlık*, and a series of chalets for the officials under Said's viziership.[95] In the gardens of his urban villa, Ahmed Süreyya Paşa (d. 1923), Abdülhamid's head clerk, added an eccentric turreted octagonal pavilion, which he later surrounded with greenhouses (fig. 70). On the harem grounds of Kamil Paşa (d. 1913), a four-time grand vizier from Cyprus, another, more traditional chalet was perched over a grotto.[96] There were even more-eccentric examples, such as a two-floor semicircular pavilion with ogee- and horseshoe-arched windows and an encircling veranda on the Beşiktaş estate of Gazi Osman Paşa (mentioned above) (fig. 71).[97] The

FIGURE 70
Colonel Ali Sami (later Aközer), Süreyya Paşa's Nişantaşı townhouse and observation (*seyir*) pavilion. İÜMK, 90647–0018.

his trusted colleague, the brilliant Russian polyglot Olga Sergeyevna Lebedeva, whom he called Madame Gülnar, visited the trifecta of buildings—Norwegian stave church, storehouse, and peasant's cottage—arranged as an open-air museum in the forest of the Oscarshall, the neo-Gothic summer palace of the Swedish court. He reported on the arduous transportation of these atavistic structures from the mountains of Norway; the manner in which they had been put together, from opening scupper holes to incising notches and interlocking pieces; their incredibly well-preserved, resin-producing fibrous wood; and the comfort of their interiors and the beauty of their ornamental carvings. His description of the interior of the peasant's cottage, its owner also its builder, with its hearth and its happy accouterments of family life, morphological singularity of Istanbul's miniature pavilions and chalets, all located in a single neighborhood of the city, suggests that the leisurely pursuits of higher-level Muslim and non-Muslim bureaucrats involved a certain degree of competition played out through architecture.

Chalets did not appeal to everyone in Abdülhamid's court. When the sultan bestowed a Nişantaşı residence—previously inhabited by Hobart Paşa (d. 1886), the British admiral of the Ottoman fleet, and among the imperial properties—on Yusuf Rıza Paşa, the head of the immigration commission, the latter requested the removal of Hobart's "imported chalet" (*getirtmiş olduğu şale*) from the premises.[98] Yusuf Rıza's 1887 appeal to the imperial treasury is nevertheless informative in specifying the cost of the structure (280 Ottoman liras) and its disassembly (10 Ottoman liras). Furthermore, the fact that Hobart owned a chalet before the 1894 earthquake helps to break the too-easy connection between the increased popularity of these portables and architectural safety, and strengthens the case for their burgeoning aesthetic appeal.

The members of Abdülhamid's extended family also embellished their gardens à la Yıldız. Abdülmecid Efendi, an amateur designer of his homes and gardens, amassed a library and architectural archive that contains, in addition to unique photographs of Yıldız's chalets under snow, similar examples of European mail-order catalogues for garden pavilions. He liked the extremely rustic products, made of untreated birch and oak, offered by a Saxon company called Voigt, whose catalogue foreword attributed to the "cultured man" (Kulturmensch), invested in the art of horticulture, a natural inclination

علمان باشاقورناغنك بغچه‌سنده خصوصی کوشك

"the free and untouched nature of the wilderness" (der freien und berührten Vegetation in der Wildnis) in his surroundings.[99] The "primitive" dragon-headed log cabins of the Norwegian prefabrication company Strömmen Traevarefabrik also seem to have held considerable appeal for this Ottoman Romantic, who kept a torn and folded catalogue page that displayed the company's thirty-fifth building type.[100]

The memoirs of Abdülhamid's niece Mevhibe Celaleddin show how compelling an influence Yıldız had over the architectural and landscaping choices of her family members. Behind a small kiosk in the groves of their Kandilli estate, her father installed "an exact replica of [Abdülhamid's artificial, winding, harem-side] lake at Yıldız" (Yıldız'daki havuzun tıpatıp eşi) and populated it with ducks, swans, and flamingos brought from Europe.[101]

FIGURE 71
Colonel Ali Sami (later Aközer), a private (*ḥuṣūṣī*) kiosk on Osman Paşa's estate. İÜMK, 90647–0014.

While Abdülhamid's court overlooked (and at times even encouraged and financed) the imitation of its architecture in the gardens of its closest statesmen, it seems to have demanded a different protocol from members of the extended family who did not have the best of relations with the sultan. When palace cronies noticed the candid imitations of the palace's dovecotes installed by Mevhibe Celaleddin's father, officials asked that they be dismantled because of their presumed role in communicating with the American college in Bebek by carrier pigeon.[102] This event did not seem to deter her father, as he soon after built a twenty-seven-room kiosk with a noticeable tower on the highest point of the grove.[103]

Towers, too, were fast becoming competitive architectural features among Istanbul's elite. Abdülmecid Efendi's architectural archives contain an unrealized project to add a Gothic minaret-like tower (with a round base, although an alternative tower with a square base is sketched on the side) to the roof of his extravagantly Alhambresque mansion in Acıbadem.[104] If Süreyya Paşa's small turret was innocuous to the court, the Hamidian vigilantes could not so easily stomach Khedive Abbas Hilmi Paşa's construction of a stately tower with art nouveau features on his Tuscan villa in the hills of Çubuklu. Once the tower's intrusiveness had been reported to the palace, Abdülhamid requested that its height be reduced from some three hundred steps to about half that, on the grounds that it aspired to compete with the city's minarets.[105] The architectural and stylistic intent of Abbas Hilmi and his wife Princess Djavidan (née Marianne May Török de Szendrő) for their Çubuklu residence was, in fact, nothing more than to replicate their beloved Alexandrian home Qasr al-Muntaza,

whose harem building supported a magnificent hybrid of a Florentine tower and a Mamluk minaret on one end and a shorter belvedere/mirador on the other.

The khedivial estate in Çubuklu was also not behind the trend in imported chalets. Like his grandfather Ismail, who had installed one on the hilltop of his sprawling Emirgan forest, Abbas Hilmi seems to have installed one on his own property, a prize-winning exhibition pavilion produced in Switzerland. It landed on the shores of the Bosphorus, with its "wooden fixtures, paneling, gabled roof, carved windowsills and balconies," in a multitude of containers. Once it had been erected, its interiors were fully refurbished in the "Turkish" style with marble cladding.[106] Princess Djavidan, a European gone native, was the only commentator on these buildings in their new, foreign environments. She contemplates the out-of-placeness of her husband's hobby-home, whose "fibrous timber and interlocked joints swelled and stretched," and describes the overall experience of a shaded grove with an Alpine structure on an Istanbul hilltop as one of make-believe.[107] Within a few short decades, however, the type that Djavidan found out of place had been so completely integrated with the Bosphorus hills and shorelines that it is today considered unassailably representative of Istanbul's nineteenth-century domestic vernacular.

Analogous to Djavidan's reading of her husband's chalet as inconsistent with its surroundings, Ahmed İhsan, the founder of the journal *Servet-i Fünūn*, reports that the chalet type was initially unwelcome to certain residents of Istanbul. In his autobiography, the journalist mentions that a Süleyman Sudi Efendi, who with his large library of Turkish and French books would inspire Ahmed

İhsan's love of literature, had built one of the first chalets in the suburb of Erenköy. This was a structure so unique for its time and place that, according to Ahmed İhsan, it managed to enrage the capital's conservatives. It was certainly not a coincidence that when news censorship was tightened under Abdülhamid II and the journalist ventured into the business of construction, he chose to manufacture chalets and ended up being incredibly successful.[108]

Few written records from the period illustrate the Ottomans' interactions with these novel, experimental buildings that they crafted for their private use, let alone the intense planning that went into their stylistic choices. Novels and memoirs structured around lives in stately konaks, yalıs, and köşks provide the most informative accounts of the centrality of these crowded, multigenerational homes to people's lives.[109] For instance, the grandson of Abdülhamid's Ottoman Greek banker Georgios Zariphis talks about garden life in his ancestral house on the shores of the Bosphorus as being spent in and around these ephemeral structures and notes that hiking between them was a particularly popular pastime for the women and children of the household. Impressionistic wanderings en plein air became part of the summertime activities of the landed gentry.[110]

Period novels also feature lengthy pastoral observations on beloved hilltop sites such as Çamlıca, which often reflect the inner worlds of their protagonists. Perhaps the most famous of these, Namık Kemal's İntibah (Rebirth), begins by linking the arrival of spring with the budding infatuation of its protagonist, Ali Bey, with the devious temptress Mahpeyker in Çamlıca's popular public park.[111] Sâmiha Ayverdi's deeply

autobiographical novel İbrahim Paşa Konağı (The mansion of İbrahim Paşa) reserves the wilder, unlandscaped part of the estate for the enjoyment of the women of the family. In the novel, they venture beyond the orchard gate of the estate to take mountain hikes in absolute silence, exhilarated by their act of trespass in the wilderness. The narrator describes the seasonal change of the mansion's flora exclusively through the eyes of these women. This unconventional family saga also touches on the expansion of the culture of teferrüc (strolling for pleasure) and indicates that such outings were led by women alone, who often breached the boundaries of their constricted outdoor lives by advancing to sites farther and farther away from their homes.[112]

If small kiosks and pavilions served as precious rest stops in the Ottoman elites' summer estates, the ones erected on the flatter grounds of Nişantaşı's bureaucratic neighborhood may have functioned as small writing retreats. Propelled by the increase in local newspapers and journals in which serials were published in different genres, the late nineteenth century saw an efflorescence in the production not only of fiction but also of more-introspective nonfiction. Growing numbers of men and, to some extent, women were writing for a living and increasingly felt the urge to document their lives and times during the accelerated upheavals of their era. The intimate interiors of these individuals' workspaces gained so much public attention that photographs of their study rooms occupied the front pages of Servet-i Fünūn in 1898: hücre-i iştiğal or hücre-i müṭālaʿa in Ottoman Turkish translated the French caption le cabinet du travail.[113]

In the context of private interiors that had become eremitic spaces for intellectual work, the ministers and scribes who inhabited the palace-owned Nişantaşı compounds for the duration of their tenure were prolific in penning reform tracts and political memoirs. In some ways their professional rivalry played out not only through these structures but also, and more directly, through their writerly output. For instance, Süreyya Paşa published his little-known *Ḥayāt-ı ʿOs̱mānī* (Ottoman existence) of 1881 as a serial in the official newspaper *Cerīde-i Ḥavādis̱*.[114] This text begins with a brief Ottoman history and continues with the state's agricultural and industrial advancements, stressing the centrality of the empire's railway systems. Kamil Paşa was even more prolific in his scholarly endeavors: he left behind a three-volume political history of the Ottoman Empire that covered its origins up to the reign of Abdülmecid, and a contrite political memoir of his viziership under Abdülhamid.[115] He also contributed to the genre of polemical texts by publishing a refutation of his rival Mehmed Said Paşa's published memoirs, which singled him out as responsible for the failings of the state.[116] Süreyya and Kamil Paşas' Nişantaşı neighbor Tunuslu Hayreddin Paşa (d. 1890) had perhaps the most lavish of these bureaucratic lodgings, the construction of which was never fully completed during his tenure, because he kept changing his mind about its architectural and stylistic elements. Most important, and certainly beyond his obvious penchant for buildings and decoration, he was recruited by Abdülhamid for the position of grand vizier due to his extremely popular reform tract of 1868, entitled *Aḳwam al-masālik fī maʿrifat aḥwāl al-mamālik* (The surest path to knowledge regarding the condition of countries), on the reasons and projected solutions for social, political, and economic decline in the Muslim world.[117]

In terms of their function, it is tempting to compare these small hermitic rooms—constructed in the gardens of Ottoman bureaucrats to serve as spaces for the contemplation of their owners' political existence and service to an aging empire—to Charles Dickens's quaint little study in his imported two-floor chalet. Charles Fechter, a Comédie-Française actor and close friend of the writer's, gifted Dickens the Swiss prefab in 1865; it "arrived from Paris in ninety-four pieces, fitting together like the joints of a puzzle, but . . . proved to be somewhat costly in setting on its legs by means of a foundation of brickwork." Installed in the forested gardens of Dickens's Gadshill residence, the chalet was reached through an underground passage and adorned with mirrors that reflected the woodland views and the River Thames. It was where Dickens would write during the summer months of his last five years.[118]

Like the Ottomans, the nineteenth-century Qajars carried their political rivalries into their Tehran residences. Analogous to emulative practices in the Ottoman capital, Nasir al-Din Shah's two rival viziers deliberately changed the names of their sprawling garden estates not only to intimate their engagement with international landscaping trends but also to proclaim their status within Iran's political community. Mirza ʿAli Khan (d. 1904), a close confidant of the shah, anti-*ulema* diarist, and follower of European sartorial and domestic customs, renamed his bāgh-i Amīn al-Dawla as pārk-i Amīn al-Dawla, a site renowned for its diplomatic banquets, which included among its several amenities a mansion constructed according to European plans.[119] Similarly, Mirza ʿAli Khan's younger rival in matters of economic reform, Mirza ʿAsghar Khan (d. 1907), who enjoyed a long period of grand viziership serving all three of the last Qajar shahs,[120] converted his garden's designation to park-i Atābak.[121]

The voluminous ʿAlī Khān Vālī album provides photographs of Mirza ʿAli Khan's Palladian villa, a multistory structure with heavyset Doric balconies, surrounded by a vast garden. The photographs of the garden focus on an octagonal pavilion surrounded by a light trellised portico, which stands on a cascading rockery with a cavernous, grotto-like opening to its ground floor (fig. 72). In the photograph's subtitle, the pavilion is called the *kulāh-ı farāngī* (European's hat), resembling Ottoman pavilions that imitated tents and were referred to as *çadır* pavilions.[122] In both Qajar and Ottoman traditions, building names were derived from the morphologies of other objects. Much like the Ottoman *çadır* pavilions that appeared in various imperial gardens (but most notably in Yıldız, Kağıthane, and Maslak), the *kulāh-ı farāngī* was a popular building configuration for a variety of Safavid and Qajar garden pavilions, generally following octagonal plans.[123] The competitive eclecticism of the Qajar homes and gardens was not lost on a female Ottoman journalist, according to whom the only other city in which homeowners invested so much effort in making their residences singular was Tehran.[124]

BUILDING PRACTICES AND ARCHITECTURAL SOURCES AND RESOURCES

Mail-order catalogues, architectural pattern books, and building manuals in circulation in nineteenth-century Istanbul offer some explanatory counterweight to the ever-problematic dearth of Ottoman architectural drawings: why can so few of these drawings be found in the archives? Still, a few examples

of actual building projects shed some light both on this scarcity and on the engagement of Ottoman builders with mass-produced architectural aids. The first two of these examples reflect almost direct transferences from paper model to full reproduction.

Abdülaziz's two forested hunting estates on either side of Istanbul (Ayazağa and Acıbadem) were both centered on compact neoclassical urban mansions almost identical to Yıldız's Mabeyn Kiosk. The two sites also contained identical wooden hunting pavilions that are strikingly similar to variants found in the architect Jean Boussard's 1881 illustrated compilation of small structures built for French gardens, *Constructions et décorations pour jardins, kiosques, orangeries, volières, abris divers*. Sarkis Balyan derived his Ottoman commissions from a fancy ibex shelter in Paris's Jardin des plantes. These pavilions,

FIGURE 72
Kulāh-ı farāngī (European's hat) pavilion in the park of Mirza ʿAli Khan's Tehran residence. From the ʿAlī Khān Vālī Album. Courtesy of Special Collections, Fine Arts Library, Harvard University.

FIGURE 73
Sultan Abdülaziz's hunting lodge at the Validebağı estate, 1867–76, attributed to Serkis Balyan. İÜMK, 90474–0024.

and clad the exteriors and interiors in painted geometric patterns from floor to ceiling. He also increased their heights to accommodate entresols for musicians, which is apparent from the grilled clerestory windows on the buildings' exteriors. Lastly, in the Ottoman version, the rustic French shed with its thatched roof was covered with brick tiles to provide better shelter (fig. 73).

The architectural projects that served the internal needs of the Ottoman court, whether for pleasure or for more mundane palace functions, appear in building and site-survey documents as cutouts from volumes like Boussard's. This, to my mind, explains why these volumes rarely survive intact and complete in library collections that belonged to the members of the court. Victor Petit's unbound lithographs in what remains of Yıldız's library are another good example. Carefully torn and appended pages from such volumes appear at random in documents from the Yıldız archives that describe imperial building commissions. A laborious list of construction specifications for a sizable aviary might be partnered with an illustration from an unknown French treatise on garden structures to guide the builder.[125] These blueprints traveled from commissioners' desks to building sites; some survived, but most did not. The documents describing the construction of a building from its foundation to its roofing often refer their audience to numbered drawings (*resim* or *resmi alınmış plan*), which were probably displaced for closer scrutiny while building.

A set of Ottoman interministerial correspondence from 1893 better reveals how court-sponsored building commissions used architectural catalogues to make formal selections.[126] These documents disclose in considerable detail the architectural preparations

like their French models, were simple square boxes with oversized hipped roofs whose hanging eaves were supported by thin columns surrounding the buildings on all sides. However, they did diverge in aspects of their ornamentation. To the small pavilions, Balyan added elaborate corbels under the eaves and wooden trellises between the columns, changed the elongated Gothic apertures of the shed to rectangular ones with shutters, undertaken for the ambitious Ottoman Exposition of Agriculture and Industry. To determine what the exposition pavilions would look like, a committee was formed from the heads of the Ministry of Forestry, Mining, and Agriculture, as well as celebrated cultural movers of the period, such as Osman Hamdi Bey, director of the Imperial Museum, and Alexandre Vallaury, an influential local architect and instructor in the capital's School of Fine Arts. This unrealized project—halted when the 1894 earthquake quickly turned the court's attention to citywide repairs—was Raimondo D'Aronco's ticket to long-term employment as architect and engineer in Abdülhamid's court and in various other state institutions.

By the time the committee decided to invite D'Aronco (*mühendis* in the documents) to supervise the project, they had already studied (the verb signified interchangeably by the Ottoman words *taṭbīḳ, tedḳīḳ,* and *ḳırāʾat*) "Italian exposition pavilions and combined aspects from their designs with ones that were drafted locally by the ministries' commissioned architects" (resim ve ṣūret ḳarārlaşdırılmaḳ üzere gerek İtalyan sergīleri resimleriniñ ve gerek ṭaraf-ı neẓāretden yapdırılmış olan resimleriñ tedḳīḳi). The committee had also predetermined the building materials: iron (the requisite for any nineteenth-century exposition), brick, and stone. The imperial arsenal would produce these permanent structures.

The foreign architect was not given sole responsibility for design and creativity; state patronage relied principally on the expertise of local actors for buildings, such as exposition pavilions, intended to announce the imperial presence or express a national idiom. The exposition's final look was a composite of carefully studied paper models and vernacular practices. In fact, the committee frequently used the word *birleşdirilmek,* meaning "conjoining," to describe the handling of catalogue models and both Vallaury's and D'Aronco's plans.

Access to architectural catalogues and pattern books, from which one could pick and choose, was not limited to state actors. When Abdülhamid II revived the Sultanahmet School of Industry (mekteb-i ṣanāyiʾ), which was founded under Âli, Fuad, and Midhat Paşas, the three standard-bearers of the Tanzimat, to serve as a vocational arts and crafts school for the city's underprivileged, its library was stocked with books for an expanded curriculum. Abdülhamid's transformation of the school was a part of a larger goal to increase the use and circulation of local products in the empire's territories.[127] The students were also expected to contribute to state projects such as the agricultural exposition, as well as to sell products such as metal knobs and wooden cabinetry at local fairs. The most successful were selected to work in the sultan's carpentry ateliers. Accordingly, the expanding collection of the school's library included volumes in Turkish and various European languages on smithery, smelting, turnery, carpentry, and small-scale architectural construction.[128]

An 1894 four-volume French work entitled *Petites constructions françaises*—published by Émile Thézard fils, a prolific publisher of illustrated construction manuals on everyday architecture and practical buildings—can be found among the still-extant library collection of this school (fig. 74).[129] On each of the quartos of *Petites constructions,* a colored elevation precedes a plan, cross section, and price sheet listing costs of materials. The key provides a description of the building's construction, starting from

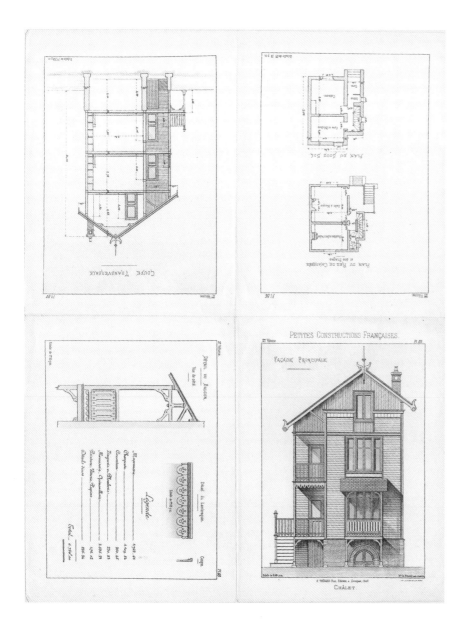

FIGURE 74
Émile Thézard, removable folio
showing details on building
a modest chalet. From *Petites
constructions françaises* (1894).
Author's collection.

exchange between patron and builder: each individual quarto is unbound and thus easily transportable from homeowner to chosen architect and from the shelves of a private library to the site of construction. The lacunae in the serially numbered models in each of the extant volumes in the school's library suggest that these sheets were indeed physically removed, used, and not returned.[130]

Like Loudon's volumes, Thézard's target members of the middle class. Most of the types bear the title *maison bourgeois* and are considerably scaled-down versions of aristocratic townhouses and country cottages, but replete with all the novelties that once defined the taste of that social class. Sample structures offer myriad possibilities for customizing one's property: landscaping ideas, towerlike projections, dovecotes, hobby rooms, ateliers, wine cellars, Gothic to neoclassical ornamental schemes, and even sculptural reliefs on entrance façades. In these volumes, too, the chalet-esque country cottage continues to dominate the aesthetic of the suburban villa.[131]

The Ottoman craftsmen were quick to acquire the skills to interpret the plans in prefab catalogues and manuals and apply them to the more sophisticated residences provided by publications like Thézard's.[132] However, it is important not to forget that Istanbul's local builders were often already proficient in woodworking. For centuries the principal structural material for residential construction in the capital had been lumber, and the predominant ornamental material had been wood—the most prestigious variety being oak (*meşe*). Two consecutive supervisors of the construction of the German embassy's summer residence in Tarabya, the renowned German archaeologist Wilhelm Dörpfeld and his successor, the younger architect Armin

its foundation and moving up through its frame, joinery, ironwork, carpentry, glazing, and paintwork. It also provides information on the various materials used, such as their sources (e.g., "stone from Hauterive," or "slate from Angers") and cost. Thézard's presentation of content to the volumes' readership is indicative of the very mobile process of

Wegner, were greatly impressed by the agility of local Greek carpenters, who displayed speed and dexterity in layering mastic on joints and cracks and in their use of nails to hold the wood together. The German architects were also fascinated by the locals' expert carving of the decorative façade features; the foreigners left it up to the builders to make the fundamental structural and stylistic choices, including the decision to build in wood rather than masonry.[133]

Around the time that foreign builders expressed their admiration for the expertise of Ottoman craftsmen, local building companies were attracting urban clientele with promises of machine-age production. In the spring months of 1896, when *konak* owners were beginning to set up their gardens for the summer, a sawmill and lumberyard in Ahırkapı with the ambitious name of Ottoman House of Industry (dārüʾṣ ṣanāyiʿ-i ʿOsmāniyye) ran a large, eye-catching illustrated advertisement in the widely circulated Ottoman newspaper *İḳdām* (Perseverance).[134] The local company promoted its manufacturing services with a quaint image of a small chalet inscribed within a baroque frame (fig. 75). Strewn on either side of this miniature house are its deconstructed parts and the tools required for its construction: a workbench, a carpenter's plane, jointers, mortisers, "moldings, carved wooden lacework" (silmeler ve oymalı dantelālar), door and window frames, and the quintessential "steam operated machine" (neccār mākineleri) that gave the factory license to call itself a house of industry. The efficiency and precision of the "machine" (mākine) and "technically advanced looms organized according to new methods [*munṭaẓam ve nev-uṣūl destgāhlar*]" are here juxtaposed with the "hand of the craftsman" (silmeci ve ṭoğramacılariñ eli ile

vücūda getireceği maʿmūlāt), "incomparable" (aṣlā muḳāyese olunamayacağı derkārdır) in its ability to systematically reproduce an ornate frame or molding. The factory makes three promises for the final product: "tastefulness" (ẓarāfet), "inexpensiveness" (ehveniyet), and "speed of construction" (surʿat-i iʿmāl).[135]

A growing industrial enterprise owned and operated by two local partners (*ḳomandīt*

FIGURE 75
Advertisement for the Ottoman House of Industry (dārüʾṣ ṣanāyiʿ-i ʿOsmāniyye). From *İḳdām* (1896).

The factory also had "its own drawing offices and architects" (kendine maḥṣūṣ resimḫānesi ve ḫuṣūṣī miʿmārları). With its swift production and design-consultation services, the company quickly adorned the popular suburbs of Istanbul, such as Göztepe, Kızıltoprak, Kuruçeşme, and Büyükada, with "elegant and graceful buildings and mansions" (ẓarīf ve laṭīf bināl ar ve kāşāneler).[136] Others continued to import structures from Europe, as did the Levantine architect Alexandre M. Raymond, whose side job was acting as the commercial agent in Istanbul for a Swedish prefabricated-house company, Hogélin & Sundström from Stockholm. Raymond advertised the company's "salubrious, economical, urban and rural dwellings" in his French-language journal *Génie civil ottoman*, for engineers and architects working in the Ottoman domains (fig. 77).

Istanbul's savvy urbanites, even those without ties to the Ottoman court and bureaucracy, were able to access various architectural styles at affordable prices when constructing their residences, and knew how to negotiate their terms. The burgeoning middle classes were not mere copyists of foreign exempla, especially when it came to their domestic surroundings. They invested great effort in making their homes appear visually distinct. A great example of this consumption frenzy over domestic types is provided in Halid Ziya's novel *Kırık Hayatlar* (Fractured Lives) of 1901. The story revolves around an Istanbul doctor's obsession with building a *köşk* on Şişli's main artery to the popular public promenade, Kağıthane. To create the perfect home for his devoted wife and daughter and to impress passersby traveling to and from Kağıthane, the novel's protagonist consults with architects, looks through architectural catalogues, and investigates built

şirketi), the journalist Rauf Bey and the owner of *Ṣervet-i Fünūn*, Ahmed İhsan, the Ottoman House of Industry sourced its wood, the sturdy and resinous *çiğdene*, from the Black Sea. An illustration of this factory from an earlier editorial foregrounds the waterfront facility with ships delivering lumber to its ateliers (fig. 76). The meandering waters of the Black Sea, along with a serpentine dragon, frame the factory building, with forests and cut lumber on one side and a chalet on the other.

examples in the fashionable neighborhoods of Moda, Tarabya, and Büyükada—the very places serviced by the Ottoman House of Industry. Once all decisions have been made, the doctor's house rises as if it were "carved out of paper like light and elegant embroidery" (kağıttan oyulmuş kadar ince, hoş oya).[137]

For the owners of the Ahırkapı lumber factory, working from samples or patterns and plans brought in by their prospective clients ("gösterilen numūne ve plan üzerine ḫāne inşāsı") came with a caveat: price negotiations were dependent ("pāzārlıḳ ile ḳarārlaşdırılacaḳ fīʾāt") on the chosen residential style. Mehmed İzzet's *Rehber* shows how ingrained and systematized house commissions had become by 1911: they were standardized legal practices incorporating a contract template to be signed by buyer and builder, the latter either a master builder (*ḳalfa*) or a contractor (*müteʿahhid*). Using images of small French urban mansions and country estates lifted from publications such as Thézard's manuals, Mehmed İzzet lists a useful step-by-step negotiation and pricing process for the home buyer in his lengthy entry on the house (*ev*).[138] However, not everything about this process was gathered from foreign manuals. In keeping with the client's economic status, Mehmed İzzet divides house types into three categories: economical (*idāreli* or *ʿādī*), moderate (*orta*), and elaborate (*mükellef*) (fig. 78). This recalls the drafting by fifteenth- and sixteenth-century Ottoman architects of three differently sized plans from which their patrons could choose.[139] Mehmed İzzet then offers a matrix that links different qualities of material, the lowest often being factory produced and standard sized, with the pricing of each of the three categories of house; the most expensive house would, of course, be built with the most

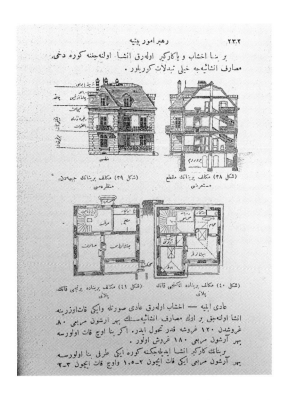

FIGURE 78
Cross-section, elevation, and plan of the "elaborate" (*mükellef*) residence in Mehmed İzzet's "house" (*ev*) entry from *Rehber-i Umūr-ı Beytīye*, vol. 2 (1907).

durable wood and with customized trimmings. The author describes the market for and sources of local as well as imported materials (especially wood, brick, and cement), indicates to which parts of a building they are best suited, and specifies the average price of each item by size and weight. His lengthy entry on the construction of residences points not only to the continued prevalence of timber over stone in civil architecture at the turn of the century but also to a firmly established empire-wide standardization of the sizes and costs of the selected materials.[140]

Sedad Hakkı Eldem, the consummate chronicler of Ottoman garden and building types, coins the phrase "Erenköy Style" to describe the eclectic wooden residences built by the growing number of nineteenth-century homeowners in the ever-expanding suburban

ثروت فنون ٣٠٠

[مائى وسیاه رسمارندن : احمد جمیل بارمقلق قوسنك یاننده کی ذبلی (صحیفه ٢٩٩) [
Noir-et-Bleu, roman de Halid Bey : Ahmed djémil hisite à sonner

FIGURE 79
Illustration for Halid Ziya's
novel *Māʾi ve Siyāh* (Blue and
Black). From *Ṣervet-i Fünūn*
(1897).

neighborhoods of Istanbul.[141] The most striking examples of wooden façade decorations
among these residences were clustered in
the vast gardens and orchards of Istanbul's
Asian district of Erenköy, which had views
overlooking its neighboring Princes' Islands.
Produced by construction companies like the
Ottoman House of Industry and catering to a
design-savvy urban clientele, these playfully
competitive, personalized structures became
so localized and ingrained in Istanbul's built
environment that they are today considered
the most iconic representatives of Ottoman Istanbul's domestic vernacular. By the
1910s, characters in the most widely read
novels naturally lived in chalet-esque homes
(fig. 79). Disappointingly, however, today's
heritage scholarship continues to refer to a
timeless Ottoman wooden-house tradition
and subsumes examples from the Hamidian period under the same decontextualized
narratives.[142]

The phenomenon of customizable, quick,
and economical construction had a much
more lasting impact on the residential types
of the United States. Twentieth-century
American catalogue-order homes manufactured by lumber-rich Midwestern companies
like Sears held considerable sway and reached
a much larger group of consumers in the
United States than in the Ottoman world.[143]
Like their European counterparts, these
American catalogues received their stylistic
inspiration from nineteenth-century pattern
books. They were initially popularized in the
United States by figures like the American
landscape designer Andrew Jackson Downing.[144] In the process of building, the Loudonian types introduced in these American
books underwent marked adaptation: they
were adjusted to local tastes and local contexts via features carried over from colonial
examples, most notably shingle cladding.[145]
Today's colonial house, the most standard
type in America's northeastern suburbs, is a
distilled—and democratizing—version of
the affordable yet individualized residences
consumed in the nineteenth century. The
contemporary Canadian novelist Annie
Proulx's *Barkskins*, a multigenerational epic
that charts the history of the destruction of
North America's native populations alongside its myriad flora and fauna, reserves a
few pages for the emergence of prefabricated
prairie houses after the Great Chicago Fire
of 1871. Proulx's architects advertise their
products at a trade exhibition in commercial
rhetoric similar to that used by the Ottoman
House of Industry: "Why, you could build a
town that way. You could have a dozen different designs of houses so people could pick the
one they liked, you could pack one or more up
and ship them to wherever on the railroad."[146]

The Last Photograph Album of the Hamidian Palace

Why were photograph albums depict-ing Ottoman imperial residences such coveted keepsakes at the turn of the century?[1] What was the role of the photographer vis-à-vis the patron in selecting and ordering images of royal edifices within an album? How did the photographer frame his *subjects of place*? And—most important for this study of a palace whose inhabitant with the longest residency was also the best-known imperial benefactor of the photographic medium in the Ottoman world—what kinds of mean-ings might have been conveyed through the photographed anatomies of the imperial royal grounds? In an attempt to elucidate a category of the still-underexplored topic of photography in the late Ottoman period, this chapter explores these intertwined questions through a previously unknown, materially lavish, and representationally unusual pho-tograph album, simply titled *Souvenir 1905* (henceforth *Souvenir*), which comprises sixty-four images that display the imperial sites of Istanbul.

The album offers ways to answer these questions through its very focus on Yıldız: it commences with thirty images of the pal-ace, which make up half of the album's overall content. Moreover, it presents the last pho-tographic trace of the imperial site before the long course of its looting, reuse, and physical fragmentation. The ordering of the photo-graphs in this album marshals these images of the capital's subsidiary imperial estates into a deliberately constructed visual narra-tive. In its purposeful sequencing, the album also makes the visual claim for Abdülhamid's conceptualization of Yıldız as his residen-tial complex much more forcefully than the sultan's earlier photographic commissions, which portrayed the palace in much more circumscribed ways.

Souvenir appeared later than the better-known and well-studied Hamidian gift albums in the collections of the Library of Congress and the British Library, which rep-resent the earlier years of Abdülhamid's reign, from the 1880s to the 1890s.[2] In these albums, in contrast with *Souvenir*, Yıldız's carefully selected buildings and sections are unin-habited, orderly, and austere, and its newly appointed picturesque gardens, all focused around the court's private quarters on the complex's hilltop, are staged as unpopulated, carefully groomed outdoor settings. Exist-ing scholarship has consistently regarded these gift albums as part and parcel of the Hamidian regime's eager exposition of its modernity to the Western world.[3] Further-more, Yıldız's vast photographic collection (from which images for these two gift albums were selected and packaged) has largely

159

FIGURE 80
Souvenir's Tarnavski binding.
İAK, Alb. 156.

been interpreted as serving the purpose of intraimperial surveillance.[4] Having based their arguments on the hermitic tendencies of its patron and thereby collapsed layers of potential meaning and context into a single imperial intention, earlier scholarship has unfortunately precluded the possibility that any Hamidian photograph or album has a discursive existence of its own.[5]

The photographs arranged in *Souvenir* stand apart from their predecessors in exhibiting a strikingly intimate picture of the last Ottoman palace. The palace complex had quickly established its presence as the empire's administrative center and, perhaps more important, had financed much of the photographic practice of the period. But though the earlier gift albums present Yıldız as an uninhabited, staged subject,[6] this practiced austerity in early photographs of Yıldız should not be attributed to Abdülhamid's elusive personality alone or to the invisible but palpable presence of the sovereign amid his court. Rather, the photographs were usually taken to document the completion, or near completion, of an imperial garden retreat's swift transformation into a palace. It is also important to note here that between the

Hamidian albums and *Souvenir*, there are no currently known photographic collections of Yıldız as a palace complex during Abdülhamid's reign. These two sets of images—the larger collection, which captures Abdülhamid's first staging of his complex and was incorporated into the gift albums, and the smaller but more personal *Souvenir*—are the only photographic evidence of the site's imperial existence. The uniqueness of *Souvenir* lies not only in its role as a visual coda to the last Ottoman palace but also in its ultimate disruption of the representational inaccessibility of the site.

The memoirs of Abdülhamid's close family members, aides-de-camp, and diplomatic visitors provide valuable insights into the life and residential world of the sultan and bolster the photograph album's visual narrative of the imperial architectural sites of the nineteenth century. Moreover, the album's biographical undertaking enlivens many of Abdülhamid's architecture-related commissions, from the renovation of the majority of the royal residences of the capital to the appointment of a court photographer to document these structures in their postrenovation splendor and a cartographer to make a topographical map that specifically outlines the imperial structures selected for *Souvenir*.

This chapter touches upon these additional sultanic imprints on the urban landscape to contextualize the album's story line. If the compositional character of the images shows how these predominantly outdoor sites were used by their visitors, it also speaks to Yıldız's centrality to the chosen buildings and their surrounding landscapes—sites that established Abdülhamid as a ruler in the guise of a wealthy landowner preoccupied with deriving both pleasure and profit from his estates. Furthermore, the album alludes to the ways in which these estates were physically separated from the rest of the city's urban environment. It also shows how the palace and its many smaller variants deliberately maintained their visual distinction by emphasizing their status chiefly as created and ordered landscapes, much as nineteenth-century parks staged their presence in cities as tracts of open country that an urbanite might unexpectedly encounter—the experience of a *ṣaḥrāʾ* (country) within an otherwise metropolitan *belde* (town), as frequently alluded to by the Ottoman writers and poets of the period.[7] The physical separators that demarcated these two zones are recurrent subjects of the images mounted in the album. Formal enclosures such as walls, hedges, and fences, which were also central topics of the nineteenth-century publications and correspondence of "gentlemen farmers," were symbols of social order that denoted gentility and property but also status, notoriety, and virtue.[8]

ORDER, MATERIALITY, AND FRAMES

Souvenir is organized as a series of coordinated interactions between Yıldız and a selection of imperial estates, accentuating the engagement between nineteenth-century architecture and nature, and the desired experience of the two together, in a sequence of landscape shots. In its dialogic representation of a catalogue of imperial structures in which one site beckons to another and the process of recollection is performed in the ordering of the images, the album serves as an architectural archive not only for the palace but also for its historically understudied formal companions, such as the large imperial farms (*çiftlikāt-ı hümāyūn*) of

Maslak and Ayazağa, which sported pleasure pavilions on the grounds of curiously configured stately country homes in the garden retreats of Kağıthane and Ihlamur (the latter was named Nüzhetiye, meaning "a restful, recreational spot," by Abdülmecid).[9] The album prompts the viewer to think of these handpicked structures relationally, as they were experienced by their royal inhabitants and visitors. Continuing the tradition of their predecessors, the sultans of the nineteenth century moved between summer and winter residences and retreats of their own choosing. These seasonal moves continued to be ingrained in the urban consciousness of the capital's subjects.

The uniqueness of the album's visual history lies in its circumspection in portraying Abdülhamid II's ideas about imperial habitation. The questions of how his royal site should appear and how it should function were linked not only to the estates he had experienced and in which he had resided but also to those he had designed and ruled over during his time as a prince and to which he wanted later to assimilate his palace complex of Yıldız. The album performs a very specific imperial architectural history, tied firmly to Abdülhamid's biography and his actual world of architecture.

The sixty-four stills of *Souvenir* are each about 19.5 by 25.5 centimeters, a standard size for albumen prints. Formally and contextually, however, it is different from its quantitatively dominant distant cousins, the Yıldız photographic collections of countless albums and unbound images, insofar as no copies of any of *Souvenir*'s contents are to be found among Abdülhamid's vast holdings. Furthermore, the album presents a great many unknowns: its photographer is not known, and there are no guiding subtitles under the shots to orient the viewer regarding the photographed subject.[10] The album's provenance is also undetermined except for a monographic trace on its silk *moiré*–centered backboard. Its materials suggest an affluent owner (as well as a wealthy patron, if it was a gift), as it bears a crowned initial *B*, is bound in rich black leather, and boasts generously applied gilding and red rocaille-patterned perimeters, delicate foliated moldings, and fore edge (fig. 80).[11] (I return to the album's possible provenance and relate its content to its intended audience after reviewing what the album reveals at first glance.)

Although only the barest traces of ownership remain, the luxurious cover offers indications as to the identities of at least two of the figures involved in the album's making. The bottom edge of the opening flyleaf bears the bookplate of the imperial bookbinder and his address in gilded Ottoman Turkish: "mücellid-i ḥażret-i şehriyārī Aġüst Tarnavski, 575 numero, Teke Beyoğlu." Had the thick flyleaf not split over time, another practitioner of the art of bookmaking might have remained unknown forever. Penciled on the flyleaf's recto side in Greek, Ottoman, and French and inscribed in an oval vignette, as if its author were sketching his own advertisement, is the insignia of one "Miltiades [fils] Crocodilos, Relieur Doreur, Constantinople," who provides two dates: May 22, 1905 (in Greek), and June 9, 1905 (in French). These dates may indicate the beginning and completion, respectively, of the gilding of the album. Tarnavski and Miltiades must have collaborated on the album, with the former outsourcing components of the job to the latter, lesser-known craftsman. The Ottoman trade journal *Annuaire oriental* (from 1903) lists Tarnavski (aka Tarnawski) twice. In the first instance, he and his business partner, J. Urhan, are named as "relieurs et fabricants de boîte en carton." The second lists him as a solo agent with a separate address: "Grande Rue de Pera, 575."[12] The second address, whose number matches that stamped on the album, was perhaps reserved for Tarnavski's services to the sultan and his court. There are stylistic reasons to speculate that an elaborately embossed leather box, almost a rare piece of furniture, containing individually leather-bound photographs of Wilhelm II's visit to Constantinople, found among the personal collection of the last caliph Abdülmecid Efendi (1868–1944), was a product of Tarnavski's collaborative box manufacturing with J. Urhan.[13]

Of the many Abdülhamid Yıldız albums extant today in Istanbul collections, fifty-nine bear Tarnavski's seal. I suspect that many more displayed the range and creativity of *Souvenir* in their cover designs but were either left unsigned/unsealed or lost their bindings during the dismantling of the library.[14] Judging from his appearance as court binder in trade journals from 1881 to 1905, Auguste Tarnavski was responsible for almost all of the Yıldız album bindings, as well as the early bindings of the *Indicateur ottoman*. The binder never once needed to advertise his business in these trade journals, because court commissions kept him occupied. The only archival document that bears his name is a petition from 1897 that he sent to the palace's scribal offices, demanding that he receive the belated amount owed to him for more than one hundred bindings he had prepared for the imperial library.[15] The same trade journals list the lesser-known Miltiades Crocodille, indexed only by his name, his self-employed status,

and his residence in Enli Yocouche (*yokuş* in Turkish meaning "ramp," thus a "ramp with girth") in Fındıklı, among the congested ateliers of craftsmen spilling behind the Tophane foundries. Whereas Tarnavski disappears from the trade journals after 1905, Crocodille, whose profession had never previously been fully listed, suddenly appears in 1909 as a proud member of the stock exchange ("membré du conseil de la bourse de fonds et valeurs").[16]

The split flyleaf also reveals that the thick sheets on which the photographs were mounted were constructed by gluing together the printed sides of recycled book leaves to allow their blank verso sides to be used for matting. The book that Tarnavski and Miltiades used to create the blank pages of the album was about the world's rarest known orchids, first published in 1854 under the directorship of the orchid-hunter Jean-Jules Linden and entitled *Pescatorea: Iconographie des orchidées* in memory of Jean-Pierre Pescatore (1793–1855) of La Celle-Saint-Cloud, France, one of the first cultivators of this family of flowers.[17] That the binders matched albums to old books with similar subjects—in this case predominantly nature—is intriguing, hinting at a highly bespoke practice in which trade secrets were inserted inside the objects created.

The front board's cloud-shaped molded-*moiré* insert, replicated on the back cover with the abovementioned single-letter monogram, announces the album's title, *Souvenir 1905*—signaling its participation in a photographic convention all too familiar for such objects, especially by that date.[18] The viewer would expect to see the selected photographs presented in the form of an excursion, perhaps one that the album's owner had already

FIGURE 81
Souvenir's opening shot, the ceremonial greeting spot (*mülākāt maḥalli*) in the Şale complex of Yıldız.

FIGURE 82
Souvenir's closing shot, the promenade of Kağıthane.

physically taken. By ordering fond yet hazy memories of the sojourn according to its most relevant moments and presenting them to the sightseer as a literal reminder, the album would act as an authorial memento of the excursion. The inherently pedantic character of the generic travel album is limited here to the retelling of the journey through the serializing of its stills according to the original itinerary. The first image, of a curious Native American way station within one of Yıldız's gates, celebrating an exploratory trip of discovery, and the last, of a crowded group of local and foreign men and children about to get into their carriages in Kağıthane on their return, deliberately bookend the trip (figs. 81–82).

Aside from its inclusion of a *telos* of travel, however, the album stands apart from the milieu of the photographic souvenir in the way that it represents the excursion. Most superficially, the album introduces movement not only between and through the images (from one site to the next) but also within a single image.[19] Just as the actual trip once exhausted its taker, almost every image in the album is framed to elicit a jolt in the armchair traveler, who is forced to participate once again in the strenuous meanderings taken along indirect routes, steep climbs, plunging vistas, and oblique approaches. It is very much a physical and experiential reminder. The mobility of the album's representations of its verdant subjects is altogether distinct from the pleasant stillness expected of nature photography. In each vertiginous still, the viewer's line of vision is drawn inward, upward, or downward. Rather than present nature in a controlled, picture-perfect manner, the photographer simulates the very experience of the photographed landscape: the deliberately coarse, overgrown terrains of the imperial estates. If the album's main theme follows the architectural genealogy of nineteenth-century Ottoman palaces, it is equally about representations of nature during that period. The album features an overwhelming number of shots of trees, focusing on the shadows they cast, the way they obscure routes and views, and their eerie anthropomorphism (fig. 83).

The album also speaks to the changing nature of Ottoman outdoor promenades. During the nineteenth century the inhabitants of Istanbul began increasingly to vary the time that they spent in nature, between the flat terrains of Kağıthane and the much more rigorous hilltops of Çamlıca or Tarabya. These two sites had popular sloping public parks. The Hungarian Orientalist Ármin Vámbéry styled his regular and demanding hikes up to Çamlıca, where he taught French to an upstart *paşazade* from the Üsküdar shore, as climbing the "Steps to Parnassus" (*Gradus ad Parnassum*).[20] The purported curative power of higher ground was partially responsible for this growing trend among a generation simultaneously intrigued by and terrified of tuberculosis and various other diseases that they were told would be cured by a "change of air" (*tebdīl-i havā*). Mehmed İzzet's home-economics encyclopedia devotes a long entry to *tebdil-i hava* (a better treatment for malaria than fish oil or quinine, the author argues), explicating the benefits and disadvantages of the respective winds and water of different suburbs and public promenades in Istanbul for ailments such as rheumatism, pleurisy, gout, and heart disease.[21]

Souvenir conveys what a private hike must have been like. The actual topography

ALB.156/22

of its photographed sites is reflected in the images.[22] The photographer probably traversed these laborious terrains with a handheld camera—used globally from the 1880s onward by both professional and amateur photographers and advertised and sold in Istanbul from the 1890s onward. A series of five images in Yıldız's park are clearly sequential snapshots. For instance,

FIGURE 83
View from Yıldız's outer garden.
From *Souvenir*.

ALB 156/16

16

The album's snapshots announce Abdülhamid II's biography of royal places by presenting all of the estates in which he spent his princely years. These places would later come to inform his vision of Yıldız as his crowning glory. Prince Abdülhamid preferred to spend his time not in the formal and largely confined spaces created for his grandfather Mahmud II and father, Abdülmecid, along Beşiktaş's shores, where he had grown up, but in and around the pavilions of Kağıthane and Tarabya (whose grounds were later given to the German embassy's summer residence), and finally those of Maslak, which were allotted to him during his uncle Abdülaziz's rule. Therefore, although Abdülhamid spent a considerable amount of time in Dolmabahçe, this site is excluded from *Souvenir*.[24]

According to Tahsin Paşa, Prince Abdülhamid preferred an active life (*faal hayat*) on the imperial estates that offered access to the "great outdoors" over a "secluded one" (*münzevi hayat*) in Dolmabahçe Palace.[25] Indeed, during his uncle's reign, Abdülhamid's penchant for the outdoor sporting life must have overstepped the bounds of acceptable courtly decorum—restrictions on a prince's social visibility were fairly relaxed during that period but still practiced in moderation.[26] When the time Abdülhamid spent on his sailboat along the Bosphorus became excessive, Abdülaziz cast him out of his princely residence on the shores of Tarabya, sending him to live instead in the hills of Maslak, which were cooler and more sparsely populated than the fashionable coastline. His daughter Ayşe Sultan recalls Abdülhamid's recollections of his exhaustively active youth, when he was a "great swimmer, horseback

FIGURE 84
One of the bridges spanning the "Pool of the Valley" (*dere ḥavūż*) inside Yıldız's outer garden. From *Souvenir*.

the cameraperson photographed not only a miniature footbridge that crossed one of Yıldız's streams (decorated with the requisite rockery and aquatic plants) (fig. 84) but also the approach to the bridge, shot while walking toward it, as well as the view below. Only a decade earlier, the Mercānof camera-equipment store in Istanbul's Sultanhamam district had furnished each of two journalists from the popular Ottoman newspaper *Servet-i Fünūn* with a small, travel-friendly Kodak ("seyāḥate maḥṣūṣ 'ḳodāḳ' denilen foṭoġraf mākinesi") for a rail trip from Istanbul to Alpuköy in Central Anatolia.[23] *Souvenir*'s photographer experiments with the aesthetics of contingency and implied movement in the same way that the journalists were able to swiftly record "important aspects" (*niḳāṭ-ı mühimme*) of the places they passed along the Anatolian railroads.

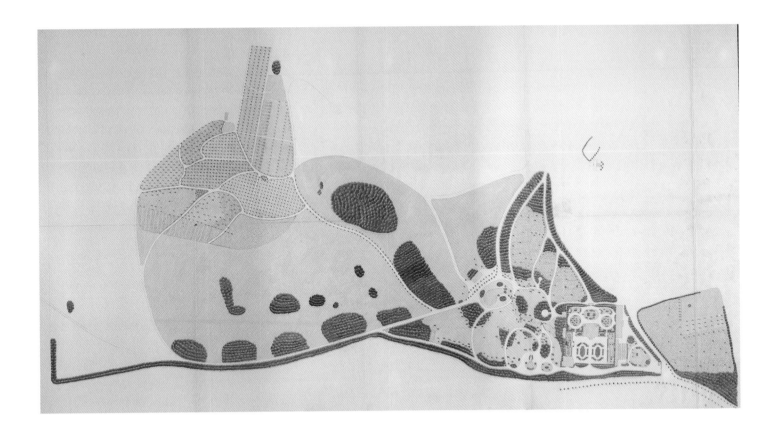

FIGURE 85
Map of the Maslak estate,
undated. İÜMK, 92586.

rider, driver, rower, sailor, shooter, marksman, hunter, and swordsman."[27]

These country estates also taught Abdülhamid how to conceptualize his domains: they had to be well manicured and simultaneously yield profit. Both his daughter and his devoted scribe speak of the prince's love for gardening. He pruned his own roses, devised designs for the flower parterres in his Tarabya and Maslak residences, and cultivated rare plants from seeds that he imported from Europe.[28] At the same time, Prince Abdülhamid learned to use sections of his properties, especially the northern pastures of his hilltop Maslak manor, which overlooked the Black Sea, for lucrative animal husbandry and stud farming. The elevated site's expansive sprawl is evident from an undated and unlabeled but cartographically precise landscaping map

(fig. 85). This site, important to Abdülhamid's development as a wealthy landowner, is the first of the subsidiary estates to follow the opening images of Yıldız in *Souvenir*.

Abdülhamid's biographers consistently portray him as the penny-pinching, industrious antithesis to his two profligate predecessors Abdülmecid and Abdülaziz. He was second in line to the throne, after his brother Murad, and had therefore sought a uniquely unassuming, private working life that combined farming (*çiftçilik*) with mining to extract white lead (*üstübeç ocağı*) at his Maslak residence.[29] On his unexpected ascension to the throne (after a series of bizarre occurrences that saw his uncle and subsequently his brother deposed), he therefore devised Yıldız's gardens not only with elaborately landscaped segments attuned to the garden trends of the picturesque but also with arable acreage that supplied goods for the large population of the palace. The palace's porcelain factory also participated in the Hamidian ideals of imperial production: it allowed for independence from expensive imports; it self-sufficiently met the needs of the court; and it reignited a distinctly Ottoman craft.[30] Archival sources reveal that a partial subsistence economy was instituted to meet the palace's nutritional needs, featuring greenhouses, dairy and livestock farms, and fruit and vegetable gardens.[31]

The album's inclusion of the imperial estates in Kağıthane, Ayazağa, and Maslak substantiates the Hamidian reformation of Yıldız as both tillable *terra* and amusing scenery. In many ways, this late nineteenth-century sultan harked back to the garden practices of his ancestors, not only in the Topkapı-like form of Yıldız's multicourt, multipavilion layout, but also in his establishment of a self-sustaining economy of supply and demand in his palace and the other estates that collectively fell under the *ḥadāʾiḳ-i ḫāṣṣa* (imperial gardens).[32]

The main building on Prince Abdülhamid's demesne in Maslak still presents as a compact rectangular unit on the hilltop. The main building is an attenuated, two-floor manor house with a simple centralized plan and pronounced Dutch gables. The arrangement of its surroundings retains the rectilinear plan of the site's built-up sections. A greenhouse, fronted by the eclectic Victorianate Mabeyn Kiosk—used by Abdülhamid's scribes and for official meetings—sits perpendicular to the left side of the lodge, while a small stream with a cascade as its centerpiece parallels it on the right, both projecting out like the manor's two arms onto the grand entranceway. A small bathhouse, adjoined by rooms for the prince's aides, is located on the manor's sloping backyard. From the unlabeled map it appears that Abdülhamid, the amateur garden designer, introduced a miniature baroque landscape with pools, grottos, serpentine streams, and oval flowerbeds ringing the main building to enhance its centrality and separate its manicured civility from the rest of the site's intentional primitiveness. The painted vignettes of bucolic Alpine vistas with snow-capped mountains, tranquil cascading streams, and rustic huts found on every walled surface in the Maslak manor indicate the colder-climate source of inspiration for the hilltop estate. The special position of this site became even more evident during Abdülhamid's three-year Thessaloniki exile after his deposition, when he petitioned for his youngest son, Abid Efendi (also under house arrest), to be given the Maslak estate. This was a paternal attempt to provide his heir with the requisite agrarian education.[33]

The only known detailed description of the site is provided by Lady Enid Layard in her Constantinopolitan memoirs. She had been invited to accompany her husband, the British ambassador Henry Austen Layard, to an intimate diplomatic gathering in the Maslak pavilions during the early years of Abdülhamid's reign. Her narrative covers the tumultuous years of the Russo-Turkish War as experienced by a foreign contact close to the Hamidian court. Her day's proceedings reveal a newly enthroned sultan who still found pleasure, solace, and pride in the home of his own making. Dolmabahçe was Abdülhamid's first sultanic residence, and although he retained it as such for less than a year, he sought out the outdoors almost every Friday, after the *selamlık*. On Lady Layard's arrival in Maslak, she was most likely accompanied on a tour by the English-speaking court marshal (*ferîk*) Eğinli Said Paşa, who furnished her with information on Abdülhamid's own hand in the making of the site's grounds.

Thursday. 30th [August 1877].... After lunch I had to dress at once to go with Henry to meet *the Sultan at his farm at Maslak*. We started at 3. Mr Zarifi lent his carriage & we had 2 mounted cavasses. Maslak is only about ½ hours drive from here on the road to Pera. On the way we met two royal guards sent out to escort us. The house at Maslak is very like a *small English Cockney villa*. Said Pasha met us & Henry & he smoked & we had coffee out of diamond zarfs. In about ¼ hour the Sultan sent for us. He was in a small room on the ground floor with a sofa & a few chairs in it. He shook hands with us & made us all sit down. Henry congratulated him on the late victories & he thanked me for what I had done about the sick & wounded—& then he & Henry went on to talk politics thro' Said P. as an interpreter for nearly 2 hours. H.M. then asked us to go & walk in the grounds where we should find the grand vizier. The sultan looked worn & thin & very anxious—he said solemnly that the late victories showed that the hand of God was with the Turks in their just cause. We found the Grand Vizier Edhem P. & Server P. & Mahmoud Damat P. in a small kiosk smoking. They came out & walked about in the grounds with us till nearly 7. The grounds are very well kept *the trees having been planted by the Sultan before he came to the throne* & there are very pretty views right away to the Black Sea. There

is a lovely conservatory with fountains, creepers & masses of lycopodium. Abt ¼ to 7 we were called to dinner wh[ich] was laid in a small Kiosque leading out of the conservatory there we found the Sultan & he motioned me to a seat on his right & put Henry on his left.... H.M. made conversation with me all the dinner time talked of England & his visit there & was very agreeable. He noticed I drank no wine & told me he did not drink any & asked me to share some pink looking sherbet with him wh[ich] I did he constantly refilling my glass himself. It got dark while we were at table but candles were lighted, as were the lamps in the conservatory. The sound of the dripping of the fountain coming thro' the open door was very cool & pleasant.[34]

From Mahmud II's reign onward, Maslak and the sultan's northern lands in the capital, along with their neighboring pastures in Ayazağa, began to be populated with imperial pavilions for courtly summer pastimes such as archery and hunting, as well as for extrapalatial procedures whereby titles were granted or revoked. It was during Abdülaziz's time that the pavilions on these sites were rebuilt, and in the process Maslak seems to have acquired a rural-manor typology, characterized by Lady Layard as the "English Cockney villa" style. The two similarly boxy Ayazağa lodges, one with more classical features than its chalet-like counterpart, began to look increasingly like buildings from European country estates, clad with the faux rusticity of brick-and-mortar banded façades. In the early years of Abdülhamid's reign, these two sites started to be associated with extensive farming activities. The photograph

FIGURE 86 (*top*)
The Maslak Pavilion. From *Souvenir*.

FIGURE 87 (*bottom*)
The stud farm in Kağıthane. From *Souvenir*.

album includes images of buildings from the Maslak site—indeed, the only image to represent its subject structure frontally is of the Maslak manor (fig. 86)—because this was the sultan's previous home. The grazing pastures around Ayazağa are incorporated as pastoral extensions of the boundless domain overseen by his manor.

During the early years of Abdülhamid's rule, when he decided to visit Maslak, he made sure to drop by to survey Ayazağa. Eğinli Said Paşa, Lady Layard's guide through the Maslak residence, records in his diary entry for March 9, 1877, that after the Friday prayers, which were held in the sixteenth-century Fındıklı Mosque, Abdülhamid ordered a leisure trip out to the Maslak farm, and then to Ayazağa for dinner in the "mansion by the big pool" (büyük havzın başındaki olan köşk). Vigorous physical exercise succeeded the meal, as the sultan and his marshal Said Paşa rowed a boat in the pool ("ba'de'-ta'âm efendimizle ben havzda bulunan sandala girip birlikte kürek çektik").[35] It was during these occasional visits that the sultan developed plans to connect the two neighboring sites into one agricultural space to ensure the maximal use of their vast territories.[36]

Imperial residences were much more than simple heraldic emblems for the sultans, and this was especially true for Abdülhamid, who most stridently publicized the symbols of his sovereignty. To each sultan certain structures in the vast imperial architectural heritage meant more than others. Their visits to their favorite sites traced distinct imperial routes through the city during their respective reigns. Fashioning himself as the fragile Romantic sovereign, Abdülmecid took solitary strolls and staged intimate gatherings in the pastoral settings of the pavilions of Ihlamur, whereas the more robust Abdülaziz, in calculated contrast with his elder brother, often satisfied his penchant for outdoor activities by hunting and wrestling in the capacious outdoor settings around his lodges in Kağıthane, Acıbadem, and Ayazağa.[37] To commemorate Abdülhamid's two predecessors, the album includes images of sites closely associated with them, one of Abdülmecid's favorite pavilions of Ihlamur, and others of the stud farms (*ḥarā*) around Kağıthane and Ayazağa that Abdülaziz had installed (fig. 87). The fact that the album presents an image not of Ihlamur's ceremonial pavilion (*merāsim köşkü*), with its rococo façade and extravagant floral reliefs—a replica in miniature of Abdülmecid's main palatial commission of the Dolmabahçe—but rather of its more subdued neoclassical twin (*ma'iyyet köşkü*), designated for private use, is another telling sign that the album engaged a knowledgeable audience (fig. 88).[38] The intended viewer was someone privy to the private world of the sovereigns, who knew the functions and meanings of their estates.

SOUVENIR'S RECIPIENT(S)

Souvenir's expensive cover, created by the court binder, its sheer quantity of stills, and the intimacy with which the sultan's dwellings are depicted in it all suggest that the album was commissioned by Abdülhamid and that it was purposed as a gift.

The crowned monogram *B* on the album's back cover, with a crescent and star on the crown's crest, indicates that it was prepared for a member of the Egyptian khedivial family, and the date suggests Behidje Hassan, granddaughter of the former khedive Ismail Paşa (r. 1863–79). The memoirs of Behidje's nephew paint her as an independent woman

of great stature who owned a large Alhambresque mansion in the Zamalek district of Cairo, insisted on speaking in French to the younger members of her family, propounded humility, and was married to the wealthy Prince Omar Toussoun (a great-grandson of Muhammad Ali and an important man of letters with deep archeological and agricultural interests).[39] Behidje's sartorial choices reflected her humble and inquisitive personality, as she wore "the simplest gowns over her stout figure" and adorned "her round homely face with no visible makeup, . . . her twinkling eyes not missing a thing behind her spectacles."[40]

Female members of the khedivial family may have had greater access to and familiarity with Istanbul's royal sites than any other official visitor. Emine Sultan, Khedive Abbas Hilmi Paşa's mother and Behidje's aunt, was a frequent and much-beloved guest of

FIGURE 88
Ma'iyyet (retinue) Kiosk on the imperial estate of Ihlamur (Nüzhetiye). From *Souvenir*.

honor in Yıldız's mansions and gardens, for whom Abdülhamid created the intriguingly gender-bending title of Valide Paşa (literally "mother of the pasha," implying the khedive's mother). Her arrival on her yacht with a large Cairene entourage to settle into her art nouveau shoreline mansion in Istanbul's Bebek neighborhood was welcomed each summer with undiminished fanfare.[41] The layout and way of life inside the parklike grounds of her mansion were similar to those at Yıldız. She roamed around her grove in an "old-style ox-drawn carriage" (eski tarzda yaldızlı bir öküz arabası) and found repose in a small pavilion built atop the site's highest point. During the celebrations of Abdülhamid's birthdays and accession anniversaries, when all of the prominent gardens along the Bosphorus were lit up, her park was the most extravagant: electrically lit, "the entire grove would turn into a cascade of red- and green-tinted lights."[42]

Although the Valide Paşa summered in Istanbul, it was also compulsory under Ottoman court decorum that she be a part of Abdülhamid's harem cortège in the Friday prayer ceremonies held every fifteen days. In her memoirs, Abdülhamid's daughter Ayşe Sultan reminisces about the post-*selamlık* leisure hours taken by the members of the harem in the vast gardens of the palace, a site affectionately referred to by the residents of the palace as *kır* (used to mean the countryside).[43] They were also relatively free to roam the Kağıthane promenades or any other outdoor site that struck their fancy in the immediate aftermath of the brief, albeit dramatic and ceremonious, public appearances of their paterfamilias.

The memoirs of female court members relate that Abdülhamid's public hour generated generous leeway for field trips for his harem. In the section of Ayşe Sultan's memoir in which she recalls the harem ladies' extensive latitude in using the grounds inside and outside the palace, she also mentions that the Şale Kiosk was designated specifically for the use of the khedive's mother on those Friday afternoons.[44] Valide Paşa would later accompany her son Abbas Hilmi and extended family to Abdülhamid's theater, where they were assigned their own box from which to view the performances. Indeed, *Souvenir* photographs forty-nine through fifty-three lead the viewer on an in-depth tour around the Şale's structure and well-manicured garden, which was laid out in the English tradition (*ingilizkārī*).

This entire album could be assessed as a depiction of one of the Friday-afternoon outings of the Sultan's harem, which the women of the khedive's court may naturally have joined; and this would certainly have made a conscientious royal gift for a female member of the court's Egyptian viceroyalty. Throughout the nineteenth century, whenever the governors of Egypt paid a visit to their Ottoman suzerains—and especially when Muhammad Ali visited his grandson Said Paşa—they would be hosted in the Fer'iye palaces (the three structures whose name literally means "secondary" or "auxiliary"), built next to Çırağan to accommodate the court's most important guests and later the princes of the court.[45] Smaller functional adjacencies, such as the kitchens serving these waterfront imperial guesthouses, were located in groves that were later, during Abdülhamid's reign, absorbed into Yıldız's park for the construction of another guesthouse (which also makes an appearance in *Souvenir*). It seems that the neighborhood around the Çırağan-Yıldız imperial complex served as a second home to the Egyptian viceroys and their large family entourages throughout the century, even after they gained their own waterfront estates, with extensive forested hills, following Ismail Paşa's acquisition of the self-invented title of khedive.

Although the Yıldız photograph albums do not provide copies or versions of any of the stills in *Souvenir*, a few prints of these stills—never bound but instead inserted into cardboard frames—have emerged from the personal archives of the last Ottoman caliph Abdülmecid Efendi. *Souvenir*'s images, then, cannot be consigned to a gendered category, compiled merely to satisfy the gaze of female members of the khedivial harem by representing their cherished outdoor pastimes. They evidence a different category within the larger Hamidian photographic project—one that yielded to a wider field of courtly gazes. I believe that these photographs were commissioned specifically for members of the extended Ottoman court, who collectively represented an imperial audience that enjoyed the closest familiarity with the photographed sites. The compilations incorporating these pictures were the sultan's gifts to his family members—hence more immediate and personal versions of the albums prepared for international audiences—and were presented to them after their participation in religious ceremonies. For the individuals invited to take part in the court processionals, these images acted as visual reaffirmations that they were esteemed and protected members of the sultan's extended family. As purposefully familial souvenirs, the albums therefore participated as valuable objects in the domestic arena of court diplomacy. The sultan shared a formalized mode of intimacy

through these objects, which in turn garnered the allegiance of his family members.

A rustic garden bench topped by a gazebo (fig. 81), which makes an appearance in a few other post-1900 albums commissioned by Abdülhamid, is *Souvenir*'s opening image and bolsters the album's theme of intimate court diplomacy within Ottoman imperial retreats (see fig. 82). Surmounted by a roof that imitated the mud roofs of Native American hogans, with the feathery tips of arrows or bulrushes at its crest, and placed on elevated ground, the structure announced its presence from afar. This outdoor furniture of cement-clad iron is ubiquitous in the albums commissioned to report on the Istanbul stay of the Qajar ruler Muzaffar al-Din Shah of Iran in 1902, on his return from his third European visit.[46] In one of these albums, the shah's entry onto the Yıldız grounds is heralded by this structure, identified in the album's extant index as an "official greeting spot" (*mülākāt mahalli*), which was placed beside the gates that opened into the gardens of the Şale Kiosk. That *Souvenir* also initiates its garden tour with this structure signals to the viewer that a diplomatic threshold is about to be crossed: it offers the exclusive, privileged access reserved for diplomatic and familial acquaintances.

The second image confirms the album's display of intimacy with the site, wherein privileged access allows the select visitor to experience not only the courtly and the processional but also the whimsical and the unexpected (fig. 89). Resting on an artificial rocky base, the second structure depicted, too, appears miniature and ephemeral. However, unlike its rustic neighbor, positioned so as to be seen, this one is hidden among the garden's foliage and fulfills its role as a

FIGURE 89
A defunct *chinoiserie*-inspired pavilion in Yıldız. From *Souvenir*.

Köşkü, discussed in chapter 4) resting slightly below it and fronted by a projecting tented entrance, all manufactured and assembled specifically for the shah's arrival and week-long stay on the palace grounds.

The fact that *Souvenir* is in such good condition—as if untouched—suggests that it may never have come into Princess Behidje's possession. The date of the album's making (May to June 1905) must have coincided too closely with Abdülhamid's attempted assassination during a *selamlık* ceremony on July 21, 1905, as the final product seems not to have reached a few of the extracourtly recipients. Although the binders completed their work in the summer, the album's photographs are likely of the previous winter: all of the trees are barren, there are glimpses of snow on the ground, and the last photograph captures a group bundled up in jackets and hats. As court ceremonies are the album's subtext, the focus on camels on Yıldız's grounds makes it likely that the images were shot around the festive month of Ramadan, which in 1904 fell in early December, right before these animals would have been paraded off to the Holy Land, carrying the substantial yearly imperial dispensation of gold for the inhabitants of Mecca and Medina along with a bevy of pilgrims (*sūrre-i hümāyūn*).[47]

SOUVENIR'S PRECEDENTS

The anonymous photographer of *Souvenir* was not the first to be allowed to photograph the imperial estates of the capital. More than twenty albums in the collection of Abdülhamid II depict Istanbul's imperial sites. These albums were either commissioned by the sultan himself or put together by local or foreign photographers and presented to him in the hope of securing his recognition and perhaps

pleasure folly waiting to be discovered. Not only the art nouveau plaques along its base but also the structure's octagonal plan and swooping roof, held up by the thinnest of columns, nod toward the *chinoiserie* fad of the eighteenth-century garden folly. The two structures that begin the album speak to the palace garden's twofold function. The pleasure grounds of the harem would sporadically be transformed into settings for intimate diplomatic visits, and the album's first two structures participated in the choreography of both. In the albums created for the Qajar shah's visit as well, the compilers liked to cluster photographs of ephemeral-looking structures within the vicinity of the Şale. Analogous to the pairing of the bench in the form of a belvedere and the *chinoiserie* folly in the 1905 album, the four albums made for the shah from 1902 consistently pair the same gazebo with a square pavilion (the ʿAcem future employment. A considerable number of albums include the same photographs arranged in different permutations, which are reproductions (*ṣūret alma*) of gift albums presented to foreign dignitaries after their visits. The Muzaffar al-Din Shah albums are of this kind.

Souvenir's impressionistic frames are peculiar in that they share nothing in common with the published corpus of landscape and monument photographs from the turn of the century and tempt the viewer to play an admittedly dangerous connoisseurial guessing game: seeking to identify the hand of the artist by other means. Available historiographic studies of Ottoman photography, which either provide the biographies of specific individuals as pioneers of the profession (early foreign importers and developers of the technique, Greek and Armenian photographers of the sultans, and commercial photographers serving the tourist market) or offer surveys integrating these monographic studies into chronological order, provide no help, because they invariably elide inquiries into the formal aspects of the photographs or the photographers' pursuit of facture.[48]

Moreover, Abdullah Frères, Gülmez Brothers, Sebah & Joaillier, Basile Kargopoulo, Guillaume Gustave Berggren, James Robertson, and Ali Sami (later Aközer)—who were all at some point employed by the sultans—often etched their insignias or negative numbers on their inventories and occasionally on the hand-painted borders of their images.[49] Leaving a mark of ownership was essential for these court-sanctioned commercial artists because they marketed their products not only through the diversity of their genres—landscapes, seascapes, streetscapes, costumed portraiture, scenes from everyday life, and

cartes de visite,[50] to name but a few—but also through the particular methods of framing that reflected their brands. The date of production of *Souvenir* falls within the period of Bogos Tarkulyan's professional career as the owner of Atelier Phébus (1882 to 1936). By June 1905 the competitive heyday of Abdullah Frères and Sebah & Joaillier was over. Tarkulyan also shot the most intimate photographs in Abdülmecid Efendi's collection, in which it is easy to find members of the caliph's colorful literary salons, including Abdülhak Hamid and Recaizade Mahmut Ekrem, in garden settings.[51]

The Ottoman Greek photographer Basilc (Vasilaki) Kargopoulo was the first of these photographers to be granted access to Yıldız. His albums in the sultan's collection bear a photographer's mark to record his privileged position. He scratched his autograph (*B. Kargopoulo* in the Latin alphabet) into each negative and occasionally titled and numbered (enumerating the specific series to which a given still belonged) what he was shooting in the lower corners of his stills. The frequency with which his autographed handiwork appears in albums of imperial places indicates that he was handpicked specifically for the visual documentation of the royal grounds. Indeed, a detailed receipt from 1879 made out to Abdülhamid first lists the photographs of panoramas and landscapes of Istanbul and Yıldız, conventional and stereoscopic, that Kargopoulo took in July of that year.[52]

A biographical study of the lives of Ottoman photographers highlights a professional rivalry between the more famous Abdullah Frères and Kargopoulo that hinged on their different religious affiliations and the respective political connotations of those affiliations at the time. Kargopoulo's rise to fame

imperial palaces and kiosks" (vues panora-
mique des intérieurs et extérieurs de tous
les palais et kiosques impériaux) in the first
issue of the Orient's trade journal from 1880.[54]
His collections concerning Istanbul's palaces
and pavilions (among them Yıldız, Dolmabahçe, Beylerbeyi, Beykoz, Göksu, Kağıthane,
Ihlamur, and occasionally Topkapı) were
the most frequently reproduced and also
dominated the court's many gift albums in
diverse permutations. The out-of-sequence
negative numbers on the stills in each album
speak to their continual replication and use
in the 1880s and 1890s.[55] Kargopoulo's images
of palatial sites, often dramatic shots of the
unpopulated exteriors and interiors, encom-
passed each structure as holistically as possible. The court apparently desired the photographic representation of its structures to be
simultaneously unambiguous and imposing,
and not at all focused on their artisanal qualities in ornamental details.

For his famed grand panoramas from
1875, Kargopoulo had to weave individual
segmented negatives into each other and
manipulate the gradational tones of each to
achieve tonal consistency in a shot that ultimately measured up to 3.5 meters in length.[56]
Kargopoulo enjoyed his designation as the
plein air photographer of the court from 1879
until his death in 1885. During that time he
fully embraced the sartorial characteristics
of his adopted artistic identity. He occasionally inserted himself into his compositions
in the guise of a wandering *flâneur*, strolling
along the scenic Bosphorus hills or in Edirne's
old palace, dressed in a full beard, artist's
overcoat, and top hat. He donned the persona of the expressionist artist upon entering
the grounds of Yıldız as the first photographer to take a visual survey of the inner

as Abdülhamid's court photographer follows
the fall from grace of the three Abdullahs, the
Armenian court photographers of the former
sultan Abdülaziz, ostensibly due to the documented involvement of Kevork Abdullah—the
more fervently nationalistic of the brothers—
with Russian diplomats during the signing
of the later unratified treaty of San Stefano
(which ended the 1877–78 Russo-Turkish
War).[53]

Ultimately, what won Kargopoulo the title
of court photographer seems to have been
his skill in photographing vast expanses—his
preoccupation with the monumental applied
to buildings as well as vistas. It is no coincidence that he boldly advertised his practice
by stressing his expertise, "stereoscopic and
panoramic views" (vues panoramas, vues ste-
reoscopiques), in the 1879 receipt and, after
receiving the court commission, "panoramic
views of the interiors and exteriors of all the

grounds. In Kargopoulo's photographs of the site, a garden palace in which landscape dictated the terms of the built environment and nature took precedence over architecture, he seems willfully to lose himself in the palace's steep and winding woods, to find momentary repose on the hilltops, to shoot partial views of rustic huts by the lake, and to allow the landscape to guide him through vistas that naturally break into partial views. The photographers of this particular palace, once introduced to the world within its walls, were incapable of producing comprehensive panoramas: Yıldız's particular topography forced these individuals, including Kargopoulo, the site's first surveyor, to capture nature's scenes on gradients, at angles, or in fragments, and therefore at times to attenuate their frames. It is partly to Kargopoulo that the unknown photographer of the 1905 album owes his quixotic eye (figs. 90–91).

ABDÜLHAMID AND ARCHITECTURAL PRESERVATION

With Abdülhamid's accession to the throne, a project for the preservation of imperial structures in the capital was placed on the state-rebuilding agenda. Instead of commissioning grand palatial structures like his two predecessors, Abdülhamid, always conscious of the pull of living history on his subjects, invested frugally in reinventing the architecture of his rule. In the process, he invigorated his persona as a preservationist sultan. He wanted the ancient buildings of the house of Osman to look unsullied and timeless. "Spared by time," they had to evince the glorious imperial past and simultaneously signal him as their caretaker. Undeniably, this preservationist aspect of his rule was in keeping with the overtly patriarchal mode

with which he would choose to commemorate his sovereignty: modest but abundant architectural markers such as clock towers and plaques on mosques and fountains were diffused all the way into the empire's smallest localities. The "world of symbols" invented and displayed in the built environment to stand vicariously for his authority often tied his sovereignty to that of his earliest ancestors. Selim Deringil describes Abdülhamid's selective accentuation and mythification of his ancestral history through restorations of the tombs of the first two sultans, Osman and Orhan, in Bursa; canonization of the tomb of Ertuğrul (Osman's father) in Söğüt via yearly reenactments of the empire's partly apocryphal origin stories; and the site's transformation into a mostly representative necropolis for Ertuğrul's wife and closest military companions.[57] The new sultan knew how to mobilize his architectural heritage.

FIGURE 91
A defunct rustic cabin in Yıldız's outer garden. From *Souvenir.*

The renovation of imperial sites in the capital began with an edict dated August 19, 1881, exactly twelve days before the fifth anniversary of Abdülhamid's accession to the throne. This edict explicitly announced the sultan's heritage-protection plans for the imperial sites in the capital. It urged the assembly of a committee of builders consisting of "benevolently inclined Serkis Bey, the head architect of the state, prosperous Mahmud Mesud Paşa, former head of the military, and fortunate Vasilaki Kalfa" (ser-mi'mār-ı devlet 'uṭūfetlü Serkiz Beǧ, erkān-ı ḥarbiyye re'īsi sābıḳ sa'ādetlü Maḥmūd Mes'ūd Paşa, ve sa'ādetlü Vāsilāki Ḳalfa), as well as "various other structural experts" (ebnīye işlerine vāḳıf icāb eden me'mūrlar), to restore, before the onset of winter, all of the palaces and pavilions, in varying degrees of decay ("ḫarāba yüz ṭutmaḳ dereceleri"), that had been erected by the sultan's more immediate predecessors for "four to five million liras" (dört beş milyon lirā ṣarfı). The emphatic nature of the edict was communicated in its opening phrase, which described "the noblest edifices of our most illustrious ancestors, our veritable benefactors" (ecdād–ı 'iẓām-ı velī-ni'met-i 'āẓamī āṣār-ı celīlesi) as on the brink of ruin because their upkeep had largely been ignored in the preceding years. The commission was assigned to produce registers detailing all of the repairs required based on inspection of the sultan's palaces and pavilions, "excluding the Palace of Çırağan" (Çırāġān sāḥilsarāy-ı hümāyūnundan mā'adā)—either because it now imprisoned his deposed and psychologically unwell brother Murad V or because it was the most recently erected palace and did not require urgent care.[58]

The spectral existence of Abdülaziz's neo-Andalusian palace during its time as the site of Murad V's house arrest is communicated in the imperial photograph albums via its puzzlingly infrequent appearances. This recurring lacuna indicates that the palace was diligently omitted from representations of the Hamidian dwellings, suggesting that its exclusion from the restoration project had more to do with its ignominious occupant than with its state of repair. Only seven images in two Yıldız albums have thus far been found to contain representations of this palace. One is a comically distant view of the European shoreline's palaces from a hilltop across the straits, where Çırağan gleams as a faint white strip, and another five, from the second album, are interior shots of the palace's ghostly main hall, all accentuating its ornamental scheme of horseshoe arches, cubes of elaborately carved column capitals, and abundant wooden and marble inlays.[59] A viewer of the latter album unfamiliar with the interiors of this structure would find it impossible to determine which imperial residence this set of five photographs depicted.

Seventy-five repair- and construction-related expense registers (*defter*s) from 1883, each either specific to a particular building on an imperial site (e.g., the quarters of the chief eunuch at Yıldız or the new imperial stables in Kağıthane) or depicting a cluster of repairs to a few buildings of an estate (e.g., the Maslak and Ayazağa kiosks and their surroundings), minutely detail the built results of this restoration project.[60] Like *Souvenir*, the registers show that the attention of the preservation commission was focused on Yıldız; its members advised on repairs but also on the erection of brand-new structures to improve on Yıldız's only recently adopted palatial status. In his memoir Eğinli Said Paşa, after only briefly mentioning the sultan's visits to the Yıldız mountain, rather abruptly announces the imperial move in an entry from April 19, 1877, thereby proclaiming the shift in Yıldız's designation from a mansion (*kaṣır*) to a palace (*sarāy*). "On this day, the imperial transfer from the Beşiktaş imperial palace to the Yıldız imperial mansion took place, and the latter was designated the Yıldız imperial palace" (Bugün Beşiktaş saray-ı hümâyunu'ndan Yıldız kasr-ı hümâyunu'na bütün bütün nakl-i hümâyun vukū' bulup Yıldız saray-ı hümâyunu ismi verilmiştir).[61] It could very well be that under the guise of a much broader preservation project and a claim of thriftiness—a concept greatly underscored in the laudatory advice narratives that two intellectuals of the period presented to Abdülhamid on his accession, Ahmed Mithat's *Üss-ı İnkılāb* (The principle of revolution) and Ahmed Cevdet Paşa's *Ma'rūżāt* (Submissions)—the sultan was legitimizing his expenditure on his chosen, underequipped palatial site.

Whether or not economic austerity was successfully implemented, with cost-cutting measures benefiting the imperial treasury's reserves in the initial years of his rule, Abdülhamid still managed to reinvoke the unity and sacrality of royal space through the architectural agenda of photographing, surveying, describing, and restoring that accompanied the preservation project. In some ways Kargopoulo's diligent architectural documentation and the architecture commission's conservation surveys were similar to the French Mission héliographique of 1851, which culled France's best photographers to chronicle the Second Republic's entire architectural patrimony, not only establishing a historical record but also using photographic evidence in a large-scale conservation project.[62]

Souvenir represents the moment of completion of Abdülhamid's restoration project and final palace, and the viewers of such picture albums understood the geography and content of the reigning sultan's memoirs of place, his refuges within the capital interconnected through his personal history.

INCLUSIONS

The album's images of Yıldız and its biographically linked sites plot a route around the northern and western stretches of the continually expanding capital. When the album's destinations are plotted on a map, the physical tour takes the viewer on a wide but easily navigable loop that emanates from a main artery, Büyükdere Road. Steadily distal to the former center of the capital, Büyükdere emerged in the nineteenth century—especially in the summer months, when the embassies moved down to their seaside palaces—as the new imperial land route, signaling a change in the landscape of Ottoman political life, which had begun to revolve around foreign affairs. During and after the Russo-Turkish War, when contact between the European embassies in Istanbul and Yıldız intensified, the scenic Büyükdere ridge connected the summer residences of foreign representatives to the palace, benefiting individuals like Lady Layard. In the summer months, this ridge also joined the khedivial family's mansions (and the beloved Valide Paşa) to the palace and offered an alternative to the busy waterways of diplomatic life between the Tarabya and Kabataş docks. For instance, Georgina Müller, the wife of the German Orientalist Max Müller, when visiting Yıldız's famed library with her husband as Abdülhamid's personal guests, took this route ("the high-road") from the summer residence of the British embassy and jotted down her impressions of it as follows: "With some difficulty we got a carriage, and drove into Yildiz. We had first a long ascent from Therapia up the wooded valley of Krio-Nero, or cold water. Once out of this ascent we were in the so-called high-road leading along the top of the hills bordering the Bosphorus, direct to Pera. The road ran too far inland for us to see the water, but all along we had lovely views of the hills on the Asiatic shore."[63] Ottoman albums began to resemble visual counterparts to specific travel routes and to illustrate the psychogeographies of Istanbul's inhabitants. Looking closely at an Abdullah Frères album entitled *Vues et types de Constantinople: Photographie d'après nature* from 1885, a recent study argues that the photographed sites imply a panorama along the lines of *Souvenir*'s implied hilltop loop.[64] Although the older album continues the photographic tradition of focusing on sites from the historical peninsula, it briefly turns its lens to the Asian shore and incorporates a few of the eastern vistas as seen from the European side of Istanbul. Some of these places are also traversed by *Souvenir*. The sites photographed in the *Vues et types de Constantinople* were connected during that period by steamboat routes, which brought them physically closer. The speedier travel and ease of access within the city afforded by these routes, which had ingrained themselves in the cognitive map of the album's viewer, would have encouraged a reading of the Abdullah Frères album as an implicit panorama of the growing city.[65] It threaded together these sites—which could now all be visited in a single day—rather than focus on a specific, more restricted segment.

A court-commissioned mammoth (216 by 216 centimeters) topographic map from 1878 that was drawn up by the military academy delineates the very route later photographically depicted in *Souvenir*: "The imperial palace of Yıldız, imperial pavilions of Ayazağa and Kağıthane, and the extant properties around them" (Yıldız sarāy-ı hümāyūnuyla Ayāzāġā ve Kāġıdḫāne ḳaṣr-ı hümāyūnları ve eṭrāf ü civārında vāḳiʿ ārāżi) (fig. 92).[66] If the preservationist edict from 1881 offers insight into the new sultan's architectural interests, the map depicts the section of the capital to which the sultan was most interested in connecting his palace. An urban landscaping project from 1874 along Büyükdere Road signaled the court's turn toward the city's unpopulated northern uplands. Gustave Deroin, Sultan Abdülaziz's head gardener at Yıldız when the site was an imperial estate and not yet a palace, planted two thousand trees on the Yıldız-Ayazağa portion of the road to enliven it.[67]

One can imagine the map being unfurled onto a large table in the palace library or in the stubby Çit Kiosk (right behind the Mabeyn Kiosk), where equally colossal "relief maps" (ḳabārtma ḫarīṭa) of the empire were exhibited and scrutinized by members of the administration.[68] The sultan would have had to walk around and hover over the massive folio to fully grasp the dizzying contour lines that marked the hilly terrain—lines interrupted only sparingly by the outlines and layouts of imperial residences, all of which, in turn, neatly bound the map's peripheries. These outlines in pink are generously depicted, surrounded by their extensive landscaping. Yıldız is delineated by the easily recognizable silhouette of Mabeyn Kiosk, yet the palace's vast grounds are, disappointingly, left out. Elsewhere, the map accents Kağıthane's attenuated spread along the river in minute detail, as well as the configuration

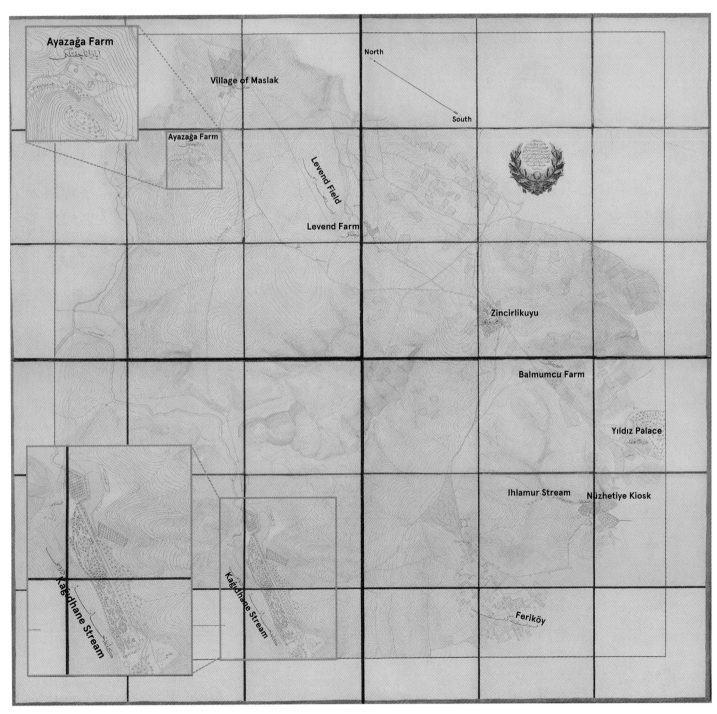

Ayazağa Farm

ايازاغا جفتلكی

Village of Maslak

Ayazağa Farm

North

South

Levend Field

Levend Farm

Zincirlikuyu

Balmumcu Farm

Yıldız Palace

Kağıdhane Stream

Kağıdhane Stream

Ihlamur Stream

Nüzhetiye Kiosk

Feriköy

FIGURE 92
"The imperial palace of Yıldız, imperial pavilions of Ayazağa and Kağıthane, and the extant properties around them" (Yıldız sarāy-ı hümāyūnuyla Ayāzāġā ve Kāġıdḫāne ḳaṣr-ı hümāyūnları ve eṭrāf ü civārında vāḳiʿ ārāżi). İÜMK, 92911.

of Ayazağa's pavilions. Cultivated land is plotted in small green squares in the village of Maslak, on either side of the Kağıthane stream, and in the vicinity of the Nüzhetiye Pavilions. The map completely elides the urban sprawl of Istanbul between these imperial sites except for some indiscriminately outlined settlements in Feriköy and a speckling of police stations (*karagol*) inconspicuously (which is unsurprising, given the anxieties of the Hamidian era) nestled in the entrances of the imperial residences.

Inside the pages of *Souvenir* this new, preferred loop along Büyükdere is rhythmically broken by a repeated return to the gardens of Yıldız. Images of the main sultanic residence function as place markers and constant reminders of the palace's centripetal presence in the newly designated imperial stretch. In an almost perfect *a-b-a-c-a-d* cadence, the album's thirty photographs of Yıldız engulf the Maslak, Ayazağa, Ihlamur, and Kağıthane sites, punctuate the narrative, and topically signal what will be exhibited next in the album. Helping to place the photographs are snippets of identifiable buildings, such as the turreted additions to the Şale Kiosk made by Raimondo D'Aronco or the steep vistas associated with the site in earlier photographs by Kargopoulo and landscape paintings by Şeker Ahmed Paşa and the Italian court painter Fausto Zonaro.[69] Not every location depicted in the photographs, however, is easily identifiable; particularly obscure are places related to farming (ox-drawn plows, flocks of sheep) and the menageries (zebras, springbok, and ostriches). This is partly because the album assumes its owner's intimacy with these places, and also because Abdülhamid saw these sites as fluidly interconnected in courtly function.

SOUVENIR'S YILDIZ

The first thirty photographs of *Souvenir* are identifiably shots of Yıldız. Among these palace photographs, the images from the third to the tenth can be grouped separately as having served a more procedural function before being serialized in the luxurious album. The snapshot effect of these particular images, and the way they frame landscaping features around an imperial structure without engaging specifically with the building, connect them with the use of photography in practices of land surveying (*mesāḥa*). For instance, the third image in the album, which presents the first stately structure modeled on an eighteenth-century French urban mansion with a strangely attenuated Mansard roof, compositionally maintains a considerable distance from the building and instead foregrounds a large pool cascading over an uneven rockery. In the next photograph, the photographer has turned around to complete the preceding image by showing where the streaming water lands, along with the cliffside boundary of the mansion's garden. Another image gives a side view of the building, with an elevated, picketed circular zone ready to receive another garden *fabrique*. When first taken, this group of photographs probably formed a visual compendium of the landscaping project in this segment of the palace's gardens—a novel way to document the completed work for the patron or bookkeeper. Although the archives have yet to yield accompanying descriptions for this project, existing accounts do show that photographs were often attached to construction and repair records for sites that belonged to the imperial treasury during Abdülhamid's reign.

The photographer of these sites could very well have been the imperial head gardener of the period, Charles Henry, or his French collaborator, the landscape artist Gustave Deroin, who was often tasked with drawing up plans for gardening projects on imperial sites. The fact that a gardening book was recycled for the photographs' matting, coupled with the photographer's eagerness to highlight the newly landscaped grounds over the individual buildings (especially in the case of Yıldız), increases the probability that a garden expert was involved in the album's making. This individual wanted to present the imperial gardens much as they were painstakingly listed in the employment registers of gardeners at the time: often hierarchically arranged, with Yıldız always appearing at the very top.

The opening images of the album present the newest and final section that Abdülhamid would introduce to his complex. Following in the footsteps of his predecessors, the sultan for decades considered the garden settings of his palace and retreats to be prime platforms for diplomatic gatherings and ceremonies. Yet it seems that the largest of these settings, that of the Şale Kiosk, was deemed insufficient at the turn of the century. To accommodate his frequent imperial guests, the sultan needed more space—a new structure that would be closer to the imperial porcelain factory and provide easier access to the large park and its two other Abdülaziz-era pavilions, Malta and Çadır, than the Şale, which now stood uncomfortably close to his private quarters. From its inception as a palace, Yıldız had to answer to the regular requests of high-placed members of the European diplomatic community to visit the imperial library, its adjacent museum, and the porcelain factory.[70] The sultan cultivated this demand by including the sites in the palace tours that he granted his foreign guests; reports of these visits fed the desire of others, who saw them as sites of privileged access. Abdülhamid may or may not have wanted greater privacy in the third decade of his rule, but whatever his motivation, he created a fully self-sufficient guest zone that fulfilled his visitors' requirements for both rest and entertainment.

The gardens of the Ferʿiye Palaces were absorbed into Yıldız to make up a large part of this new segment. The album's photographer documents the structures that delineated the boundaries of this newly appropriated area. The new imperial guesthouse, depicted in the album's third image, which looks like an eighteenth-century French urban mansion, was built on the foundations of the single-story home of the former imperial head gardener Christian Sester, which until the 1890s had fallen outside Yıldız's imperial grounds. Sester's residence was incorporated into this new section, along with the gardens belonging to Ferʿiye, and commanded the highest point of its northwesterly edge. If the photographer, or the person responsible for commissioning at least the first set of images in the album, did indeed belong to the gardening profession, the images of this site in *Souvenir* take on new poignancy, documenting as they do a change of hands in the gardener's office—a transition from German to French authority over the imperial post. By reworking an area and neighborhood that had been closely associated with the first head gardener, the newcomer laid claim to the sites newly under his jurisdiction.

This set of images not only helps to identify the exact location of Abdülhamid's last imperial commission in Yıldız by providing shots of its boundaries and of its vistas overlooking Ortaköy's shoreline, but also reveals something about the pragmatism of architectural patronage, even at the sultanic level. It seems that commissions were not always site specific. The French *hôtel*-type first appears among an eclectic assortment of residential plans drafted in 1900 by the prolific Levantine architect Alexandre Vallaury for Abdülhamid's five sons and intended to be strung along the suburban garden retreat of Kurbağalı Dere on the Asian shores of the Kadıköy neighborhood—a pleasure garden first bestowed on Abdülaziz by his brother Abdülmecid during the latter's tenure as sultan.[71] Although plots earmarked for these mansions can be found on the Pervititch maps from the 1920s, they were never built. Instead, a modified version of the last Vallaury project was recycled for Abdülhamid's new guest lodge, which replaced Sester's home (map 3, no. 67) (see fig. 43).[72] To fit the site's sloping topography and orientation toward the Bosphorus, the narrower side of the planned building was turned into the main façade of the built version. The structure retained its three stories (excluding the service floor in an elevated basement), but its attenuated attic floor was replaced with blank conical decorative projections that framed the dormer windows in the design's elevation. The Serlian windows in the design were broken up on the building's second floor by rectangular ones. Overall, the decorative reliefs that bracketed most of the apertures of the projected building were reduced in the built version to their bare minimum: the Mansard roof lost its scaled slates and widow's walks, the corners of the façade's tripartite arrangement had no brick articulations, chimney bases were deprived of their intended vase-shaped reliefs, and second-floor windows lost their voussoirs. White paint replaced the

banded rustication that wrapped around the projected façade, and the pilasters breaking up the series of windows on the third floor received Corinthian capitals flatter than those on the paper version of the building. The internal arrangement of the rooms, especially the main halls in the original plan, were probably shrunk to fit the new, narrower orientation facing the commanding Ortaköy views of the subimperial *yalı*s appointed by the sultan to his daughters.

It is difficult to read the hand of Vallaury in these unself-conscious modifications, which resulted in an idiosyncratic version of the miniature Versailles presented on paper. The *Annuaire oriental* from 1900 lists Vasilaki Kalfa's son Yanko ("Yanco Eff. Joannidi") as the palace's chief architect, and D'Aronco as his assistant; were they, therefore, involved in this adaptation of a retreat for princes to a site much more visible to an intended audience of international visitors?[73] Vallaury and D'Aronco had a history of collaborating on civic projects in an inventive Neo-orientalist idiom for the state's Ministry of Pious Endowments (*evḳāf neẓāreti*).[74] The flexibility observed in the use of plans and the implementation of projects was in practice similar to that exercised by the imperial commissions in their accommodation of collaborations between the palace's in-house architects and independent architects like Vallaury, who was hired to design not only residences for members of the Ottoman court but also some of the most important civic structures of the period.

If the album's first layer of meaning, especially in the opening ten shots, can be found in the way newly built areas of the palace were documented for bureaucratic purposes, the second lies in the intention to take the album's audience—the court's privileged visitor—on a tour of this guest zone, illustrating the physical connections between the new imperial building and various points of interest within the garden. The photographer's first stop is the porcelain factory, the structure closest to the new mansion; he then proceeds into the park to visit its ivy-covered pavilions, painstakingly mapping the routes along the way. As he takes his walking tour, he reveals not only a transition from more-private to more-public spaces but also a visible widening of the camera lens in the scenes he captures, from specific buildings and garden features to vaster vistas, finally offering a complete picture of the cherished Hamidian estates.

PARTITIONS

This album neither retains the ordering impulses of its distant cousins, in which each photograph validates a single fact about the empire's many material advances and ever-stoic glory, nor depicts the vast and austere expanses against which modernity's objects (e.g., battleships or railways) and subjects (e.g., students or patients) were foregrounded. Rather, it solicits an impressionistic and familial eye from its viewer, attuned to the interplay of light, color, and movement yet also percipient enough to discern the intention behind the sequenced narrative of Abdülhamid's private turf and personal preference for royal dwellings in the capital. In other words, the contents of this album present no simple visual certification of a monolithic edifice or a stately yet indistinct panoramic landscape of the capital, but a photographic narrative that requires the viewer to associate each image with the next and intuit the imperial program behind the sites depicted.

By calibrating the lens more pensively, compared with the reductive way in which the city's foreign audience focused on the picturesque (with each perfectly manicured landscape pronouncing an individual structure), this album asks its viewer to labor over meanings (of land), be considerably more introspective (about the photographic content), and form associations (concerning empire). Its unknown photographer places Yıldız in its Hamidian architectural lineage by summoning the irrevocable link between the Ottoman imperial edifice and the abundant verdancy of the city. Drawing from travel writings on the empire's capital, all prefaced with similar expressions of awe before nature, Ahmet Hamdi Tanpınar speaks as if to the album's heart when he writes, "Not only is Istanbul a city abundant in monuments and monument-like edifices, but the city's nature aids in the display of these structures."[75]

The album's shots of particularly knobby and tufted segments of gardens and pastures signal the impending appearance of structures in such a way as to give the impression that they were discovered during a series of nature walks. The photographer uses these nature shots to multifarious effect to illustrate that what sustains the Hamidian house is the fecundity of its land: the possession of both fertile and scenic nature supports the royal dwelling. The frequency of these shots also blurs the transitions between the sites represented in the album. The photographer intensifies the idea of the boundlessness of the sultan's domains in the capital by arbitrarily ending the viewer's time in one and moving on to another. Despite being representationally incongruous with the photographs of picturesque meanderings in the album, images of farming are factored into

ALB.156/5

5

FIGURE 93
Picket fences of the menagerie belonging to Yıldız's expanded section. From *Souvenir*.

he foregrounds gates, walls, bridges, and fences, which distinguish the two zones in each estate. In one instance, with what appears to be a dog scurrying out of the shot in the lower left-hand corner, the photographic plane is separated into two sections by a picket fence, while the plunging vista draws the eye to the Ortaköy shoreline palaces of the immediate members of the court, including that of Gazi Osman Paşa and the demure, neoclassical residences of Abdülhamid's daughter Zekiye Sultan (fig. 93). In another photograph, fences that delimit Yıldız's grazing pastures occupy the foreground of an image that intimates the outlines of small residential pavilions in the hilly background. This peculiar fascination with the physical demarcations of land—between urban and rural, man-made and natural, the palace and its domains—comes up frequently in the novels and memoirs of the Ottoman intellectuals of the period.

While serving as a scribe in the Ottoman embassy in London, Abdülhak Hamid, one of the most illustrious Ottoman poets of the second half of the nineteenth century, reflected on the city's ability to conjoin the town (*belde*) and country (*sahra*). He observed that the only thing separating Piccadilly Street's prosperous (*mamur*) urban sprawl from the royal parks around Buckingham Palace (Green Park and St. James Park) was a railing (*parmaklık*). Through this simple partition the city dweller accessed civilized country living (*sahra-ı medeniyet*), a space that performed rusticity without any of its potentially displeasing inconveniences: "It is *as if* those parks are like villages in every sense" (Sanki o parklar her mânâsıyla rustâidir).[76]

In a similar vein, Recaizade Mahmud Ekrem, Hamid's literary mentor, begins his

these nature walks precisely to highlight Abdülhamid's dual conception of nature as beautiful and bountiful.

To further accentuate the duality of the imperial estate, containing both artificial and natural terrains, the photographer obsessively captures partitions between the two. From the fourth image in the album, well-known satirical novel *Araba Sevdası* (The carriage affair), of 1896, with a detailed cartographic description of the walled exteriors of Çamlıca gardens, Istanbul's first public park. Imagining himself as "a bird gliding over the famous hilltop" (*yüksekten kuş bakışı bir nazarla bakmak mümkün olsa*), Recaizade's omniscient narrator describes this urban intervention as cutting an elongated conical segment (*şekl-i mahrūtī*) out of the otherwise virgin landscape. The novel's first subjects are the very partitions—walls (*duvār ile muhāṭ*) and wires (*teller uzatılarak muhāfaza*)—that mark the park's plot, protect this "civilized country" from prying eyes and animals, and separate it from the derelict rocky cemetery of Şarı Ḳaya (the Tawny Rock) on its northernmost borders.[77] Here, for the first time, a public space was constructed out of land that was never actually inaccessible to the residents of the city. Indeed, many adventurous climbers would use this very spot to survey Istanbul's European cityscape. What mattered to the park's builders was how this space could perform civility in nature; the peculiar, paradoxical phrase *sahra-ı medeniyet* used by Hamid to describe London's parks makes sense in this context. For that performance, the borders and partitions had to be pronounced and visible. Nature's turn to artifice must have caught Recaizade's attention and impelled him to write this almost tiresomely punctilious analysis of its boundaries. Indeed, the first illustration of the serialized novel, which was made by the celebrated military painter Halil Paşa (d. 1939), offers a perspectival view of the park's iron entrance gates (fig. 94). It is only after the narrator surveys the site's boundaries that he walks his readers into the safety of an idyllic Rousseauian park with "small hut-like buildings" (*ḳulübe ṭarzında*

ufak ufak binālar), gazebos (*ḳameriyeler*), a lake (*lāḳ*), a pleasing island (*dilnişīn bir adacıḳ*), and "bridges molded out of irregular hedges" (*ṣūret-i ġayr-ı muntaẓamada çitten yapılmış ṭabiʿī güzel köprüler*)—in no way different from *Souvenir*'s photographs of Yıldız, particularly of the English-style, rustic make-believe of the Şale's environs.[78]

Many Ottoman literary opponents to Abdülhamid's rule, especially following his

FIGURE 94
Halil Paşa's painting of the entrance to the Çamlıca garden. From Recaʾizāde Maḥmūd Ekrem, *ʿAraba Sevdāsı, Muṣavver Millī Ḥikāye* (1314 [1896]).

dissolution of the short-lived first constitutional period (1876–77), saw partitions as deeply troubling metaphors. Writing about the sultan's commission of Yıldız, they focused on his erection of imposing, impenetrable walls around its perimeters—"walls so high that only birds who trust the might of their wings can fly over" (üzerinden ancak kanatlarına güvenen kuşlar geçebilecek kadar yüksek duvarlar). These barriers were presented as a metaphor for Abdülhamid's descent into despotism, alienating his subjects, once and for all, from representational rights, even as he sealed himself off from their world.[79]

Souvenir and the twenty other albums in the imperial collection are a testament to how royal space was continually represented and reproduced through the photographic medium. In a way, the photographic book became a new kind of imperial chronicle in the Hamidian period, during which traditional chronicle writing came to a halt, largely due to the speed with which information began to be shared and to Abdülhamid's decision to sustain a chronicler only on principle. His rule was only retrospectively and vitriolically elaborated, by his successor's historians.[80]

Undeniably, Abdülhamid II invested deeply in the power of the photographic image; its positivist representation, magnified by imperial tunnel vision, was a stand-in for *his* carefully manipulated truth. No better illustration of Abdülhamid's conception of an image can be found than the oft-repeated quotation, recorded by his scribe Tahsin Paşa in his memoirs, in which the sultan explains his penchant for browsing images from foreign newspapers and journals: "Every image

[*resim*] is a thought. One image can prompt [*telkin*] political and sentimental meanings [*siyâsî ve hissî manalar*] that a hundred-page text cannot. That is why I benefit more from images than contents recorded in writing [*tahrirî münderecâtlar*]."[81] I have claimed that certain images from Abdülhamid's vast collection—mostly photographs, but also some lithographs of paintings and engravings, which were often bound alongside instances of their competitor medium—were primary informants of his architectural decisions. It is therefore best to understand Abdülhamid's conception of *resim* as broadly and as inclusively as possible; the term should not be considered to designate photographs alone but should be applied to a larger group of visual media, releasing the photographic medium from its role as the ultimate visual proof for the period and liberating the sultan's biography from at least one overly proclaimed fixation.

Abdülhamid may have accrued an ever-growing collection of photographs with which to survey the nineteenth-century world from hermetic repose. Indeed, Samuel Cox, the one-time American ambassador to Ottoman Istanbul, offers a brief vignette of the sultan quietly perusing photographs of Native Americans inside one of his *Atala*-inspired rustic huts in Yıldız's parks and describes the closely guarded *cartes de visite* of the German emperor and empress on Abdülhamid's side table. Moreover, the sultan simultaneously created a modern visual documentary treasury, all preserved in red binding, "so that at once the *entente cordiale* is established between the various volumes,"[82] and servicing the conjoined acts of collecting, compiling, and consulting. Each *resim*, often instrumentalized for the production of another related medium (e.g., murals, porcelain tableaus, or paintings on canvas), should also be understood within this grand repository. His collection, augmented by commissions, bearers of gifts, and keepers of his library, could perhaps even be considered a monumental, comprehensive *mecmūʿa* (an often-personal album or scrapbook with mixed contents) of his nineteenth-century world.[83]

Under its sumptuous cladding, *Souvenir* is a unique historical document that exhibits Yıldız's genealogical links, through the sultan's intercession, to other structures within the larger repertoire of Ottoman ancestral architecture. The album's contents stage a textless, pictorial exchange between the palace and other deliberately selected imperial residences of the capital with which it shared structural affinities and, for its patron Abdülhamid, lived experiences that merited special commemorative documentation. By decoding these affinities through *Souvenir*'s deliberately ordered images, we gather insights into the palace's otherwise seemingly idiosyncratic configuration, the various forms of its individual structures, and its use. In short, the album provides a more compelling explanation than any narrative description of why Yıldız took the shape it did in the latter half of the nineteenth century.

Coda

PALACE MOSQUE, PALACE THEATER

For Abdülhamid II, royal spectacle came in two sharply contrasting forms: intimately private and ceremoniously public. Although he made sure that his weekly *selamlık*, during which he took center stage riding alone in a carriage, wearing a modest suit (fig. 95, an oft-reproduced but hollow image), was always a well-attended public event, he was, by and large, invisible to most of his subjects. He was much more readily available to visiting heads of state, ambassadors, and delegates, especially those with whom he was eager to form an alliance. Even his harshest critics agree that he played the game of diplomacy exceptionally well, knowing how to please his would-be allies and skillfully but deferentially evade his detractors.[1]

Although Abdülhamid's court ceremonies and diplomatic receptions were ostentatious, grand, and meticulously planned, the two structures in which he presented himself most frequently—his mosque and theater— were scaled down and intimate, not unlike the types for administrative and residential structures he chose for his palace. From September 1885 imperial prayers unfailingly took place on Fridays in the Hamidiye Mosque, which was conveniently located just outside the palace, opposite the Mabeyn Kiosk. Each week people from all walks of life poured into this mosque on the outskirts of the

palace's hilltop to witness their sultan and members of his family make their absurdly short descent down the hill, escorted by an overblown military cortège. The forced theatricality of the Hamidian *selamlık* was not lost on a palace scribe who referred to the weekly event as a traditional performance centered on improvisational storytelling acted out by individuals in gold-embroidered costumes ("sırmalı ortaoyunu").[2] A privileged few, following the ceremony from an elevated imperial box, were allowed inside the palace to continue the festivities in the sultan's small theater and, during intermissions, resume their ministerial or diplomatic appeals.

Hamidiye was conceptualized as a palace mosque, not unlike the Bezm-i Alem Valide Sultan Mosque outside the gates of Dolmabahçe Palace. Hamidiye, too, is modest in size, not intended for large congregations, and conceptually resembles a royal family chapel; the architectural historian Doğan Kuban reads it as a replica of a compact Byzantine church.[3] Typologically, however, the structure of this devotional space derived from the cozy residential buildings of the late Tanzimat period. The sultan's kiosk (*hünkar köşkü*), in particular, and its identical counterpart for the *valide*, flanking the north and south sides of the higher mosque structure, were conceived as separate compact residential units with canopied double-staired entrances, much like Yıldız's many kiosks and pavilions (see fig. 5).[4] In contrast, the two portals of the mosque's central rectangular structure were designed as monumental *ivan*s topped with crowns of low-relief ornamentation to complement the unusual high-drummed dome.[5] Attenuated arched windows replete with latticework grilles augment the unabashedly Gothic ornamentation of the structure's three volumes. The building's commission report designates its style (*üslūb*) as a studied but inventive amalgamation of Islamic elements, namely Turkish, Arabesque, and Gothic, perfectly aligned with the late nineteenth-century Ottoman architectural formulations of the ideal medieval form.[6] Indeed, the same document informs its makers that the *miḥrāb*, *minbār*, and pulpit (*kürsü*) should closely resemble those of the late fourteenth-century Great Mosque of Bursa, with its multicolored marble. Instructors from the Imperial School of Engineering were mobilized to retrieve photographs of the Great Mosque's interiors to aid Yıldız's artisans in crafting these objects. A report addressed to the sultan by the grand vizier Küçük Said Paşa voices disappointment in the scale, crudeness, and plainness of some of these features. The extent to which they were amended is unknown, with the exception of increased ornamentation on the architraves and column capitals supporting the dome.

Situated in the transitional zone between the Mabeyn Kiosk and the harem's residential quarters, Yıldız's tiny theater had once been a rudimentary carriage house servicing the *valides*' estate (see fig. 17).[7] Hence, its façade is inconspicuous—as if it had been squeezed in as an afterthought between other structures—and its interiors are relatively underlit, with

pastel hues and curiously understated panels of gilded rococo acanthus and laurel scrolls (fig. 96). A small foyer leads to the level of the parterre for the orchestra and guests and a raised stage, whose platform bears murals depicting idyllic Bosphorus scenes. The second floor, containing a gallery of boxes, rests on twelve columns. The sultan's spacious box was located on this floor, facing the stage; off to the side, four boxes set behind *jali* screens patterned with stars were reserved for the sultan's female relatives. These women were able to access the theater without having to step outside, passing instead through the hallways that opened into the building from the residence of the queen mother on the left of the theater or from the servants' quarters on its right.

Ernesto Rossi, a touring Italian performer recruited by İlyas Bey, the keeper of the sultan's wardrobe (whose job expanded over time to the equivalent of a master of private ceremonies, staging acts from *Othello* and *The Merchant of Venice* to *Sullivan*, a contemporary French comedy based on a Shakespearean actor), described the theater's interior with a Latin term, "Achaico" (meaning Achaean, or Greek).[8] The Khedivial Opera House in Cairo, built in the early 1870s, and its exemplar, the Naum Theater in Istanbul, also followed this Greek style, "*scène classique avec salle classique*," which allowed audience members to gaze at each other while viewing the stage.[9] Rossi also observed that the second-level gallery, where the sultan and his family sat, took the form of theater boxes ("a guisa di palchi"). He found the stage restrictive, except for its Greek proscenium arch, which established the physical and metaphorical "fourth wall" between the actors and audience. Although small, Yıldız's stage,

FIGURE 95
One of Sultan Abdülhamid II's
last *selamlık* ceremonies,
ca. 1908. Bahattin Öztuncay
Collection.

which Rossi called *"quadro di Arlecchino"* (Harlequin's canvas), was designed to accentuate the principal actor and his or her unmediated effect on the principal audience member, the sultan.[10] The recollections of Rossi and others dwell intently on their inability to gauge the reactions of spectators, as the orchestra seats often remained empty and an overwhelming silence was observed during performances. It was up to İlyas to convey the sultan's observations to the actors after every act.

A Verdi enthusiast and an avid consumer of quirky musical inventions such as the Aeolian pneumatic player piano, Abdülhamid was directly involved in the management of the imperial military band (*mızıka-ı hümāyūn*, led by Aranda Paşa), which subsumed the palace orchestra, the theater's Italian opera troupe (run by the Neapolitan actor Arturo Stravolo), and a polyphonic men's chorus (chosen from the band's most talented voices). The sultan preferred music in clear and upbeat major keys over that in introverted, darker-toned minor keys, and comedies over tragedies— he often left the theater before impending scenes of death.[11] On Fridays and Wednesdays the members of the court religiously attended performances at the theater. Like the gardening corps (discussed in chapter 3), the in-house actors and musicians were arranged

FIGURE 96
View of the stage from the
sultan's box inside the palace
theater.

into military units and had to perform on short notice for various audiences.[12] Some of the period's most popular operas were performed so frequently—and sometimes in Turkish—that their names became part of an internal palace parlance: Jacques Offenbach's *La belle Hélène* became the "opera about the shepherd," while Verdi's *Il trovatore* was the "blacksmith's opera" and his *Rigoletto* the "kingly daughter's opera" (kral kız operası).[13] During his exile, Abdülhamid obsessively reminisced about his Italian opera troupe (hoping that its members had been treated well since his deposition) and its beautiful *prima donna*.[14] As sultan, he was also keen to recruit the period's most famous entertainers to perform on his stage, with the famed French actor

Sarah Bernhardt topping the roster.[15] Original Turkish plays, librettos, Ahmed Vefik Paşa's celebrated Molière translations, and even a ballet by Ahmed Midhat were also frequently staged.[16] On warm days, the performances were relocated to the harem garden for members of the court residing in the palace.

The interiors of the mosque and the theater show an uncanny resemblance, reflective of the typological slippages between intimate residential spaces and austere devotional or ceremonial ones that marked Abdülhamid II's architectural patronage. They were either designed by the same architect or the result of collaborative planning. The identity of the theater's architect is still contested, although anecdotes in the lively memoirs of Pera's

FIGURE 97
Interior view of the Hamidiye
Mosque, Istanbul. Photograph
courtesy of M. Göktuna.

cosmopolitan inhabitants name Yanko Ioannidis, the son of Abdülhamid's trusted *kalfa*
Vasilaki.[17] While Vasilaki held high-ranking
posts within the state bureaucracy, such as
head architect of the imperial arsenal, his
son took over the title of palace architect,
replacing Sarkis Balyan. The designer of the
Hamidiye Mosque has recently been identified as Nikolaos Tzelepis (d. 1905), who hailed
from a line of court-affiliated Ottoman Greek
builders and, like most architects of the
period, including the Ioannidises, learned his
trade through an apprenticeship at the imperial arsenal.[18] While designing the mosque,
Tzelepis, or Nikolaki *kalfa* as per his designation in official Ottoman documentation, must
have been supervised by Yanko. The memoirs
of an Ottoman Greek acquaintance of the

Ioannidis family indicate that Yanko built
the wooden dome of the Hamidiye Mosque,
to the great satisfaction of Abdülhamid II,
which won him his post as palace architect.[19]
Although Yanko was the palace's registered
architect, tasked with the project's completion, he must have recruited members of his
own religious affiliation through an unofficial
system of allegiance; they were employed as
*kalfa*s in other state institutions, such as the
Ebniye-i Seniyye Müdüriyeti (Directorate of
Royal Buildings) and the Emlāk-i Hümāyūn
(Sultanic Properties). Nikolaki belonged to the
former. He gained piecemeal, if not uncom-
mon, training in carpentry, engineering, and
architecture in various state schools and later
through apprenticeships. He acquired professional versatility on the job but was also

extremely well versed in molding the global trends of the Gothic and the Alhambresque into Ottoman historical forms.

Yanko and Nikolaki conceived of the domed ceilings of the mosque and theater as stretches of sky. They are both painted blue—although the mosque, as a much larger and better-lit structure, acquired a darker shade than the small, boxy theater—and covered in gilded stars. (Incidentally, the dome of the mosque in the Orhaniye barracks has a similar pattern.) The airiness of the interiors of the Hamidiye Mosque and the palace theater is imparted by tapered wooden columns, which hold up the second-story balconies of the theater and the dome of the mosque. It is unclear when the theater was built (documents related to its construction are oddly scarce), but one surely inspired the other. To the sultan's family members and court officials, who joined him in prayer in the Hamidiye Mosque and to watch performances in the theater, the decorative and architectural continuity of the two spaces must have been obvious. The palace's foreign guests were able to enter the theater, not the mosque. For them, however, access to the theater—joining the sultan and his retinue in watching operas on the nights after the *selamlık*—was compensation for their exclusion from the communal religious experience of the sultan's Friday prayers, in which they only partially partook. Of course, the sultan's place in both of these buildings was on the second level, away from prying eyes. In its earlier version, the sultan's theater box had a screen just like the cedar screens of his elevated loge in the Hamidiye Mosque (fig. 97). It is also important to note that Abdülhamid experienced these spaces, especially the theater's stage and mosque's *mihrab*, from an elevated level. Their interiors were conceived predominantly with his sightlines in mind.

Following in the footsteps of the nineteenth-century *valide*s from whom he inherited his palace, Abdülhamid overemphasized the symbolism of Yıldız's name—not just by covering the ceilings of the two sites of his courtly spectacle with stars but also through religious metaphors. In the time of the queen mothers, the site's celestial metaphors were derived from astronomical or meteorological phenomena; for the sultan, who always tactically underscored his caliphal role in his symbolic choices, they—although similarly straightforward—were religious in nature. calling for a reinterpretation of the literal meaning of Yıldız as star.

Abdülhamid keenly followed the progress of his mosque's construction. He asserted his desire not only for allusions to features of medieval Ottoman structures but for the mosque's blueprint to be "in a creative dialogue"[20] with the reversed T-plan mosques found in the dynasty's early settlements and considered to be *sui generis*, that is, not derived from other building traditions. He also commissioned the journalist and tastemaker Ebüzziya Tevfik—who, amid the mid-nineteenth-century global fad for the Alhambra, had promoted Kufic, the oldest calligraphic script widely used in early Ottoman monuments (after its reviver Armenian calligrapher Köçeoğlu Kirkor)—to inscribe the Hamidiye's dome with the first three verses of the fifty-third surah, entitled "The Star" ("Al-Najm").[21] It has also been asserted that Abdülhamid's selection of a newly revived *Ur*-script to adorn his "medieval" mosque, signifying a return to an unblemished Ottoman/Muslim past, augmented his reenergized caliphal claims.[22]

The Koranic passage in the dome reads as follows: "By the star when it sets, Your Companion [Prophet Muhammad] is neither astray nor being misled; nor does he speak from [his own] inclination."[23] Koranic exegetes have interpreted the word "star" as a reference either to the act of revealing one verse at a time (*nücūm*) to Muhammad or, more directly, to the prophet's own return to the Earth following his ascent to heaven to convene with God (which the subsequent verse of the same surah highlights).[24] The surah is an unusual and learned choice for the empire's last sultanic mosque; it reflects on the very ontology of the Koran by referring to the process of its revelation, while also drawing the physical boundaries of the garden-like paradise where God received his prophet. The surah's fourth verse, reserved for the mosque's endowment deed, further conveys the indomitability of the ultimate source of the revelation.[25] The private assemblies that Abdülhamid held to discuss Koranic passages, as well as the continuity of the Koranic passages between the mosque and its deed, may lie behind his unusual surah selection.

The memoirs of a member of Yıldız's scribal team identify the palace as the empire's direction of prayer (*kıble*). Once completed, in 1886, the sultan's mosque substantiated the religious centrality of his role as caliph.

Abdülhamid fruitfully combined extant symbols with new commemorative monuments across his caliphate. He commissioned D'Aronco to design an obelisk-like sculpture supporting a miniature Hamidiye, to be placed in a prominent square in Damascus to commemorate the beginning of construction of the Hejaz railway line and the completion of the telegraph line. The mosque, like

the Hamidian clock towers spread across the remaining Ottoman lands, was a reminder of his reign. Among a few other Hamidiye mosques in the empire's peripheries, the one built in Thessaloniki in 1902 for the new Hamidiye neighborhood allocated to the *Dönme* community (Sephardic Jewish converts to Islam) resembles its Istanbul predecessor in both its stylistic eclecticism and the distribution of architectural features on its façades (fig. 98).[26] The architect of the Thessaloniki mosque was Vitaliano Poselli, a Sicilian employed by the Ottoman government, who also designed the Allatini Palace, which would house the exiled Abdülhamid in Thessaloniki after 1909.[27] The mosque's Seljukid *pishtaq*, although a replica of that in Yıldız's Hamidiye, features a horseshoe-arched doorway, pointing even more clearly to its medieval sources and their Orientalist interpretations. This mosque's more pronounced Spanish references speak to the makers' presumed familiarity with and appeal to the formerly Jewish community for whom the mosque was built; the synagogues of the Sephardic Jewish diaspora at the turn of the century also derived their architectural and ornamental elements from the Alhambresque.[28]

The ornamental star motif was crucial in emphasizing the connection between Yıldız's central mosque and its Thessaloniki successor. In the latter, six-pointed stars are found at the center of the portal's stucco pediment (like that on the portal of Yıldız's mosque), on the keystone of the horseshoe-arched doorway, on the marble parapets of the roof, and on balustrades above the narthex and the pew designated for women. The meaning of the six-pointed star is as layered as it is culturally specific, extending to the Hermetic tradition to stand in for the microcosmos, the beginning and end of the universe, and the concept of dualism. Nevertheless, its universal recognizability must have appealed to the mosque's patron and designers. In the Hamidiye Mosque in Yıldız, the star was a Seljuk motif as well as the seal of Solomon (*mühr-i Süleyman*), and therefore both an ornamental reference to the dynasty's Turkic origins and a talismanic staple for Islam. For the new Jewish converts, however, it might have been read as the sovereign's gesture acknowledging the Star of David's continued importance to their community.[29] The symbol's Solomonic connection stretched to Abdülhamid himself, especially as the builder of a devotional structure intended to be the centerpiece of his sovereignty and in his rekindled role as the spiritual leader of an empire. The Istanbul mosque's distribution of structures—the central tall rectilinear volume with two smaller units on either side—even resembles nineteenth-century reconstitutions of the mythical temple of Solomon.[30] Solomonic allusions to Abdülhamid's rule further intensified during the year marking the twenty-fifth anniversary of his accession. In particular, gifts from family members such as framed calligraphic inscriptions highlighted his quarter-century rule as *dehr-i Süleyman*, indicating Solomon's unquantifiable but lengthy period of rule.[31]

Theater and opera spectatorship was part of Abdülhamid's courtly life from his princely years onward. Accompanying his uncle, the then sultan Abdülaziz, on his European tour in 1867, Abdülhamid witnessed performances in London and Paris. As noted in chapter 3, his father, Abdülmecid, had installed in Mahmud II's Çırağan a palace theater that enjoyed views of both the Bosphorus and Sester's gardens on the hills behind

it. On ceremonial and diplomatic occasions, this space hosted abridged versions of touring performances staged in Istanbul's public theaters, as well as shows by magicians and athletes. The nineteenth-century sultans, like their European and khedivial counterparts, used the ceremonial power of their gaze (while themselves being observed) during performances, part of a strategy to legitimize political power in what Ruth Berenson calls the "operatic state."[32] Adam Mestyan identifies

FIGURE 98
Hamidiye Mosque built in Thessaloniki to commemorate the twenty-fifth anniversary of Sultan Abdülhamid II's accession, 1901/2. BOA, Y_EE_d_00410.

this imperial ideology in Egypt under Khedive Ismail, who installed and controlled the functions of all novel spaces of sociability in Cairo, and most importantly the Khedivial Opera House, inaugurated at the opening of the Suez Canal. He reads the intensification of the use of European aesthetics in Egypt as a deliberate khedivial choice to mitigate the country's geopolitical dependency on the Ottomans. It was through these popular state institutions and Ismail's burgeoning elite/bourgeois courtiers, Mestyan argues, that Arab patriotism emerged, much as an invented Ottomanism developed among Abdülhamid's bureaucrats. Following in the footsteps of his nineteenth-century predecessors as well as the court's Egyptian rivals, Abdülhamid, too, used the notion that his body, beyond its physical constitution, was the "animate representation" of Ottoman sovereignty.[33] The miniature palace mosque and theater, then, were two sides of the same coin, conceived and experienced as structures housing the ultimate, coveted, and rare rituals of physical display.

Despite calculated efforts to maintain Ottoman ceremonial protocol as a timeless and invariable imperial performance that presented even a late nineteenth-century sultan as an invisible yet omnipresent sovereign, modernity's material manifestations often complicated this once indomitable image. Extending the Tanzimat project, practices of decorum were constantly refitted over novel forms. In the process, palace posts were invented, and chronograms were composed about gardens rather than new palaces.

The quaint demountable structures that so well suited Yıldız's hills also pointed to the nuclearization of the harem, the dynasty's literal navel and ultimate source of survival. As a site that continually manufactured objects bearing images of itself and the empire as well as items for its own upkeep, the Hamidian palace was in perpetual production flux. This—to many outside observers—messy dynamism often encroached upon the traditional functions of the palatial zones. Binding ateliers and photography studios were set inside the sultan's inner garden, with artisans circulating between their desirable, if precarious, workspaces and the image repositories, libraries and factories on the outer courtyard. Photographs surveying construction sites that complemented building manuals were quickly inserted into gift albums that now narrativized imperial sightseeing tours for a privileged gaze. That the most cohesive physical depictions of the site emerged from repurposed photographs, makeshift structures of diplomacy, and infrastructural maps is a testament to the accelerated and ceaseless pace of the palace's renewal and re-creation. These seemingly ephemeral and fragmentary representational choices and modes of habitation demonstrated ingenuity in making flexible, practical, and economic decisions in an empire that suffered sweeping territorial, political and financial losses. For all their relative intangibility, however, these choices and modes collectively preserved a potency and durability of meaning for the most sustained and longest-serving imperial site of the empire's last century.

Introduction

1. Kreil, "Magnetische und geographische Orts-bestimmungen," 25–26.

2. By 1858 these instruments not only produced standard units of measurement but also were fairly portable. See Multhauf and Good, *Brief History of Geomagnetism*, 22.

3. Coen, *Climate in Motion*, 92–104.

4. The toise, roughly corresponding to two meters, or six feet, was the fundamental unit of measurement of length in the French *ancien régime*.

5. Sester's global ambition should be seen in the larger, international domain of Ottoman profession-alization of sciences in this period, best articulated in S. Çelik, "Science," 85 and 89, and Yalçınkaya, *Learned Patriots*.

6. Skarlatos Byzantios (d. 1878), the dili-gent annalist of Mahmud's Istanbul, too, views the deep valley between Beşiktaş and Ortaköy amphitheatrically (αμφιθεατροειδώς). Byzantios, *Hē Kōnstantinoupolis*, 2:96.

7. For the important assertion that Mahmud II's Çırağan—also known at the time as Beşiktaş Palace—was the first palace of the nineteenth century that signified the sultan's reforms, see Girardelli, "Dolma-bahçe and the Old Çırağan Palace."

8. The conception of Abdülhamid II as a bour-geois sultan and his palace as an idealist bourgeois microcosm is first introduced in Georgeon, *Abdulha-mid II*, 136–46.

9. For a succinct examination of Yıldız as Abdül-hamid II's palace, see Özlü, "Merkezin Merkezi."

10. While scholars have contested Arthur Conan Doyle's claim to have attended an audience with the sultan to receive a medal of honor, the Arme-nian novelist Yervant Odyan penned a fictionalized account-cum-whodunit in 1911, *Abdülhamid and Sherlock Holmes*, centered on Abdülhamid's meeting with Doyle's protagonist.

11. For the palace's conversion into a military academy, see Ezgü, *Yıldız Sarayı Tarihçesi*, 77–83.

12. Ahmed İhsan, "Yakında Açılacak Olan Yıldız İstanbul Belediye Gazinosu," 290–93.

13. For an abridged version of this chapter, see Türker, "'I Don't Want Orange Trees.'" For the reprint of this essay and its companions from a special issue of the *International Journal of Islamic Architecture* as an anthology and Peter Christensen's theoretical

grounding of expertise in the nineteenth-century non-West, see Christensen, *Expertise and Architecture*.

14. Harmanşah, "Deep Time and Landscape His-tory," 47.

15. This chapter expands on two seminal studies on Ottoman-garden histories, especially sections on the nineteenth century: Evyapan, *Tarih İçinde Formel Bahçenin Gelişimi*, 26–27, and Atasoy, *Garden for the Sultan*, 299–302.

16. Türker, "Prefabs, Chalets, and Home Making."

17. For this type's international popularity, see White, *Cottages Ornés*, and Galinou, *Cottages and Villas*.

18. Marchand, *Porcelain*, especially 2–3 and 240–90.

19. For an Ottoman art-historical context for the notion of decorum (*ādāb*), see Necipoğlu, *Age of Sinan*, 115–26.

20. Şenyurt, "Political Relations," 539–48, and Şenyurt, *İstanbul Rum Cemaatinin Osmanlı Mimari-sindeki Temsiliyeti*, 151–55.

21. Erkmen, *Geç Osmanlı Dünyasında Mimarlık ve Hafıza*, 20–75.

22. For recent explorations of the heterogeneous use of novel media in the Hamidian archives and its multivalent actors, see Ahmet Ersoy, "Ottomans and the Kodak Galaxy"; Türker, "'Every Image Is a Thought'"; and Nolan, "Gift of the Abdülhamid II Albums."

23. Necipoğlu, *Architecture, Ceremonial, and Power*.

24. Babaie, *Isfahan and Its Palaces*, 15–29.

25. Artan, "Architecture as a Theatre of Life."

26. Hamadeh, *City's Pleasures*.

27. Artan, "Boğaziçi'nin Çehresini Değiştiren Soylu Kadınlar ve Sultanefendi Sarayları."

28. Z. Çelik, *Remaking of Istanbul*.

29. Ersoy, *Architecture*.

30. While Bouquet's work centers on the state-documented professional profiles of nineteenth-century Ottoman bureaucrats, he includes their extracurricular interests where he can find them; Bouquet, *Pachas du sultan*, 420–50.

31. On other potential markers of an "Ottoman" bourgeoisie, see E. Eldem, "Bourgeoisie of Istanbul." See also Göçek, *Rise of the Bourgeoisie*.

32. Stephanov, *Ruler Visibility*, 3–5.

33. Hanioğlu, *Brief History*, 205.

34. Doyle, *Inter-imperiality*, 11.

35. This attention to wider networks of art and architectural patronage is exemplified, for instance, most recently by Büke Uras in his magisterial volume *Balyanlar*, which demonstrates the monumental impact of the Armenian family of architects on Istanbul's nineteenth-century urban developments.

36. Two scholars have provided valuable starting points in opening up the intellectual and material world of the Ottoman bureaucracy: M. Burak Çetintaş, in *Dolmabahçe'den Nişantaşı'na*, and Şemsettin Şeker, in *Ders ile Sohbet Arasında*.

37. Dejung, Motadel, and Osterhammel, *Global Bourgeoisie*.

38. I borrow the notion of the versatile nineteenth-century image for the Ottoman visual domain from the approach taken by scholars to the Qajar material culture in Roxburgh and McWilliams, *Technologies of the Image*. On a recent anthropological inquiry into Ottoman visual history, see Gürsel, "Picture of Health."

Chapter 1

1. McCullagh, *Fall of Abd-ul-Hamid*, 262. On the multifaceted work of this itinerant journalist, see Horgan, "Journalism, Catholicism, and Anti-Communism."

2. McCullagh, *Fall of Abd-ul-Hamid*, 287.

3. On Nadir Ağa, the palace eunuch who collaborated with the Young Turk government and whose life was thus spared, see Erdem, *Slavery in the Ottoman Empire*, 148, and Toledano, *As If Silent and Absent*, 53. For his intimate tell-alls, see Çapanoğlu, "Abdülhamid'in En Yakın Adamı"; Ertuğ, "Musahib-i Sani Hazret-i Şehriyari Nadir Ağa'nın Hatıratı-I," 9–15; and Ertuğ, "Musahib-i Sani Hazret-i Şehriyari Nadir Ağa'nın Hatıratı-I," 6–14.

4. McCullagh, *Fall of Abd-ul-Hamid*, 287. For the inventories of this commission, see Candemir, *Yıldız'da Kaos ve Tasfiye*. For the contents of Yıldız's imperial museum itemized by the commission, see Kutluoğlu and Candemir, *Bir Cihan Devletinin Tasfiyesi*. On the formation and early work of the commission, see Uşaklıgil, *Saray ve Ötesi*.

5. McCullagh, *Fall of Abd-ul-Hamid*, 297. On the penchant of the nineteenth-century sultans for Victorian technological equipment, see Karahüseyin, *Chandeliers and Lamps*; F. Y. Yılmaz, *Heating Devices in the National Palaces*; and Sezgin, *Sanayi ve Teknoloji Araçları*.

6. Şakir, *İkinci Sultan Hamit*, 328.

7. McCullagh, *Fall of Abd-ul-Hamid*, 257.

8. Ibid., 258.

9. Ibid., 254.

10. Especially for the palace- and garden-related sections, Osman Nuri translated indiscriminately from Bernhard Stern's *Abdul Hamid II, seine Familie und sein Hofstaat, nach eigenen Ermittelungen*, published in 1901. Another red flag signaling the unreliability of Nuri's text is the invented names of many palace employees.

11. In the Koran, the garden city that Şeddād built is called İrem (Iram). According to Şeref, Abdülhamid resembled this notorious ancient oppressor, and Yıldız's high, impenetrable walls were the pillars of İrem. Both tyrannical rulers were doomed to fall, along with their ostentatious dwellings. See Abdurrahman Şeref, *Son Vak'anüvis Abdurrahman Şeref Efendi Tarihi*, 9.

12. In its sensationalism, the European counterpart to Osman Nuri's work is Georges Dorys [pseud.], *Abdul-Hamid intime*. This scathing pseudonymous biography was written by Anastase Adossidis, an early member of the Young Turks and the son of a former governor of Crete. Hanioğlu, *Young Turks in Opposition*, 183 and 189, and Karpat, *Politicization of Islam*, 444.

13. H. Y. Şehsuvaroğlu, "Abdülhamid'in Yıldız'daki Hususi Dairesi," 1005–7.

14. Among the architectural histories that dismiss Yıldız for an alleged lack of architectural cohesion, monumentality, and "palatial magnificence" is Doğan Kuban's entry on the site in his *Ottoman Architecture*, 626–28. Although Kuban's interpretation is largely unenthusiastic, he does identify Yıldız as a trendsetting site in the garden culture of the late nineteenth century. Others in the genre of heritage studies seek to raise cultural awareness of the fragmented palace; see Sözen, *Devletin Evi: Saray*, 201–2.

15. McCullagh, *Fall of Abd-ul-Hamid*, 299.

16. The most famous of these serialized recollections of life in Yıldız are A. Osmanoğlu, *Babam Abdülhamid*; Tahsin Paşa, *Yıldız Hatıraları*; and Mayakon, *Yıldız'da Neler Gördüm?* The beauty of this triad is that the authors represent different groups within the palace: Ayşe Osmanoğlu was the sultan's daughter and in her account views the site as her home; Tahsin Paşa was its principal administrator and a functionary working closely with Abdülhamid; and Mayakon was a lowly scribe. An overlooked but equally informative serial-cum-memoir is Örikağasızade Hasan Sırrı's *Sultan Abdülhamit Devri Hatıraları ve Saray İdaresi*.

17. Celâlettin, *Geçmiş Zaman Olur ki*, 126–27.

18. İrtem, *Abdülhamid Devrinde Hafiyelik ve Sansür*; Gör, *II. Abdülhamid'in Hafiye Teşkilatı*. See also Mayakon, *Yıldız'da Neler Gördüm?*, 179–88.

19. Pervititch, *Istanbul in the Insurance Maps*, 40–41, 46–48.

20. Ezgü, *Yıldız Sarayı Tarihçesi*.

21. For a brief history of the site's fragmentation, see Gülersoy, "Yıldız Parkı."

22. Ahmed İhsan, *Yildiz*.

23. Bardakçı, "Yıldız Sarayı."

24. For the earliest overview of the diverse nature of these archives, see S. J. Shaw, "'Yıldız' Palace Archives."

25. I rely on the 1901 English translation of Dorys's *Abdul-Hamid intime*; see Dorys, *Private Life*, 118.

26. Ibid., 118–19.

27. Âtıf Hüseyin Bey, *Sultan II. Abdülhamid'in Sürgün Günleri*, 340. This underused text is a much more reliable source on Abdülhamid's character than the apocryphal autobiographies written after his deposition: *II. Abdülhamid'in Hatıra Defteri* and Bozdağ, *İkinci Abdülhamid'in Hatıra Defteri*.

28. Âtıf Hüseyin Bey, *Sultan II. Abdülhamid'in Sürgün Günleri*, 151–52.

29. Dodd, *Palaces of the Sultan*, 71.

30. Dorys, *Private Life*, 121.

31. Cambon, *Correspondance*, 1:23.

32. Georgeon, *Abdülhamid II*, 130–32.

33. Âtıf Hüseyin Bey, *Sultan II. Abdülhamid'in Sürgün Günleri*, 221–22 and 337.

34. There are a number of courtyard-centered descriptions of Yıldız. Afife Batur's encyclopedia entry and Fuad Ezgü's brief history, for example, follow this architectural principle in analyzing the site. See also Bilgin, "Yıldız Sarayı."

35. Selim Deringil's seminal work on Abdülhamid's separate and meticulously crafted appeals to his subjects and foreign allies highlights the strategic symbols of his rule; see Deringil, *Well-Protected Domains*.

36. McCullagh, *Fall of Abd-ul-Hamid*, 259.

37. Babaie, *Isfahan and Its Palaces*, 224–25.

38. In the nineteenth century a sovereign's fear of assassination was only too real. Most famously, multiple attempts were made on Queen Victoria's life. See Murphy, *Shooting Victoria*.

39. Muẓaffar al-Dīn Shāh, *Safarnāmah-i Farangistān*, 220.

40. Gülersoy, *Yıldız Parkı ve Malta Köşkü*.

41. Nāṣir al-Dīn Shāh, *Diary of H. M. the Shah of Persia*, 221.

42. Muẓaffar al-Dīn Shāh Qājār, *Safarnāmah-i Farangistān*, 221–22.

43. Georgeon, *Abdülhamid II*, 128–29.

44. Ibid.

45. Scarce, "Architecture and Decoration."

46. Dodd, *Palaces of the Sultan*, 82 and 74.

47. Ibid., 74–75.

48. Dorys, *Private Life*, 120.

49. Dodd, *Palaces of the Sultan*, 49, 50.

50. Ibid., 88.

51. A. Batur, "Yıldız Sarayı," 1050.

52. Ibid.

53. "Une ville dans la ville," in Georgeon, *Abdülhamid II*, 130–31.

54. Muẓaffar al-Dīn Shāh, *Safarnāmah-i Farangistān*, 221.

55. Mıntzuri, *İstanbul Anıları*, 31.

56. Georgeon, *Abdülhamid II*, 134–35.

57. On Yıldız Palace's transformation into the empire's administrative heart, see Findley, *Bureaucratic Reform*, 239–69.

58. Tahsin Paşa, *Yıldız Hatıraları*, 226–27.

59. BOA, Y. PRK. HH. 34/38.

60. Esatlı, *Saray ve Konakların Dilinden Bir Devrin Tarihi*, 91–92 and 94–95; most recently, on the salon-like gatherings and cultured discussions in these mansions of the Ottoman elite, see Şeker, *Ders ile Sohbet Arasında*. For an intimate eyewitness account of life in the mansions of the *paşa*s, see Mümtaz, *Eski İstanbul Konakları*.

61. Mayakon, *Yıldız'da Neler Gördüm?*, 11.

62. Mıntzuri, *İstanbul Anıları*, 42–43.

63. Ibid., 55.

64. Adıvar, *Memoirs of Halidé Edib*, 36.

65. Ibid.

66. Tuğlacı, *Osmanlı Mimarlığında Batılılaşma Dönemi*, 288–316.

67. Ibid., 195.

68. Akyıldız, "Mâbeyn-i Hümâyun," 284.

69. Wasti, "Last Chroniclers of the Mabeyn."

70. On Osman Paşa's formal and extremely fettered relationship with Abdülhamid and the palace, see Mümtaz, *Tarihimizde Hayal Olmuş Hakikatler*, 98–101.

71. Although this structure cannot be identified today, an unrealized project for an imperial archive in Yıldız resembling a Roman sarcophagus might have been planned to replace this old one. See Godoli, "D'Aronco e Vienna," 189. See also Şakir, *İkinci Sultan Hamit*, 361.

72. Tahsin Paşa, *Yıldız Hatıraları*, 226–27.

73. For vibrant recollections of the grueling Mabeyn shifts and the young palace clerks' conception of their workplace as an extension of their time as students at the Imperial School of Public Service, see Özgül, *Ali Ekrem Bolayır'ın Hâtıraları*, 319–28.

74. Şemseddin Sâmī, *Ḳāmūs-ı Türkī*, 1:601.

75. Tahsin Paşa, *Yıldız Hatıraları*, 20–28.

76. Mayakon, *Yıldız'da Neler Gördüm?*, 180.

77. Ş. Osmanoğlu, *Babam Sultan Abdülhamid*, 21.

78. Âtıf Hüseyin Bey, *Sultan II. Abdülhamid'in Sürgün Günleri*, 294.

79. Ibid., 220.

80. Tahsin Paşa, *Yıldız Hatıraları*, 40; Deringil, "Legitimacy Structures in the Ottoman State."

81. The sultan's inauguration of the Imperial School for Tribes to educate and integrate the sons of these leaders for governmental jobs was another aspect of his tightening grip on the empire's remaining and predominantly Muslim provinces; Rogan, "Asiret Mektebi."

82. Mıntzuri, *İstanbul Anıları*, 24–25.

83. "Ziynetsiz, külfetsiz bir ibadetgâh," in Mayakon, *Yıldız'da Neler Gördüm?*, 113.

84. Tekçe, *Zafir Konağında Bir Tuhaf Zaman*, 98–103.

85. ʿOsmān Nūrī, *ʿAbdülḥamīd-i Sānī ve Devr-i Salṭanatı*, 2:451.

86. Mayakon, *Yıldız'da Neler Gördüm?*, 134–41.

87. Ibid., 117–24.

88. Ibid., 119.

89. ʿOsmān Nūrī, *ʿAbdülḥamīd-i Sānī ve Devr-i Salṭanatı*, 2:401.

90. Necipoğlu, *Architecture, Ceremonial, and Power*, 56–60 and 91–96.

91. A. Osmanoğlu, *Babam Abdülhamid*, 90–91.

92. On the sultan's processional to visit the Prophet's mantle in Topkapı Palace and on the grand *bayrām* receptions for the ʿīd-i fıṭr (feast marking the end of the fasting month of Ramadan) and ʿīd-i aẓḥā (the Feast of the Sacrifice), see Karateke, *Padişahım Çok Yaşa!*, 82–92 and 195–99.

93. Müller, *Letters from Constantinople*, 52.

94. Dodd, *Palaces of the Sultan*, 75.

95. Müller, *Letters from Constantinople*, 54–55.

96. Ibid., 55.

97. Ibid., 57–58. Aside from the main library, many of Yıldız's residential buildings contained their own library rooms, one of which was reserved for Abdülhamid's collection of books from his princely years. The initial reconnaissance reports by Abdurrahman Şeref, after the deposition of Abdülhamid, identify at least four of these spaces. See Candemir, *Son Yıldız Düşerken*, 144–46.

98. Layard, *Twixt Pera and Therapia*, 253.

99. BOA, HH. d. 16536.

100. Zonaro, *Abdülhamid'in Hükümdarlığında Yirmi Yıl*, 161.

101. Örikağasızade Hasan Sırrı, *Sultan Abdülhamit Devri Hatıraları*, 149–52; for the medieval town analogy, see A. Batur, "Yıldız Sarayı," 522.

102. Âtıf Hüseyin Bey, *Sultan II. Abdülhamid'in Sürgün Günleri*, 245.

103. Muẓaffar al-Dīn Shāh, *Safarnāmah-i Farangistān*, 224.

104. Ibid., 225, and Kilerci, "Ottoman-Qajar Relations Through Photography," 104.

105. Nasir al-Din Shah seems also to have installed two railroad cars in the gardens of his palace, which, according to the French ambassador Paul Cambon (d. 1924), resembled "our first-class cars," with "three compartments upholstered in gray fabric." These two coaches, stored in a purpose-built hangar and without rails on which to travel, were revealed only when distinguished guests visited the grounds. These guests were encouraged to spend time inside the railcars, "opening and closing the doors, or playing with the windows." Cambon, *Correspondance*, 1:386.

106. Ibid.

107. A. Batur, "Yıldız Sarayı," 1050.

108. For a detailed on-site archaeological study of the palace's inner garden, see Şen, "Yıldız Sarayı Selamlık Bahçe Düzeni," and her *Yıldız Sarayı Selamlık Bahçesi*.

109. For wooden scale models of the imperial railcars produced for Sultan Abdülaziz during the construction of the İzmir-Aydın line and the Rumelia line, see Şentürk, *Iron Track*, 44 and 46.

110. Christensen, *Germany and the Ottoman Railways*; see also Özyüksel, *Osmanlı İmparatorluğu'nda Nüfuz Mücadelesi*, 22–26.

111. On these gift albums, see Ertem and Öztuncay, *Ottoman Arcadia*.

112. Necipoğlu, *Architecture, Ceremonial, and Power*, 40–49. It is important to note here that although electrical illumination was tried in small scale inside the palace's Şale from 1889 onwards, the complex was by and large illuminated and heated by town gas (*havagazı*) produced and disseminated from the gasworks in nearby Dolmabahçe until 1914. At least in the 1900s, the palaces on the European shore used 500,000 cubic meters of gas per year, an undisclosed sum of which was consumed by Yıldız. See Kayserilioğlu, Mazak, and Kon, *Osmanlı'dan Günümüze Havagazının Tarihçesi*, 1:55, 61, and, for Yıldız's brief electrification, 2:300–308. On the town gas's primary use as a source of illumination, see Mazak, *Gündelik Hayattan Renklerle Eski İstanbul*, 135–78.

113. Kutluoğlu and Candemir, *Bir Cihan Devletinin Tasfiyesi*, 103.

114. Âtıf Hüseyin Bey, *Sultan II. Abdülhamid'in Sürgün Günleri*, 297–98.

115. Kutluoğlu and Candemir, *Bir Cihan Devletinin Tasfiyesi*, 193.

116. Ibid., 71.

117. Ibid., 158.

118. For an extensive analysis of the palace's holdings of living birds and other animals, including those that contributed to the site's subsistence economy, see Çakılcı, "Sultan II. Abdülhamid'in Hayvan Merakı."

119. Kutluoğlu and Candemir, *Bir Cihan Devletinin Tasfiyesi*, 126–27.

120. For the plan of the photography studio, see Türker, "'Every Image Is a Thought,'" 64. The location of this small photography studio inside the harem garden is confirmed in Tepeyran, *Hatıralar*, 323.

121. Candemir, *Yıldız'da Kaos ve Tasfiye*, 153–58.

122. Tahsin Paşa, *Yıldız Hatıraları*, 30.

123. A. Osmanoğlu, *Babam Abdülhamid*, 113; Ali Said, *Saray Hâtıraları*, 29–32.

124. McCullagh, *Fall of Abd-ul-Hamid*, 288; A. Osmanoğlu, *Babam Abdülhamid*, 84.

125. Örikağasızade Hasan Sırrı, *Sultan Abdülhamit Devri Hatıraları*, 168–69; A. Osmanoğlu, *Babam Abdülhamid*, 77–82.

126. Örikağasızade Hasan Sırrı, *Sultan Abdülhamit Devri Hatıraları*, 169.

127. The pronounced cornice on the first-floor level, similar to the one found on the Çit Kiosk, indicates that when it was first built, it was a one-floor structure, adhering to the general typology of buildings subsidiary to imperial *konak*s, like the Mabeyn from the reigns of Abdülmecid and Abdülaziz.

128. Tahsin Paşa, *Yıldız Hatıraları*, 141.

129. Ali Said, *Saray Hâtıraları*, 32; ʿOs̱mān Nūrī, ʿAbdülḥamīd-i S̱ānī ve Devr-i Salṭanatı, 2:476–95.

130. Ali Said, *Saray Hâtıraları*, 40; A. Osmanoğlu, *Babam Abdülhamid*, 68; Sevengil, *Saray Tiyatrosu*, 117–39.

131. Şakir, *İkinci Sultan Hamit*, 289–90; and Saz, *Harem'in İçyüzü*, 131–33.

132. Şakir, *İkinci Sultan Hamit*, 290–91.

133. Ibid.; A. Osmanoğlu, *Babam Abdülhamid*, 45–49.

134. Ali Said, *Saray Hâtıraları*, 44.

135. A. Osmanoğlu, *Babam Abdülhamid*, 58.

136. ʿOs̱mān Nūrī, ʿAbdülḥamīd-i S̱ānī ve Devr-i Salṭanatı, 2:452.

137. McCullagh, *Fall of Abd-ul-Hamid*, 263.

138. Komara, "Concrete and the Engineered Picturesque."

139. ʿOs̱mān Nūrī, ʿAbdülḥamīd-i S̱ānī ve Devr-i Salṭanatı, 2:454.

140. Müller, *Letters from Constantinople*, 53.

141. Tahsin Paşa, *Yıldız Hatıraları*, 316.

142. ʿOs̱mān Nūrī, ʿAbdülḥamīd-i S̱ānī ve Devr-i Salṭanatı, 2:453. An archival document dated 1880 suggests that a kiosk named after this artificial lake, the Derehavuz Kiosk, was built in the valley of Yıldız; BOA, Y. PRK. HH. 12/27.

143. Çeçen, *İstanbul'un Vakıf Sularından Taksim ve Hamidiye Suları*, 169.

144. Ibid., 169–94.

145. ʿOs̱mān Nūrī, ʿAbdülḥamīd-i S̱ānī ve Devr-i Salṭanatı, 2:453.

146. Ali Haydar Mithat, *Hâtıralarım*, 125–27; Uzunçarşılı, *Midhat Paşa ve Yıldız Mahkemesi*, 134, 167, 171–72, 221, 231–35, 253, 268, 296, and 307.

147. For Şevkefza's highly publicized competition with Abdülaziz's mother, Pertevniyal, see Örik, "İki Valide Sultan Arasında," in *Bilinmeyen Yaşamlarıyla Saraylılar*, 74–80.

Chapter 2

1. Uğurlu, "Selim III's Istanbul," 261.

2. Necipoğlu, "Suburban Landscape of Sixteenth-Century Istanbul." Artan's "Architecture as a Theatre of Life" documents the structural and formal continuations and transformations of the early modern royal gardens into more-full-fledged palaces, as well as their increasingly variegated proprietors (with prominent women most significant among these new elite groups). I borrow the phrase "pastoral ethos" from Shirine Hamadeh to describe the continuation of this practice—especially, and most poignantly, by queen mothers—in the nineteenth century; Hamadeh, *City's Pleasures*, 55.

3. *Evliyâ Çelebi Seyahatnâmesi*, 1:191.

4. On the prolific architectural patronage of the high-ranking women of the Ottoman court in Eyüp, see Artan, "Eyüp'ün Bir Diğer Çehresi," and Artan, "Boğaziçi'nin Çehresini Değiştiren Soylu Kadınlar ve Sultanefendi Sarayları."

5. Information on the tastes, social lives, and internal worlds of these imperial women is often limited to the fictionalized narratives of twentieth-century popular history. For an overly dramatized biography of Fatma Sultan, see Aḥmed Refīḳ, *Tarihte Kadın Simaları*, 59–127. Artan traces the property ownership of eighteenth-century princesses through groundbreaking archival research; for Fatma Sultan's Çırağan, see Artan, "Theatre of Life," 368–69.

6. Aḥmed Refīḳ, *Tarihte Kadın Simaları*, 109–13.

7. Artan, "Istanbul in the 18th Century." On the origins of this tactical practice and shifts in the empire's marriage-based political alliances, see Peirce, *Imperial Harem*.

8. Byzantios, *Hē Kōnstantinoupolis*, 2:98–99.

9. S. H. Eldem, *Köşkler ve Kasırlar*, 2:213–22.

10. Ibid., 214.

11. Selim III's daily memoirist, Sırkâtibi Ahmed Efendi, refers to the site as the *yalı* of Çırağan on which was built the waterfront mansion of Beyhan Sultan (the word *yalı* most likely meaning the plot of waterfront land rather than the structure itself): "Beyhân Sultan Sâhilsarâyı olan Çırâgân Yâlısı." Ahmed Efendi also indicates that Selim visited the site to inspect the construction in the spring months of 1794. See Ahmed Efendi, *III. Selim'in Sırkâtibi Ahmed Efendi Tarafından Tutulan Rûznâme*, 184. Two foreign travelers (among many) to describe Beyhan Sultan's Çırağan were James Dallaway, in *Constantinople Ancient and Modern*, 138–41, and John Cam Hobhouse, in *Journey Through Albania and Other Provinces of Turkey*, 2:860.

12. Artan, "From Charismatic Leadership to Collective Rule."

13. Hafız Hüseyin Ayvansarayî, *Garden of the Mosques*, 274–75; Artan, "Composite Universe."

14. A shorter version of Artan's article "Composite Universe" analyzes the decorative vocabulary that these women selected for themselves; see Artan, "From Charismatic Leadership to Collective Rule," 569–80. For Hatice Sultan's Neşetabad Pavilion, see Melling, *Constantinople et de rives de Bosphore*.

15. Perot, Hitzel, and Anhegger, *Hatice Sultan ile Melling Kalfa.*

16. Artan, "From Charismatic Leadership to Collective Rule," 575. For their collectors' identities, see Artan, "Eighteenth-Century Ottoman Princesses as Collectors."

17. Artan, "From Charismatic Leadership to Collective Rule," 81.

18. Karal, *Osmanlı Tarihi,* 5:96; Melek-Hanum, *Thirty Years in the Harem,* 30; and Artan, "From Charismatic Leadership to Collective Rule," 66–68.

19. Artan, "From Charismatic Leadership to Collective Rule," 70–73.

20. Ibid., 62.

21. Ibid., 53–94. For the genesis of this income allocation to the women of the court, see Peirce, *Imperial Harem,* 126–27, 212–16, 247–48.

22. Peirce, *Imperial Harem,* 91. Artan identifies a pronounced hierarchy of public visibility favoring the sultans' daughters over their sons-in-law; the prestige of the latter group dwindled even further over the course of the eighteenth century; Artan, "Theatre of Life," 381. On the final and definitive removal of power from the sons-in-law during the reign of Abdülhamid II, see the journalistic tell-all Örik, *Bilinmeyen Yaşamlarıyla Saraylılar,* 11–32.

23. N. Yıldırım, *Gureba Hastanesi'nden Bezmiâlem Vakıf Üniversitesi'ne,* 38–55.

24. For Mahmud I's prolific yet understudied architectural patronage, see Rüstem, *Ottoman Baroque,* 57–110. See also Hamadeh, *City's Pleasures,* 76–78.

25. Şem'dânî-zâde, *Mür'i't-Tevârih,* 1:30.

26. Ibid., 31.

27. Câbî Ömer Efendi, *Câbî Târihi,* 1:49.

28. Kahraman, *Osmanlı Devleti'nde Spor,* 416–17. For Selim III's rifle-shooting and archery hobbies, see Ü. Yücel, *Türk Okçuluğu.* For the site's renowned winds, see the description of Ortaköy in Meḥmed Rāʿif, *Mirʾāt-ı İstānbul,* 287.

29. Şânî-zâde Târîhî, 1:1113–114.

30. Cezar, *Sanatta Batı'ya Açılış,* 1:110.

31. A baroque fountain with an attenuated trunk and exaggerated eaves still remains from the time of Mihrişah's Yıldız Kiosk; the landscape designers employed by Abdülhamid II at the end of the nineteenth century used this fountain as the focal monument when they redesigned the interior, the harem, and the surrounding artificial lake.

32. The redesign of Topkapı's harem seems to have been undertaken first by Ahmed III on the court's return from Edirne to Istanbul. On the changes to the queen mother's quarters during the reign of Abdülhamid I, specifically the new aesthetic in wall paintings, see Renda, *Batılılaşma Döneminde Türk Resim Sanatı,* 89–108. For Selim III's

transformations of and extensions to the harem, see Türker, "Ottoman Horticulture After the Tulip Era."

33. For a modest but insightful study of Ottoman Istanbul's orchard types, see Göncüoğlu, *Üsküdar ve Boğaziçi.*

34. A measurement of the volumetric flow of water, one *masura* was one quarter of a *lüle* (26 cubic meters), therefore about 6.5 cubic meters of water per day. While *masura* was the preferred indicator of quantity in judicial documents, *lüle* was the preferred designation for allusions to an abundance of water in prose; see Pakalın, *Osmanlı Tarih Deyimleri ve Terimleri Sözlüğü,* 2:372.

35. Egemen, *İstanbul'un Çeşme ve Sebilleri,* 601. The fountain was originally across from the Topal Hoca Mescid in Çırağan, no longer extant. The inscription stone was later moved to an apartment's entrance façade on Sinan Paşa Mescidi Sokak.

36. I thank Gülru Necipoğlu for pointing out that the eighteenth-century Ottomans probably continued to enact a geographical hierarchy of decorum on Istanbul's landscape through their building patterns. While shore space was given to the princesses, the more remote elevated estates were reserved for the mother; this was perhaps an act of respectful veneration through a removal from the public gaze that emphasized the mother's much loftier status.

37. Mihrişah's orchard estate is mentioned with great frequency in the diary of Selim III's unnamed scribe; see Beyhan, *Saray Günlüğü,* 122–26, 128–29, 145–46, 148, 150, 152, 154.

38. Halman, *Rapture and Revolution,* 281; for Selim III's patronage of the convent, see Hafız Hüseyin Ayvansarayî, *Garden of the Mosques,* 422–23.

39. The intertwining of courtly pastimes with practices of faith in Eyüp was first beautifully observed by Artan, in "Eyüp'ün Bir Diğer Çehresi." Mihrişah built her interconnected tomb and *imaret,* a delicate baroque complex, in Eyüp; see Uğurlu, "Selim III's Istanbul," 177–200, and Gültekin, "Mihrişah Valide Sultan Külliyesi." For a published account of Mihrişah's endowments, see İnan, "Mihrişah Sultan İmareti," 720.

40. Whether Mihrişah's, Nakş-ı Dil's, and Pertevniyal's Validebağ estates were one and the same or inhabited the same plot of land is currently unclear. However, they seem to have been incredibly close, based on the superimposition of Helmuth von Moltke's Istanbul map (1839) onto a scaled representation of the still extant Validebağ. The plot given to Nakş-ı Dil was expanded for Pertevniyal, just as Mihrişah's Yıldız estate was expanded for Abdülmecid's mother, Bezm-i Alem. Today, Validebağ's ownership is assigned solely to Abdülaziz's sister Adile Sultan, with no mention of the succession of queen mothers who owned and cultivated the

site—an oversight all the more surprising given that the site's designated name is derived from the *valides*' title. Tanman, "Korular." A brief entry for "Valide Sultan Sarayı" places the mansion of Selim III's mother, Mihrişah Sultan, in Çamlıca in Kısıklı; Konyalı, *Âbideleri ve Kitâbeleriyle Üsküdar Tarihi*, 2:273.

41. The apocryphal nineteenth-century stories that align Nakş-ı Dil with Empress Josephine's missing cousin, Aimée du Buc de Rivéry, have a riveting history of their own; see Sakaoğlu, *Bu Mülkün Kadın Sultanları*, 355–61. Although the Nakş-ı Dil–Aimée connection has long been refuted, it continues to be replicated in less circumspect histories; see Uluçay, *Padişahların Kadınları ve Kızları*, 107–8.

42. For Nakş-ı Dil and her sanatorium-like estate in Çamlıca, see the introduction by Rahşan Gürel to the *divan* of the court poet Vasıf, *Enderunlu Osman Vâsıf Bey ve Dîvânı*, 106.

43. Carpenter, *Health, Medicine, and the Society*, 54–70.

44. Byrne, *Tuberculosis and the Victorian Literary Imagination*, 21–30.

45. This Yıldız-Çamlıca connection through the *valide* estates is attributed to Vasıf's *kaside*, as cited in H. Y. Şehsuvaroğlu, "Yıldız Kasrı," 5.

46. Vasıf, *Enderunlu Osman Vâsıf Bey ve Dîvânı*, 255.

47. More specifically, Vasıf calls the retreat built for him by Mahmud II's mother "shelter of the just one," *me'vā-yı ʿadlī*; *ʿadlī* was the sultan's pen name.

48. *Şânî-zâde Târîhî*, 1:474.

49. H. Y. Şehsuvaroğlu, *Asırlar Boyunca İstanbul*, 138.

50. Hâfız Hızır İlyas, *Osmanlı Sarayında Gündelik Hayat*, 165; İrtem, *II. Mahmud Devri ve Türk Kemankeşleri*.

51. A *gez* is sixty-six centimeters. An archer qualified for the title of *kemankeş* or *tirendaz* (master bowman) once he could shoot as far as eight hundred *gez* with arrows having metal spearheads (*azmayiş oku*) and as far as nine hundred *gez* with arrows having bone-edged tips (*peşrev oku*). Ü. Yücel, *Türk Okçuluğu*, 399; Pakalın, *Osmanlı Tarih Deyimleri ve Terimleri Sözlüğü*, 1:664.

52. Kuşoğlu, *Türk Okçuluğu ve Sultan Mahmud'un Ok Günlüğü*.

53. Mahmud II commissioned his archery tutor and chamberlain Mustafa Kânî Bey to compile a comprehensive guide, which was then transcribed by the period's most celebrated calligrapher, Yesarizade Mustafa İzzet Efendi (d. 1849); Mustafa Kânî Bey, *Okçuluk Kitabı: Telhîs-i Resâ'ilât-ı Rumât*.

54. Ahmed Sâdık Zîver Paşa, *Dîvân ve münşe'ât*, 388–89. For the poet's biography, see İnal, *Son Asır Türk Şairleri*, 3:2090–94.

55. S. H. Eldem, *Türk Bahçeleri*, 30. For an architectural history of the meadow, see Gülersoy, *Beşiktaş'da Ihlamur Mesiresi ve Tarihî Kitabeler*. For an illustrated study of Mahmud II's recorded arrow and rifle shots, see M. Ş. Acar, *Osmanlı'da Sportif Atıcılık*. For the geography of the sites Mahmud II selected for archery and later for shooting, see Kahraman, *Osmanlı Devleti'nde Spor*, 579–85.

56. The diary refers to the cemetery rather imprecisely as the "infidel cemetery" (*kâfir mezarlığı*); it was probably one of the two Armenian cemeteries close to Yıldız at this time. Alternatively, the diary may have been referring to the Jewish cemetery bordering the Armenian cemetery adjacent to the park. The diary is occasionally more specific about location names, and records at one point that the sultan shot arrows in the direction of the Jewish cemetery by the Ortaköy stream.

57. Karal, *Osmanlı Tarihi*, 5:107–24.

58. *Şânî-zâde Târîhî*, 2:1260.

59. Ibid., 1131–35.

60. Ahmed Sâdık Zîver Paşa, *Dîvân ve münşe'ât*, 518. For the Nakşî designation, see Uluçay, *Padişahların Kadınları ve Kızları*, 107–8.

61. For a recent biographical account on Bezm-i Alem, see Baytar, *19. Yüzyıl Sarayında Bir Valide Sultan*.

62. Stephanov, "Sultan Abdülmecid's 1846 Tour."

63. Muḥabbetden Muḥammed oldu ḥāṣıl
Muḥammedsiz muḥabbetden ne ḥāṣıl
Ẓuhūrundan bezm-i ʿālem oldu vāṣıl.

64. Carpenter, *Health, Medicine, and the Society*, 103.

65. Alpgüvenç, *Hayırda Yarışan Hanım Sultanlar*, 161.

66. Ibid., 165.

67. Slade, *Turkey and the Crimean War*, 87–88.

68. Alpgüvenç, *Hayırda Yarışan Hanım Sultanlar*, 167.

69. Ahmed Sâdık Zîver Paşa, *Dîvân ve münşe'ât*, 427, 455.

70. Uluçay, *Harem'den Mektuplar*, 1:150–64.

71. Notably, one of the earliest portrayals of Bezm-i Alem can be found in the letters of an Austrian physician, Siegmund Spitzer, who served as Abdülmecid's personal doctor from 1845 to 1850: Spitzer, "Am Hofe Sultan Abdul Medjid's," 123–24.

72. For a complete list of her fountains, see Egemen, *İstanbul'un Çeşme ve Sebilleri*, 208–15.

73. Ibid., 208. See also Çetintaş, *Dolmabahçe'den Nişantaşı'na*, 139–40.

74. For an amusing biography of this lesser-known scribe, see İnal, *Son Asır Türk Şairleri*, 2:1365–69. İbrahim Raşid's *divan* has been transcribed, although the list of his chronograms is incomplete because it was compiled early in the poet's career

(1835); see Çetin, "Râşid (?–1310 [1892]) ve Divanı İnceleme-Tenkidli Metin."

75. İnal, *Son Asır Türk Şairleri*, 3:2092.

76. Ahmed Sâdık Zîver Paşa, *Dîvân ve münşe'ât*, 470. András Riedlmayer points out that some of the poem's words have double meanings. For instance, *burc* means both "constellation" and "battlement," and *yıldız* is both the polestar and the name of the estate. Thus, the building's architecture and layout are equated in their height and nobility with a group of stars in the sky.

77. Pherkad: a bright star in the constellation of Ursa Minor that appears to revolve around the polestar in the night sky. For the role of Pherkad/ Farqadān in celestial navigation, see Glick, Livesey, and Wallis, *Medieval Science, Technology, and Medicine*, 365–66.

78. The extant wooden plaque is stored in the Dolmabahçe Palace Museum, Istanbul.

79. Hagar, the mother of Abraham's firstborn son, Ismā'īl (Ishmael), a forebear of the Prophet Muhammad.

80. Şıddīķa, meaning "truthful, veracious": "a title of honor given to Mary, the mother of Jesus, and to Ã'isha, wife of the Prophet Muhammad." Redhouse, *Turkish and English Lexicon*, 1172.

81. Rābi'a al-'Adawiyya, Muslim saint and Sufi poetess; see Smith, *Rābi'a the Mystic*. İbrahim Raşid seems to have used the model of Rābi'a frequently in the funerary chronograms he composed for women; see Çetin, "Raşid," 91–92.

82. The Arch of Chosroes (Ṭāķ-ı Kisrā), a sixth-century Sasanian monument from the ancient city of Ctesiphon, in today's Iraq, is perhaps the most commonly used archetype for palatial architecture in poetry from the Islamic world, along with the castle of Khawarnaq. The structure's monumental arch, one of its only remaining segments, boasted the largest single-span brick vault of its time. Not only was the building a source of inspiration for poetry, it was a source of both inspiration and spolia for actual building practices, starting with the Lakhmids and the Abbasids. See Bier, "Sasanian Palaces," 59–60. See also Hoffman, "Between East and West," 123.

83. For the legend of the Greek architect Sinimmār, the Lakhmid king Nu'mān ibn Imru al-Qays, and the building of the castle of Khawarnaq, see *Encyclopaedia Iranica*, s.v. "Ḳawarnaq," http://www .iranicaonline.org/articles/kawarnaq. See also Necipoğlu, "Outline of Shifting Paradigms," 4.

84. Raşid seems to have composed an incomplete chronogram (*tamiyeli tarih*), in that the sum of the letters in the final line is intentionally seven short, that is, 1251. The seven planets of classical Islamic astrology, heralds of fortune, which are mentioned in the penultimate line, enter and add the missing

figure and thus give the total of 1258, which equals the date of construction of the queen mother's pavilion. However, when the numerical values of the letters in the last line are added up, they give the date 1241, which is ten short. If the final vowel of *Ķamerdir* were spelled with a *yā* (numerical value 10), this would supply the amount missing from the total. But *-dir plene* is also the less common spelling, so perhaps the woodcarver followed the more usual orthography, and by the time the implications were noticed, it was too late to redo the entire inscription.

85. Şehinşāh-ı cihān Abdülmecīd Ḫān-ı felek-pāye
O şāhıñ māderidir Bezm-i 'Ālem nām-ı 'ālī-şān
O Hācer-haşlet Şıddīķa-'iffet Rābi'a-ṭab'ıñ
Yed-i cūdu riyāż-ı dehre oldu menba'-ı iḥsān
Edince Yıldız'a raġbet 'aceb ṭaġ üstü bāġ oldu
Ki yapdı hem de bir ḳaṣr-ı müzeyyen şāmiḫü'l-erkān
Nesīmi cānfezā ābı laṭīf neżżāresi ā'lā
Bunuñ yanında ḳaldı Ṭāḳ-ı Kisrā bir kühen bünyān
Zehî kāḫ-ı mu'allā resm-i vālā baġ-ı ra'nā kim
Sinimmār ṭarḥını görse olur engüşt-i leb-i ḥayrān
Nişīn olduḳça yā Rabb 'āfiyetle ol kerem-pīrā
Derūnuñda şefādan başķa bir şey görmeye her ān
Du'āsıñ bendesi Rāşid gibi vird-i zebān eyler
Gülistānıñda dā'im bekleyen hep bülbül-i gūyān
Gelüb seyyāre-i seb'a bu gūnā söyledi tārīḫ
Ķamerdir Yıldız'a gūyā bu ḳaṣr-ı vālide sulṭān
1258 [1842]

86. Necipoğlu, *Age of Sinan*, 280–92.

87. "Before the above-mentioned lady established these charitable buildings, their site and environs had been vacant plots. With the construction of new housing, they attracted around them a large population, and they augmented Üsküdar's inhabited region by at least one-third." Aşık Mehmed's description of the site, cited in Necipoğlu, *Sinan*, 292.

88. When von Moltke's map is overlaid onto a scaled plan of today's extant Yıldız structures, Bezm-i Alem's new pavilion coincides with the Azizian Mabeyn, and the site of Selim III's Yıldız Kiosk is held by Abdülhamid II's private residence.

89. H. Y. Şehsuvaroğlu, "Yıldız Kasrı," 6.

90. Terzioğlu, "Hekimbaşı Salih Efendi"; Günergun and Baytop, "Hekimbaşı Salih Efendi (1816–1895)"; E. Yücel, "Hekimbaşı Salih Efendi Yalısı."

91. Tokgöz, *Matbuat Hatıralarım*, 31. The journalist remembers his instructor as follows: "When he presented us with scientific explanations of the plant

lives of flowers and leaves that he culled from his garden, he would wipe clean our minds, filled with empty beliefs." See also Mardin, *Religion, Society, and Modernity in Turkey*, 113.

92. H. Y. Şehsuvaroğlu, *Asırlar Boyunca İstanbul*, 171. For a transcription of this orchard's contents, see Kut, "Meyve Bahçesi."

93. Hâfız Hızır İlyas, *Osmanlı Sarayında Gündelik Hayat*, 316.

94. Bezm-i Alem erected this fountain on the outer wall of the Yıldız complex, between the site of her new pavilion and the farmlands belonging to her estate. The fountain was located across from the Hamidiye clock tower, a corner that probably marked the entrance to Bezm-i Alem's Yıldız complex. Egemen, *İstanbul'un Çeşme ve Sebilleri*, 211–12. See also Koçu, "Bezmiâlem Vâlidesultan Çeşmesi."

95. Direct iconographic connections could be established between Bezm-i Alem's globe and the fountain surmounted by a marble globe at the tomb complex of her husband, Mahmud II, as symbols of court-coordinated Tanzimat enlightenment; see Akın, "Tanzimat ve Bir Aydınlanma Simgesi."

96. Egemen, *İstanbul'un Çeşme ve Sebilleri*, 214.

97. Aracı, *Donizetti Paşa*, 127–33, and his "'Each Villa on the Bosphorus,'" 624.

98. Ahmed Cevdet Paşa, *Tezâkir*, 1:20.

99. Ibid., 2:131.

100. Ibid., 3–4, 8, 59, 64–65, 100, 131.

101. A number of revisionist family histories have been published in recent years. One such modest publication makes a good attempt at clearing Serfiraz's name; see H. Açba, *Kadınefendiler*, 71–73.

102. My argument that women were frequently scapegoated during times of economic downturn is inspired by Artan, "Eighteenth-Century Ottoman Princesses as Collectors," 138–39.

103. Pertevniyal's patronage pattern closely resembled that of Bezm-i Alem. The former established a women's-only hospital in Mecca, opened another preparatory school in Istanbul, and donated to her mosque in Aksaray a library of manuscripts even larger than that of Bezm-i Alem to her school; Alpgüvenç, *Hayırda Yarışan Hanım Sultanlar*, 172–78.

104. It is not necessary to attribute unusual decorative motifs to distinctly gendered tastes, as does Bates, "Women as Patrons of Architecture in Turkey," 249–50.

105. H. Y. Şehsuvaroğlu, *Asırlar Boyunca İstanbul*, 155; Sakaoğlu, *Bu Mülkün Kadın Sultanları*, 392.

106. Ahmed Lütfî Efendi, *Vak'a-nüvis*, 14:15–16.

107. Sakaoğlu, *Bu Mülkün Kadın Sultanları*, 392.

108. Aksüt, *Sultan Azizin Mısır ve Avrupa Seyahati*; Kutay, *Sultan Abdülaziz'in Avrupa Seyahati*.

109. Gürfırat, "Pertevniyal Valide Sultan'ın Hâtıratı: Sergüzeştname." For another fictionalized account, see Coral, *Konstantiniye'nin Yitik Günceleri*, 85–108.

110. A. Osmanoğlu, *Babam Abdülhamid*, 112. On Queen Victoria as the archetypal eternal widow, see Jalland, *Death in the Victorian Family*, 318–38; also Cannadine, "War and Death, Grief and Mourning," 190–91.

111. Ahmed Lütfî Efendi, *Vak'a-nüvis*, 14:122.

112. Ibid., 47–48 and 137; also ibid., 15:21.

113. The title, meaning "mother of the governor of Egypt," conferred considerable status because the Egyptian khedive was the highest ranking of all Ottoman *paşa*s. The *valide paşa* came after the Ottoman *valide* in court ceremonies.

114. Ahmed Cevdet Paşa, *Tezâkir*, 4:91–93, 120–23, 126–27, 132–33, 152.

115. The coffin of the sultan's daughter, referred to as *ṭāsasız Rāżiye* (Raziye without sorrow), shares a space with that of her spiritual guide. Meḥmed Rāʿif, *Mirʿāt-ı İstānbul*, 291; H. Y. Şehsuvaroğlu, *Asırlar Boyunca İstanbul*, 146; Uluçay, *Padişahların Kadınları ve Kızları*, 39.

116. H. Y. Şehsuvaroğlu, *Asırlar Boyunca İstanbul*, 147–48.

117. Artan, "Theatre of Life," 81.

118. Hafız Hüseyin Ayvansarayî, *Garden of the Mosques*, 424–25.

119. Inchichean, *XVIII. Asırda İstanbul*, 114.

120. Sevgen, *Beşiktaşlı Şeyh Yahya Efendi*, 5.

121. Āşık Çelebi, *Meşâʿirüʾş-şuʿarâ*, 2:796.

122. Yahya Efendi cited in Meḥmed Rāʿif, *Mirʿāt-ı İstānbul*, 293.

123. *Evliyâ Çelebi Seyahatnâmesi*, 1:192.

124. Vasıf, *Enderunlu Osman Vâsıf Bey ve Dîvânı*, 579.

125. Duran, *Tarihimizde Vakıf Kuran Kadınlar*, 537–47.

126. Süleyman Hayri Bey (d. 1891), a bureaucrat educated in the palace school (*enderun mektebi*), was known for the eulogies he composed annually for Sultan Abdülaziz; see İnal, *Son Asır Türk Şairleri*, 2:606–10.

127. Şakir, *İkinci Sultan Hamit*, 76–77.

128. Hüseyin Vassaf, *Sefîne-i Evliyâ*, 1:259–60.

129. H. Açba, *Kadınefendiler*, 43, 56, 62, 87, 142.

130. L. Açba, *Bir Çerkes Prensesinin Harem Hatıraları*.

131. Esatlı, *Saray ve Konakların Dilinden Bir Devrin Tarihi*, 345.

132. For descriptions and photographs of the Maçka mansion of the last *valide*, Perestu, see Çetintaş, *Dolmabahçe'den Nişantaşı'na*, 240–41, and Esatlı, *Saray ve Konakların Dilinden Bir Devrin Tarihi*, 440–41.

133. Ahmed Sâdık Zîver Paşa, *Dîvân ve münşeât*, 422–23.

Chapter 3

1. Uzunçarşılı, *Osmanlı Devletinin Saray Teşkilâtı*, 465–87. For an overview of the Ottoman gardens and their varied types in the capital, see Necipoğlu, "Suburban Landscape of Sixteenth-Century Istanbul."

2. Ahmed Lütfî Efendi, *Vak'anüvîsî*, 1:146–47.

3. Mangone, "Nicola Carelli in Constantinople," 104.

4. Quataert, "Clothing Laws, State, and Society," 413.

5. For a broader range of Mahmud's depictions, see Kangal and Işın, *Sultan's Portrait*, 449–52.

6. Tomas, Merlin, and Tourret, *Jean-Michel Dalgabio*, 156–57. Although Paolo Girardelli suggests that this harem plan belonged to Mahmud's new palace (in large part because Dalgabio titles it indistinctly as "plan du palais de l'empereur à Constantinople"), it might in fact be of Bezm-i Alem's new kiosk on the Yıldız hilltop, which was completed in 1842; Girardelli, "Dolmabahçe and the Old Çırağan Palace," 250. Furthermore, judging from extant engravings, the harem of Mahmud's Çırağan was cruciform.

7. For a laudatory description of Mahmud's palace, see Byzantios, *Hē Kōnstantinoupolis*, 2:98–99.

8. Fergusson, *History of the Modern Styles of Architecture*, 2:317.

9. Biographical studies of Fethi Paşa are divided. Positive ones focus on his diverse cultural enterprises to rekindle empire-wide artisanal production; see Ayaşlı, *Dersaâdet*, 109–10. For a less laudatory version, see Ahmed Cevdet Paşa, *Ma'rûzât*, 10.

10. BOA, D. DRB. İ 2/12.

11. Sester's credentials as a garden director in Vienna are described in his obituary: A.W., "Ein unterfränkischer Landsmann," 1194.

12. Ibid.

13. Ibid. For Schönbusch's garden history, see Kreisel, *Schönbusch bei Aschaffenburg*. For a description of Schönbusch in the wider context of Weimar landscaping, see Hunt, *Picturesque Garden in Europe*, 163–64.

14. A.W., "Ein unterfränkischer Landsmann," 1194.

15. Ibid.

16. For an overview of a European head gardener's training trajectory and so-called journeyman years in the eighteenth and nineteenth centuries, see Musgrave, *Head Gardeners*, 75–78.

17. Sckell, *Das königliche Lustschloß Nymphenburg*.

18. "Wohlgefallen des türkischen Kaisers an englischen Gärten," *Frauendorfer Blätter*, July 3, 1845, 202–3.

19. Herder, "Kalligenia, die Mutter der Schönheit." For the broader historical context of the German Romantics and their intellectual pursuits of ancient Eastern cultures, see Marchand, *German Orientalism in the Age of Empire*. For the strong interconnection between German aesthetic theory and landscape design, see Lee, *German "Mittelweg."*

20. "Wohlgefallen des türkischen Kaisers an englischen Gärten," 203.

21. Linda B. Parshall, introduction to Pückler-Muskau, *Hints on Landscape Gardening*, 11.

22. Ibid., 14.

23. "Retrospect of German Literature," *Monthly Magazine; or, British Register* 14, no. 2 (1803): 653.

24. Hirschfeld, *Theory of Garden Art*, 145.

25. In Sester's obituary Mahmud declares, "Ich will keine Orangenbäume, ich will Etwas was Andere nicht haben"; see A.W., "Ein unterfränkischer Landsmann," 1195.

26. Necipoğlu, "Sources, Themes, and Cultural Implications of Sinan's Autobiographies," in *Sinan's Autobiographies*, x.

27. Sester's aid in forming lazarettos in the capital is mentioned in a postmortem report: *Beiträge zur Allgemeinen Zeitung*, January 30, 1866, 482. Indeed, the Ottoman government implemented quarantine reforms and maritime facilities against the plague in 1838. Though Sester is not mentioned, an Austrian doctor, Anton Lago, and his treatise on the plague (*risāle-i ḳarḳāntina*) seem to have propelled them. See Bulmuş, *Plague, Quarantines, and Geopolitics*, 2 and 11.

28. "Konstantinopel," *Allgemeine Zeitung München*, October 9, 1852, 4523.

29. A.W., "Ein unterfränkischer Landsmann," 1194. On Ensle's renovations, see Türker, "Ottoman Horticulture After the Tulip Era."

30. BOA, HH. 19355.

31. "Wohlgefallen des türkischen Kaisers an englischen Gärten," 202. Although the exact location of Rıza Paşa's waterfront mansion remains unknown, the account of an English woman's visit to his inland mansion and her interactions with his wife "Madame Riza," who describes the newly constructed gardens of her *yalı* to her foreign guest, are revealing: "There are hanging gardens with a stream leaping from rock to rock amongst the orange-trees.... There are also beautiful fountains, and rose-gardens." Hornby, *In and Around Stamboul*, 258.

32. Rbg., "Sr. Hoheit Sultans Abdul Medschid in seine Residenz: Im Juni 1846," *Allgemeine Theaterzeitung*, July 13, 1846, 662.

33. İAK, PVSE 757, 1086, 1125, 1126, and 1128.

34. By selecting *ṭıbāḳ*, the poet not only alludes to the overall harmony of the design, matching the garden of paradise, but also emphasizes that it was physically stacked like plates, a reiteration of the phrase *ḳat ḳat*, which appears in the previous line.

35. Nev-bahar-ı bâğ-ı şevket Ḥażret-i Maḥmūd Ḫān.

Eyledi bu baġçeyi nev gülşen-i pür-zîb ü şān.

Ḳat ḳat bu ravżayı tezyîne fermân idicek.
Oldı maḥsûd-ı ṭıbaḳ-ı bâġ-ı cennet
bî-gümân.

Ahmed Sâdık Zîver Paşa,
Dîvân ve münşe'ât, 452.

36. Gyllius, *De Bosphoro Thracio*, libri II, 90–93.

37. Pardoe, *Beauties of the Bosphorus*, 20.

38. A.W., "Ein unterfränkischer Landsmann," 1195.

39. Koch, *Wanderungen im Oriente*, 1:368.

40. Hahn-Hahn, *Letters from the Holy Land*, 246.

41. Léopold II, *Voyage à Constantinople*, 56–57: "Après déjeuner, nous descendîmes en caïk le Bosphore jusqu'aux jardins et kiosques de Tschéragan. Ce jardin, tracé par un Allemand, est grand et joliment établi. On voit Constantinople, le Bosphore, et même un peu de la mer de Marmara. Le sol, rocailleux ici, n'est pas excessivement favorable à la végétation, aussi le jardin ne possède pas d'ombre. Tout près d'ici, dans un fond, se trouve un autre kiosque du Sultan, tout en marbre blanc et orné d'une façon très riche, mais de mauvais goût."

42. For Mıgırdıç Melkon, see Kürkman, *Armenian Painters in the Ottoman Empire*, 2:619–31.

43. Uras, *Balyanlar*, 59. Uras cites an article from the Armenian journal *Hayasdan* that puzzlingly describes this new structure as "moorish" (*moresko*), inspired by Chinese architectural features.

44. Türker, "On Dokuzuncu Yüzyıl Diplomasisinin Bir Kristal Saray Serüveni." See also S. Can, *Belgelerle Çırağan Sarayı*, 30–31.

45. Bossoli, *War in Italy*, and Vernizzi et al., *Carlo Bossoli*.

46. R. D., "Aus Konstantinopel," *Allgemeine Theaterzeitung*, October 30, 1846, 1040.

47. The seventy-five notebooks begin with BOA, HH. d. 18928, and end with 22266. In Sester's seal, the name of the palace is misspelled *Çerāġañ*, when it should have been *Çerāġān*.

48. BOA, HH. d. 18928–22266.

49. Frankl, *Nach Jerusalem!*, 1:173.

50. Ibid., 174.

51. BOA, A.}MKT.NZD. 65/79.

52. A.W., "Ein unterfränkischer Landsmann," 1196.

53. On the dormitories of the gardening corps and the office of the head gardener (*bostancı çardağı*, or the gardener's arbor) inside Topkapı, see Necipoğlu, *Topkapı Palace*, 207.

54. Aracı, *Donizetti Paşa*, 54.

55. Two examples of the military formations implemented for gardeners installed in the various imperial gardens of the capital can be observed in the Ottoman imperial treasury registries BOA, Y. PRK. SGE. 11/45 from December 20, 1908, and Y. PRK. SGE. 39/19 from the same year.

56. İÜMK 93332 and 93405. For a third, see İAK 5908.

57. On this regiment, composed of Northern (Gheg) Albanians, see Karateke, *Padişahım Çok Yaşa!*, 256n32 and 272. Abdülhamid II also kept a turban-wearing *zouave* regiment made up of North African Arabs, adopted from Napoleon's Algerian footmen; see ibid., 278.

58. Uşaklıgil, *Saray ve Ötesi*, 199.

59. Ibid.

60. Nogel, *Utazása Keleten*, 28.

61. Kutluoğlu and Candemir, *Bir Cihan Devletinin Tasfiyesi*, 125–26.

62. Frankl, *Nach Jerusalem!*, 1:174.

63. Bertsch, *Anton Prokesch von Osten*, 388: "unwissend, launisch, herzlos, und boshaft."

64. Frazee, *Catholics and Sultans*, 256–74, offers the most cogent overview of these complicated divisions. On the Catholic *amira* families, see Dadyan, *Osmanlı'da Ermeni Aristokrasisi*.

65. *Protokolle der Deutschen Bundesversammlung vom Jahre 1856*, Sitzung 1 bis 33, 15.

66. Csorba, "Hungarian Emigrants of 1848–49," 227–28.

67. On Orbán's club for Hungarian émigrés, see Tóth, *Exiled Generation*, 186–91, 228.

68. Orbán, "Külföldi életemből."

69. For a biography of Sipos, see Gaboda, "Conclusions historiques."

70. For a discussion of the Teutonia Club, see Manz, *Constructing a German Diaspora*, 54–55. See also Radt, *Geschichte der Teutonia*.

71. "Ein schönes Familienfest," *Passavia, Zeitung für Niederbayern*, October 23, 1845. The newspaper item lists the remaining members of the Sester family by vocation. Notably, two of Sester's brothers also continued the family trade: Jakob Sester was gardener to a Herr von Bethmann in Frankfurt, and Joseph Sester was an art and trade gardener in Aschaffenburg. Christian Sester's sister, Julia Rinz, was married to a municipal and trade gardener by the name of Jakob.

72. Schrott, *Prinzregent*, 30–32.

73. Granville, *Spas of Germany*, 1:7.

74. BOA, A. MKT. MHM 210/56. Sester was most likely among the first set of honorees of the Mecidiye, as it was instituted in 1851, the date of the monumental garden project's completion.

75. "Ein schönes Familienfest." The Turkish medal of honor to which the news item refers was the Order of Glory (*nişān-ı iftiḫār*), founded by Mahmud II in 1831; see E. Eldem, *Pride and Privilege*, 110–25.

76. Blackbourn, "Fashionable Spa Towns."

77. "Ein schönes Familienfest."

78. Granville, *Spas of Germany*, 1:33.

79. Ibid., xxxii.

80. Granville lists all the disorders cured miraculously by the Bad Gastein waters, but stresses that

they were particularly good for diseases of the nervous system; ibid., 329–30.

81. "Ein schönes Familienfest."

82. A.W., "Ein unterfränkischer Landsmann," 1195.

83. Gräffer, *Historische Raritäten*, 2:168.

84. Frankl, *Nach Jerusalem!*, 1:179.

85. Granville, *Spas of Germany*, 1:166, 254–55, and 209. See also Walsh, *Riding and Driving*, 67–68.

86. *La Turquie*, no. 273, December 19, 1866.

87. Marmara, *Pancaldi*, 206.

88. Del Giorno, *Chroniques*, 1:478.

89. Ibid., 89–90.

90. Ibid., 3:1378.

91. Ibid.

92. BOA, HR. TO., 164/90.

93. BOA, A.}MKT.MHM. 210/56.

94. "Telegraphische Berichte: Türkei," *Allgemeine Zeitung München*, April 5, 1865.

95. Saz, *Imperial Harem of the Sultans*, 36–39.

96. Ibid., 36; Frankl, *Nach Jerusalem!*, 1:179. Within a garden late eighteenth-century German landscape architects created sections, called rooms, much like painterly vignettes, that provided individual, differentiated vistas; see Lee, *German "Mittleweg,"* 59–112. In fact, Skell and Pückler-Muskau had developed the picturesque term "garden scenes" to capture the experience of the landscaped garden as *Raumkontinuum*, or a sequence of rooms, which they aligned with the gardener's heightened agency as a capable modifier of a terrain; see Lauterbach, "Werdende Bilder im Übergange," 45–47.

97. Saz, *Imperial Harem of the Sultans*, 30.

98. Ibid., 36.

99. Pischon, *Einfluss des Islâm*, 33. Pischon also managed the German Hospital while in Istanbul during the Crimean War and was in correspondence with Florence Nightingale.

100. C. K. S., "Vom Goldenen Horn."

101. Bachmann, "Epochenwandel am Bosporus," 121–22.

102. Klausmeier and Pahl, "Zur Geschichte des Parks."

103. For Petzold, see Rohde, *Von Muskau bis Konstantinopel*.

104. Klausmeier and Pahl, "Zur Geschichte des Parks," 120.

105. Mühle cited in Bachmann, "Epochenwandel am Bosporus," 68.

106. C. K. S., "Vom Goldenen Horn," 604. For the arduous production process of these insurance maps, see Sabancıoğlu, "Jacques Pervititch and His Insurance Maps."

107. BOA, Y. PRK. MYD. 2/39.

108. For the region's non-Muslim ethno-demographic composition, see Inchichean, *XVIII. Asırda İstanbul*, 114–15.

109. BOA, I . . DH . . 848/68081.

110. "Personal-Nachrichten," *Gartenflora* 48 (1899): 87.

111. On Romeo Scanziani and his brother, court dragoman Angelo Bey Scanziani, see Grange, *L'Italie et la Méditerranée*, 1:491.

112. BOA, Y. PRK. SGE. 10/36 and Y. PRK. HH. 39/19.

113. Stern, *Abdul Hamid II*, 24–25.

114. BOA, Y. PRK. HH. 39/19.

115. BOA, Y. PRK. SGE. 10/36.

116. This documentary practice was of course rooted in earlier *defter*s registering janissary conscripts; see Uzunçarşılı, *Osmanlı Devleti Teşkilâtından Kapıkulu Ocakları*, 1:16–17. For a sample of near-identical, contemporaneous *sicil*s for the district of Kastamonu, see Abdulkadiroğlu, Aksoyak, and Duru, *Kastamonu Jurnal Defteri (1252–1253/1836–1837)*.

117. The village of Kızara is in the district of Safranbolu, in the northern Anatolian province of Kastamonu. See Karakaya, Yücedağ, and Yılmaz, *Arşiv Belgelerinde Karabük*, 193.

118. At the time, Nikšić was part of the Ottoman province of İşkodra (Shkodër). In the disastrous war of 1877–78, a few years before this register of palace gardeners was compiled, Nikšić was lost to the Ottoman Empire, taken by the Montenegrin army, as was the Adriatic seaport of Bar, the hometown of Hāşim Aġā's colleague Rüstem Aġā bin Edhem. Most of the local Muslim inhabitants—Albanians, Bosniaks, and Turks—were either killed or forced to flee. Sultan Abdülhamid II's fondness for surrounding himself with Muslim Albanians was not merely sentimental but also an embodiment of his worries about the shrinking frontiers of his empire.

119. BOA, HH. 17679.

Ḳasṭamonu sāncāġında Zāʿferānbolu [Safranbolu] ḳaṣabasında
Ḳızāra ḳaryesinde Cānbozoġlu, uzūn boylu, elā gözlü, ḳumrāl (?)
bıyıḳlı Ḥüseyin Aġā bin Ḥasan,
sinn 40
duḫūlu 1 Ḥazīrān 96, mʿaāşa nāʾili 1 Nīsān 1301 [1300?]

İşkodra'ya tābʿī Nikşīk ḳaṣabasında
orta boylu, elā gözlü, az bıyıḳlı
Hāşim Aġā bin ʿAbdullāh
sinn 28
duḫūlu 27 Teşrīn-i şānī 300, mʿaāşa nāʾili 27 Teşrīn-i şānī 300

İşkodra'ya tābʿī Bār ḳaṣabasında
orta boylu, elā gözlü, ḳumrāl (?) bıyıḳlı Rüstem Aġā
bin Edhem
sinn 55
duḫūlu 12 Şubāṭ 86, mʿaāşa nāʾili 12 Şubāṭ 86

120. For Abdülhamid's strategic appeal to the Albanian Muslim subjects of his empire, see Gawrych, *Crescent and the Eagle*.

121. For the most recent demographic composition of the gardeners in Ottoman Istanbul's market gardens, and the workers' Black Sea and Albanian origins, see Kaldjian, "Istanbul's Bostans," 286 and 292.

122. BOA, Y. PRK. MM. 1/36. See also Stern, *Der Sultan*, 25.

123. Henry, "Les jardins de Yildiz," 57.

124. Noyan, *Prizren-Dersaadet*, 50–54.

125. "Death of the Sultan's Gardener," *Gardener's Chronicle*, February 16, 1907, 105. See also "Bilder als aller Welt," *Die Woche* 9, February 2, 1907, 222. The latter provides a photograph of Adam Schlerff in his Ottoman regalia.

126. Stern, *Abdul Hamid II*, 23.

127. C. K. S., "Vom Goldenen Horn," 605.

128. BOA, Y. PRK. SGE. 11/54.

129. BOA, Y. PRK. HH. 39/19.

130. Stern, *Abdul Hamid II*, 25.

131. "Liste des membres," *Journal de la Société impériale et centrale d'horticulture* 10 (1864): xxxvi.

132. BOA, Y. PRK. HH. 16/63.

133. BOA, Y. PRK. HH. 39/19.

134. Tinayre, *Notes d'une voyageuse en Turquie*, 286–91.

135. Henry, "Les jardins de Yildiz," 57. "Il ne faut pas considérer les jardins en Orient comme nous les considérons chez nous; a l'encontre des nôtres, qui sont regardés comme lieux de repos et d'agrément, ils ne sont, en réalité, que des annexes aux constructions hermétiquement closes, dans lesquelles se passe la vie des Orientaux; c'est ce qui explique la très petite quantité de beaux jardins que l'on voit dans ces pays."

136. Ibid., 55.

137. BOA, Y. PRK. SGE. 11/22.

138. The Ottoman translation of Henry's trip is provided in Çuluk, "Bahçıvanbaşı Charles Henry'nin Bursa Çevresinde Araştırma Gezisi."

139. BOA, Y. PRK. SGE. 11/22.

140. Tinayre, *Notes d'une voyageuse en Turquie*, 290.

141. Henry, "Les jardins de Yildiz," 58.

142. Guerville, *New Egypt*, 116–19.

143. For André's professional life, see Padilla, "Édouard François André." Of André's many publications, the most prominent is his treatise on garden designs, *L'art des jardins*.

144. In an article on cultivating flowering yucca in Koubbeh's park, Henry talks about André's introduction of these plants to the gardens six years before the gardener took up the post. Henry, "Dasylirion Glaucophyllum."

145. On Abdülhamid II's court-appointed head calligrapher, see Derman, *Letters in Gold*, 128.

146. Mehmed İzzet, *Rehber-i Umūr-ı Beytīye*, vol. 3. The first volume was published in 1901 by the publisher of the newspaper *İḳdām*; the second was published in 1907, and the third in 1909.

147. Cevat Rüştü, *Türk Çiçek ve Ziraat Kültürü*, 332.

148. The most prominent of these elegiac memoirs are Abdülhak Şinasi Hisar's *Boğaziçi Mehtapları* (1942) and *Boğaziçi Yalıları; Geçmiş Zaman Köşkleri* (1968). Also noteworthy are Semih Mümtaz's *Tarihimizde Hayal Olmuş Hakikatler* (1948) and Münevver Ayaşlı's *Dersaâdet* (1993).

Chapter 4

1. Only a few scholars mention Yıldız's prevalent chalet aesthetic; see Barillari and Godoli, *Istanbul 1900*, 70, and Girardelli, "Power or Leisure?," 42. For a scorching description of Abdülhamid's life in the palace, depicting the palace's chalets as the sultan's individual harems, see Kélékian, "Life at Yildiz."

2. Lamartine, *Nouveau voyage en Orient*, 1:78. For Lamartine's ill-fated farm in Izmir, see Aḥmed Refīk, *Lāmārtīn*.

3. Örikağasızade Hasan Sırrı, *Sultan Abdülhamit Devri Hatıraları*, 186–87. According to this author, the building, in its later, stone incarnation, was used for intimate diplomatic gatherings between the sultan and visiting diplomats after Friday prayer ceremonies. It also contained a map room for meetings of the Hamidian war commissions. Overall, however, it served as a transitional space between the sultan's private quarters and the official, public courtyard of the Mabeyn. It had a door that opened into the palace's harem quarters. Precisely due to the building's interstitial position between the Mabeyn and the sultan's private domain, commentaries on Koranic verses (*ḥuẓūr dersleri*) were delivered here in the form of a *meclis* for eight days during the holy month of Ramadan, attended by Abdülhamid, the highest functionaries of his *mabeyn*, cabinet members, and the sultan's sons and sons-in-law; see Tahsin Paşa, *Yıldız Hatıraları*, 177–78. For the eighteenth-century origins, see Zilfi, "*Medrese* for the Palace."

4. Moüy, *Lettres du Bosphore*, 250.

5. Frank, "Air Cure Town."

6. Kennedy, *Magic Mountains*, 3, 105, and 163.

7. Abdülaziz frequented the site with his mother during the hot summer months. A *defter* from his time details the cost of furnishing the Yıldız Kiosk before Pertevniyal Valide Sultan's arrival and refers to the site as a summer residence (*ṣayfīye*); BOA, HH. d. 12570.

8. For the ultimate satire on the bourgeois fad for estate building, see Flaubert, *Bouvard et Pécuchet*.

9. Eastlake, *History of the Gothic Revival*; Maudlin, *Idea of the Cottage in English Architecture*.

10. For Petit's titles more specifically, and for volumes related to architecture and landscape design,

I have consulted the library catalogue registered under BOA, Y. EE. d. 400.

11. A. Osmanoğlu, *Babam Abdülhamid*, 103.

12. Borgese, *Autunno di Costantinopoli*, 73.

13. Abdülhamid II appears to have inherited his interest in woodworking from his father, Abdülmecid, and learned the skill from his father's instructor, Halil Efendi. The carpentry tools of the two sultans bore the insignia of this master. According to his daughter, Abdülhamid liked to work in wood and mother-of-pearl inlay and was skilled enough to produce scenes of "country life" in wood intarsia as well as intricate miniature furniture. He reportedly gifted an ebony desk to his minister of foreign affairs, Tevfik Paşa. A. Osmanoğlu, *Babam Abdülhamid*, 26–27; see also ʿOs̱mān Nūrī, *ʿAbdülḥamīd-i S̱ānī ve Devr-i Salṭanatı*, 2:540.

14. Although this structure was built to serve as a summer residence for Abdülaziz and had the central *sofa* layout traditional to Ottoman domestic architecture, it was expanded and converted into the palace's main governmental space once Abdülhamid had moved his court to Yıldız. For renderings of the Hamidian Mabeyn and its structural constituents, see S. H. Eldem, *Köşkler ve Kasırlar*, 1:444–47, and Kılıçoğlu, "Yıldız Sarayı Büyük Mabeyn Köşkü Oda-ı Ali Restorasyonu."

15. In many of the accounts of Abdülhamid's "camarilla," the weight of infamy heaped on İzzet Holo Paşa (sometimes referred to as Arap İzzet Paşa) from Damascus stems in large part from his closeness to the sultan. Although this office building has not survived, a photograph of the structure reveals its likeness to its neighbor, housing the office of the aides-de-camp, built by D'Aronco. On this much-resented personality, see Örikağasızade Hasan Sırrı, *Sultan Abdülhamit Devri Hatıraları*, 143–44, and Tahsin Paşa, *Yıldız Hatıraları*, 184–88. For a German account of İzzet Paşa's place in the palace hierarchy, which refers to him as *der Vice-Sultan*, see Stern, *Abdul Hamid II*, 131–40.

16. For a discussion and examples of D'Aronco's early studies for this building, see Barillari and Godoli, *Istanbul 1900*, 72–75.

17. Türkgeldi, *Görüp İşittiklerim*, 292.

18. See, by A. Batur, "Art Nouveau," "D'Aronco, Raimondo Tommaso," and "İstanbul Art Nouveau'su."

19. The Şale, in its tertiary expansion by D'Aronco after 1898, was referred to as the Ceremonial Apartments (Merāsim Dāʾiresi). For its multiphase construction and expansion, see Gezgör and İrez, *Yıldız Sarayı, Şale Kasr-ı Hümâyunu*. For a nuanced reading of D'Aronco's additions and his awareness of the structural elements of Sarkis Balyan's first version of the building, see A. Batur, "Şale Köşkü." The elusive *hususi daire*—which burned down during Vahdeddin's reign and is often confused either with the prefabricated pavilion later erected temporarily on the platform to receive the *hususi daire* or with the ceremonial pavilion (known as Sester's or Gardener's Kiosk) built in the early 1900s in the palace's Ortaköy expansion—is best discussed by the architect Can Binan; see his "Yıldız Sarayı Yanmış Hususi Daire Kuzey Avlusu." On the builders, approximate location, inhabitants, and interior decoration of the *hususi daire*, see A. Osmanoğlu, *Babam Abdülhamid*, 103–4. A little-known photograph taken from Üsküdar's Sultantepe shows Çırağan's shoreline and Yıldız's hilltop settlement and captures the commanding position of Abdülhamid's private residence; see S. H. Eldem, *Boğaziçi Anıları*, 50–51.

20. BOA, Y. PRK. MM. 1/39, dated July 20, 1889, a few short months before Wilhelm's visit, refers to an old chalet and an extension to the Şale Kiosk. The old chalet, no longer extant, was probably a cottage—with a clock placed centrally in one gable end, just below the roof—that rested atop the cascading stream, perpendicular to the earliest (1878) version of the Şale. This old chalet was taken down to accommodate the extension introduced by D'Aronco.

21. C. Can, "Tanzimat and Architecture." Can argues that the Swiss-Italian architect Gaspare Fossati's Russian embassy in Istanbul became the prototype for the civic architecture of the Ottoman Tanzimat.

22. The pre-Hamidian sultan's pavilion, likely a reformatted version of the first Yıldız kiosk, is now the main administrative office of the Yıldız Technical University and is inaccessible. It is attached to the palace theater and during the Hamidian era was occupied by the sultan's adopted mother. Köse, "Yıldız Sarayı Hünkar Dairesi." Information is also lacking on the so-called Sunken Palace. A plaque on its façade claims it was used by the widowed and unmarried members of the Hamidian harem. This structure was the second largest residential structure in Abdülhamid's palace after the expanded Şale; Görgülü, "Çukur Saray Yapısı."

23. Örikağasızade Hasan Sırrı comments on the arduous twenty-five-minute walk from the gate beside the Mabeyn, which was open to the palace functionaries, to the mountain gate. Örikağasızade Hasan Sırrı, *Sultan Abdülhamit Devri Hatıraları*, 188.

24. Of the six extant kiosks constructed for the princes, five were balloon framed with walls of either cement-plastered galvanized wire or lath and plasterwork (*baġdādī*); only one of them, known today as the "Pink Kiosk," was constructed from wood paneling. For individual analyses of these six kiosks, see Arapoğlu, "Yıldız Sarayı Şehzade Köşkleri."

25. Ünüvar, *Saray Hâtıralarım*, 18.

26. Georgeon, *Abdülhamid II*, 142–46.

27. A. Osmanoğlu, *Babam Abdülhamid*, 103–4.

28. Ibid.

29. İnal, *Son Asır Türk Şairleri*, 1:44–47. For a Turkish transcription of the fourteen-*defter* manuscript of Abdülaziz Efendi's study, see ʿAbdüʾl-ʿazīz Bey, *Ādāt ü Merāsim-i Ḳadīme*, 163.

30. Hahn-Hahn, *Letters from the Holy Land*, 70.

31. Özsezgin, *Collection of Istanbul Museum of Painting and Sculpture*, 522–23.

32. Mehmet Memduh Paşa, *Tanzimattan Meşrutiyete*, 102–3.

33. It is safe to assume that Sarkis Balyan introduced the chalet type to the court; see Tuğlacı, *Role of the Balian Family*, 492–94, and Wharton, *Architects of Ottoman Constantinople*, 41–42.

34. Caston, "Grand mouvement architectural," 408.

35. The use of portable objects or patterns as sources for permanent structures was by no means a nineteenth-century novelty. For the transmission of architectural inspiration from transferable ephemera to solid buildings in the medieval world, and the global residential idiom that they helped to create, see Redford, "Portable Palaces."

36. *Seyyār* and *ḳurma*, meaning "portable" in Ottoman Turkish, appear in the same *defter* in the Yıldız Palace Library that contains the volumes by Viktor Petit. Within these bound volumes the Ottoman cataloguer indiscriminately included mail-order catalogues, loose plans, and images of chalets and other building types. See note 10 above for the *defter*'s archival record.

37. Kuban, "Wooden Housing Architecture of Istanbul," 16–17.

38. S. M. P., "The Wooden House from Norway," *The Builder*, January 27, 1877.

39. Wærn, "Scandinavia: Prefabrication as a Model of Society."

40. "Wooden Architecture of Norway," *The Builder*, November 3, 1894. This article was, in fact, a comprehensive review of a Norwegian publication that, much like *L'architecture ottomane* with respect to Ottoman architecture, resulted from a collaborative historical inquiry into the fundamentals of Norse architecture: Dietrichson and Munthe, *Die Holzbaukunst Norwegens*.

41. Vernes, "Le chalet infidèle."

42. Hahn-Hahn, *Letters from the Holy Land*, 6. For the centrality of these churches to imperial architectural revivalism in Scandinavian and German countries, see Donnelly, *Architecture in the Scandinavian Countries*, 36–37, and Lane, *National Romanticism*.

43. Viollet-le-Duc, *Habitations of Man in All Ages*, 386–87.

44. Ersoy, "Architecture and the Search for Ottoman Origins," and his "Ottoman Gothic."

45. Z. Çelik, *Displaying the Orient*, 96–97; Avcıoğlu, *Turquerie and the Politics of Representation*, 266.

46. For Giovanni Battista Barborini, the little-known principal architect of the Ottoman buildings of 1867, see Girardelli and Can, "Giovanni Battista Barborini à Istanbul."

47. Ersoy, *Architecture*, 61.

48. Dana, *Swiss Châlet Book*, 13.

49. Ibid., 16.

50. Herbert, *Pioneers of Prefabrication*, 41–42. On Mahmud II's patronage of ironworks from England, see Fairbairn, *Treatise on Mills and Millwork*, 1:116.

51. Türker, "On Dokuzuncu Yüzyıl Diplomasisinin Bir Kristal Saray Serüveni."

52. Silver, *Renkioi*. For a detailed discussion of the production of military huts in England during the Crimean War, see Herbert, *Pioneers of Prefabrication*, 75–96.

53. "Muḳavvā İnşāāt," *Servet-i Fünūn*, no. 25 (February 27, 1892).

54. Ibid.

55. Wærn, "Scandinavia: Prefabrication as a Model of Society."

56. Şakir, *İkinci Sultan Hamit*, 365–66.

57. The main article appears in *Servet-i Fünūn*, no. 326 (June 10, 1895); photographic illustrations of the site and its employees were made available much later, in *Servet-i Fünūn*, nos. 329–31 (1897).

58. Playfair, *Handbook to the Mediterranean*, 53.

59. Fontane, *Voyage pittoresque*, 74–76. This publication contains lithographs of these buildings made from watercolors by Édouard Riou (d. 1900), the French illustrator of Jules Verne's novels.

60. Huber, *Channelling Mobilities*, 66; Grey, *Journal of a Visit to Egypt*, 142–43.

61. For detailed descriptions of the chalet's construction and the panoramic views it afforded, see Fontane, *Voyage pittoresque*, 59–61, 66, and 139.

62. The narrator of Joseph Conrad's *Heart of Darkness* (1899), who is fascinated by and longs to find rivets to patch up vessels and buildings, predicts the impending colonization of the Congo River Basin by towns containing buildings that need none, being made of wood blocks that fit together like puzzle pieces.

63. On Christian Thams, see Nyberg, "Fenomenet Thams"; Gran, "Magnate and His Manor"; and Reiersen, "Scandinavians in Colonial Trading Companies."

64. Lisianskii, *Vsia Odessa*, part 2, p. 54. For another prefab supplied by Shcherbakov as an imperial residence outside of Yıldız, see Damla Acar's important dissertation, "19. Yüzyılın İkinci Yarısında İstanbul'da Ahşap Yapım Sistemlerinin Değişimi," 289, 292–98.

65. BOA, Y. EE. d. 400.

66. For Shcherbakov's portable harem structure, I have consulted BOA, Y. MTV. 169/103 and HH. d. 26595; for his negotiations on building a hospital and his later disappearance, see BOA, BEO. 529/39656, BEO. 1615/121074, BEO. 1637/122729, BEO. 1821/136562, and BEO. 2025/151809.

67. Tahsin Paşa, *Yıldız Hatıraları*, 419, relays Abdülhamid's own reflections and views on Dresset Paşa.

68. BOA, HH. d. 30226.

69. On Vasilaki Kalfa, see Hocaoğlu, *Abdülhamit Han'ın Muhtıraları*, 224; also Şenyurt, *İstanbul Rum Cemaatinin Osmanlı Mimarisindeki Temsiliyeti*, 146–51.

70. BOA, Y. PRK. MF. 1/11.

71. This kind of taste-reflecting marginalia appears frequently in the extant catalogues of chalet manufacturers. The collection at Harvard University's Fine Arts Library contains one such remarkable example, in which the printed plans and elevations of chalets are annotated with the patron's selections and calculations: *Schweizer Châlet Fabrik Chur*.

72. Gloag, *Victorian Comfort*; Brown, *Bourgeois Interior*.

73. The Ottoman tendency to resort to wooden construction in the aftermath of earthquakes was not unprecedented. After the 1509 earthquake, called the "Little Apocalypse" (*kıyāmet-i şuğrā*), Bayezid II commissioned a timber-framed palace (*çatma sarāy*) for shelter inside the Topkapı Palace. See Necipoğlu, "'Virtual Archaeology,'" 320. For early modern examples of prefabricated-home production after natural disasters in Istanbul, see Necipoğlu, "Volatile Urban Landscapes," 213.

74. A. Osmanoğlu, *Babam Abdülhamid*, 93.

75. Toğral, "Osmanlı'da Japon Kültürü." For a wider analysis of the cultural agency of this Japanese merchant, Torajirō Yamada, in Istanbul, see Esenbel, "*Fin de Siècle* Japanese Romantic," and Esenbel, Girardelli, and Küçükyalçın, *Crescent and the Sun*.

76. Bein, "Istanbul Earthquake of 1894."

77. Genç and Mazak, *İstanbul Depremleri*, 96–97; Ürekli, *İstanbul'da 1894 Depremi*, 40.

78. Ürekli, *İstanbul'da 1894 Depremi*, 40.

79. Acar and Mazlum, "Timber-Framed Houses," 618.

80. Ibid., 619.

81. Ibid. The elevation of this 1894 structure is preserved in BOA. HH. d. 27830.

82. For an evaluation of the pronounced downscaling of Hamidian protocol into frequent *tête-à-têtes*, see Karateke, *Padişahım Çok Yaşa!*, 190–93.

83. Demirel, *Son Ziyaretler, Son Ziyafetler*, 73–76.

84. Küçükerman, *Hereke Fabrikası*, 117; Gezgör, "Hereke Fabrika-i Hümayunu'nda Halı Üretimi," 174; Y. Yılmaz, "Osmanlı'nın Hediye Sunumlarında Önem Taşıyan Bir Fabrika," 134–36.

85. Demirel, *Son Ziyaretler, Son Ziyafetler*, 89–108.

86. Muẓaffar al-Dīn Shāh, *Safarnāmah-i Farangistān*, 219–20.

87. The photograph album may be found in Yıldız's library. During the German Third Reich, Rominten became Hermann Göring's favorite retreat; Neumärker and Knopf, *Görings Revier*. For the lodge's afterlife, see Frevert, *Rominten*.

88. The album, containing twenty-five photographs, has the catalogue number İÜMK 91380.

89. Bernard, *Rush to the Alps*.

90. Norberg-Schulz, *Nightlands*, 127–28.

91. Arıkan et al., *Seçilmiş Nadir Basma Kitaplar Sergisi*, 6. The German volume is *Esaias Tegnérs Frithiofsage*.

92. Findley, "An Ottoman Occidentalist in Europe."

93. Ahmet Mithat Efendi, *Avrupa'da Bir Cevelan*, 291–96.

94. The blending of the court's architectural taste with that of the extracourtly vernacular had precedents in the eighteenth century, when Ahmed III was inspired to build his palaces in the likeness of the wooden townhouses of his court officials and favored timber over stone. See Rāşid Efendi, *Tārīḫ-i Rāşid*, 3:307.

95. BOA, Y. A. HUS. 352/22. See also Şenyurt, *İstanbul Rum Cemaatinin Osmanlı Mimarisindeki Temsiliyeti*, 152.

96. For a photograph of this modest chalet, see İÜMK, 90646–0005.

97. For a detailed study of the locations and characteristics of these no-longer-extant *konak*s of the Hamidian bureaucrats, see Çetintaş, *Dolmabahçe'den Nişantaşı'na*, 230–331. Others, too, were built on their suburban estates on the capital's Asian side. For the domed and galleried—Islamicized—pavilion, surrounded by porticoes (*revak*), built by Rıdvan Paşa (d. 1906) specifically for his daughter Nuriye, see B. N. Şehsuvaroğlu, *Göztepe*, 67–70.

98. BOA, Y. MTV. 28/75.

99. The Dolmabahçe Palace Museum has assigned to this catalogue no. 2009.

100. This undigitized and uncatalogued item is stored in his intact library inside the Dolmabahçe Palace Museum.

101. Celâlettin, *Geçmiş Zaman Olur ki*, 70–71.

102. Ibid., 72–73.

103. Ibid., 73.

104. This drawing is also among Abdülmecid Efendi's undigitized and uncatalogued archives in the Dolmabahçe Palace Museum.

105. Tanman, *From the Shores of the Nile to the Bosphorus*, 148–53; Gülersoy, *Hidiv'ler ve Çubuklu Kasrı*. See also Oral, *Yazı ve Resimlerde Beykoz*, 222–23. For the official court documentation on the request to

lower the tower, see BOA, I .. HUS. 142/1324 and Y .. A ... HUS. 503/83.

106. Prenses Cavidan, *Harem Hayatı*, 235. This incongruity between the exteriors and interiors of chalets was particular to the Ottoman case, but these structures, whose interiors arrived untreated, were conducive to the decorative whims and tastes of their diverse owners. Abdülhamid's catalogue-inspired Cihannüma chalet bore decorative elements of *chinoiserie* in its living room, while the Şale Kiosk's interiors were in equal part rococo and Alhambresque.

107. Ibid., 236.

108. Tokgöz, *Matbuat Hatıralarım*, 91–93.

109. For a study of domestic spaces in Tanzimat novels, see İnci, *Roman ve Mekân*; on the Ottoman novel as a source on consumption history, see Mardin, "Super Westernization in Urban Life."

110. Zarifi, *Hatıralarım*, 137–39.

111. Ayverdi, *İbrahim Efendi Konağı*, 163–65.

112. Ibid., 168.

113. For instance, the covers of *Servet-i Fünūn*, nos. 368, 376, and 378 from 1898, exhibit the private studies of the artist Halil Bey and the physicians Besim Ömer Bey and Cemil Paşa (later Topuzlu), respectively.

114. On connections between political tracts and social engagement, see Artan, "Topkapı Sarayı Arşivi'ndeki Bir Grup Mimari Çizimin Düşündürdükleri," 17–18. Ahmed Süreyya Paşa's deeply pan-Ottomanist tract was later published as a book under the title *Ḥayāt-ı ʿOs̱māniye Bir Naẓar* (A view on Ottoman existence) in 1908.

115. *Tārīḫ-i Siyāsī-i Devlet-i ʿAliye-i ʿOs̱māniye* (1325) and *Ḥāṭırāt-ı Ṣadr-ı esbaḳ Kāmil Paşa* (1329).

116. Çağalı-Güven, *II. Abdülhamid'in Sadrazamları*.

117. For Hayreddin's acclaimed treatise, see Tunisi, *Réformes nécessaires aux États musulmans*. See also Mardin, *Genesis of Young Ottoman Thought*, 387.

118. Forster, *Life of Charles Dickens*, 2:151–52.

119. Farmayan, "Amīn-al-Dawla, Mīrzā ʿAlī Khan."

120. Calmard, "Atābak-e Aʿẓam, Amīn-al-Solṭān."

121. Sheikholeslami, "Integration of Qajar Persia," 290.

122. The album of photographs by the Qajar governor ʿAlī Khān Vālī (1845–1902), consisting of 1,412 albumen photographs, is housed in the Special Collections of Harvard University's Fine Arts Library.

123. Scarce, "Arts of the Eighteenth to Twentieth Centuries," 906–7. Scarce identifies a Zand dynasty (1750–94) example of a *kulāh-ı farāngi* in the palace annex of Karim Khan Zand (d. 1779) in his capital, Shiraz. The designation seems also to have been used later for Qajar pavilions, and although it often seems to refer to a specific type (an "octagonal structure with a shallow dome and overhanging eaves"), it is at times assigned indiscriminately to garden pavilions in general; see P. Hobhouse, *Gardens of Persia*, 125 and 140.

124. Ayaşlı, *Dersaâdet*, 91.

125. İÜMK 93209.

126. BOA, İ .. DUİT. 136/12, İ .. DUİT. 136/13, İ .. DUİT. 136/14, and İ .. OM .. 2/1312.

127. Ersoy, *Architecture*, 60.

128. M. A. Yıldırım, *Dersaâdet Sanayi Mektebi*, 79–118.

129. This set of books, with lavish green Yıldız bindings, is displayed in the school's museum, Cumhuriyet Müzesi. Another Thézard publication is the *Petites villas de 3.000 à 10.000 fr.; la maison pour tous*.

130. For instance, the Canadian Center for Architecture also lacks a complete set of the original plates.

131. On the striking range of wooden residential structures, see Tuğlacı, *Tarih Boyunca İstanbul Adaları*; Ekdal, *Kapalı Hayat Kutusu*; and Balcı, *Eski İstanbul Evleri ve Boğaziçi Yalıları*.

132. For an example of the local mastery in carpentry, see Ali Tal'at, *Sanâyi'-i İnşâiye ve Mi'mâriyeden Doğramacılık*.

133. Bachmann, "Summer Residence."

134. *İḳdām*, March 12, 1896. For in-depth analysis of this firm's operations, see Acar, "19. Yüzyılın İkinci Yarısında İstanbul'da Ahşap Yapım Sistemlerinin Değişimi."

135. These three virtues reflected the selling points of the aforementioned Norwegian frame houses; Lowzow, "Norwegian Style of Building," 706.

136. "Dārü's-Ṣanāyī'-i ʿOs̱māniyye," *Servet-i Fünūn*, October 12, 1899.

137. Uşaklıgil, *Kırık Hayatlar*, 30.

138. Mehmed İzzet, *Rehber-i Umūr-ı Beytīye*, 1:231–46.

139. Necipoğlu, "Plans and Models," 230.

140. For an illustration of the empire-wide standardization of materials during the construction of the Hejaz Railway, see Raymond, *Notes pratiques et résumés*.

141. S. H. Eldem, *Türk Bahçeleri*, ii. See also Kalafatoğlu, "'Viktorya Tarzı' Sayfiye Konutları."

142. Ciner, "İstanbul Ahşap Konutlarında Cephe Bezemeleri."

143. Schweitzer and Davis, *America's Favorite Homes*.

144. Downing, *Architecture of Country Houses*. Downing found competition in enterprising builders like A. J. Bicknell and William Ranlett. See Ranlett, *Architect: A Series of Original Designs*, and Bicknell, *Specimen Book of One Hundred Architectural Designs*.

145. For an important critique of Vincent Scully's *Shingle Style & the Stick Style* (1955) via emphasis on

the influence of European pattern books on the so-called Stick Style, see Landau, "Richard Morris Hunt."

146. Proulx, *Barkskins*, 546.

Chapter 5

1. Although scholarship on photographic practices in the Ottoman territories of the nineteenth and twentieth centuries is still in its infancy, innovative work has begun to suggest frameworks that eschew the discursively stifling designation of "Ottoman photography" in their approach to the material. For a critique of national designations for photographic practices in the nineteenth-century Middle East, see Roberts, "Limits of Circumscription," and Micklewright, "Personal, Public, and Political (Re)Constructions."

2. For the first studies on the gift albums, see Allen, "Abdul Hamid II Collection," and Gavin, *Imperial Self-Portrait*. In recent years Istanbul's municipality has published thematic groupings from the more than thirty thousand photographs that make up the Yıldız Palace Library Collections; see Genç and Çolak, *Photographs of İstanbul from the Archives of Sultan Abdülhamid II*; Yılmaz, *Family Album of Sultan Abdülhamid II*; and city-specific annual publications such as Eren, *Bursa in Photographs of the Period of Sultan Abdulhamid II*, and Eren, *Manisa in Photographs from Sultan Abdulhamid II Period*. Aside from the serializing project of the municipality, see Dördüncü, *II. Abdülhamid Yıldız Albümleri: Mekke-Medine*, and Atasoy, *Yıldız Sarayı Fotoğraf Albümlerinden Yadigâr-ı İstanbul*.

3. For a recent reevaluation of Hamidian photographic representation as having aims beyond promoting the materiality of modernization, see Çelik and Eldem, *Camera Ottomana*.

4. For photography's use in state surveillance, see Tagg, *Burden of Representation*. For the Hamidian context of reconnaissance, see Gigord, *Images d'empire*, 26.

5. When "imperial surveillance" is the primary explanatory focus, a large group of albums that were gifts to the imperial library are neglected, as are a miscellaneous body of single photographs and scrapbook-like albums made up of different media like engravings, sketches, and photographs. Wendy Shaw's assessment of the early use of photography in the Ottoman Empire as a technology serving the "nineteenth-century positivist drive for information" is analogously reductive in cutting out the formal aspects and sociohistorical currents that make up a single image; Shaw, "Ottoman Photography of the Late Nineteenth Century."

6. The more intimate selection of photographs of the Ottoman court appeared in the households of the extracourtly elite; see Öztuncay, *Dynasty and Camera*. Qajar Shah Nasir al-Din made bolder, more intimate photographic choices for his palace; see Chi, *Eye of the Shah*, and Sarayian and Semsar, *Golestan Palace Photo Archive*.

7. The relationship between town and country or city and scenery was a central preoccupation of the renowned nineteenth-century Ottoman poet Abdülhak Hamid Tarhan (d. 1937). See Abdülḥak Ḥāmid, *Ṣaḥrāʾ, Bir Manẓūmedir*, and his *Dīvāneliklerim, Yāḥūd Belde*. For textual analyses of these poems, see Enginün, *Abdülhak Hâmid Tarhan*, and her *Yeni Türk Edebiyatı*.

8. Bourcier, "'In Excellent Order.'"

9. On Kağıthane, see S. H. Eldem, *Saʾdabad*; for cursory treatments of the pavilions of Ihlamur (Nüzhetiye) and others, see Pekin, Yücel, and Rifat, *Milli Saraylar*, and Ağın, *Beşiktaş İlçesi, Dolmabahçe Sarayı—Ihlamur Kasrı*. On the pavilions of Maslak, see Toğral, "Maslak Kasırları Yerleşim Düzeni ve Kullanımı," and his "Maslak Kasrı Askerî Prevantoryumu Yerleşim Düzeni ve Kullanımı." On the Ayazağa estate, see Eyice, "Ayazağa Kasrı," and A. Batur, "Ayazağa Kasırları." For in-depth typological (but ahistorical) analyses of the nineteenth-century Ottoman pavilions, see Turhan, "Osmanlı Çağında İstanbul'da Av Köşkleri-Kasırları," and Çelikbilek, "Beykoz Kasrı ve 19. Yüzyıl Kasırları."

10. For an analogous close reading of an album with an anonymous author, see Micklewright, "Picturing the 'Abode of Felicity.'"

11. On the composition of a nineteenth-century album, see Horton, "Historical Photo Albums and Their Structures."

12. Cervati, *Annuaire oriental* (1903), 830. Tarnavski is mentioned alongside two other Istanbul binders, George Christodoulos and Emmanuel Horn; Öztuncay, *Photographers of Constantinople*, 1:297.

13. Başaran, "Abdülmecid Efendi Kütüphanesi Koleksiyonu'ndan Cilt Sanatı Örnekleri."

14. Candemir, *Son Yıldız Düşerken*, 137–88.

15. BOA, BEO 996/74667.

16. Cervati, *Annuaire oriental* (1909), 373.

17. That a book about gardening was recycled to form the pages of the album supports my suggestion in the following pages that the anonymous photographer may have been Yıldız's last head gardener.

18. For travel albums as complete narrative constructs, see Armstrong, *Scenes in a Library*; in the context of the Middle East, see Micklewright, *Victorian Traveler in the Middle East*.

19. A refreshing exception to this recurrent reading can be found in Akcan, "Off the Frame."

20. Vámbéry, *Story of My Struggles*, 1:123.

21. Mehmed İzzet, *Rehber-i Umūr-ı Beytīye*, 3:384–91.

22. On the landscape—and especially the stereoscopic—photograph's expectations of the viewer, see Krauss, "Photography's Discursive Spaces."

23. Ahmed İhsan, "Ḥaydarpāşā'dan Ālpū Köyü'ne."

24. Öztuna, *Devletler ve Hânedanlar*, 2:297–329.

25. Tahsin Paşa, *Yıldız Hatıraları*, 7–8.

26. Artan, "Topkapı Sarayı Arşivi'ndeki Bir Grup Mimari Çiziminin Düşündürdükleri."

27. A. Osmanoğlu, *Babam Abdülhamid*, 27.

28. Âtıf Hüseyin Bey, *Sultan II. Abdülhamid'in Sürgün Günleri*, 151–52.

29. A. Osmanoğlu, *Babam Abdülhamid*, 27–28; Âtıf Hüseyin Bey, *Sultan II. Abdülhamid'in Sürgün Günleri*, 215.

30. The archives offer extremely limited information on Yıldız's porcelain factory; see Küçükerman, *Dünya Saraylarının Prestij Teknolojisi*, and Acar, "Yıldız Çini ve Porselen Fabrikası'nda Endüstriyel Araçların ve Mimari Yapının Değişimi." For examples of the factory's high-end products, see Küçükerman, *Milli Saraylar Koleksiyonu'nda Yıldız Porseleni.*

31. For instance, well-documented registers cover the supply of the palace's dairy farm, containing Swedish and Egyptian cows, adjacent to the Malta Kiosk; see BOA, Y. PRK. HH. 4–7; BOA, Y. HH. d. 16848.

32. Necipoğlu, "Suburban Landscape of Sixteenth-Century Istanbul," 34. The imperial imagery of a bountiful palace garden as a microcosmic stand-in for the productivity of the empire at large stretches far back in time; see Winter, *On Art in the Ancient Near East*, 2:199–226.

33. Âtıf Hüseyin Bey, *Sultan II. Abdülhamid'in Sürgün Günleri*, 108.

34. Layard, *Twixt Pera and Therapia*, 54, emphasis added.

35. İngiliz Said Paşa, *II. Abdülhamid'in İlk Mâbeyn Ferîki*, 130–31.

36. On both the local and the European proposals for the farm conversions, see BOA, Y. PRK. OMZ. 1/3 and Y. PRK. HH. 5/28.

37. Oscanyan, *Sultan and His People*, 182–83.

38. Artan, "Ihlamur Kasrı."

39. Hassan, *In the House of Muhammad Ali*, 60, 98, and 127; Hamouda, *Omar Toussoun*, 13.

40. Hassan, *In the House of Muhammad Ali*, 127.

41. Ulunay, *Bu Gözler Neler Gördü?*, 105–7.

42. Ibid., 107.

43. A. Osmanoğlu, *Babam Abdülhamid*, 56.

44. Ibid.

45. Önel, "Fer'iye Sarayları." That these three structures were designated for the viceroys of Egypt can be gleaned from the refurbishment expenses of the Ottoman treasury. See BOA, TS. MA. d. 333 (for Muhammad Ali), 295 (for Abbas Paşa and his mother), 2756 (for kitchen expenses during Abbas Paşa's first visit as the newly appointed governor of Egypt, in 1849). For the latter, see also Ahmed Lütfî Efendi, *Vak'anüvîs*, 8:1268.

46. The gift albums prepared for the shah's visit are in İÜMK (90508, 90509, 90510, and 90511). The *Levant Herald and Eastern Express* reports that after having received a photograph album from Abdülhamid II documenting his visit, Muzaffar al-Din Shah was "so pleased with the gift that he asked for a dozen more albums, and the photographer Sami Bey [later Aközer] is now engaged in preparing the photographs." "The Shah," *Levant Herald and Eastern Express*, October 3, 1900, 1. This must be the reason for the considerable repetition in each of the albums housed in Istanbul University Library. Sami had earlier been appointed to accompany the German emperor on his 1898 visit to the Holy Land.

47. Karateke, *Padişahım Çok Yaşa!*, 206–7.

48. For biographical compilations of "Ottoman" photographers, see Özendes, *Photography in the Ottoman Empire*; Özendes, *Photographer Ali Sami*; Öztuncay, "Ernest De Caranza"; Öztuncay, *Robertson*; Özendes, *Abdullah Frères*; Özendes, *From Sébah & Joaillier to Foto Sabah*; Öztuncay, *Vassilaki Kargopoulo*; and Öztuncay, *Photographers of Constantinople.*

49. The surge of monographic studies centered on individual photographers and studios was initiated by Allen, "Sixty-Nine Istanbul Photographers."

50. For the allure of portrait photography in the Ottoman context, see Öztuncay, *Hatıra-ı Uhuvvet.*

51. Tarkulyan leaves behind a candid description of his time as a photographer of the Ottoman elite in Kandemir, "Febüs Anlatıyor."

52. BOA, Y. PRK. MYD. 1/33, and BOA, İ .. DH .. 931/73778.

53. Kevork Abdullah's published biography is first mentioned in Öztuncay, *Photographers of Constantinople*, 1:232. The full citation of this understudied book is Esayi Tayets'i, *Hushagir kenats' ew gortsunēut'ean nakhkin kayserakan lusankarich' Gēorg Aptullahi* (Venice: S. Ghazar, 1929).

54. *Indicateur ottoman illustré* (1880).

55. The largest of Kargopoulo's court-commissioned albums is İÜMK 90751, with ninety-two stills.

56. Öztuncay, *Photographers of Constantinople*, 1:248.

57. Deringil, *Well-Protected Domains*, 31–32.

58. BOA, Y. EE. d. 1030 to Y. EE. d. 1105.

59. Photographic representations of Çırağan are extremely rare in the Yıldız albums: one photograph (no. 28) in İÜMK 90474 and five in album 90853.

60. BOA, Y. EE. d. 1030 to Y. EE. d. 1105.

61. İngiliz Said Paşa, *II. Abdülhamid'in İlk Mâbeyn Ferîki*, 142.

62. On this failed imperial project, see Boyer, "*La Mission Héliographique*." For monograph studies of the two photographers central to the French undertaking, see Daniel, *Photographs of Édouard Baldus*, and Aubenas and Baldwin, *Gustave Le Gray.*

63. Müller, *Letters from Constantinople*, 94–95.

64. Akcan, "Off the Frame," 106.

65. Ibid., 108.

66. For a military artist's cartographic memories, see Arseven, *Sanat ve Siyaset Hatıralarım*, 113.

67. BOA, İ.DH 691/48286.

68. BOA, BEO. 3705/277817.

69. For Şeker Ahmed Paşa, see Şerifoğlu and Baytar, *Şeker Ahmed Paşa*. For Zonaro's Istanbul years, see Öndeş and Makzume, *Fausto Zonaro*, and Şerifoğlu, *Ottoman Court Painter Fausto Zonaro*.

70. Ottoman officials employed under the office of court ceremonies (*teşrīfāt neẓāreti*) repeatedly relayed to the palace's administrative body (*bāşkitābet dāʾiresi*) specific requests (*irāde*) made by foreign heads of state to see the library, museum, and porcelain factory. For Şeker Ahmed Paşa's role in the office of court ceremonies, see Kaya, "Başyaver Şeker Ahmed Paşa."

71. Artan, "Topkapı Sarayı Arşivi'ndeki Bir Grup Mimari Çizimin Düşündürdükleri." On Vallaury, see Akpolat, "Architect Alexandre Vallaury," and Kula Say, "Post-1908 Project of Vallaury."

72. Another episode of recycling and adapting at will that awaits detailed study is the conversion of D'Aronco's unbuilt jubilant little building project for the sultan's grand master of ceremonies to house the palace's rifle factory, with a faux-grotto water fountain and projecting side doors with triangular pediments; for D'Aronco's sketch, see Barillari and Godoli, *Istanbul 1900*, 75.

73. Cervati, *Annuaire oriental* (1900), 24.

74. Barillari and Godoli, *Istanbul 1900*, 46–64.

75. Tanpınar, *Beş Şehir*, 165.

76. Enginün, *Abdülhak Hâmid'in Hatıraları*, 311–12, emphasis added.

77. Recāʾizāde Maḥmūd Ekrem, ʿAraba Sevdāsı, Muṣavver Millī Ḥikāye, 3–4.

78. Ibid., 5.

79. Uşaklıgil, *Saray ve Ötesi*, 193.

80. For instance, Abdurrahman Şeref, *Son Vakʿanüvis Abdurrahman Şeref Efendi Tarihi*.

81. Tahsin Paşa, *Yıldız Hatıraları*, 356.

82. Cox, *Diversions of a Diplomat in Turkey*, 39.

83. For the most recent work on earlier text-based versions of such compilations, see Aynur et al., *Mecmûa*.

Coda

1. "He has shown perfect knowledge of the little tricks of diplomacy. He knows how to neutralize the claims of the Powers by sowing discord among them." Dorys, *Private Life*, 75.

2. Özgül, *Ali Ekrem Bolayır'ın Hâtıraları*, 479.

3. Kuban, *Ottoman Architecture*, 640.

4. S. Batur, "Yıldız Camii," 514; S. Can, "Yıldız Camii."

5. Pertevniyal's mosque in Aksaray showcases the earliest experiments with high-drummed and monumental crowned portals (embedded in the mosque's façades); see Ersoy, "Aykırı Binanın Saklı Kalfası," 112.

6. S. Can, "Yıldız Hamidiye Camii'nin İnşası ve Mimarına İlişkin Yeni Bilgiler."

7. A. Batur, "Yıldız Sarayı Tiyatrosu"; Sevengil, *Saray Tiyatrosu*, 117–18.

8. Rossi, *Quarant'anni di vita artistica*, 3:227.

9. Mestyan, *Arab Patriotism*, 94. Mestyan cites the French phrase describing this type of theater from Louis and George Leblanc's *Traité d'aménagement des salles de spectacles* (1950).

10. Rossi, *Quarant'anni di vita artistica*, 3:227–28.

11. And, *Tanzimat ve İstibdat Döneminde Türk Tiyatrosu*, 249.

12. Toker, "Yıldız'da Operalar Nasıl Hazırlanırdı?," 4.

13. Sevengil, *Saray Tiyatrosu*, 122.

14. Âtıf Hüseyin Bey, *Sultan II. Abdülhamid'in Sürgün Günleri*, 298 and 307.

15. Tahsin Paşa, *Yıldız Hatıraları*, 17–20.

16. Sevengil, *Saray Tiyatrosu*, 150.

17. For a biography of the Ioannidis family of architects and *kalfa*s, see Şenyurt, *İstanbul Rum Cemaatinin Osmanlı Mimarisindeki Temsiliyeti*, 146–55.

18. On the different architects and builders involved in the building of the Hamidiye Mosque and the actual designer of the structure, see Ersoy, "Aykırı Binanın Saklı Kalfası."

19. Zarifi, *Hatıralarım*, 341. Indeed, Yanko Ioannidis seems to have been an expert in dome building. He also designed the celebrated domed main hall of the Çağlayan (Cascade) Pavilion in Kağıthane. Sevengil, *Saray Tiyatrosu*, 118, asserts that Yanko Ioannidis was the theater's architect. The *Annuaire oriental* confirms Yanko's title as palace architect. He also directed the work of Raimondo D'Aronco, who is listed in the same trade journal as an architect working under the orders of Ioannidis. Having discovered references to a project to renovate the theater at Yıldız in the D'Aronco archives in Udine, Afife Batur attributes the theater to D'Aronco; A. Batur, "Yıldız Sarayı," 523.

20. Ersoy, "Aykırı Binanın Saklı Kalfası," 113.

21. Schick, "Revival of *Kūfī* Script."

22. Ibid., 133–35.

23. The translation here is based on Abdullah Yusuf Ali's English translation of the Koran: https://www.quranyusufali.com/53.

24. Two complementary interpretations (*tafsīr*) of this surah inform my take on its selection by Abdülhamid II: the fifteenth-century Sunni exegesis *al-Jalalayn* and the seventh-century *Tanwir al-Miqbas*, by Ibn ʿAbbas, a cousin of the Prophet Muhammad's and one of the earliest Koranic scholars.

25. The endowments of the Orhaniye Mosque (the centerpiece of the barracks on the north of Yıldız) and the Hamidiye Mosque were joined with the endowment of the Ertuğrul Mosque, which also contained the convent assigned to Shaykh Zafir. Two copies of the mosque's endowment are kept in the archives of the Directorate General of Foundations (VGMA) in Ankara under K. 181 and K. 183. See A. Batur, "Yıldız Serencebey'de Şeyh Zafir Türbe, Kitaplık ve Çeşmesi," 108. See also Çınar, "Sultan II. Abdülhamid'in Vakıf, Hayrat ve Akaratı," 284.

26. Şenyurt, "Selanik Hamidiye Cami."

27. Colonas, "Vitaliano Poselli." See also Colonas, "Italian Architects in Thessaloniki."

28. Şenyurt, "Selanik Hamidiye Cami," 191–92. See also Bush, "Architecture of Jewish Identity."

29. Pala, "Mühr-i Süleyman."

30. Here I have in mind German architect Konrad Schick's involvement as city planner in Jerusalem under Ottoman rule. In this context Schick built for Abdülhamid II a multilayered model of the Temple Mount that contains a hypothetical reconstruction of Solomon's Temple. See Goldhill, *Temple of Jerusalem*, 132. For Abdülhamid II's patronage of the Temple Mount, see St. Laurent and Riedlmayer, "Restorations of Jerusalem," 81–82.

31. H. Y. Şehsuvaroğlu, "Yıldız Sarayındaki Müze," 14 and 32.

32. Berenson's concept of the "operatic state" is cited in Mestyan, *Arab Patriotism*, 89.

33. Ibid., 114.

Period Journals and Newspapers
Allgemeine Theaterzeitung, Vienna
Allgemeine Zeitung München
Annuaire oriental, Istanbul
Aschaffenburger Zeitung, Aschaffenburg
Beiträge zur Allgemeinen Zeitung
The Builder, London
The Building News, London
The Contemporary Review, London
Frankfurter Allgemeine Zeitung, Frankfurt
Frauendorfer Blätter, Frauendorf
The Gardener's Chronicle, London
Gartenflora, Erlangen
Die Gartenkunst, Stuttgart
Die Gartenwelt, Berlin
Le génie civil, Istanbul
İḳdām, Istanbul
L'Illustration, Paris
Indicateur oriental, Istanbul
Indicateur ottoman illustré, Istanbul
Journal de la Société impériale et centrale d'horticulture, Paris
Journal of the Society of Arts, London
The Levant Herald and Eastern Express, Istanbul
The Levant Times, Istanbul
Le Monde illustré, Paris
The Monthly Magazine; or, British Register, London
Passavia, Zeitung für Niederbayern, Passau
Revue horticole, Paris
Ṣervet-i Fünūn, Istanbul
La Turquie, Istanbul
Die Woche, Berlin

Unpublished Theses and Dissertations
Acar, Damla. "19. Yüzyılın İkinci Yarısında İstanbul'da Ahşap Yapım Sistemlerinin Değişimi: Gelenekselin Rasyonelleştirilmesi." PhD diss., İstanbul Teknik Üniversitesi, 2015.
Akpolat, Mustafa Servet. "The French Origin Levantine Architect Alexandre Vallaury." MA thesis, Hacettepe Üniversitesi, 1991.
Arapoğlu, Güçlü. "Yıldız Sarayı Şehzade Köşkleri ve Şehzade Burhaneddin Efendi Köşkü Restitüsyonu." MArch thesis, Yıldız Teknik Üniversitesi, 2005.
Artan, Tülay. "Architecture as a Theatre of Life: Profile of the Eighteenth Century Bosphorus." PhD diss., Massachusetts Institute of Technology, 1988.

Bilgin, Bülent. "Türk Saray Mimarisinin Gelişmesi Çerçevesinde Yıldız Sarayı." PhD diss., İstanbul Üniversitesi, 1993.
Binan, Can. "Yıldız Sarayı Yanmış Hususi Daire Kuzey Avlusu Mekansal Oluşumu Sorunlar ve Değerlendirilmesi Üzerine Bir Araştırma." MArch thesis, Yıldız Teknik Üniversitesi, 1984.
Çelikbilek, Diğdem. "Beykoz Kasrı ve 19. Yüzyıl Kasırları Üzerine Bir İnceleme." MArch thesis, Yıldız Teknik Üniversitesi, 1988.
Çetin, Kamile. "Raşid (?–1310 [1892]) ve Divanı İnceleme-Tenkidli Metin." PhD diss., Sivas Devlet Üniversitesi Sosyal Bilimler Enstitüsü, 2006.
Ciner, Semra. "Son Osmanlı Dönemi İstanbul Ahşap Konutlarında Cephe Bezemeleri." MArch thesis, İstanbul Üniversitesi Mimarlık Fakültesi, 1982.
Görgülü, Hakime Esra. "Yıldız Teknik Üniversitesi (Yıldız Sarayı) Çukur Saray Yapısı Koruma ve Restorasyonu Üzerine Bir Araştırma." MArch thesis, Yıldız Teknik Üniversitesi, 2004.
Kilerci, Başak. "Ottoman-Qajar Relations Through Photography: Mozaffar al-Din Shah's İstanbul Visit." MA thesis, Boğaziçi University, 2013.
Kılıçoğlu, Selda. "Yıldız Sarayı Büyük Mabeyn Köşkü Oda-ı Ali Restorasyonu." MArch thesis, Yıldız Teknik Üniversitesi, 1984.
Köse, Aslı Özge. "Yıldız Sarayı Hünkar Dairesi: Valide Sultan Kasrı." MA thesis, Yıldız Teknik Üniversitesi, 2002.
Kurtay, Nevin. "Yıldız Sarayı Üzerine Yapılan Çalışmaların Değerlendirilmesi." PhD diss., İstanbul Teknik Üniversitesi, 1994.
Şen, Münevver Dağgülü. "Yıldız Sarayı Selamlık Bahçe Düzeni." MA Thesis, Yıldız Teknik Üniversitesi, 1984.
Turhan, Hasan. "Osmanlı Çağında İstanbul'da Av Köşkleri-Kasırları." MArch thesis, Yıldız Teknik Üniversitesi, 1981.
Uğurlu, Ayşe Hilal. "Selim III's Istanbul: Building Activities in the Light of Political and Military Transformations." PhD diss., İstanbul Teknik Üniversitesi, 2012.

Published Works
A.W. "Ein unterfränkischer Landsmann als Gartendirektor des Sultans." *Erheiterungen:*

Belletristisches Beiblatt zur Aschaffenburger Zeitung, December 17, 1867.

Abdulkadiroğlu, Abdulkerim, İ. Hakkı Aksoyak, and Necip Fazıl Duru. *Kastamonu Jurnal Defteri (1252–1253/1836–1837): Metin ve Tıpkıbasım.* Ankara: T.C. Başbakanlık Devlet Arşivleri Genel Müdürlüğü, 1998.

Abdurrahman Şeref. *Son Vak'anüvis Abdurrahman Şeref Efendi Tarihi: II. Meşrutiyet Olayları, 1908–1909.* Ankara: Türk Tarih Kurumu Basımevi, 1996.

ʿAbdüʾl-ʿazīz Bey. *Ādāt ü Merāsim-i Ḳadīme, Ṭaʿbirāt ü Muʿāmelāt-ı Ḳavmīye-i ʿOs̠mānīye.* Istanbul: Tarih Vakfı Yurt Yayınları, 1995.

Abdülḥaḳ Ḥāmid. *Dīvāneliklerim, Yāḫūd Belde.* Istanbul: Dīḳrān Ḳarabetyān Maṭbaʿası, 1303 [1886].

———. *Ṣaḥrāʿ, Bir Manẓūmedir.* Istanbul: Mihrān, 1296 [1879].

Abdülhamid II. *II. Abdülhamid'in Hatıra Defteri.* Ankara: Kardeş Matbaası, n.d.

Acar, Damla. "Yıldız Çini ve Porselen Fabrikası'nda Endüstriyel Araçların ve Mimari Yapının Değişimi." *Milli Saraylar Dergisi* 9 (2012): 13–36.

Acar, Damla, and Deniz Mazlum. "Timber-Framed Houses Built for the Court Members After the 1894 Earthquake in Istanbul: Rationalization of Construction Techniques." *International Journal of Architectural Heritage* 10, no. 5 (2016): 604–19.

Acar, M. Şinasi. *Osmanlı'da Sportif Atıcılık: Nişan Taşları.* Istanbul: YEM Yayın, 2013.

Açba, Harun. *Kadınefendiler, 1839–1924.* Istanbul: Profil, 2007.

Açba, Leyla. *Bir Çerkes Prensesinin Harem Hatıraları.* Istanbul: L & M Yayınları, 2004.

Adıvar, Halide Edib. *Memoirs of Halidé Edib.* New York: Arno Press, 1972.

Ağın, Ahmed. *Beşiktaş İlçesi, Dolmabahçe Sarayı—Ihlamur Kasrı.* Vol. 2 of *Saraylarımız.* Istanbul: Tan Gazetesi ve Matbaası, 1965.

Ahmed Cevdet Paşa. *Maʿrûzât.* Istanbul: Çağrı Yayınları, 1980.

———. *Tezâkir.* 2nd ed. Ankara: Türk Tarih Kurumu Basımevi, 1986.

Ahmed Efendi, Sırkâtibi. *III. Selim'in Sırkâtibi Ahmed Efendi Tarafından Tutulan Rûznâme.* Ankara: Türk Tarih Kurumu Basımevi, 1993.

Ahmed İhsan. "Ḥaydarpāşāʾdan Ālpū Köyü'ne ʿOs̠mānlı Anādolu Demiryol Ḥaṭṭinda Bir Seyāḥat." *Servet-i Fünūn*, no. 75 (August 18, 1892): 354–55.

———. "Yakında Açılacak Olan Yıldız İstanbul Belediye Gazinosu ve Yıldız Hatıraları." *Servet-i Fünūn*, September 23, 1926.

———. *Yildiz, the Municipal Casino of Constantinople: The Historical Past of the Palace and Park of Yildiz.* 2nd ed. Constantinople: Ahmed İhsan, 1926.

Ahmed Lütfî Efendi. *Vak'anüvîs Ahmed Lûtfî Efendi Tarihi.* Vols. 1–8. Istanbul: Türkiye Ekonomik ve Toplumsal Tarih Vakfı, Yapı Kredi Yayınları, 1999.

———. *Vak'a-nüvis Ahmed Lûtfî Efendi Tarihi.* Vols. 9–15. Edited by M. Münir Aktepe. Ankara: Türk Tarih Kurumu Basımevi, 1988.

Ahmed Sâdık Zîver Paşa. *Dîvân ve Münşe'ât.* Sivas: Cumhuriyet Üniversitesi, 2009.

Aḥmed Refīḳ. *Lāmārtīn: Türkiyeye muhāceret ḳarārı, İzmirdeki çiftliği, 1849–1853.* Istanbul: Orḫāniye Maṭbaʿası, 1925.

———. *Tarihte Kadın Simaları.* Istanbul: Muallim Ahmet Halit Kitaphanesi, 1931.

Ahmed Süreyya Paşa. *Ḥayāt-ı ʿOs̠mānīye Bir Naẓar.* Istanbul: Kāmil Maṭbaʿāsı, 1324 [1908].

Ahmet Mithat [Ahmed Midhat] Efendi. *Avrupa'da Bir Cevelan.* Istanbul: Dergâh Yayınları, 2015.

Akcan, Esra. "Off the Frame: The Panoramic City Albums of Istanbul." In Behdad and Gartlan, *Photography's Orientalism*, 93–114.

Akın, Günkut. "Tanzimat ve Bir Aydınlanma Simgesi." In *Osman Hamdi Bey ve Dönemi: Sempozyumu, 17–18 Aralık 1992*, edited by Zeynep Rona, 123–31. Istanbul: Tarih Vakfı Yurt Yayınları, 1993.

Aksüt, Ali Kemalî. *Sultan Azizin Mısır ve Avrupa Seyahati.* Istanbul: A. Sait Oğlu Kitapevi, 1944.

Akyıldız, Ali. "Mâbeyn-i Hümâyun." In *DİA*, 27:283–86.

Ali Haydar Mithat. *Hâtıralarım, 1872–1946.* Istanbul: M. Akçit Yayını, 1946.

Ali Said. *Saray Hâtıraları: Sultan Abdülhamid'in Hayatı.* Istanbul: Nehir Yayınları, 1994.

Ali Tal'at. *Sanâyi'-i İnşâiye ve Mi'mâriyeden Doğramacılık, Marangoz ve Silicilik İ'malatına Âid Mebâhis.* Edited by Süleyman Faruk Göncüoğlu and Davut Türksever. Istanbul: Kiptaş, 2008.

Allen, William. "The Abdul Hamid II Collection." *History of Photography* 8, no. 2 (1984): 119–45.

———. "Sixty-Nine Istanbul Photographers, 1887–1914." In *Shadow and Substance: Essays on the History of Photography in Honor of Heinz K. Henisch*, edited by Kathleen Collins, 127–36. Bloomfield Hills, MI: Amorphous Institute Press, 1990.

Alpgüvenç, Can. *Hayırda Yarışan Hanım Sultanlar: Araştırma.* Istanbul: Kaynak Kitaplar, 2010.

And, Metin. *Tanzimat ve İstibdat Döneminde Türk Tiyatrosu, 1839–1908.* Ankara: Mars Basımevi, 1972.

André, Édouard François. *L'art des jardins: Traité général de la composition des parcs et jardins.* Paris: G. Masson, 1879.

Aracı, Emre. *Donizetti Paşa: Osmanlı Sarayının İtalyan Maestrosu.* Istanbul: Yapı Kredi Yayınları, 2006.

———. "'Each Villa on the Bosphorus Looks a Screen New Painted, or a Pretty Opera Scene': Mahmud II (r. 1808–1839) Setting the Ottoman Stage for Italian Opera and Viennese Music." In *Ottoman Empire and European Theatre*, vol. 2, *The Time of Joseph Haydn: From Sultan Mahmud I to Mahmud II (r. 1730–1839)*, edited by Michael Hüttler and Hans Ernst Weidinger, 621–30. Vienna: Hollitzer, 2014.

Arıkan, Aykut, et al., eds. *Yıldız Sarayı Kütüphanesi'nden Seçilmiş Nadir Basma Kitaplar Sergisi Kataloğu*. Istanbul: İstanbul Üniversitesi Kütüphane ve Dokümantasyon Daire Başkanlığı, 1995.

Armstrong, Carol M. *Scenes in a Library: Reading the Photograph in the Book, 1843–1875*. Cambridge: MIT Press, 1998.

Arseven, Celâl Esad. *Sanat ve Siyaset Hatıralarım*. Istanbul: İletişim Yayınları, 1993.

Artan, Tülay. "Boğaziçi'nin Çehresini Değiştiren Soylu Kadınlar ve Sultanefendi Sarayları." *İstanbul Dergisi* 3 (October 1992): 106–18.

———. "A Composite Universe: Arts and Society in Istanbul at the End of the Eighteenth Century." In *Ottoman Empire and European Theatre*, vol. 1, *The Age of Mozart and Selim III (1756–1808)*, edited by Michael Hüttler and Hans Ernst Weidinger, 751–94. Vienna: Hollitzer, 2013.

———. "Eighteenth-Century Ottoman Princesses as Collectors: Chinese and European Porcelains in the Topkapı Palace Museum." *Ars Orientalis* 39 (2010): 113–47.

———. "Eyüp'ün Bir Diğer Çehresi: Sayfiye ve Sahilsaraylar." In *Eyüp: Dün/Bugün; Sempozyum, 11–12 Aralık 1993*, edited by Tülay Artan, 106–14. Istanbul: Tarih Vakfı Yurt Yayınları, 1994.

———. "From Charismatic Leadership to Collective Rule: Gender Problems of Legalism and Political Legitimation in the Ottoman Empire." In *Histoire économique et sociale de l'Empire ottoman et de la Turquie (1326–1960): Actes du sixième congrès international tenu à Aix-en-Provence du 1er au 4 juillet 1992*, edited by Daniel Panzac, 569–80. Paris: Peeters, 1995.

———. "From Charismatic Leadership to Collective Rule: Introducing Materials on Wealth and Power of Ottoman Princesses in the Eighteenth Century." *Toplum ve Ekonomi* 4 (1993): 53–94.

———. "Ihlamur Kasrı." In *DBİA*, 4:111–12.

———. "Istanbul in the 18th Century: Days of Reconciliation and Consolidation." In *From Byzantion to Istanbul: 8000 Years of a Capital*, edited by Koray Şevki Durak, 300–312. Istanbul: Sakıp Sabancı Museum, 2010.

———. "Topkapı Sarayı Arşivi'ndeki Bir Grup Mimari Çizimin Düşündürdükleri." In *Topkapı Sarayı Müzesi Yıllık 5*, 7–52. Istanbul: Topkapı Sarayı Müdürlüğü ve Topkapı Sarayı Müzesini Sevenler Derneği, 1992.

Âşık Çelebi. *Meşâ'irü'ş-şu'arâ: İnceleme, Metin*. 3 vols. Edited by Filiz Kılıç. Istanbul: İstanbul Araştırmaları Enstitüsü, 2010.

Atasoy, Nurhan. *A Garden for the Sultan: Gardens and Flowers in the Ottoman Culture*. Istanbul: Aygaz, 2002.

———. *Yıldız Sarayı Fotoğraf Albümlerinden Yadigâr-ı İstanbul*. Istanbul: Akkök Yayınları, 2007.

Âtıf Hüseyin Bey. *Sultan II. Abdülhamid'in Sürgün Günleri, 1909–1918: Hususi Doktoru Âtıf Hüseyin Bey'in Hatıratı*. Edited by M. Metin Hülagü. Istanbul: Pan Yayıncılık, 2007.

Aubenas, Sylvie, and Gordon Baldwin, eds. *Gustave Le Gray, 1820–1884*. Los Angeles: J. Paul Getty Museum, 2002.

Avcıoğlu, Nebahat. Turquerie *and the Politics of Representation, 1728–1876*. Farnham: Ashgate, 2010.

Ayaşlı, Münevver. *Dersaâdet*. 2nd ed. Istanbul: Bedir Yayınevi, 1993.

Aynur, Hatice, Müjgan Çakır, Hanife Koncu, Selim Sırrı Kuru, and Ali Emre Özyıldırım, eds. *Mecmûa: Osmanlı Edebiyatının Kırkambarı*. Istanbul: Turkuaz, 2011.

Ayverdi, Sâmiha. *İbrahim Efendi Konağı*. Istanbul: Baha Matbaası, 1964.

Babaie, Sussan. *Isfahan and Its Palaces: Statecraft, Shiʿism and the Architecture of Conviviality in Early Modern Iran*. Edinburgh: Edinburgh University Press, 2008.

Bachmann, Martin. "Epochenwandel am Bosporus: Die bauliche Entwicklung auf dem Gelände der deutschen Sommerresidenz in Tarabya." In *Deutsche Präsenz am Bosporus: 130 Jahre Kaiserliches Botschaftspalais, 120 Jahre historische Sommerresidenz des deutschen Botschafters in Tarabya*, edited by Matthias von Kummer, 117–36. Istanbul: Generalkonsulat der Bundesrepublik Deutschland, 2009.

———. "The Summer Residence of the German Embassy." In Bachmann and Tanman, *Wooden Istanbul*, 309–17.

Bachmann, Martin, and M. Baha Tanman, eds. *Wooden Istanbul: Examples from Housing Architecture*. Istanbul: Suna ve İnan Kıraç Vakfı İstanbul Araştırmaları Enstitüsü, 2008.

Balcı, Perihan. *Eski İstanbul Evleri ve Boğaziçi Yalıları*. Istanbul: Apa Ofset, 1980.

Bardakçı, Murat. "Yıldız Sarayı 'Cumhurbaşkanlığı İstanbul Külliyesi' Oluyor." *Habertürk Gazetesi*, November 8, 2015.

Barillari, Diana, and Ezio Godoli. *Istanbul 1900: Art Nouveau Architecture and Interiors*. New York: Rizzoli, 1996.

Başaran, Naciye Uçar. "Abdülmecid Efendi Kütüphanesi Koleksiyonu'ndan Cilt Sanatı Örnekleri." *Milli Saraylar Dergisi* 7 (2011): 111–20.

Bates, Ülkü. "Women as Patrons of Architecture in Turkey." In *Women in the Muslim World*, edited by Lois Beck and Nikki R. Keddie, 245–60. Cambridge: Harvard University Press, 1978.

Batur, Afife. "Art Nouveau." In *DBİA*, 1:327–33.

———. "Ayazağa Kasırları." In *DBİA*, 1:470–71.

———. "D'Aronco, Raimondo Tommaso." In *DBİA*, 2:550–51.

———. "İstanbul Art Nouveau'su." In *TCTA*, 4:1086–88.

———. "Şale Köşkü." In *DBİA*, 7:132–35.

———. "Yıldız Sarayı." In *DBİA*, 7:520–27.

———. "Yıldız Sarayı." In *TCTA*, 4:1048–154.

———. "Yıldız Sarayı Tiyatrosu." In *DBİA*, 7:527.

———. "Yıldız Serencebey'de Şeyh Zafir Türbe, Kitaplık ve Çeşmesi." In *Anadolu Sanatı Araştırmaları*, 1:103–36. Istanbul: İstanbul Teknik Üniversitesi Mimarlık Fakültesi, 1968.

Batur, Selçuk. "Yıldız Camii." In *DBİA*, 7:514–16.

Baytar, İlona. *19. Yüzyıl Sarayında Bir Valide Sultan: Bezm-i Âlem*. Istanbul: Milli Saraylar İdaresi Başkanlığı, 2019.

Behdad, Ali, and Luke Gartlan, eds. *Photography's Orientalism: New Essays on Colonial Representation*. Los Angeles: Getty Research Institute, 2013.

Bein, Amit. "The Istanbul Earthquake of 1894 and Science in the Late Ottoman Empire." *Middle Eastern Studies* 44, no. 6 (2008): 909–24.

Bernard, Paul B. *Rush to the Alps: The Evolution of Vacationing in Switzerland*. Boulder, CO: East European Quarterly, 1978.

Bertsch, Daniel. *Anton Prokesch von Osten (1795–1876), ein Diplomat Österreichs in Athen und an der Hohen Pforte: Beiträge zur Wahrnehmung des Orients im Europa des 19. Jahrhunderts*. Munich: Oldenbourg, 2005.

Beyhan, Mehmet Ali. *Saray Günlüğü: 25 Aralık 1802–24 Ocak 1809*. Istanbul: Doğu Kütüphanesi, 2007.

Bicknell, A. J. *Specimen Book of One Hundred Architectural Designs: Showing Plans, Elevations, and Views*. New York: A. J. Bicknell, 1878.

Bier, Lionel. "The Sasanian Palaces and Their Influence in Early Islam." In "Pre-Modern Islamic Palaces," special issue, *Ars Orientalis* 23 (1993): 57–66.

Bilgin, Bülent. "Yıldız Sarayı." In *DİA*, 43:541–44.

Blackbourn, David. "Fashionable Spa Towns in Nineteenth-Century Europe." In *Water, Leisure, and Culture: European Historical Perspectives*, edited by Susan C. Anderson and Bruce H. Tabb, 9–21. New York: Berg, 2002.

Borgese, Giuseppe Antonio. *Autunno di Costantinopoli*. Milan: Treves, 1929.

Bossoli, Carlo. *The War in Italy*. London: Day & Son, 1859.

Bouquet, Olivier. *Les pachas du sultan: Essai sur les agents supérieurs de l'État ottoman (1839–1909)*. Leuven: Peeters, 2007.

Bourcier, Paul G. "'In Excellent Order': The Gentleman Farmer Views His Fences, 1790–1860." *Agricultural History* 58, no. 4 (1984): 546–64.

Boyer, M. Christine. "*La Mission Héliographique*: Architectural Photography, Collective Memory, and the Patrimony of France, 1851." In *Picturing Place: Photography and the Geographical Imagination*, edited by Joan M. Schwartz and James R. Ryan, 21–54. New York: I. B. Tauris, 2003.

Bozdağ, İsmet, ed. *İkinci Abdülhamid'in Hatıra Defteri*. Istanbul: Selek Yayınevi, 1960.

Brown, Julia Prewitt. *The Bourgeois Interior*. Charlottesville: University of Virginia Press, 2008.

Bulmuş, Birsen. *Plague, Quarantines, and Geopolitics in the Ottoman Empire*. Edinburgh University Press, 2012.

Bush, Olga. "The Architecture of Jewish Identity: The Neo-Islamic Central Synagogue of New York." *Journal of the Society of Architectural Historians* 63, no. 2 (June 2004): 180–201.

Byrne, Katherine. *Tuberculosis and the Victorian Literary Imagination*. New York: Cambridge University Press, 2011.

Byzantios, Skarlatos D. *Hē Kōnstantinoupolis ē perigraphē topographikē, archaiologikē kai historikē tēs periōnymou tautēs megalopoleōs*. Vol. 2. Athens: Andreos Koromila, 1862.

C. K. S. "Vom Goldenen Horn." *Die Gartenwelt* 11 (1907): 604–5.

Câbî [Cabi] Ömer Efendi. *Câbî Târihi: Târîh-i Sultân Selîm-i Sâlis ve Mahmûd-i Sânî: Tahlîl ve Tenkidli Metin*. Edited by Mehmet Ali Beyhan. 2 vols. Ankara: Türk Tarih Kurumu Basımevi, 2003.

Çağalı-Güven, Gül, ed. *II. Abdülhamid'in Sadrazamları, Kamil Paşa ve Said Paşa'nın Anıları, Polemikleri*. 2nd ed. Istanbul: Arba, 1991.

Çakılcı, Diren. "Sultan II. Abdülhamid'in Hayvan Merakı: Yıldız Sarayı'nda Kuşluk-ı Hümâyûn Teşkilatı." *Tarih Dergisi* 68 (2018): 57–100.

Calmard, J. "Atābak-e A'zam, Amīn-al-Solṭān." In *Encyclopædia Iranica*, vol. 2, fasc. 8, 878–890. https://www.iranicaonline.org/articles/atabak-e-azam.

Cambon, Paul. *Correspondance, 1870–1924*. Vol. 1. Paris: Grasset, 1940.

Can, Cengiz. "Tanzimat and Architecture." In *7 Centuries of Ottoman Architecture: "A Supra-national Heritage,"* edited by Nur Akın, Afife Batur, and Selçuk Batur, 135–43. Istanbul: YEM Yayın, 1999.

Can, Selman. *Belgelerle Çırağan Sarayı*. Ankara: T. C. Kültür Bakanlığı, 1999.

———. "Yıldız Camii." In *DİA*, 43:540–41.

———. "Yıldız Hamidiye Camii'nin İnşası ve Mimarına İlişkin Yeni Bilgiler." In *Nurhan Atasoy'a Armağan*, edited by M. Baha Tanman, 59–66. Istanbul: Lale Yayıncılık, 2014.

Candemir, Murat. *Son Yıldız Düşerken*. Istanbul: Çamlıca, 2011.

———. *Yıldız'da Kaos ve Tasfiye*. Istanbul: İlgi Kültür Sanat, 2007.

Cannadine, David. "War and Death, Grief and Mourning in Modern Britain." In *Mirrors of Mortality: Studies in the Social History of Death*, edited by Joachim Whaley, 187–242. New York: St. Martin's Press, 1982.

Çapanoğlu, Münir Süleyman. "Abdülhamid'in en Yakın Adamı Nadir Ağa Eski Efendisi için Neler Söylüyor." *Yedigün* 83 (1934): 19–21.

Carpenter, Mary Wilson. *Health, Medicine, and Society in Victorian England*. Santa Barbara: Praeger, 2010.

Caston, Alfred de. "Le grand mouvement architectural dans l'Empire ottoman." *Revue de Constantinople* 1 (March 7, 1875): 395–421.

Çeçen, Kâzım. *İstanbul'un Vakıf Sularından Taksim ve Hamidiye Suları*. Istanbul: T. C. İstanbul Büyükşehir Belediyesi, 1992.

Celâlettin [Celaleddin], Mevhibe. *Geçmiş Zaman Olur ki, Prenses Mevhibe Celalettin'in Anıları*. Edited by Sara Ertuğrul Korle. Istanbul: Çağdaş Yayınları, 1987.

Çelik, Semih. "Science, to Understand the Abundance of Plants and Trees: The First Ottoman Natural History Museum and Herbarium." In *Environments of Empire: Networks and Agents of Ecological Change*, edited by Ulrike Kirchberger and Brett M. Bennett, 85–102. Chapel Hill: University of North Carolina Press, 2020.

Çelik, Zeynep. *Displaying the Orient: Architecture of Islam at Nineteenth-Century World's Fairs*. Berkeley: University of California Press, 1992.

———. *The Remaking of Istanbul: Portrait of an Ottoman City in the Nineteenth Century*. Seattle: University of Washington Press, 1986.

Çelik, Zeynep, and Edhem Eldem, eds. *Camera Ottomana: Photography and Modernity in the Ottoman Empire, 1840–1914*. Translated by Hande Eagle. Istanbul: Koç University Press, 2015.

Cervati, Raphael C. *Annuaire oriental du commerce, de l'industrie, de l'administration et de la magistrature*. Istanbul: J. Pallamary, 1900–1909.

———. *Indicateur ottoman illustré: Annuaire-almanach du commerce, de l'industrie, de l'administration et de la magistrature*. Constantinople: Cervati Frères & D. Fatzea, 1883.

Çetintaş, M. Burak. *Dolmabahçe'den Nişantaşı'na: Sultanların ve Paşaların Semtinin Tarihi*. Istanbul: Antik, 2005.

Cevat Rüştü. *Türk Çiçek ve Ziraat Kültürü Üzerine: Cevat Rüştü'den Bir Güldeste*. Istanbul: Kitabevi, 2001.

Cezar, Mustafa. *Sanatta Batı'ya Açılış ve Osman Hamdi*. 2nd ed. 2 vols. Istanbul: Erol Kerim Aksoy Kültür, Eğitim, Spor ve Sağlık Vakfı, 1995.

Chi, Jennifer Y., ed. *The Eye of the Shah: Qajar Court Photography and the Persian Past*. New York: Institute for the Study of the Ancient World at New York University, 2015.

Christensen, Peter H., ed. *Expertise and Architecture in the Modern Islamic World: A Critical Anthology*. Chicago: Intellect, 2018.

———. *Germany and the Ottoman Railways: Art, Empire, and Infrastructure*. New Haven: Yale University Press, 2017.

Çınar, Hüseyin. "Sultan II. Abdülhamid'in Vakıf, Hayrat ve Akaratı: 1888 Tarihli Vakfiyesine Göre." In *Bir Sultan, Bir Paşa: Sultan II. Abdülhamid ve Gazi Osman Paşa*, edited by Coşkun Yılmaz, 277–328. Istanbul: Gaziosmanpaşa Belediyesi, 2018.

Coen, Deborah R. *Climate in Motion: Science, Empire, and the Problem of Scale*. Chicago: University of Chicago Press, 2018.

Colonas, Vassilis. "Italian Architects in Thessaloniki: New Elements About the Work of Vitaliano Poselli and Pietro Arrigoni." In Girardelli and Godoli, *Italian Architects and Builders*, 149–59.

———. "Vitaliano Poselli: An Italian Architect in Thessaloniki." *Environmental Design: Journal of the Islamic Environmental Design Research Centre* (1990): 162–71.

Conrad, Joseph. *Heart of Darkness; with, The Congo Diary*. London: Penguin, 2000.

Coral, Mehmet. *Konstantiniye'nin Yitik Günceleri*. Istanbul: Doğan Kitapçılık, 1999.

Cox, Samuel Sullivan. *Diversions of a Diplomat in Turkey*. New York: C. L. Webster, 1887.

Csorba, György. "Hungarian Emigrants of 1848–49 in the Ottoman Empire." In *The Turks*, edited by Hasan Celâl Güzel, C. Cem Oğuz, and Osman Karatay, 4:224–32. Ankara: Yeni Türkiye, 2002.

Çuluk, Sinan. "Bahçıvanbaşı Charles Henry'nin Bursa Çevresinde Araştırma Gezisi." *Arşiv Dünyası Dergisi* 7 (2006): 43–45.

Dadyan, Saro. *Osmanlı'da Ermeni Aristokrasisi*. Istanbul: Everest Yayınları, 2011.

Dallaway, James. *Constantinople Ancient and Modern: With Excursions to the Shores and Islands of the Archipelago and to the Troad*. London: Printed by T. Bensley, for T. Cadell Junr. & W. Davies, 1797.

Dana, William Sumner Barton. *The Swiss Châlet Book: A Minute Analysis and Reproduction of the Châlets of Switzerland, Obtained by a Special Visit to That Country, Its Architects, and Its Châlet Homes.* New York: William T. Comstock, 1913.

Daniel, Malcolm R. *The Photographs of Édouard Baldus.* New York: Metropolitan Museum of Art, 1994.

Dejung, Christof, David Motadel, and Jürgen Osterhammel, eds. *The Global Bourgeoisie: The Rise of the Middle Classes in the Age of Empire.* Princeton: Princeton University Press, 2019.

Del Giorno, Sac. Ph. Victor. *Chroniques de la basilique cathédrale du Saint-Esprit.* 3 vols. Ankara, 1983.

Demirel, Fatmagül. *Dolmabahçe ve Yıldız Saraylarında Son Ziyaretler, Son Ziyafetler.* Istanbul: Doğan Kitap, 2007.

Deringil, Selim. "Legitimacy Structures in the Ottoman State: The Reign of Abdülhamid II (1876–1909)." *International Journal of Middle East Studies* 23, no. 3 (1991): 345–59.

———. *The Well-Protected Domains: Ideology and the Legitimation of Power in the Ottoman Empire, 1876–1909.* New York: I. B. Tauris, 1998.

Derman, M. Uğur. *Letters in Gold: Ottoman Calligraphy from the Sakıp Sabancı Collection, Istanbul.* New York: Metropolitan Museum of Art, 1998.

Dietrichson, Lorentz, and Henrik Munthe. *Die Holzbaukunst Norwegens in Vergangenheit und Gegenwart.* Berlin: Schuster & Bufleb, 1893.

Dodd, Anna Bowman. *In the Palaces of the Sultan.* New York: Dodd, Mead, 1903.

Donnelly, Marian C. *Architecture in the Scandinavian Countries.* Cambridge: MIT Press, 1992.

Dördüncü, Mehmet Bahadır, ed. *II. Abdülhamid Yıldız Albümleri: Mekke-Medine.* Istanbul: Yitik Hazine Yayınları, 2006.

Dorys, Georges. *The Private Life of the Sultan of Turkey.* Translated by Arthur Hornblow. New York: D. Appleton, 1901.

Downing, A. J. *The Architecture of Country Houses; Including Designs for Cottages, Farm-Houses, and Villas, with Remarks on Interiors, Furniture, and the Best Modes of Warming and Ventilating.* New York: D. Appleton, 1853.

Doyle, Laura. *Inter-imperiality: Vying Empires, Gendered Labor, and the Literary Arts of Alliance.* Durham: Duke University Press, 2020.

Dünden Bugüne İstanbul Ansiklopedisi (DBİA). 8 vols. Istanbul: Kültür Bakanlığı ve Tarih Vakfı, 1993.

Duran, Tülây, ed. *Tarihimizde Vakıf Kuran Kadınlar: Hanım Sultan Vakfiyyeleri.* Istanbul: İstanbul Araştırma Merkezi, 1990.

Eastlake, Charles L. *A History of the Gothic Revival: An Attempt to Show How the Taste for Mediaeval Architecture, Which Lingered in England During the Two Last Centuries, Has Since Been Encouraged and Developed.* London: Longmans, Green, 1872.

Egemen, Affan. *İstanbul'un Çeşme ve Sebilleri: Resimleri ve Kitabeleri ile 1165 Çeşme ve Sebil.* Istanbul: Arıtan Yayınevi, 1993.

Ekdal, Müfid. *Kapalı Hayat Kutusu: Kadıköy Konakları.* Istanbul: Yapı Kredi Yayınları, 2004.

Eldem, Edhem. *Pride and Privilege: A History of Ottoman Orders, Medals, and Decorations.* Istanbul: Ottoman Bank Archives and Research Centre, 2004.

———. "(A Quest for) the Bourgeoisie of Istanbul: Identities, Roles, and Conflicts." In *Urban Governance Under the Ottomans: Between Cosmopolitanism and Conflict*, edited by Ulrike Freitag and Nora Lafi, 159–86. London: Routledge, 2014.

Eldem, Sedad Hakkı. *Boğaziçi Anıları.* Istanbul: Aletaş Alarko Eğitim Tesisleri, 1979.

———. *Köşkler ve Kasırlar.* 2 vols. Istanbul: Devlet Güzel Sanatlar Akademisi, 1969.

———. *Sa'dabad.* Ankara: Kültür Bakanlığı, 1977.

———. *Türk Bahçeleri.* Ankara: Kültür Bakanlığı, 1976.

Enginün, İnci, ed. *Abdülhak Hâmid'in Hatıraları.* Istanbul: Dergâh Yayınları, 1994.

———. *Abdülhak Hâmid Tarhan.* Ankara: Kültür ve Turizm Bakanlığı, 1986.

———. *Yeni Türk Edebiyatı: Tanzimat'tan Cumhuriyet'e, 1839–1923.* Istanbul: Dergâh Yayınları, 2006.

Erdem, Y. Hakan. *Slavery in the Ottoman Empire and Its Demise, 1800–1909.* London: Palgrave Macmillan, 1996.

Eren, Halit, ed. *Bursa in Photographs of the Period of Sultan Abdulhamid II.* Istanbul: IRCICA, 2011.

———. *Manisa in Photographs from Sultan Abdulhamid II Period.* Istanbul: IRCICA, 2013.

Erkmen, Alev. *Geç Osmanlı Dünyasında Mimarlık ve Hafıza: Arşiv, Jübile, Âbide.* Istanbul: Metis Yayınları, 2011.

Ersoy, Ahmet A. *Architecture and the Late Ottoman Historical Imaginary: Reconfiguring the Architectural Past in a Modernizing Empire.* Burlington, VT: Ashgate, 2015.

———. "Architecture and the Search for Ottoman Origins in the Tanzimat Period." *Muqarnas* 24, no. 1 (2007): 117–39.

———. "Aykırı Binanın Saklı Kalfası: Hamidiye Camisi ve Nikolaos Tzelepis (Celepis)." In *Batılılaşan İstanbul'un Rum Mimarları*, edited by Hasan Kuruyazıcı and Eva Şarlak, 104–17. Istanbul: Zağrofyan Lisesi Mezunları Derneği, 2010.

———. "Ottoman Gothic: Evocations of the Medieval Past in Late Ottoman Architecture." In *Manufacturing Middle Ages: Entangled History of Medievalism in Nineteenth-Century Europe,* edited by Patrick J. Geary and Gábor Klaniczay, 217–38. Boston: Brill, 2013.

———. "Ottomans and the Kodak Galaxy: Archiving Everyday Life and Historical Space in Ottoman Illustrated Journals." *History of Photography* 40, no. 3 (2016): 330–57.

Ertem, Özge, and Bahattin Öztuncay, eds. *Ottoman Arcadia: The Hamidian Expedition to the Land of Tribal Roots (1886)*. Istanbul: Koç University Press, 2018.

Ertuğ, Hasan Ferit. "Musahib-i Sani Hazret-i Şehriyari Nadir Ağa'nın Hatıratı-I." *Toplumsal Tarih* 49 (January 1998): 9–15.

———. "Musahib-i Sani Hazret-i Şehriyari Nadir Ağa'nın Hatıratı-I." *Toplumsal Tarih* 50 (February 1998): 6–14.

Esatlı, Mustafa Ragıp. *Saray ve Konakların Dilinden Bir Devrin Tarihi*. Istanbul: Bengi, 2010.

Esenbel, Selçuk. "A *Fin de Siècle* Japanese Romantic in Istanbul: The Life of Yamada Torajirō and His *Toruko Gakan*." *Bulletin of the School of Oriental and African Studies* 59, no. 2 (1996): 237–52.

Esenbel, Selçuk, Miyuki Aoki Girardelli, and Erdal Küçükyalçın. *The Crescent and the Sun: Three Japanese in Istanbul; Yamada Torajirō, Itō Chūta, Ōtani Kōzui*. Istanbul: İstanbul Araştırmaları Enstitüsü, 2010.

Evliyâ Çelebi. *Evliyâ Çelebi Seyahatnâmesi: Topkapı Sarayı Kütüphanesi Bağdat 304 Numaralı Yazmanın Transkripsiyonu, Dizini*. Edited by Robert Dankoff, Yücel Dağlı, and Seyit Ali Kahraman. Vol. 1. Istanbul: Yapı Kredi Yayınları, 2010.

Evyapan, Gönül Aslanoğlu. *Tarih İçinde Formel Bahçenin Gelişimi ve Türk Bahçesinde Etkileri*. Ankara: Orta Doğu Teknik Üniversitesi, 1974.

Eyice, Semavi. "Ayazağa Kasrı." In *DİA*, 4:205–6.

Ezgü, Fuad. *Yıldız Sarayı Tarihçesi*. Istanbul: Harb Akademileri Komutanlığı, 1962.

Fairbairn, William. *Treatise on Mills and Millwork*. 2nd ed. Vol. 1. London: Longman, Green, Longman, Roberts & Green, 1864.

Farmayan, H. F. "Amīn-al-Dawla, Mīrzā ʿAlī Khan." In *Encyclopædia Iranica*, vol. 1, fasc. 9, 843–45. https://www.iranicaonline.org/articles/amin-al-dawla-mirza-ali-khan.

Fergusson, James. *History of the Modern Styles of Architecture*. 3rd ed., rev. Vol. 2. London: Murray, 1891.

Findley, Carter V. *Bureaucratic Reform in the Ottoman Empire: The Sublime Porte, 1789–1922*. Princeton: Princeton University Press, 1980.

———. "An Ottoman Occidentalist in Europe: Ahmed Midhat Meets Madame Gülnar, 1889." *American Historical Review* 103, no. 1 (1998): 15–49.

Flaubert, Gustave. *Bouvard et Pécuchet: Oeuvre posthume*. Paris: A. Lemerre, 1881.

Fontane, Marius. *Voyage pittoresque à travers l'isthme de Suez*. Paris: P. Dupont, 1870.

Forster, John. *The Life of Charles Dickens; in 2 Volumes*. New ed. New York: Dutton, 1969.

Frank, Alison F. "The Air Cure Town: Commodifying Mountain Air in Alpine Central Europe." *Central European History* 45, no. 2 (2012): 185–207.

Frankl, Ludwig August. *Nach Jerusalem!* 2 vols. Leipzig: Baumgärtner, 1858.

Frazee, Charles A. *Catholics and Sultans: The Church and the Ottoman Empire, 1453–1923*. New York: Cambridge University Press, 1983.

Frevert, Walter. *Rominten: Das ostpreußische Jagdparadies*. Munich: blv, 2008.

Gaboda, Péter. "Conclusions historiques (et muséologiques) du trajet d'une statue égyptienne." *Bulletin du Musée hongrois des beaux-arts* 82 (1995): 21–30.

Galinou, Mireille. *Cottages and Villas: The Birth of the Garden Suburb*. New Haven: Yale University Press, 2011.

Gavin, Carney E. S., ed. *Imperial Self-Portrait: The Ottoman Empire as Revealed in the Sultan Abdul-Hamid II's Photographic Albums Presented as Gifts to the Library of Congress (1893) and the British Museum (1894); A Pictorial Selection with Catalogue, Concordance, Indices, and Brief Essays*. Cambridge, MA: Harvard University, Office of the University Publisher, 1989.

Gawrych, George Walter. *The Crescent and the Eagle: Ottoman Rule, Islam, and the Albanians, 1874–1913*. New York: I. B. Tauris, 2006.

Genç, Adnan, and Orhan M. Çolak, eds. *Photographs of İstanbul from the Archives of Sultan Abdülhamid II*. Istanbul: İstanbul Büyükşehir Belediyesi, 2008.

Genç, Mehmet, and Mehmet Mazak, eds. *İstanbul Depremleri: Fotoğraf ve Belgelerde 1894 Depremi*. Istanbul: İGDAŞ Genel Müdürlüğü, 2000.

Georgeon, François. *Abdulhamid II: Le sultan calife (1876–1909)*. Paris: Fayard, 2003.

Gezgör, Vahide. "Hereke Fabrika-i Hümayunu'nda Halı Üretimi." In *Milli Saraylar Koleksiyonu'nda Hereke Dokumaları ve Halıları*, edited by Mehmet Kenan Kaya, 173–77. Istanbul: TBMM Milli Saraylar Daire Başkanlığı, 1999.

Gezgör, Vahide, and Feryal İrez, eds. *Yıldız Sarayı, Şale Kasr-ı Hümâyunu*. Istanbul: TBMM Milli Saraylar Daire Başkanlığı, 1993.

Gigord, Pierre de. *Images d'empire: Aux origines de la photographie en Turquie*. Edited by Nazan Ölçer. Istanbul: Institut d'études françaises d'Istanbul, 1993.

Girardelli, Paolo. "Dolmabahçe and the Old Çırağan Palace in European Sources." In *150. Yılında Dolmabahçe Sarayı Uluslararası Sempozyumu:*

Bildiriler, edited by Kemal Kahraman, 247–56. Istanbul: TBMM Milli Saraylar, 2007.

———. "Power or Leisure? Remarks on the Architecture of the European Summer Embassies on the Bosphorus Shore." *New Perspectives on Turkey* 50 (2014): 29–58.

Girardelli, Paolo, and Cengiz Can. "Giovanni Battista Barborini à Istanbul." *Observatoire urbain d'Istanbul* 8 (October 1995): 2–7.

Girardelli, Paolo and Ezio Godoli, eds. *Italian Architects and Builders in the Ottoman Empire and Modern Turkey: Design Across Borders*. Newcastle upon Tyne: Cambridge Scholars Publishing, 2017.

Glick, Thomas F., Steven J. Livesey, and Faith Wallis, eds. *Medieval Science, Technology, and Medicine: An Encyclopedia*. New York: Routledge, 2005.

Gloag, John. *Victorian Comfort: A Social History of Design from 1830–1900*. London: A. & C. Black, 1961.

Göçek, Fatma Müge. *Rise of the Bourgeoisie, Demise of Empire: Ottoman Westernization and Social Change*. New York: Oxford University Press, 1996.

Godoli, Ezio. "D'Aronco e Vienna: Un dialogo a distanza." In *Atti del Congresso internazionale di studi su "Raimondo D'Aronco e il suo tempo,"* 185–94. Udine: Istituto per l'Enciclopedia del Friuli Venezia Giulia, 1982.

Goldhill, Simon. *The Temple of Jerusalem*. Cambridge: Harvard University Press, 2005.

Göncüoğlu, Süleyman Faruk. *Üsküdar ve Boğaziçi*. Istanbul: İstanbul Büyükşehir Belediyesi, 2015.

Gör, Emre. *II. Abdülhamid'in Hafiye Teşkilatı ve Teşkilat Hakkında Bir Risale Örneği "Hafiyelerin Listesi."* Istanbul: Ötüken Neşriyat, 2015.

Gräffer, Franz. *Historische Raritäten*. Vol. 2. Vienna: Tendler und v. Manstein, 1823.

Gran, Gunnar. "A Magnate and His Manor." *Norseman*, no. 1 (2003): 58–63.

Grange, Daniel J. *L'Italie et la Méditerranée, 1896–1911: Les fondements d'une politique étrangère*. 2 vols. Rome: École française de Rome, 1994.

Granville, Augustus Bozzi. *The Spas of Germany*. Vol. 1. London: Henry Colburn, 1837.

Grey, Mrs. William. *Journal of a Visit to Egypt, Constantinople, the Crimea, Greece &c.: In the Suite of the Prince and Princess of Wales*. London: Smith, Elder, 1869.

Guerville, A. B. de. *New Egypt*. New York: E. P. Dutton, 1906.

Gülersoy, Çelik. *Beşiktaş'da Ihlamur Mesiresi ve Tarihî Kitabeler*. Istanbul: Türkiye Turing ve Otomobil Kurumu Yayınları, 1962.

———. *Hidiv'ler ve Çubuklu Kasrı*. Istanbul: Türkiye Turing ve Otomobil Kurumu, 1985.

———. "Yıldız Parkı." In *DBİA*, 7:519–20.

———. *Yıldız Parkı ve Malta Köşkü*. Istanbul: Türkiye Turing ve Otomobil Kurumu Yayını, 1979.

Gültekin, Gülbin. "Mihrişah Valide Sultan Külliyesi." In *DBİA*, 5:459–61.

Günergun, Feza, and Asuman Baytop. "Hekimbaşı Salih Efendi (1816–1895) ve Botanikle İlgili Yayınları." *Osmanli Bilimi Araştırmaları* 0, no. 2 (1998): 293–317.

Gürfırat, Baha. "Pertevniyal Valide Sultan'ın Hâtıratı: Sergüzeştname." *Belgelerle Türk Tarihi Dergisi* 2 (1967): 57–59.

Gürsel, Zeynep Devrim. "A Picture of Health: The Search for a Genre to Visualize Care in Late Ottoman Istanbul." *Grey Room* 72 (2018): 36–67.

Gyllius, Petrus. *De Bosphoro Thracio*. Libri II. Venice, 1565.

Hâfız Hızır İlyas. *Osmanlı Sarayında Gündelik Hayat: Letâif-i Vekâyi'-i Enderûniyye*. Edited by Ali Şükrü Çoruk. Istanbul: Kitabevi, 2011.

Hafız Hüseyin Ayvansarayî. *The Garden of the Mosques: Hafiz Hüseyin al-Ayvansarayī's Guide to the Muslim Monuments of Ottoman Istanbul*. Translated by Howard Crane. Boston: Brill, 2000.

Hahn-Hahn, Ida. *Letters from the Holy Land*. London: J & D. A. Darling, 1849.

Halman, Talât Sait. *Rapture and Revolution: Essays on Turkish Literature*. Syracuse: Syracuse University Press, 2007.

Hamadeh, Shirine. *The City's Pleasures: Istanbul in the Eighteenth Century*. Seattle: University of Washington Press, 2008.

Hamouda, Sahar. *Omar Toussoun: Prince of Alexandria*. Alexandria: Bibliotheca Alexandria, 2005.

Hanioğlu, M. Şükrü. *A Brief History of the Late Ottoman Empire*. Princeton: Princeton University Press, 2010.

———. *The Young Turks in Opposition*. New York: Oxford University Press, 1995.

Harmanşah, Ömür. "Deep Time and Landscape History: How Can Historical Particularity Be Translated?" In *Timescales: Thinking Across Ecological Temporalities*, edited by Bethany Wiggin, Carolyn Fornoff, and Patricia Eunji Kim, 39–54. Minneapolis: University of Minnesota Press, 2020.

Hassan, Hassan. *In the House of Muhammad Ali: A Family Album, 1805–1952*. Cairo: American University in Cairo Press, 2000.

Henry, Charles. "Dasylirion Glaucophyllum." *Revue horticole* 83 (1911): 87.

———. "Les jardins de Yildiz au temps d'Abdul-Hamid." *Revue horticole* 84 (1912): 54–57.

Herbert, Gilbert. *Pioneers of Prefabrication: The British Contribution in the Nineteenth Century*.

Baltimore: Johns Hopkins University Press, 1978.

Herder, Johann Gottfried von. "Kalligenia, die Mutter der Schönheit: Ein Traum." In *Johann Gottfried von Herders sämtliche Werke: Zur schönen Literatur und Kunst*, 6:224–34. Carlsruhe: Bureau der Deutschen Klassiker, 1821.

Hirschfeld, Christian Cajus Lorenz. *Theory of Garden Art*. Translated by Linda B. Parshall. Philadelphia: University of Pennsylvania Press, 2001.

Hisar, Abdülhak Şinasi. *Boğaziçi Mehtapları*. Istanbul: Hilmi Kitabevi, 1942.

———. *Boğaziçi Yalıları; Geçmiş Zaman Köşkleri*. Istanbul: Varlık Yayınevi, 1968.

Hobhouse, John Cam. *A Journey Through Albania and Other Provinces of Turkey in Europe and Asia, to Constantinople, During the Years 1809 and 1810*. 3 vols. Philadelphia: M. Carey, 1817.

Hobhouse, Penelope. *The Gardens of Persia*. San Diego: Kales Press, 2004.

Hocaoğlu, Mehmet. *Abdülhamit Han'ın Muhtıraları: Belgeler*. Istanbul: Oymak Yayınları, 1975.

Hoffman, Eva R. "Between East and West: The Wall Paintings of Samarra and the Construction of Abbasid Princely Culture." *Muqarnas* 25 (2008): 107–32.

Horgan, John. "Journalism, Catholicism, and Anti-Communism in an Era of Revolution: Francis McCullagh, War Correspondent, 1874–1956." *Studies: An Irish Quarterly Review* 98, no. 390 (2009): 169–84.

Hornby, Edmund. *In and Around Stamboul*. Philadelphia: J. Challen & Son, Lindsay & Blakiston, 1858.

Horton, Richard W. "Historical Photo Albums and Their Structures." In *Conservation of Scrapbooks and Albums: Postprints of the Book and Paper Group / Photographic Materials Group Joint Session at the 27th Annual Meeting of the American Institute for Conservation of Historic and Artistic Works, June 11, 1999, St. Louis, Missouri*, edited by Shannon Zachary, 13–27. Washington, DC: Book and Paper Group [and] Photographic Materials Group, American Institute for Conservation of Historic and Artistic Works, 2000.

Huber, Valeska. *Channelling Mobilities: Migration and Globalisation in the Suez Canal Region and Beyond, 1869–1914*. New York: Cambridge University Press, 2013.

Hunt, John Dixon. *The Picturesque Garden in Europe*. New York: Thames & Hudson, 2002.

Hüseyin Vassaf. *Sefine-i Evliyâ*. Vol. 1. Istanbul: Şeha Neşriyat, 1990.

İnal, İbnülemin Mahmut Kemal. *Son Asır Türk Şairleri: Kemâlü'ş-Şuarâ*. 5 vols. Ankara: Atatürk Kültür Merkezi Başkanlığı, 1999–2000.

İnan, Ahmet. "Mihrişah Sultan İmareti." In *Eyüp Sultan Tarihi*, edited by Mehmet Nermi Haskan, 2:720–24. Istanbul: Eyüp Belediyesi, 2008.

Inchichean, Ghukas. *XVIII. Asırda İstanbul*. Translated by Hrand D. Andreasyan. 2nd ed. Istanbul: Baha Matbaası, 1976.

İnci, Handan. *Roman ve Mekân: Türk Romanında Ev*. Istanbul: Arma Yayınları, 2003.

İngiliz [Eğinli] Said Paşa. *II. Abdülhamid'in İlk Mâbeyn Ferîki: Eğinli Said Paşa'nın Hâtırâtı, I–II, 1876–1880*. Istanbul: Bengi Yayınları, 2011.

İrtem, Süleyman Kâni. *Abdülhamid Devrinde Hafiyelik ve Sansür: Abdülhamid'e Verilen Jurnaller*. Istanbul: Temel Yayınları, 1999.

———. *II. Mahmud Devri ve Türk Kemankeşleri*. Istanbul: Temel Yayınları, 2005.

Jalland, Patricia. *Death in the Victorian Family*. New York: Oxford University Press, 1996.

Kahraman, Âtıf. *Osmanlı Devleti'nde Spor*. Ankara: T. C. Kültür Bakanlığı, 1995.

Kalafatoğlu, Pelin E. "Yüzyıl Dönümü İstanbul Mimarlığında 'Viktorya Tarzı' Sayfiye Konutları." In *Geç Osmanlı Döneminde Sanat Mimarlık ve Kültür Karşılaşmaları*, edited by Gözde Çelik, 119–32. Istanbul: Türkiye İş Bankası Kültür Yayınları, 2016.

Kaldjian, Paul. "Istanbul's Bostans: A Millennium of Market Gardens." *Geographical Review* 94, no. 3 (2004): 284–304.

Kâmil Paşa. *Ḫāṭırat-ı Ṣadr-ı Esbāḳ Kāmil Paşa*. Istanbul: Maṭbaʿa-ı Ebużżiyā, 1329 [1911].

———. *Tārīḫ-i Siyāsī-yi Devlet-i ʿĀlīye-i ʿOsmānīye*. Istanbul: Maṭbaʿa-ı Aḥmed İḥsān, 1325 [1907–8].

Kandemir, Feridun. "Febüs Anlatıyor." *Aydabir* 7 (March 1, 1936): 53–55.

Kangal, Selmin, and Priscilla Mary Işın, eds. *The Sultan's Portrait: Picturing the House of Osman*. Istanbul: İşbank, 2000.

Karahüseyin, Güller. *Chandeliers and Lamps in the National Palaces*. Istanbul: TBMM Milli Saraylar Daire Başkanlığı, 1998.

Karakaya, Recep, İsmail Yücedağ, and Nâzım Yılmaz, eds. *Arşiv Belgelerinde Karabük*. Istanbul: Karabük Valiliği Kültür Yayınları, 2013.

Karal, Enver Ziya. *Osmanlı Tarihi*. Vol. 5, *Nizam-ı Cedit ve Tanzimat Devirleri (1789–1856)*. Ankara: Türk Tarih Kurumu, 1961.

Karateke, Hakan T. *Padişahım Çok Yaşa! Osmanlı Devletinin Son Yüz Yılında Merasimler*. Istanbul: Kitap Yayınevi, 2004.

Karpat, Kemal H. *The Politicization of Islam: Reconstructing Identity, State, Faith, and Community in the Late Ottoman State*. New York: Oxford University Press, 2001.

Kaya, Gülsen S. "Başyaver Şeker Ahmed Paşa ve Sara-yın Yabancı Konukları." In Şerifoğlu and Baytar, *Şeker Ahmed Paşa*, 71–79.

Kayserilioğlu, Sertaç, Mehmet Mazak, and Kadir Kon. *Osmanlı'dan Günümüze Havagazının Tarihçesi*. 3 vols. Istanbul: İGDAŞ Genel Müdürlüğü, 1999.

Kélékian, Diran. "Life at Yildiz." *Contemporary Review* 70 (December 1896): 784–92.

Kennedy, Dane Keith. *The Magic Mountains: Hill Stations and the British Raj*. Berkeley: University of California Press, 1996.

Klausmeier, Axel, and Andreas Pahl. "Zur Geschichte des Parks des ehemaligen Sommersitzes der deutschen Botschaft in Tarabya am Bosporus." *Die Gartenkunst* 19, no. 1 (2007): 109–26.

Koch, Karl Heinrich Emil. *Wanderungen im Oriente, während der Jahre 1843 und 1844*. 2 vols. Weimar: Druck und Verlag des Landes-Industrie-Comptoirs, 1846.

Koçu, Reşat Ekrem. "Bezmiâlem Vâlidesultan Çeşmesi." İn *İstanbul Ansiklopedisi*, 5:2736–2737. Istanbul: İstanbul Ansiklopedisi ve Neşriyat Kollektif Şirketi, 1961.

Komara, Ann. "Concrete and the Engineered Picturesque: The Parc des Buttes Chaumont (Paris, 1867)." *Journal of Architectural Education* 58, no. 1 (2004): 5–12.

Konyalı, İbrahim Hakkı. *Âbideleri ve Kitâbeleriyle Üsküdar Tarihi*. 2 vols. Istanbul: Türkiye Yeşilay Cemiyeti, 1976–77.

Krauss, Rosalind. "Photography's Discursive Spaces: Landscape/View." *Art Journal* 42, no. 4 (1982): 311–19.

Kreil, Karl. "Magnetische und geographische Ortsbestimmungen im südöstlichen Europa und einigen Küstenpunkten Asiens." *Denkschriften der Kaiserlichen Akademie der Wissenschaften: Mathematisch-naturwissenschaftliche Klasse* 20 (1862): 1–94.

Kreisel, Heinrich. *Schönbusch bei Aschaffenburg: Amtlicher Führer*. Aschaffenburg: Verlag der Wailandtschen Druckerei, 1932.

Kuban, Doğan. *Ottoman Architecture*. Translated by Adair Mill. Woodbridge, Suffolk: Antique Collector's Club, 2010.

——. "Wooden Housing Architecture of Istanbul." In Tanman and Bachmann, *Wooden Istanbul*, 14–18.

Küçükerman, Önder. *Anadolu'nun Geleneksel Halı ve Dokuma Sanatı İçinde Hereke Fabrikası: Saray'dan Hereke'ye Giden Yol*. Ankara: Sümerbank Genel Müdürlüğü, 1987.

——. *Dünya Saraylarının Prestij Teknolojisi: Porselen Sanatı ve Yıldız Çini Fabrikası*. Ankara: Sümerbank Genel Müdürlüğü, 1987.

——. *Milli Saraylar Koleksiyonu'nda Yıldız Porseleni*. Istanbul: TBMM Milli Saraylar Daire Başkanlığı Yayını, 1998.

Kula Say, Seda. "A Post-1908 Project of Vallaury: Customs House in Thessaloniki." In *14th International Congress of Turkish Art: Proceedings*, edited by Frédéric Hitzel, 449–58. Ankara: Republic of Turkey Ministry of Culture and Tourism, 2013.

Kürkman, Garo. *Armenian Painters in the Ottoman Empire, 1600–1923*. 2 vols. Istanbul: Matüsalem Publications, 2004.

Kuşoğlu, Mehmet Zeki. *Türk Okçuluğu ve Sultan Mahmud'un Ok Günlüğü*. Istanbul: Ötüken Neşriyat, 2006.

Kut, Günay. "Meyve Bahçesi." In "Festschrift in Honor of Eleazar Birnbaum," edited by Virginia Aksan, special issue, *Journal of Turkish Studies* 29 (2005): 201–56.

Kutay, Cemal. *Sultan Abdülaziz'in Avrupa Seyahati*. Istanbul: Boğaziçi Yayınları, 1991.

Kutluoğlu, Muhammed H., and Murat Candemir, eds. *Bir Cihan Devletinin Tasfiyesi: Yıldız Sarayı Müzesi Tasfiye Komisyonu Defteri*. Istanbul: Çamlıca, 2010.

Lamartine, Alphonse de. *Le nouveau voyage en Orient*. Vol. 1. Paris: Administration, 1851.

Landau, Sarah Bradford. "Richard Morris Hunt, the Continental Picturesque, and the 'Stick Style.'" *Journal of the Society of Architectural Historians* 42, no. 3 (October 1983): 272–89.

Lane, Barbara Miller. *National Romanticism and Modern Architecture in Germany and the Scandinavian Countries*. New York: Cambridge University Press, 2000.

Lauterbach, Iris. "Werdende Bilder im Übergange: Gartenkunst und Landschaftsmalerie." In *Parkomanie: Die Gartenlandschaften des Fürsten Pückler in Muskau, Babelsberg und Branitz*, edited by Agnieszka Lulińska, 40–53. Munich: Prestel, 2016.

Layard, Enid. *Twixt Pera and Therapia: The Constantinople Diaries of Lady Layard*. Istanbul: Isis Press, 2010.

Leblanc, Louis, and Georges Leblanc. *Traité d'aménagement des salles de spectacles*. Vol. 2. Paris: Vincent, Fréal, 1950.

Lee, Michael G. *The German "Mittelweg": Garden Theory and Philosophy in the Time of Kant*. New York: Routledge, 2007.

Léopold II. *Voyage à Constantinople, 1860*. Brussels: Éditions Complexe, 1997.

Lisianskii, L. A., ed. *Vsia Odessa: Adresnaia i spravochnaia kniga vsei Odessi na 1904–5-i god*. Part 2. Odessa: L. A. Lisianskago, 1905.

Lowzow, P. "Norwegian Style of Building." *The Builder*, May 26, 1883, 705–6.

Mangone, Fabio. "Nicola Carelli in Constantinople and in the Levant: Some Notes." In Girardelli and Godoli, *Italian Architects and Builders*, 97–110.

Manz, Stefan. *Constructing a German Diaspora: The "Greater German Empire," 1871–1914*. New York: Routledge, 2014.

Marchand, Suzanne L. *German Orientalism in the Age of Empire: Religion, Race, and Scholarship*. New York: Cambridge University Press, 2009.

———. *Porcelain: A History from the Heart of Europe*. Princeton: Princeton University Press, 2020.

Mardin, Şerif. *The Genesis of Young Ottoman Thought: A Study in the Modernization of Turkish Political Ideas*. 1st Syracuse University Press ed. Syracuse: Syracuse University Press, 2000.

———. *Religion, Society, and Modernity in Turkey*. Syracuse: Syracuse University Press, 2006.

———. "Super Westernization in Urban Life in the Ottoman Empire in the Last Quarter of the Nineteenth Century." In *Turkey: Geographic and Social Perspectives*, edited by Peter Benedict, Erol Tümertekin, and Fatma Mansur, 403–46. Leiden: Brill, 1974.

Marmara, Rinaldo. *Pancaldi: Quartier levantin du XIXe siècle*. Istanbul: Éditions Isis, 2004.

Maudlin, Daniel. *The Idea of the Cottage in English Architecture, 1760–1860*. New York: Routledge, 2015.

Mayakon, İsmail Müştak. *Yıldız'da Neler Gördüm?* Istanbul: Sertel Matbaası, 1940.

Mazak, Mehmet. *Gündelik Hayattan Renklerle Eski İstanbul*. Istanbul: Yeditepe Yayınevi, 2016.

McCullagh, Francis. *The Fall of Abd-ul-Hamid*. London: Methuen, 1910.

Mehmed İzzet. *Rehber-i Umūr-ı Beytīye: Eve müteʿalliḳ bi'l-cümle umūruñ rehberidir*. Vol. 1. Istanbul: Ferīdiye Maṭbaʿāsı, 1319 [1901].

———. *Rehber-i Umūr-ı Beytīye: Eve müteʿalliḳ bi'l-cümle umūruñ rehberidir*. Vol. 2. Istanbul: Ḫānımlara Maḫṣūṣ Gazete Maṭbaʿāsı, 1325 [1907].

———. *Rehber-i Umūr-ı Beytīye: Eve müteʿalliḳ bi'l-cümle umūruñ rehberidir*. Vol. 3. Istanbul: Maḥmūd Bey Maṭbaʿāsı, 1327 [1909].

Meḥmed Rāʾif. *Mirʾāt-ı İstānbul*. Istanbul, 1314 [1896].

Mehmet Memduh Paşa. *Tanzimattan Meşrutiyete (Mirʾât-ı Şuûnât)*. Istanbul: Nehir Yayınları, 1990.

Melek-Hanum. *Thirty Years in the Harem: or, The Autobiography of Melek-Hanum, Wife of H. H. Kibrizli-Mehemet-Pasha*. London: Chapman & Hall, 1872.

Melling, Antoine-Ignace. *Voyage pittoresque de Constantinople et de rives de Bosphore, d'après les dessins de M. Melling*. Facsimile of the MM. Treuttel et Würtz edition. Istanbul: Ertuğ & Kocabıyık, 2003.

Mestyan, Adam. *Arab Patriotism: The Ideology and Culture of Power in Late Ottoman Egypt*. Princeton: Princeton University Press, 2017.

Micklewright, Nancy C. "Personal, Public, and Political (Re)Constructions: Photographs and Consumption." In *Consumption Studies and the History of the Ottoman Empire, 1550–1922: An Introduction*, edited by Donald Quataert, 261–87. Albany: State University of New York Press, 2000.

———. "Picturing the 'Abode of Felicity' in 1919: A Photograph Album of Istanbul." In *Envisioning Islamic Art and Architecture: Essays in Honor of Renata Holod*, edited by David J. Roxburgh, 250–78. Boston: Brill, 2014.

———. *A Victorian Traveler in the Middle East: The Photography and Travel Writing of Annie Lady Brassey*. Burlington, VT: Ashgate, 2003.

Mıntzuri, Hagob. *İstanbul Anıları, 1897–1940*. 3rd ed. Translated by Silva Kuyumcuyan. Edited by Necdet Sakaoğlu. Istanbul: Tarih Vakfı Yurt Yayınları, 1998.

Moüy, Charles de. *Lettres du Bosphore: Bucarest, Constantinople, Athènes*. Paris: E. Plon, 1879.

Müller, Georgina A. *Letters from Constantinople*. New York: Longmans, Green, 1897.

Multhauf, Robert P., and Gregory Good. *A Brief History of Geomagnetism and a Catalog of the Collections of the National Museum of American History*. Washington, DC: Smithsonian Institution Press, 1987.

Mümtaz, Semih. *Eski İstanbul Konakları*. Istanbul: Kurtuba Kitap, 2011.

———. *Tarihimizde Hayal Olmuş Hakikatler*. Istanbul: İbrahim Hilmi Çığıraçan, 1948.

Murphy, Paul Thomas. *Shooting Victoria: Madness, Mayhem, and the Rebirth of the British Monarchy*. New York: Pegasus Books, 2012.

Musgrave, Toby. *The Head Gardeners: Forgotten Heroes of Horticulture*. London: Aurum, 2007.

Mustafa Kânî Bey. *Okçuluk Kitabı: Telhîs-i Resâʾilât-ı Rumât*. Istanbul: İstanbul Fetih Cemiyeti, 2010.

Muẓaffar al-Dīn Shāh [Muzaffar al-Din Shah]. *Safarnāmah-i Farangistān: Safar-i avval*. Tehran: Intishārāt-i Sharq 1363 [1984].

Nāṣir al-Dīn Shāh [Nasir al-Din Shah]. *The Diary of H. M. the Shah of Persia During His Tour Through Europe in A.D. 1873*. Translated by James W. Redhouse. London: J. Murray, 1874.

Necipoğlu, Gülru. *The Age of Sinan: Architectural Culture in the Ottoman Empire*. Princeton: Princeton University Press, 2005.

——. *Architecture, Ceremonial, and Power: The Topkapı Palace in the Fifteenth and Sixteenth Centuries.* Cambridge: MIT Press, 1991.

——. "An Outline of Shifting Paradigms in the Palatial Architecture of the Pre-modern Islamic World." *Ars Orientalis* 23 (1993): 3–24.

——. "Plans and Models in 15th- and 16th-Century Ottoman Architectural Practice." *Journal of the Society of Architectural Historians* 45, no. 3 (1986): 224–43.

——, ed. *Sinan's Autobiographies: Five Sixteenth-Century Texts.* Critical edition and translation by Howard Crane and Esra Akın. Boston: Brill, 2006.

——. "The Suburban Landscape of Sixteenth-Century Istanbul as a Mirror of Classical Ottoman Garden Culture." In *Gardens in the Time of the Great Muslim Empires: Theory and Design*, edited by Attilio Petruccioli, 32–71. New York: Brill, 1997.

——. "'Virtual Archaeology' in Light of a New Document on the Topkapı Palace's Waterworks and Earliest Buildings, Circa 1509." *Muqarnas Online* 30, no. 1 (2014): 315–50.

——. "Volatile Urban Landscapes Between Mythical Space and Time." In *A Companion to Early Modern Istanbul*, edited by Shirine Hamadeh and Çiğdem Kafescioğlu, 197–232. Leiden: Brill, 2021.

Neumärker, Uwe, and Volker Knopf. *Görings Revier: Jagd und Politik in der Rominter Heide.* Berlin: Ch. Links Verlag, 2007.

Nogel, István. *Utazása Keleten.* Pest: Beimel József, 1847.

Nolan, Erin Hyde. "The Gift of the Abdülhamid II Albums: The Consequences of Photographic Circulation." *Trans-Asia Photography* 9, no. 2 (Spring 2019): https://quod.lib.umich.edu/t/tap/7977573.0009.207/—gift-of-the-abdulhamid-ii-albums-the-consequences?rgn=main;view=fulltext.

Norberg-Schulz, Christian. *Nightlands: Nordic Building.* Cambridge: MIT Press, 1996.

Noyan, Abbas Erdoğan. *Prizren-Dersaadet: Sultan II. Abdülhamid'in Yıldız Sarayı Muhafızlığına Getirilen Arnavut Taburunun Öyküsü.* Istanbul: Profil, 2012.

Nyberg, Klas. "Fenomenet Thams." *Scandinavian Journal of History* 34, no. 1 (2009): 108–9.

Öndeş, Osman, and Erol Makzume. *Fausto Zonaro: Ottoman Court Painter.* Istanbul: Yapı Kredi Yayınları, 2002.

Önel, Emine. "Fer'iye Sarayları." In *DBİA*, 3:294.

Oral, Ünver. *Yazı ve Resimlerde Beykoz.* Istanbul: Veli, 2007.

Orbán, Balázs. "Külföldi életemből." *Ellenzék*, December 1–28, 1881.

Örik, Nahid Sırrı. *Bilinmeyen Yaşamlarıyla Saraylılar.* Istanbul: Türkiye İş Bankası Kültür Yayınları, 2002.

Örikağasızade Hasan Sırrı. *Sultan Abdülhamit Devri Hatıraları ve Saray İdaresi.* Istanbul: Dergâh Yayınları, 2007.

Oscanyan, Christopher. *The Sultan and His People.* New York: Derby & Jackson, 1857.

'Oṣmān Nūrī [Osman Nuri]. *'Abdülḥamīd-i Sānī ve Devr-i Salṭanatı, Ḥayāt-ı Ḫuṣūṣīye ve Siyāsīyesi.* 3 vols. in 1. Istanbul: Kitāb ḫāne-i İslām ve 'askerī, İbrāhīm Hilmi, 1327 [1911].

Osmanoğlu, Ayşe. *Babam Abdülhamid.* Istanbul: Güven Yayınevi, 1960.

Osmanoğlu, Şâdiye. *Babam Sultan Abdülhamid: Saray ve Sürgün Yılları.* Istanbul: L & M Yayınları, 2007.

Özendes, Engin. *Abdullah Frères: Ottoman Court Photographers.* Istanbul: Yapı Kredi Yayınları, 1998.

——. *From Sébah & Joaillier to Foto Sabah: Orientalism in Photography.* Istanbul: Yapı Kredi Yayınları, 1999.

——. *Photographer Ali Sami: 1866–1936 = Fotoğrafçı Ali Sami: 1866–1936.* Istanbul: Haşet Kitabevi, 1989.

——. *Photography in the Ottoman Empire, 1839–1919.* Istanbul: Haşet Kitabevi, 1987.

Özgül, Metin Kayahan, ed. *Ali Ekrem Bolayır'ın Hâtıraları.* Ankara: Kültür Bakanlığı, 1991.

Özlü, Nilay. "Merkezin Merkezi: Sultan II. Abdülhamid Döneminde Yıldız Sarayı." *Toplumsal Tarih*, no. 206 (February 2011): 2–13.

Özsezgin, Kaya. *The Collection of Istanbul Museum of Painting and Sculpture, Mimar Sinan University.* Istanbul: Yapı Kredi Yayınları, 1996.

Öztuna, Yılmaz. *Devletler ve Hânedanlar.* Vol. 2. Ankara: Kültür Bakanlığı, 1989.

Öztuncay, Bahattin. *Dynasty and Camera: Portraits from the Ottoman Court, Ömer M. Koç Collection.* Istanbul: Aygaz, 2011.

——. "Ernest De Caranza: Member of the Société française de photographie." *History of Photography* 15, no. 2 (1991): 139–43.

——. *Hatıra-i Uhuvvet: Portre Fotoğrafların Cazibesi, 1846–1950.* Istanbul: Aygaz, 2005.

——. *The Photographers of Constantinople: Pioneers, Studios, and Artists from 19th Century Istanbul.* 2nd ed. 2 vols. Istanbul: Aygaz, 2006.

——. *Robertson: Photographer and Engraver in the Ottoman Capital.* Istanbul: Vehbi Koç Foundation, 2013.

——. *Vassilaki Kargopoulo: Photographer to His Majesty the Sultan.* Istanbul: BOS, 2000.

Özyüksel, Murat. *Osmanlı İmparatorluğu'nda Nüfuz Mücadelesi: Anadolu ve Bağdat Demiryolları.* Istanbul: Türkiye İş Bankası Kültür Yayınları, 2008.

Padilla, V. "Édouard François André: Explorer, Botanist, Gardener, City Planner, and Landscape Designer." *Pacific Horticulture* 45, no. 3 (1984): 2–7.

Pakalın, Mehmet Zeki. *Osmanlı Tarih Deyimleri ve Terimleri Sözlüğü.* 3 vols. Istanbul: Millî Eğitim Basımevi, 1946–56.

Pala, İskender. "Mühr-i Süleyman." In *DİA*, 31:524–26.

Pardoe, Miss [Julia]. *The Beauties of the Bosphorus.* London: George Virtue, 1839.

Peirce, Leslie P. *The Imperial Harem: Women and Sovereignty in the Ottoman Empire.* New York: Oxford University Press, 1993.

Pekin, Ersu, İhsan Yücel, and Samih Rifat. *Milli Saraylar.* Istanbul: TBMM Vakfı, 1987.

Perot, Jacques, Frédéric Hitzel, and Robert Anhegger. *Hatice Sultan ile Melling Kalfa: Mektuplar.* Translated by Ela Güntekin. Istanbul: Tarih Vakfı Yurt Yayınları, 2001.

Pervititch, Jacques. *Istanbul in the Insurance Maps of Jacques Pervititch.* Istanbul: Tarih Vakfı, 2000.

Pischon, Carl Nathanael. *Die Einfluss des Islâm auf das häusliche, sociale und politische Leben seiner Bekenner.* Leipzig: F. A. Brockhaus, 1881.

Photographs of İstanbul from the Archives of Sultan Abdülhamid II. Istanbul: İstanbul Büyükşehir Belediyesi Kültür and IRCICA, 2007.

Playfair, R. Lambert. *Handbook to the Mediterranean: Its Cities, Coasts, and Islands.* 2nd ed. London: J. Murray, 1892.

Prenses Cavidan [Princess Djavidan] Hanım. *Harem Hayatı.* Edited by Seda Hauser. Istanbul: İnkılap, 2009.

Protokolle der Deutschen Bundesversammlung vom Jahre 1856. Sitzung 1 bis 33. Frankfurt am Main: Bundes-Präsidial-Druckerei, 1856.

Proulx, Annie. *Barkskins.* London: 4th Estate, 2016.

Pückler-Muskau, Hermann, Fürst von. *Hints on Landscape Gardening.* Translated by John Hargraves. Basel: Birkhäuser, 2014.

Quataert, Donald. "Clothing Laws, State, and Society in the Ottoman Empire, 1720–1829." *International Journal of Middle East Studies* 29, no. 3 (1997): 403–25.

Radt, Barbara. *Geschichte der Teutonia: Deutsches Vereinsleben in Istanbul 1847–2000.* Würzburg: Ergon, 2001.

Ranlett, William H. *The Architect: A Series of Original Designs, for Domestic and Ornamental Cottages and Villas, Connected with Landscape Gardening, Adapted to the United States, Illustrated by Drawings and Ground Plots, Plans, Perspective Views, Elevations, Sections, and Details.* 2 vols. New York: William H. Graham, 1847–49.

Rāşid Efendi. *Tārīḫ-i Rāşid.* 6 vols. in 3. Istanbul: Maṭbaʿa-ı ʿĀmire, 1865.

Raymond, Alexandre M. *Notes pratiques et résumés sur l'art du constructeur en Turquie: Contenant 180 croquis et 15 planches hors texte.* Alessandria: Typolithographie centrale I. Della Rocca, 1908.

Recāʾizāde Maḥmūd Ekrem, ʿAraba Sevdāsı, Muṣavver Millī Ḥikāye.* Istanbul: ʿĀlem Maṭbaʿası, 1314 [1896].

Redford, Scott. "Portable Palaces: On the Circulation of Objects and Ideas About Architecture in Medieval Anatolia and Mesopotamia." *Medieval Encounters* 18, nos. 4–5 (2012): 382–412.

Redhouse, James W. *A Turkish and English Lexicon: Shewing in English the Significations of the Turkish Terms.* [New ed.] Beirut: Librairie du Liban, 1996.

Reiersen, Elsa. "Scandinavians in Colonial Trading Companies and Capital-Intensive Networks: The Case of Christian Thams." In *Navigating Colonial Orders: Norwegian Entrepreneurship in Africa and Oceania*, edited by Kirsten Alsaker Kjerland and Bjørn Enge Bertelsen, 267–90. Oxford: Berghahn, 2015.

Renda, Günsel. *Batılılaşma Döneminde Türk Resim Sanatı, 1700–1850.* Ankara: Türk Tarih Kurumu Basımevi, 1977.

Roberts, Mary. "The Limits of Circumscription." In Behdad and Gartlan, *Photography's Orientalism*, 53–74.

Rogan, Eugene L. "Aşiret Mektebi: Abdülhamid II's School for Tribes (1892–1907)." *International Journal of Middle East Studies* 28, no. 1 (1996): 83–107.

Rohde, Michael. *Von Muskau bis Konstantinopel: Eduard Petzold, ein europäischer Gartenkünstler, 1815–1891.* Dresden: Verlag der Kunst, 1998.

Rossi, Ernesto. *Quarant'anni di vita artistica.* Vol. 3. Florence: L. Niccolai, 1890.

Roxburgh, David J., and Mary McWilliams, eds. *Technologies of the Image: Art in 19th-Century Iran.* Cambridge, MA: Harvard Art Museums, 2017.

Rüstem, Ünver. *Ottoman Baroque: The Architectural Refashioning of Eighteenth-Century Istanbul.* Princeton: Princeton University Press, 2019.

Sabancıoğlu, Müsemma. "Jacques Pervititch and His Insurance Maps of Istanbul." *Dubrovnik Annals* 7 (2003): 89–98.

Sakaoğlu, Necdet. *Bu Mülkün Kadın Sultanları: Valide Sultanlar, Hatunlar, Hasekiler, Kadınefendiler, Sultanefendiler.* Istanbul: Oğlak Yayıncılık, 2008.

Şakir, Ziya. *İkinci Sultan Hamit: Şahsiyeti ve Hususiyetleri.* Istanbul: Anadolu Türk Kitap Deposu, 1943.

Şânî-zâde Mehmed ʿAtâ'ullah Efendi. *Şânî-zâde Târîhî: 1223–1237/1808–1821.* 2 vols. Edited by Ziya Yılmazer. Istanbul: Çamlıca, 2008.

Sarayian, Fatima, and Mohammed Hasan Semsar. *Golestan Palace Photo Archive: Catalogue of Selected Qajar Photographs*. [In Persian.] Tehran, 2003.

Saz, Leylâ. *Harem'in İçyüzü*. Istanbul: Milliyet Yayınları, 1974.

———. *The Imperial Harem of the Sultans: Daily Life at the Çırağan Palace During the 19th Century*. Istanbul: Peva Publications, 1994.

Scarce, Jennifer M. "The Architecture and Decoration of the Gulistan Palace: The Aims and Achievements of Fath ʿAli Shah (1797–1834) and Nasir al-Din Shah (1848–1896)." *Iranian Studies* 34, nos. 1–4 (2001): 103–16.

———. "The Arts of the Eighteenth to Twentieth Centuries." In *The Cambridge History of Iran*, vol. 7, *From Nadir Shah to the Islamic Republic*, edited by Peter Avery, Gavin Hambly, and Charles Melville, 890–958. Cambridge: Cambridge University Press, 1991.

Schick, İrvin Cemil. "The Revival of *Kūfī* Script During the Reign of Sultan Abdülhamid II." In *Calligraphy and Architecture in the Muslim World*, edited by Mohammad Gharipour and İrvin Cemil Schick, 119–38. Edinburgh: Edinburgh University Press, 2014.

Schrott, Ludwig. *Der Prinzregent: Ein Lebensbild aus Stimmen seiner Zeit*. Munich: Süddeutscher Verlag, 1962.

Schweitzer, Robert, and Michael W. R. Davis. *America's Favorite Homes: Mail-Order Catalogues as a Guide to Popular Early 20th-Century Houses*. Detroit: Wayne State University Press, 1990.

Schweizer Châlet Fabrik Chur. Switzerland, 188–?

Sckell, Carl Ludwig von. *Das königliche Lustschloß Nymphenburg und seine Gartenanlagen: Mit einem Plane*. Munich: George Jaquet, [1837–40?].

Scully, Vincent, Jr. *The Shingle Style & the Stick Style: Architectural Theory & Design from Downing to the Origins of Wright*. New Haven: Yale University Press, 1955.

Şehsuvaroğlu, Bedi N. *Göztepe*. Istanbul: Turing, 1969.

Şehsuvaroğlu, Halûk Y. "Abdülhamid'in Yıldız'daki Hususi Dairesi ve Orada Yaşayış Tarzı." *Resimli Tarih Mecmuası* 22, no. 2 (1951):1005–9.

———. *Asırlar Boyunca İstanbul: Sarayları, Camileri, Abîdeleri, Çeşmeleri*. Istanbul: Cumhuriyet Gazetesi, 197–.

———. "Yıldız Kasrı." *Cumhuriyet Gazetesi*, July 5, 1952.

———. "Yıldız Sarayındaki Müze." *20. Asır Mecmuası* 85 (196?).

Şeker, Şemsettin. *Ders ile Sohbet Arasında: On Dokuzuncu Asır İstanbulu'nda İlim, Kültür ve Sanat Meclisleri*. Istanbul: Zeytinburnu Belediyesi Kültür Yayınları, 2013.

Şem'dânî-zâde, Süleyman Efendi. *Şem'dânî-zâde Fındıklılı Süleyman Efendi Târihi Mür'i't-Tevârih*. Translated by M. Münir Aktepe. Vol. 1. Istanbul: Edebiyat Fakültesi Matbaası, 1976.

Şemseddin Sâmî. *Ḳāmūs-ı Türkī*. 2 vols. Istanbul: İḳdām, 1317–18 [1899–1900].

Şen, Münevver Dağgülü. *Yıldız Sarayı Selamlık Bahçesi: Has Bahçe-İç Bahçe (Tespit ve Envanter Çalışması)*. Istanbul: Yıldız Teknik Üniversitesi, 1993.

Şentürk, Şennur, et al. *Iron Track: Age of the Train*. Istanbul: Yapı Kredi Kültür Sanat Yayıncılık, 2003.

Şenyurt, Oya. "II. Abdülhamit Döneminde İki Ünlü Saray Mimarının Siyasi İlişkileri / Political Relations of Two Famous Palace Architects During Abdülhamid II Epoch." *Uluslararası Sosyal Araştırmalar Dergisi / The Journal of International Social Research* 3, no. 2 (Spring 2010): 539–48.

———. *İstanbul Rum Cemaatinin Osmanlı Mimarisindeki Temsiliyeti*. Istanbul: Doğu Kitabevi, 2012.

———. "Selanik Hamidiye Cami: II. Abdülhamid Döneminde Mimaride Geleneksel Yaklaşımlar ve Oryantalizm." *KOSBED* 31 (2016): 185–208.

Şerifoğlu, Ömer Faruk, ed. *Ottoman Court Painter Fausto Zonaro on His 150th Birth Anniversary*. Istanbul: Yapı Kredi Yayınları, 2004.

Şerifoğlu, Ömer Faruk, and İlona Baytar, eds. *Şeker Ahmed Paşa: 1841–1907*. Istanbul: TBMM Saraylar Daire Başkanlığı, 2008.

Sevengil, Refik Ahmet. *Saray Tiyatrosu*. Istanbul: Millî Eğitim Basımevi, 1962.

Sevgen, Nazmi. *Beşiktaşlı Şeyh Yahya Efendi: Hayatı, Menkıbeleri, Şiirleri*. Istanbul: Türkiye Basımevi, 1965.

Sezgin, Candan, ed. *Sanayi Devrimi Yıllarında Osmanlı Saraylarında Sanayi ve Teknoloji Araçları*. Istanbul: Yapı Kredi Kültür Sanat Yayıncılık, 2004.

Shaw, Stanford J. "The 'Yildiz' Palace Archives of 'Abdülhamit II.'" *Archivum Ottomanicum* 3 (1971): 211–37.

Shaw, Wendy M. K. "Ottoman Photography of the Late Nineteenth Century: An 'Innocent' Modernism?" *History of Photography* 33, no. 1 (February 2009): 80–93.

Sheikholeslami, Ali Reza. "Integration of Qajar Persia in the World Capitalist System." *Iranian Journal of International Affairs* 12, pt. 2 (Spring 2000): 285–312.

Silver, Christopher. *Renkioi: Brunel's Forgotten Crimean War Hospital*. Sevenoaks, Kent: Valonia Press, 2007.

Slade, Adolphus. *Turkey and the Crimean War: A Narrative of Historical Events*. London: Smith, Elder, 1867.

Smith, Margaret. *Rābi'a the Mystic and Her Fellow-Saints in Islām: Being the Life and Teachings of Rābi'a Al-'Adawiyya Al-Qaysiyya of Baṣra Together with Some Account of the Place of the Women Saints in Islām.* New York: Cambridge University Press, 1984.

Sözen, Metin. *Devletin Evi: Saray.* Istanbul: Sandoz Kültür Yayınları, 1990.

Spitzer, Siegmund. "Am Hofe Sultan Abdul Medjid's." *Deutsche Rundschau* 99 (June 1899): 115–28.

Stephanov, Darin N. *Ruler Visibility and Popular Belonging in the Ottoman Empire, 1808–1908.* Edinburgh: Edinburgh University Press, 2018.

———. "Sultan Abdülmecid's 1846 Tour of Rumelia and the Trope of Love." *Journal of Ottoman Studies* 44 (2014): 475–501.

Stern, Bernhard. *Abdul Hamid II, seine Familie und sein Hofstaat, nach eigenen Ermittelungen.* Budapest: Deutsch, 1901.

———. *Der Sultan [Abdul Hamid II] und seine Politik: Erinnerungen und Beobachtungen eines Journalisten.* Leipzig: Verlag von B. Elischer Nachfolger, 1906.

St. Laurent, Beatrice, and András Riedlmayer. "Restorations of Jerusalem and the Dome of the Rock and Their Political Significance, 1537–1928." *Muqarnas* 10 (1993): 76–84.

Tagg, John. *The Burden of Representation: Essays on Photographies and Histories.* Minneapolis: University of Minnesota Press, 1993.

Tahsin Paşa. *Sultan Abdülhamid: Tahsin Paşa'nın Yıldız Hatıraları.* Istanbul: Boğaziçi Yayınları, 1990.

Tanman, Baha M., ed. *From the Shores of the Nile to the Bosphorus: Traces of Kavalalı Mehmed Ali Pasha Dynasty in Istanbul.* Istanbul: Suna ve İnan Kıraç Vakfı, İstanbul Araştırmaları Enstitüsü, 2011.

———. "Korular." In *DBİA,* 3:72–75.

Tanpınar, Ahmet Hamdi. *Beş Şehir: Deneme.* 6th ed. Istanbul: Yapı Kredi Yayınları, 2003.

Tanzimat'tan Cumhuriyet'e Türkiye Ansiklopedisi (TCTA). 6 vols. Istanbul: İletişim Yayınları, 1985.

Tayets'i, Esayi. *Hushagir kenats' ew gortsunēut'ean nakhkin kayserakan lusankarich' Gēorg Aptullahi.* Venice: S. Ghazar, 1929.

Tegnér, Esaias. *Esaias Tegnérs Frithiofsage.* Munich: Verlagsanstalt für Kunst und Wissenschaft, 1885.

Tekçe, Güngör. *Zafir Konağında Bir Tuhaf Zaman: Anı.* Istanbul: Yapı Kredi Yayınları, 2007.

Tepeyran, Ebubekir Hâzim. *Hatıralar.* Istanbul: Pera Yayıncılık, 1998.

Terzioğlu, Arslan. "Hekimbaşı Salih Efendi ve Onun Prof. Dr. Joseph Hyrtl'e Yazdığı Fransızca Bir Mektup." *Tarih ve Toplum: Aylık Ansiklopedik Dergi,* no. 118 (October 1993): 30–36.

Thézard, Émile. *Petites villas de 3.000 à 10.000 fr.; la maison pour tous.* Paris: Émile Thézard, 1910.

Tinayre, Marcelle. *Notes d'une voyageuse en Turquie: Jours de bataille et de révolution; choses et gens de province; premiers jours d'un nouveau règne; la vie au harem.* Paris: Calmann-Lévy, 1910.

Toğral, Tahsin. "Maslak Kasrı Askerî Prevantoryumu Yerleşim Düzeni ve Kullanımı Üzerine Kronolojik İnceleme." *Milli Saraylar Dergisi* 9 (2012): 95–116.

———. "Maslak Kasırları Yerleşim Düzeni ve Kullanımı Üzerine İnceleme." *Milli Saraylar Dergisi* 7 (2011): 131–50.

———. "Osmanlı'da Japon Kültürü." *Milli Saraylar Dergisi* 6 (2010): 169–76.

Toker, Metin. "Yıldız'da Operalar Nasıl Hazırlanırdı?" *Cumhuriyet,* September 24, 1938.

Tokgöz, Ahmet İhsan. *Matbuat Hatıralarım.* Istanbul: İletişim Yayınları, 1993.

Toledano, Ehud R. *As If Silent and Absent: Bonds of Enslavement in the Islamic Middle East.* New Haven: Yale University Press, 2007.

Tomas, François, Bernard Merlin, and Jean-Marc Tourret, eds. *Jean-Michel Dalgabio: Lyon, Athènes, Constantinople; Les dessins du voyage de 1843.* Saint-Etienne: Publications de l'Université de Saint-Etienne, 2002.

Tóth, Heléna. *An Exiled Generation: German and Hungarian Refugees of Revolution, 1848–1871.* New York: Cambridge University Press, 2014.

Tuğlacı, Pars. *Osmanlı Mimarlığında Batılılaşma Dönemi ve Balyan Ailesi.* Istanbul: İnkılâp ve Aka, 1981.

———. *The Role of the Balian Family in Ottoman Architecture.* Istanbul: Yeni Çığır Bookstore, 1990.

———. *Tarih Boyunca İstanbul Adaları.* Istanbul: Say, 1995.

Tunisi, Khayr al-Din al-. *Réformes nécessaires aux États musulmans: Essai formant la première partie de l'ouvrage politique et statistique intitulé la plus sure direction pour donnaître l'état des nations.* Paris: Paul Dupont, 1868.

Türker, Deniz. "'Every Image Is a Thought': Nineteenth-Century Gift Albums and the Hamidian Visual Archive." In Ertem and Öztuncay, *Ottoman Arcadia,* 64–83.

———. "'I Don't Want Orange Trees, I Want Something That Others Don't Have': Ottoman Head-Gardeners After Mahmud II." In "Conception and Use of Expertise in the Architecture of the Islamic World Since 1800," special issue, *International Journal of Islamic Architecture* 4, no. 2 (2015): 257–85.

———. "On Dokuzuncu Yüzyıl Diplomasisinin Bir Kristal Saray Serüveni." *Milli Saraylar Belgeler Dergisi,* no. 2 (2014): 83–98.

———. "Ottoman Horticulture After the Tulip Era: Botanizing Consuls, Garden Diplomacy, and the First Foreign Head Gardener." In *The Botany of Empire in the Long Eighteenth Century*, edited by Yota Batsaki, Sarah Burke Cahalan, and Anatole Tchikine, 307–36. Washington, DC: Dumbarton Oaks Research Library and Collection, 2016.

———. "Prefabs, Chalets, and Home Making in 19th-Century Istanbul." Interview by Taylan Güngör. *Ottoman History Podcast.* Podcast audio. February 12, 2017. https://www.ottomanhistorypodcast.com/2017/02/turker.html.

Türkgeldi, Ali Fuat. *Görüp İşittiklerim.* Ankara: Türk Tarih Kurumu Basımevi, 1949.

Türkiye Diyanet Vakfı İslam Ansiklopedisi (DİA). 44 vols. Istanbul: Türkiye Diyanet Vakfı, 1988–2013.

Uluçay, M. Çağatay. *Harem'den Mektuplar.* Vol. 1. Istanbul: Vakit Matbaası, 1956.

———. *Padişahların Kadınları ve Kızları.* Ankara: Türk Tarih Kurumu Basımevi, 1980.

Ulunay, Refi' Cevad. *Bu Gözler Neler Gördü?* Istanbul: Sebil Yayınevi, 2004.

Ünüvar, Safiye. *Saray Hâtıralarım.* Istanbul: Bedir Yayınevi, 2000.

Uras, Büke. *Balyanlar: Osmanlı Mimarlığı give Balyan Arşivi.* Istanbul: Korpus, 2021.

Ürekli, Fatma. *İstanbul'da 1894 Depremi.* Istanbul: İletişim Yayınları, 1999.

Uşaklıgil, Halit Ziya. *Kırık Hayatlar.* Istanbul: Orhaniye Matbaası, 1924.

———. *Saray ve Ötesi: Anılar.* Istanbul: Özgür Yayınları, 2003.

Uzunçarşılı, İsmail Hakkı. *Midhat Paşa ve Yıldız Mahkemesi.* Ankara: Türk Tarih Kurumu Basımevi, 1967.

———. *Osmanlı Devletinin Saray Teşkilâtı.* 3rd ed. Ankara: Türk Tarih Kurumu Basımevi, 1988.

———. *Osmanlı Devleti Teşkilâtından Kapukulu Ocakları.* Vol. 1. Ankara: Türk Tarih Kurumu Basımevi, 1943.

Vámbéry, Ármin. *The Story of My Struggles: The Memoirs of Arminius Vambéry.* Vol. 1. London: T. F. Unwin, 1904.

Vasıf. *Enderunlu Osman Vâsıf Bey ve Dîvânı: Dîvan-ı Gülşen-i Ekfâr-ı Vâsıf-ı Enderûnî.* Edited by Rahşan Gürel. Istanbul: Kitabevi, 1999.

Vernes, Michel. "Le chalet infidèle ou les dérives d'une architecture vertueuse et de son paysage de rêve." *Revue d'histoire du XIXe siècle* 32 (2006): 111–36.

Vernizzi, Cristina, Carlo Pischedda, Ada Peyrot, and Rosanna Maggio Serra, eds. *Carlo Bossoli: Cronache pittoriche del Risorgimento (1859–1861) nella collezione di Eugenio di Savoia, principe di Carignano.* Turin: Artema, 1998.

Viollet-le-Duc, Eugène-Emmanuel. *The Habitations of Man in All Ages.* Translated by Benjamin Bucknall. Boston: J. R. Osgood, 1876.

Wærn, Rasmus. "Scandinavia: Prefabrication as a Model of Society." In *Home Delivery: Fabricating the Modern Dwelling*, edited by Ron Broadhurst, 27–31. New York: Museum of Modern Art, 2008.

Walsh, J. H. *Riding and Driving.* London: Routledge, Warne, & Routledge, 1863.

Wasti, S. Tanvir. "The Last Chroniclers of the Mabeyn." *Middle Eastern Studies* 32, no. 2 (April 1996): 1–29.

Wharton, Alyson. *The Architects of Ottoman Constantinople: The Balyan Family and the History of Ottoman Architecture.* London: I. B. Tauris, 2015.

White, Roger. *Cottages Ornés: The Charms of the Simple Life.* New Haven: Yale University Press, 2017.

Winter, Irene J., ed. *On Art in the Ancient Near East.* 2 vols. Boston: Brill, 2010.

Yalçınkaya, M. Alper. *Learned Patriots: Debating Science, State, and Society in the Nineteenth-Century Ottoman Empire.* Chicago: University of Chicago Press, 2014.

Yıldırım, Mehmet Ali. *Dersaâdet Sanayi Mektebi: İstanbul Sanayi Mektebi, 1868–1926.* Istanbul: Kitabevi, 2012.

Yıldırım, Nuran. *Gureba Hastanesi'nden Bezmiâlem Vakıf Üniversitesi'ne.* Istanbul: Bezmiâlem Vakıf Üniversitesi, 2013.

Yılmaz, F. Yaşar. *Heating Devices in the National Palaces.* Istanbul: TBMM Milli Saraylar Daire Başkanlığı Yayını, 1998.

Yılmaz, Hakan. *The Family Album of Sultan Abdülhamid II.* Istanbul: Kültür, 2010.

Yılmaz, Yaşar. "Osmanlı'nın Hediye Sunumlarında Önem Taşıyan Bir Fabrika: Hereke Fabrika-ı Hümâyûnu ve Hereke Köşkü." In *İki Dost Hükümdar: Sultan II. Abdülhamid, Kaiser II. Wilhelm*, edited by İlona Baytar, 131–40. Istanbul: TBMM Milli Saraylar Daire Başkanlığı, 2010.

Yücel, Erdem. "Hekimbaşı Salih Efendi Yalısı." In *DBİA*, 3:41–42.

Yücel, Ünsal. *Türk Okçuluğu.* Ankara: Atatürk Kültür Merkezi Başkanlığı, 1999.

Zarifi, Yorgo L. *Hatıralarım: Kaybolan Bir Dünya; İstanbul 1800–1920.* Translated by Karin Skotiniyadis. Istanbul: Literatür, 2005.

Zilfi, Madeline C. "A *Medrese* for the Palace: Ottoman Dynastic Legitimation in the Eighteenth Century." *Journal of the American Oriental Society* 113, no. 2 (April–June 1993): 184–91.

Zonaro, Fausto. *Abdülhamid'in Hükümdarlığında Yirmi Yıl: Fausto Zonaro'nun Hatıraları ve Eserleri.* Istanbul: Yapı Kredi Yayınları, 2008.